LES
X mas
'99

The
CHESAPEAKE BAY
Book
A Complete Guide

David Trozzo

THE CHESAPEAKE BAY BOOK

A Complete Guide

Fourth Edition

Allison Blake
with Tracy Sahler

Berkshire House Publishers
Lee, Massachusetts

On the cover and frontispiece
Front cover: *Skipjack, Chesapeake Bay Maritime Museum, St Michaels, Maryland,*
photo © Bill Howe.
Frontispiece: *The majestic great blue heron thrives in the Chesapeake's tidal marshes and bays,*
photo © David Trozzo.

The Chesapeake Bay Book: A Complete Guide
Copyright © 1992, 1996, 1997, 1999 by Berkshire House Publishers
Cover photograph © Bill Howe.
Interior photographs © 1992, 1996, 1997, 1999 by David Trozzo.

*Permission to use historic photographs was courteously granted by the Maryland State
Archives, Annapolis.*

Library of Congress Cataloging-in-Publication Data
Blake, Allison, 1960-
   The Chesapeake Bay book: a complete guide / Allison Blake with Tracy Sahler. —
4th ed.
      p.   cm. — (The great destinations series, ISSN 1056-7968)
   Includes bibliographical references and index.
   ISBN 1-58157-005-8
   1. Chesapeake Bay Region (Md. and Va.)—Guidebooks. I. Sahler, Tracy. II. Title.
III. Series.
F187.C5 B54   1999   98-46737
917.55'180443—dc21   CIP

ISBN 1-58157-005-8
ISSN 1056-7968

Editor: Constance Lee Oxley. Managing Editor: Philip Rich. Text design and layout:
Dianne Pinkowitz. Cover design: Jane McWhorter. Maps: Matt Paul/Yankee Doodles.

Berkshire House books are available at substantial discounts for bulk purchases by cor-
porations and other organizations' promotions and premiums. Special personalized
editions can also be produced in large quantities. For more information, contact:

Berkshire House Publishers
480 Pleasant St., Ste. 5; Lee, Massachusetts 01238
800-321-8526
E-mail: info@berkshirehouse.com
Web: www.berkshirehouse.com
Manufactured in the United States of America
First Printing 1999
10 9 8 7 6 5 4 3 2 1

*No complimentary meals or lodgings were accepted by the author and reviewers in gathering
information for this work.*

Berkshire House Publishers'
Great Destinations™ travel guidebook series

Right on the money.

— THE NEW YORK TIMES

Smart, literate, well-reported, and incredibly comprehensive.

— MID-ATLANTIC COUNTRY

. . . a crisp and critical approach, for travelers who want to live like locals.

— USA TODAY

Great Destinations™ guidebooks are known for their comprehensive, critical coverage of regions of extraordinary cultural interest and natural beauty. The authors in this series are professional travel writers who have lived for many years in the regions they describe. Each title in this series is continuously updated with each printing, in order to insure accurate and timely information. All of the books contain over 100 photographs and maps.

Neither the publisher, the authors, the reviewers, nor other contributors accept complimentary lodgings, meals, or any other consideration (such as advertising) while gathering information for any book in this series.

Current titles available:
The Adirondack Book
The Berkshire Book
The Charleston, Savannah & Coastal Islands Book
The Chesapeake Bay Book
The Coast of Maine Book
The Hamptons Book
The Monterey Bay, Big Sur & Gold Coast Wine Country Book
The Nantucket Book
The Newport & Narragansett Bay Book
The Napa & Sonoma Book
The Santa Fe & Taos Book
The Sarasota, Sanibel Island & Naples Book
The Texas Hill Country Book
Wineries of the Eastern States

If you are traveling to, moving to, residing in, or just interested in any (or all!) of these enchanting regions, a **Great Destinations™** guidebook is a superior companion. Honest and painstakingly critical, full of information only a local can provide, **Great Destinations™** guidebooks give you all the practical knowledge you need to enjoy the best of each region. Why not own them all?

Contents

CHAPTER ONE
"A Very Goodly Bay"
HISTORY
1

CHAPTER TWO
Of Ferries & Freeways
TRANSPORTATION
20

CHAPTER THREE
Bed & Breakfast & Boat
LODGING
35

CHAPTER FOUR
Catch of the Bay
RESTAURANTS & FOOD PURVEYORS
79

CHAPTER FIVE
The Best of the Bay
CULTURE
130

CHAPTER SIX
Water, Water Everywhere
RECREATION
182

CHAPTER SEVEN
Antiques, Boutiques & Inlet Outlets
SHOPPING
239

CHAPTER EIGHT
The Right Connections
INFORMATION
267

CHAPTER NINE
Urban Bay Neighbors
BALTIMORE & NEARBY ATTRACTIONS
283

Acknowledgments

To all those who assisted in this highly detailed effort, I issue many hearty thanks.

First among the many is Tracy Sahler, the contributing author of this edition who researched the Eastern Shore and brought new insights to the region, particularly the Lower Shore, and built upon the work of her two predecessors. Longtime Annapolis area photographer David Trozzo brought his keen eye to another edition, while Kathryn Flynn checked all the facts. Claire Papanastasiou wrote and updated the Baltimore chapter, while Jay Votel updated the Eastern Shore sections of the information and transportation chapters (and also pinch-hitted in a restaurant review).

Thanks also to editor Constance Oxley and all the folks at Berkshire House: publisher Jean Rousseau, managing editor Philip Rich, marketing director Carol Bosco Baumann, and office manager Mary Osak. Everyone's been great.

Readers are in good hands with the restaurant reviewers, veterans of the local scene with credentials to match. Yours truly, who also ate her way through portions of Virginia's Tidewater, was joined on the Western Shore by Amy Argetsinger, the aforementioned Ms. Flynn, and Gwyn Novak, who also sampled many restaurants on the Eastern Shore. Also reviewing on the Eastern Shore: Pat Vojtech, Tracy Sahler, Anne Stinson, Melissa Midgett, and Pete Nelson. Jack Chamberlain contributed from the Northern Neck.

When writing a fourth edition of a collaborative work such as this, the expertise of those who've gone before must be acknowledged, especially former contributing authors Eric Mills and Tom Dove, and former editor Sarah Novak. A host of former restaurant reviewers provided local insight that we have built upon over time.

Also thanks to Bess Gillelan and Kate Naughten for help with my environmental reporting.

From Tracy, many thanks to husband Erick and exchange daughter, Lea Mercier of Göttingen, Germany, for their patience — and for putting up with the pressing schedule. Also, thanks to Dave's wife Cathy for all of her help.

Finally, let me thank the folks closest to me for putting up with my absence (even if it was just a mental departure), or factoring in my obligations. My mom, Miriam Thompson Blake, wanted to go out for lunch for my birthday. We ended up going on a research trip to the Northern Neck. Her insights proved invaluable, particularly when enhancing the lodging chapter introduction, which addresses unforeseen issues for those staying in B&Bs.

Greatest thanks of all goes to my patient mate and husband, Joshua Thomas Gillelan II, named for his grandfather who was, in turn, named for the Parson of the Islands. They know who he is, around Bay Country.

Introduction

Down on Kitty Duval Creek in Annapolis, the blue heron rules the marsh even if the red-winged blackbirds stake out cattail quadrants of their own. A barn owl lived one summer in the white boathouse across the way and swooped by from time to time when we rowed past in the doubled-ended dory. An ambitious day in the dory finds us clear to the mouth of the South River, where stands the famed Thomas Point Light. An unambitious day means poking around the cove around the corner. Afterwards, we'll order a dozen hard-shell crabs. If it's Memorial Day, we'll pick 'em out in the backyard, looking up as the Blue Angels, in town for the U.S. Naval Academy graduation, scream overhead. If it's Saturday night, we might hop in the car and drive to Washington, D.C. or Baltimore within an easy hour.

Therein lies the great beauty of life on the Chesapeake: it's the best of both worlds. You can live out of the way. You can live an urban life. Some people would rather be out of the way. They live in corners of the Eastern Shore or down in Virginia's placid Northern Neck and Middle Peninsula. Urban dwellers who secretly wish that they had the nerve to live there all the time keep big houses on the creeks and rivers and invite their friends down on the weekends.

Visitors who find themselves in Crisfield, Maryland — the nation's Crab Capital — find a town that's not so different from the downtowns of childhood, but for the dock opening wide onto the vast water. Storefronts line the streets; locals cruise past after dinner on summer nights. In the town parking lot, a waterman's pickup easily might be parked alongside a suburban Volvo in town from chic Annapolis. If you drive south through Virginia along the Shore's narrowing peninsula, you'll pass through the green rural tidewater, flat and calm and a good bit more Tennessee Williams than you'll find at the head of the Bay in Havre de Grace. Up there, it's starting to feel ever so slightly Northeast industrial. Still, the sailors from Wilmington and Philadelphia arrive wearing boat shoes; the Bay and the Susquehanna River meet at Havre de Grace, and water is in view everywhere you turn.

Old steamship lines served the Chesapeake Bay well into this century, a lifeline to history as rich as anywhere in this relatively young country. Forebears to oysters, now ordered at a raw bar, fed our native forebears; George Washington did sleep here, maybe in the colonial, four-poster in your room at the B&B.

And the Bay, which scientists know suffered from our early farming settlers, is turning around ecologically. The huge, local and federal cleanup effort, rallied by the "Save the Bay" battle cry, is making headway. Back on Kitty Duval Creek, that means that the red-winged blackbirds shouldn't miss a migratory beat.

Allison Blake
Bowie, Maryland

THE WAY THIS BOOK WORKS

Geographically, we've divided the Bay area into five regions. **HEAD OF THE BAY** starts past Aberdeen, Maryland, circles around the tip of the Bay to the Sassafras River, and includes Chesapeake City and historic Havre de Grace. Below the Head of the Bay, on the western side, we've designated the area south of the Magothy River to the Potomac River and west to Rte. 301, as the **ANNAPOLIS/WESTERN SHORE** area. Virginia's **NORTHERN NECK/MIDDLE PENINSULA** area runs down to Gloucester Point, west to Rte. 301 at the northern end of the area, and Rte. 17 farther south.

On the other side of the Bay is the **UPPER EASTERN SHORE,** from the Sassafras River south to the Choptank River, east to the Delaware line. South of the Choptank River to Virginia's Cape Charles, with a side trip through Berlin to Assateague Island, is the **LOWER EASTERN SHORE.**

Information is presented according to these five regions. Within each region, towns are listed alphabetically, with lodgings, restaurants, and other places of interest in each town also given alphabetically. The book covers sections of both Maryland and Virginia, with Maryland, of course, having the greater percentage of territory and, therefore, more entries. So whenever we cross the border into Virginia, we'll remind you by specifying that in the address, which accompanies each set of listings.

The helpful, little blocks of salient information that accompany the listings and reviews have been updated as close to publication as possible, but we can't control changes in operating hours or prices. Please accept out apologies in advance for any details that may have changed, and be sure to call ahead when planning a visit.

For the same reason, we've usually avoided listing specific prices, preferring instead to indicate a range of prices (see below). Restaurant prices cover an average dinner for one, including appetizer, entrée, and dessert, but not including cocktails, wine, tax, or tip.

PRICE CODES

	Lodging	Dining
Inexpensive	Up to $55	Up to $15
Moderate	$56 to $85	$16 to $22
Expensive	$86 to $125	$23 to $32
Very Expensive	Over $125	Over $32

Credit cards are abbreviated as follows:

AE – American Express   DC – Diners Club
CB – Carte Blanche   MC – MasterCard
D – Discover   V – Visa

The
CHESAPEAKE BAY
Book
A Complete Guide

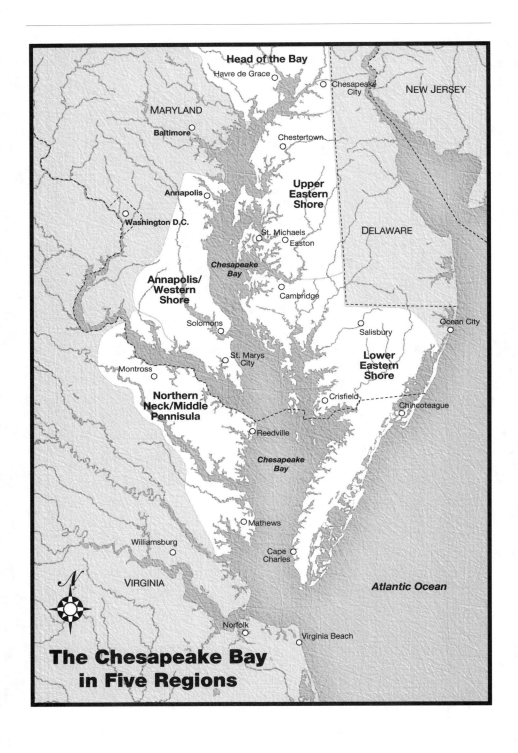

Head of the Bay
Havre de Grace ○
Chesapeake City ○
NEW JERSEY

MARYLAND

Baltimore ○

Chestertown ○

Upper Eastern Shore

Annapolis ○

Washington D.C. ●

DELAWARE

St. Michaels ○
Easton

Chesapeake Bay

Annapolis/ Western Shore

Cambridge ○

Solomons ○

Salisbury ○

Ocean City ○

St. Marys City ○

Lower Eastern Shore

Montross ○

Northern Neck/Middle Pennisula

Crisfield ○

Chincoteague ○

Reedville ○

Chesapeake Bay

Mathews ○

Williamsburg ○

Cape Charles ○

VIRGINIA

N

Atlantic Ocean

Norfolk ○

Virginia Beach ○

The Chesapeake Bay in Five Regions

CHAPTER ONE
"A Very Goodly Bay"
HISTORY

There is but one entrance by Sea into this Country, and that is at the mouth of a very goodly Bay, 18 or 20 myles broad. The cape on the South is called Cape Henry, in honour of our most notable Prince. The North Edge is called Cape Charles, in honour of the worthy Duke of Yorke. Within is a country that may have the prerogative over the most pleasant places. Heaven and earth never agreed better to frame a place for man's habitation. Here are mountains, hills, plaines, valleyes, rivers, and brookes, all running into a faire Bay, compassed but for the mouth, with fruitful and delightsome land.

Capt. John Smith, 1607

Archaeologists dig-ging in this cradle of U.S. history have unearthed countless rem-nants of an even deeper past. Layered in sand and clay along Chesa-peake Bay shores are oyster shells, some thou-sands of years old. The largest cache was a thirty-acre Indian shell midden spread across Pope's Creek, off the Potomac River. Long before Chesapeake water-men took up their tongs, the Bay was feeding her people.

Maryland State Archives

An 1890 fleet of skipjacks — still the country's oldest fishing fleet under sail — stands at the dock in Cambridge, Maryland.

The native inhabitants called her Chesapeake Bay, "the Great Shellfish Bay." In the sixteenth century, a Jesuit priest sailed through the Virginia capes described by John Smith and bestowed a second name: La Bahía de la Madre de Dios — the Bay of the Mother of God.

The Chesapeake has always looked after those who lived here. Just as the Native Americans thrived on Bay oysters, so early European settlers grew crops in rich Bay soil. As the indigenous peoples paddled canoes from encampment to encampment, so ferries linked later settlements.

Today, the waters of this ancient river valley fan out into a complex network of urban bridges and rural lanes. Here endures the heart of the modern MidAtlantic megalopolis and the soul of nineteenth-century fishing villages. U.S. history here is old; geological history is young.

The Chesapeake Bay is bookended by two major metropolitan areas in two states: Baltimore, Maryland's largest city, and Norfolk-Newport News-Hampton Roads in Virginia's Tidewater. Both are major Atlantic ports. Near John Smith's Virginia capes, now spanned by the 17.6-mile Chesapeake Bay Bridge-Tunnel, the Norfolk Naval Air Station presides over a strong Navy presence throughout Tidewater.

David Trozzo

Canada geese at the Blackwater National Wildlife Refuge, premiere Bay birding in Cambridge, Maryland.

Much of Maryland's Western Shore life looks to urban centers, as city dwellers willing to endure the hour-long commute to Washington, D.C. or Baltimore emigrate to Annapolis or Kent Island. For their highway-bound hours during the week, these government insiders are repaid with long sails on the Bay or hours anchored in secluded "gunkholes," shallow coves where green and great blue herons fly from nearby marshes. On the Eastern Shore, fishing, farming, tourism, and the retirement business spur local economic life.

Up the Bay's major tributaries are the major cities of the region: Washington, D.C., on the Potomac; Richmond, Virginia, on the James; and Baltimore,

Maryland, on the Patapsco. Maryland's capital, Annapolis, stands at the mouth of the Severn River, near where the William Preston Lane Memorial Bridge, or Bay Bridge, links the Eastern and Western Shores.

Even as the Chesapeake is defined by her waters, so she is defined by her history. A stop at Maryland's Statehouse in Annapolis, where Washington resigned his Continental Army commission, is as integral to a Chesapeake country visit as a charter boat fishing trip from Tilghman Island. In 1607, the first permanent colonial English settlement was at Jamestown, Virginia. The first Catholic settlers landed farther north, on the Potomac, and established Maryland at St. Marys City in 1634. George Washington and his peers used the Bay first to transport their tobacco, the region's first sizable cash crop, and then used the Bay to their military advantage as they plotted their navigational comings and goings during the Revolutionary War.

For all of the Bay's history and enduring navigability, however, she shares a problem with virtually every other heavily populated estuary. A confluence of pressures has threatened the health of her rich waters since the European settlers chopped down forests to create fields to farm. Soil from the fertile lands lining the Bay's shores has slipped into the water, silting in harbors and obscuring marshy invertebrate nurseries. Damage has been compounded by twentieth-century wastes: fertilizers, air pollution, and sewage.

Many say the magnificent Chesapeake is at the most crucial crossroads of her most recent geological incarnation. A massive assault against pollution is well underway and is producing some good results. Perhaps, like the estuary's flushing by fresh water from the north and by saltwater tides from the south, the diverse mix of urban and rural can maintain a beneficial balance in La Bahía de la Madre de Dios.

NATURAL HISTORY

Cargo ships journeying the 200-mile length of the Chesapeake Bay travel in a deep channel that more than 10,000 years ago cradled the ancient Susquehanna River. The mighty river flowed south to the ocean, drawing in the waters of many tributaries but for one independent soul: the present-day James River. Then came the great shift in the glaciers of the last Ice Age, when the thick sheets of ice that stopped just north of the Chesapeake region — in what is now northern Pennsylvania and New York state — began to melt under warming temperatures. As the Pleistocene Era ended, torrents of released water flowed, filling the oceans. The Susquehanna River Valley flooded once, twice, and probably more, settling eventually within the bounds of the present-day Chesapeake Bay.

The Bay as it now exists is the largest estuary in the U.S. — some say in all North America. Estuaries are schizophrenic bodies of water, mixing the fresh waters of inland mountain streams and rivers with salty ocean waters. The undulating brew of fresh and salt stirs a habitat that supports a huge range of creatures. Clams, crabs, oysters, striped bass (known hereabouts as rockfish), menhaden, and more have always thrived in these waters, living a solitary life in the deep as bottom dwellers, bedding down in the shallows, or navigating north to the fresh water to spawn.

The Susquehanna River, supplying fifty percent of the Chesapeake's fresh water, flows into the head of the Bay. The Potomac River adds another twenty percent. Even the renegade James River has joined the other Chesapeake tributaries, helping to nourish the vast mix of species living in the Bay.

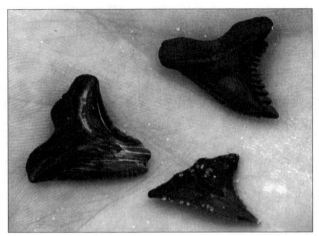

Evidence of the prehistoric sea that once covered the Bay is sometimes uncovered along its shores. These shark's teeth were found in Calvert County, Maryland.

David Trozzo

Solid evidence of a prehistoric past lies layered along the Western Shore of the Bay, perhaps most famously at Calvert Cliffs, located eighty miles south of Annapolis. From here to the Virginia side of the Potomac River, shark's teeth and other fossils still wash up from time to time. These are twelve- to seventeen-million-year-old forebears to the Bay's crab, menhaden, and oysters that lived in a Miocene Era sea that stretched to present-day Washington, D.C. Crocodile, rhinoceros, and mastodon lived along the cliffs that were once the uplands of the ancient Susquehanna River Valley.

WHERE LAND & WATER MEET

The modern-day Chesapeake boasts impressive statistics. The Bay surface is 2,200 square miles, but her 150 tributaries, including all manner of coves, creeks, and tidal rivers double that area. The total system is filled by eighteen-trillion gallons of water — the fresher water in the upper Bay, the saltier farther south.

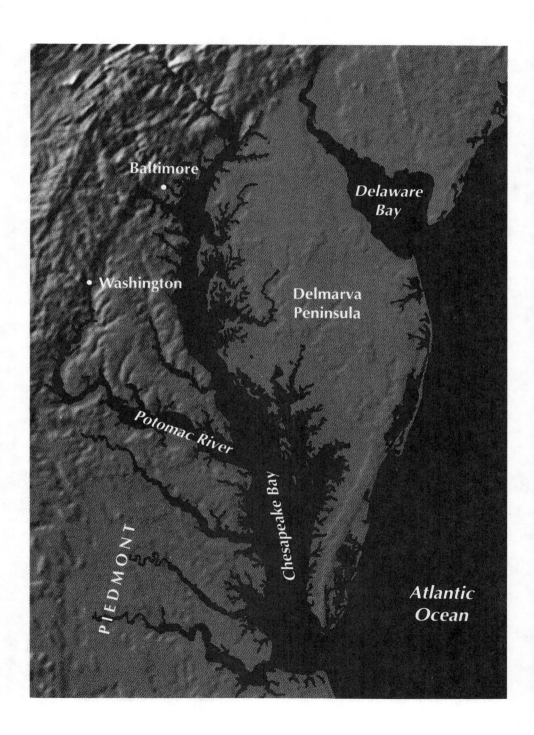

The Bay's width ranges from four miles at Annapolis to thirty miles at Point Lookout, Maryland, where the Potomac River meets the Bay, dividing Maryland and Virginia. Despite the enormity of this expansive body of water, the Chesapeake is surprisingly shallow. Its average depth is twenty-one feet, although at the so-called "Deep Trough," off Kent Island, depths reach 160 feet.

Beyond the waters of the Bay, within her 64,000-square-mile watershed, is geological diversity: the metamorphic rock of the Appalachian plateau, the weathered, iron-rich soil of the piedmont, and the sandy coastal plain.

Meanwhile, a shoreline that seems to snake forever along marshes, creeks, or mighty rivers amounts to as many miles as the number of history books that tell of this Bay. Estimates of total shoreline reach 6,000 miles. A variety of wildlife lives here. Muskrats were hunted and trapped commonly — and still are; but nutria, a similar South American species, have taken over much of their habitat since a few escaped from an Eastern Shore breeding operation back in the 1940s or 1950s. Overhead each fall come the migratory waterfowl — swans, Canada geese, brant, and of course, ducks: mallards, pintail, canvasbacks, and teal — following the Atlantic Flyway. The mighty osprey is common, back from its severely threatened status after the insecticide DDT was banned in the early 1970s.

David Trozzo

Sunset over the Blackwater National Wildlife Refuge, deep in Dorchester County's lowlands.

The Eastern Shore, in particular, historically has been a haven for hunters. Hunting is still popular, but so is bird-watching. Down in the lowlands of Dorchester County, the brackish marshes of the Blackwater National Wildlife Refuge welcome the red-cockaded woodpecker, peregrine falcon, and the endangered bald eagle, which breeds here. The great horned owl likewise breeds in this marshy backwater, and the rare Delmarva fox squirrel also makes it his home.

The Chesapeake's salt marshes are crucial creature nurseries once thought to be useless. Here, as elsewhere in early America, settlers harvested "salt hay" for their livestock's winter food. Grasses tough enough to withstand this strange habitat between land and sea grew profusely, sheltering molting blue crabs and protecting the sea from land and vice versa.

Waterman Ken Watts carries on the crabber's tradition at Chesapeake Beach, Maryland.

David Trozzo

Talk to a salty waterman who has worked the Bay and her rivers for a few decades, though, and he'll tell you the once-prolific underwater Bay grasses aren't what they once were. Environmentalists studying the Bay watch the grasses, known officially as "submerged aquatic vegetation," as a sort of clarity gauge of the Bay. Efforts to bring back these protectors have been fairly successful in recent years, giving fish and fowl, and even the shores of the Bay, one more ally against the rush of wind against bare sea and land.

Even with the slow return of the underwater protectors, the Chesapeake as a fishery, heavy with menhaden and blue crabs, comes in about third among the nation's eight regions where landings are counted. The blue crab, mainstay of a Chesapeake summer diet, officially is considered to be fully exploited — meaning fishing is at capacity — following a population drop in the mid-1990s that prompted intensive management measures by Maryland and Virginia. Whether the decline was due to a natural drop in the life cycle or something else altogether, fisheries managers now keep a close eye on the crab. Meanwhile, tables still fill at Chesapeake crab houses, and recreational crabbers still take nets down to local piers.

The story of the formerly endangered rockfish could signal a brighter future for the blue crab. Commercial fishermen who had enjoyed steady catches of five-million pounds of fish annually saw the stocks drop to two-million pounds in the late 1970s. By 1985, Maryland imposed a fishing moratorium. Virginia followed in 1989. Since then, a limited catch-and-release season has expanded each year, and stocks were officially declared restored in January 1995 by the body that governs coastal catches, the Atlantic States Marine Fisheries Commission. Scientists continue to monitor the rockfish's road to recovery, fishermen are thrilled, and devotees have been pleased to find this sweet, flavorful fish return to local menus.

One reason that fishing pressures are up for the blue crab has been the plunge among the native oysters that breathed economic life into the Eastern Shore for decades. A century after they were first dangerously overfished, harvestable oysters had dropped to an all-time low in the early 1990s. In recent years, a combination of threats has undermined efforts to help restore what were once bounteous oyster bars: overfishing, disease, habitat destruction, and pollution. Bright spots have arisen as scientists test various techniques to build productive oyster bars, with some small success. The debate over just how to bring the oysters back will continue — and not only to retain the popular, historic fishery. Oysters filter pollutants from the water and may be a key to restoring the Bay's overall water quality.

As the oyster population has swelled and dropped, so has the Bay shoreline itself. The lapping and crashing of water against her edges have always caused erosion: marshes fill, harbors shift, and over the years, islands and peninsulas have disappeared.

Colonial-era Sharp's Island, off the mouth of the Eastern Shore's Choptank River, was once the site of one of William Claiborne's string of trading posts founded in the 1630s. A 600-acre plantation once was established here, but now the entire island is gone. Apparently, the island eroded away quickly, for there are old-timers along the Shore who still remember it. A similar fate befell Holland Island at Tangier Sound, once the site of a small village, home to 300. The shoreline began to slip by 1900, and its residents moved away two decades later.

SAVING THE BAY

Even as time and tide send shoreline slipping into the Bay, human debris has followed. In addition to chemical fertilizers from farms throughout the vast watershed, waste discharged from aging sewage plants, until recently, flowed into the estuary. The challenge ahead lies in maintaining improved pollution levels.

Industrial and residential development has likewise sped erosion. Waste-produced nutrients, primarily phosphorous and nitrogen, poured into the Bay, feeding algal blooms that cut oxygen and light to the flora and fauna on the

Bay floor during the spring and summer. Air pollution adds as much as one-quarter of the nitrogen, scientists say. The goal now is to cut polluting phosphorus and nitrogen dramatically. Given the growing population of this popular region, it will be incumbent on all of us to pitch in.

Efforts to clean up Chesapeake Bay stretch back over decades, although formal federal and state programs weren't organized until 1977. In 1964, President Lyndon B. Johnson announced the federally supported beginnings of an effort to clean up the Potomac River, one of the Bay's best-known tributaries. The $1-billion project is considered a great success story, perhaps inspiration to the many agencies and organizations now spending millions of dollars and countless hours to save the Bay.

"Save the Bay" is the rallying cry for the nonprofit Chesapeake Bay Foundation, even as continuing efforts by state and federal government programs are working to improve the Bay. Research begun in 1977 led to the Chesapeake Bay Agreement of 1983, signed by the states of Maryland, Virginia, and Pennsylvania, the District of Columbia, the Environmental Protection Agency, and the Chesapeake Bay Commission, a group of area legislators. The landmark agreement established the nuts-and-bolts programs for cleaning up a deteriorating habitat. At that point, the focus was on cleaning the Bay per se; an updated agreement in 1987 shifted the focus from improving water quality to conserving Bay flora and fauna. Now scientists are shifting their concerns not only to cleaning up air pollution harming the Bay, but also to projects for restoring wetlands, encouraging landowners to plant trees along watershed streams, and creating experimental oyster bars.

The results of the Bay cleanup are mixed. Launched in the early 1980s, apparent improvements began with submerged aquatic grasses that have spread considerably since the 1980s. Concern remains for the hopefully stabilized blue crab population. The shad fishing moratoria seem to have prompted signs of improvement to those stocks, and major efforts to open historical anadromous fish spawning rivers bode well for the future.

Meanwhile, visitors can expect to see enthusiastic local support for the Bay, from the annual Bay Bridge Walk from Annapolis to Kent Island in late spring to Maryland's "Treasure the Chesapeake" specialty license plates. Half the proceeds from the sales of the special plates go to Bay cleanup efforts.

In the years since the cleanup began, the Bay's health has improved. Sailing and boating thrive; recreational fishers still go after striped bass. The central effort for all Bay lovers is to help restore the estuary and nurture it as the MidAtlantic region continues to grow.

SOCIAL HISTORY

The first settlers of the Chesapeake region lived here during the last Ice Age. These Paleo-Indians were hunters, following mammoth and bison on their migrations. The melting of the glaciers marked the beginning of the Archaic period, when these forebears of the Piscataway and Nanticoke tribes convened in villages and began to eat oysters and other shell- and finfish from the Bay. About 3,000 years ago, they began to farm these shores, raising maize, ancestor of the Eastern Shore's now popular Silver Queen corn, and tobacco, which the English settlers later converted to the region's early economic foundation.

EARLY SETTLERS

D utch and Spanish explorers of the sixteenth century were reportedly the first Europeans to sail into the Bay, and Vikings may have visited even earlier. The first Europeans to settle permanently, however, were the English. In 1607, Capt. Christopher Newport left England, crossed the Atlantic to the West Indies, then sailed north into the Bay. He navigated up what would come to be called the James River. Those aboard Newport's three-ship fleet, the forty-nine-foot *Discovery*, the sixty-eight-foot *Godspeed*, and the 111-foot *Susan Constant*, settled Jamestown.

Long before Europeans settled the Chesapeake, woodland Native Americans lived here. Their tools are displayed at St. Marys City, site of Maryland's first capital.

David Trozzo

The new colony, chartered by the Virginia Company, proved to be a near disaster. Hostiles and disease either drove off or killed many of the original settlers. Among the survivors was Capt. John Smith, by all accounts an adventurer. It was here that Smith's fabled rescue by the maiden Pocahontas took place — an event recorded in Smith's journal, but questioned by scholars. As the story goes, the young captain was captured and taken to a village where the old "powhatan," or chief, was to preside over Smith's execution. Even as the warriors threatened with raised clubs, the chief's young daughter threw herself upon the English captain, thus saving him from a brutal fate. Smith was also the first Englishman to explore the Bay and indeed charted it rather accurately. He set out from Jamestown on his exploration in 1608, accompanied by fourteen men on an open barge. They sailed first up the "Easterne Shore," where sources of fresh water proved poor. While still in what came to be called Virginia, Smith wrote, ". . . the first people we saw were 2 grimme and stout Salvages upon Cape-Charles, with long poles like Javelings, headed with bone. They boldly demanded what we were, and what we would, but after many circumstances, they in time seemed very kinde . . ." Smith learned from them "such descriptions of the Bay, Isles, and rivers, that often did us exceeding pleasure." The party then went on across the Bay to its western shore, sailing as fast as they could ahead of a fearsome storm. "Such an extreame gust of wind, rayne, thunder, and lightening happened, that with great danger we escaped the unmercifull raging of that Ocean-like water," wrote Smith.

Early Jamestown survived as Virginia's colonial capital to the end of the seventeenth century. Meanwhile, English migration across the Atlantic continued. In 1631, William Claiborne established his trading post at Kent Island, mid-Bay, setting himself up to become arguably the first settler of Maryland. In ensuing years, on behalf of the Virginia Company, he provided ample rivalry for Maryland's "proprietors," or royal grant holders, the Calverts.

George Calvert, the first Lord Baltimore, hoped to settle his own "Avalon." He first sought to establish a colony in Newfoundland, but soon abandoned the harsh northern land. A second grant for a new colony passed to his son, the second Lord Baltimore, Cecil Calvert. The younger Calvert, a Catholic, knew that Virginia would not welcome the new settlement and feared that enemies in England would try to undermine his colony. He put his younger brother, Leonard, in charge of the settlers who boarded the ships *Ark* and *Dove* and sailed off to found Maryland, named in honor of Charles I's queen at St. Clement's Island, near the mouth of the Potomac River.

The 128 hardy souls aboard the two ships landed on March 25, 1634, after taking a route similar to that taken by Christopher Newport. Upon landing, Leonard Calvert, as governor, led a party of men up the river to meet the "tayac," or leader, of the Piscataways. The tayac gave the settlers permission to settle where they would; their village was to become Maryland's first capital, St. Marys City. They also taught the English settlers how to farm unfamiliar lands in an unfamiliar climate.

Among the Marylanders' first crops was tobacco, soon to be the staple of a Chesapeake economy and already being harvested farther south along the Virginia Bay coast. In the years that followed, farmers would discover just how damaging tobacco proved to be in costs to both the land and humans; the crop sapped the soil's nutrients. Without fertilizers, a field was used up after a couple of seasons, so more land constantly had to be cleared and planted. This called for labor. While some Englishmen indentured themselves to this life in exchange for transatlantic passage to the colonies, tobacco farming was nevertheless responsible for the beginnings of African slave labor along the Chesapeake. By the late seventeenth century, wealthy planters had begun to "invest" in slaves as "assets."

Up and down the Chesapeake grew a tobacco coast, fueled by demand from English traders. From its beginnings as a friendly home to new settlers, the Bay grew into a seagoing highway for the burgeoning tobacco trade. Soon came fishing and boatbuilding.

A rural manorial society grew up around St. Marys City, which was never itself very large. Perhaps a dozen families lived within five square miles. Planters raised tobacco, a fort was established, and government business eventually brought inns and stables. In 1650, about 100 miles to the north, a settlement was established near what is now Annapolis, named Providence. In 1695, the new governor, Francis Nicholson, moved Maryland's capital near the mouth of the Severn River to Annapolis. By 1720, St. Marys City was gone. That colony's heyday has been re-created, however, in a living museum complete with wild Ossabaw pigs. Archaological work continues on the site. In recent years, three lead coffins holding the remains of members of the Calvert clan were unearthed and authenticated.

The Statehouse in Annapolis is the country's oldest capitol building in continuous use.

David Trozzo

Nicholson's Annapolis, considered America's first baroque-style city, is still evident. From two circles, State Circle and Church Circle, radiate the streets of today's historic district. Three statehouses have stood in State Circle, the most recent begun in 1772. This was the building used as the national capitol during the period of the Articles of Confederation and is the state capitol in longest continual use. From the center of Church Circle rises the spire of St. Anne's Church, the third on the site since 1696. Known also as "the Ancient City," Annapolis grew into a thriving late seventeenth- and eighteenth-century town. It became renowned as the social gathering spot for colonial gentlemen and ladies. Here, the Provincial Court and the Legislature met. Planters "wintered" here amid fashionable society; the witty men of the Tuesday Club gathered at the homes of its members for music and poetry.

Elsewhere along the Chesapeake, seaport settlements were rising from the sandier Eastern Shore. Chestertown was established as a seaport and Kent County seat in 1706. Near the head of the Bay, "Baltimore Town" was first carved from sixty acres owned by the wealthy Carroll family in 1729. Those who couldn't survive the fluctuations of the tobacco market turned to tonging for oysters, to fishing for herring, or to shipbuilding.

THE CHESAPEAKE IN WARTIME

During the Revolutionary War, Annapolis's central port location drew blockade runners and Continental colonels alike. Both Americans and British used the Bay to transport troops. War meetings that included George Washington and the Marquis de Lafayette were held beneath the Liberty Tree, still standing today on the campus of St. John's College and thought to be 400 to 600 years old. (The college, founded in 1696 as King William's School, still holds graduation ceremonies there.)

The gardens at the home of William Paca, signer of the Declaration of Independence, were painstakingly reconstructed from archaeological digs.

David Trozzo

Three Annapolitans, Samuel Chase, William Paca, and Charles Carroll of Carrollton, signed the Declaration of Independence in 1776; their colonial-era homes have been preserved and are open for public tours. In 1781, the war finally ended at Yorktown, Virginia, near Jamestown. Reinforcements traveled south along the Bay to meet up with Washington's gathering troops, and French Admiral de Grasse barricaded the mouth of the Bay. Lord Cornwallis, the British commander, surrendered.

In 1783, during a meeting of the Continental Congress in the Maryland Statehouse in Annapolis, George Washington resigned his Army commission; visitors may still see the chamber. This is also where the Treaty of Paris was ratified in 1784, formally ending the war. Likewise, Annapolis itself soon saw an end to its glittery social role. The city soon fell quiet, awakened only by the 1845 establishment of the U.S. Naval Academy, which overshadowed much of city life for at least the next century.

Peace with the British after the Revolution was short-lived. Soon came the War of 1812, the only war in U.S. history when unfriendly foreign troops reached our shores. The British established their operations center at Tangier Island, and many battles and skirmishes ensued upon the Bay. The citizens of the young nation were not eager to bow to the British, including those at the shipbuilding center of St. Michaels. Blockade runners routinely left the Eastern Shore port, and hostility ran high. Late on the night of August 9, 1813, amid rumors of an impending British attack, the good citizens of St. Michaels blew out their lanterns. Just before dawn, the British attacked a nearby fort. The wily Shorefolk were ready. They hoisted their lanterns into the treetops, the British fired too high, and the town, except the now-renowned "Cannonball House," was saved. For this, St. Michaels calls itself "The Town That Fooled the British."

A year later came the war's decisive battle. In September 1814, a man watched the fire of cannons and guns as the Americans successfully defended Fort McHenry, which guards the entrance to Baltimore Harbor. The next morning, Francis Scott Key saw a tattered U.S. flag flying and, inspired, penned the words to "The Star-Spangled Banner." It became the national anthem in 1931.

NINETEENTH-CENTURY LIFE

Once this second war ended, the denizens of nineteenth-century Chesapeake country turned to building their economy. Tobacco declined; shipbuilding grew. Smaller Chesapeake shore towns, such as Chestertown and Annapolis, lost commercial prominence to Baltimore, which grew into the Upper Bay region's major trade center. Steamships were launched, and the Baltimore & Ohio Railroad more speedily connected the region to points west. Exported were Eastern Shore-grown wheat and the watermen's catch of oysters, menhaden, and more. By all accounts, there was no love lost between the landed gentry, who controlled the region, and the Chesapeake watermen. These scrappy individualists may have been one-time small farmers down on their luck or were descendants of released indentured servants who had once served the wealthy class.

The shoals of the Chesapeake saw their first aids to navigation in this era. Lightships were sent out to warn passing ships of the worst sandbars. In 1819, Congress made provisions to set two lightships in Virginia waters. This experiment in safety was popular, and by 1833, ten lightships stood sentinel at the mouth of the Rappahannock River and elsewhere in the Bay. The mid-nineteenth century saw construction of the distinctive screw-pile lighthouses, with

David Trozzo

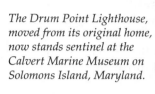

The Drum Point Lighthouse, moved from its original home, now stands sentinel at the Calvert Marine Museum on Solomons Island, Maryland.

their pilings that could be driven securely into the muddy bottom of the Bay. Today, only three stand — two at maritime museums at Solomons and St. Michaels, Maryland, and one in action in the Bay just southeast of Annapolis, off Thomas Point. The Thomas Point Light was manned until automation came in 1986.

As the Bay became easier to travel, the people who spent the most time on the water discovered perhaps her greatest wealth. In the nineteenth century, demand increased for the famous Chesapeake oysters. Watermen went after them in an early ancestor to many "Bay-built" boat designs, the log canoe. Boats like the fast oceangoing schooners known as "Baltimore clippers" already were being built, but oyster dredging and tonging required boats that could skip over shoals, run fast, and allow a man to haul gear over the side. Log canoes have unusually low freeboard; crab pots and oyster tongs can be worked over their sides. These successors to dugout canoes were given sails and shallow-draft hulls to navigate shoals. With their top-heavy sails and low sides, log canoes now present one of a yachtsman's greatest challenges. Shifting their weight just ahead of the wind, sailors race log canoes most summer weekends on the Eastern Shore.

The Bay's 120-year steamboat era arrived in 1813, seven years after packets first carried passengers on a ship-and-stagecoach journey from Baltimore to Philadelphia. The steamboat *Chesapeake* paddled out of Baltimore Harbor on June 13, 1813, for Frenchtown, Maryland, a now-extinct town at the head of the Bay. Within a week, a trip was offered to Rock Hall, Maryland, on the Eastern Shore, for seventy-five cents. By 1848, the steamship company that came to be called the Old Bay Line ran the 200-mile length of the Bay, from Baltimore to Norfolk. Steamships ran in the Bay into the 1960s.

THE CIVIL WAR & SLAVERY

Even as the Chesapeake Bay fueled a growing nineteenth-century economy, these were the years of growing North-South hostility. The Chesapeake region was largely slaveholding, although the nearby Mason-Dixon Line (the southern boundary of Pennsylvania) to the north beckoned many slaves to freedom. Historical accounts say this tended to moderate the behavior of many Maryland slaveholders who feared their slaves would run away.

The history of slavery here had started with tobacco farming in the late 1600s; by 1770, tobacco exports reached 100-million pounds in the Western Shore region. When the tobacco trade declined in the nineteenth century, the services of many slaves were no longer needed. Abolitionist Quakers living in the Bay area campaigned to free many slaves, and free blacks were not uncommon in Annapolis and Baltimore in the first half of the nineteenth century. Many Eastern Shore watermen were free blacks, who mixed with white watermen in mutual contempt for the wealthy.

In 1817, abolitionist and writer Frederick Douglass was born into slavery in Talbot County, Maryland. As a boy, he worked at the Wye Plantation, owned by Edward Lloyd V, the scion of a political dynasty in Maryland. Following alternately civil treatment in Baltimore and brutal treatment as an Eastern Shore field hand, Douglass escaped to Philadelphia at age 21 and became a free man. Because the upper reaches of the Bay were so close to freedom, the Underground Railroad thrived here. The best-known local conductor was Harriet Tubman, an escaped slave from Dorchester County, Maryland, who led nearly 300 slaves north during her lifetime.

When the Civil War broke out in 1861, the Virginia half of the Chesapeake quickly turned to Richmond, located at the head of navigation of the James River. Maryland struggled over its political loyalties. Many Chesapeake families would be divided by the North-South rivalries.

Naval warfare changed forever on the waters of the Civil War Bay, when the *Monitor* and the *Merrimack* met at Hampton Roads. The *Merrimack*, having been salvaged, rebuilt as an ironclad, and renamed *Virginia* by the Confederates, had already rammed and sunk the Union *Cumberland* and disabled the *Congress*, which burned and sank. The next day, the ironclad *Monitor*, with her two guns protected in a swiveling turret, arrived to engage the *Merrimack's* fixed guns. Neither ship sank the other; neither side won, but the encounter was the first battle between armored battleships.

Ironically, when the Emancipation Proclamation went into effect in January 1863, slaves laboring on the Virginia shores of the Chesapeake were freed where federal law — via Union occupation — prevailed; slaves in Union Maryland were not. The Proclamation freed only those in the states "in rebellion against the United States." It wasn't until September 1864, when Maryland voted for its own new constitution, that those in bondage in the state were freed.

THE OYSTER BOOM

In the years before the war, shrewd Baltimore businessmen had opened oyster packing plants. With the war over, enterprising Chesapeake business was renewed. The fertile oyster bars of the Bay's famed shoals fueled a much-needed economic spurt for the Eastern Shore.

Chesapeake oyster production peaked at more than 11-million bushels during the great oyster boom of the 1870s. The Eastern Shore Railroad snaked down through the flatlands to Dorchester County, where one John Crisfield, former Maryland congressman, set about capitalizing on his new railroad. At the head of Tangier Sound, where watermen were dredging or tonging millions of oysters from the rich waters, Crisfield built a town that still calls itself the "Crab Capital of the World." The town was literally built upon millions of oyster shells. An enormous wharf stretched along Somer's Cove, and the railroad depot stood nearby. Shuckers and packers set to work once the daily catch was landed; the cargo was shipped out on the railroad line; newly developed refrigeration techniques kept it fresh on its way deep into the nation's interior.

Like Crisfield, Solomons, Maryland, sprang from the oyster rush. Isaac Solomon came from Baltimore, taking his patented pasteurizing canning process to the tiny village, where he set up a successful packing plant.

From this gold mine grew greed, and the famed Chesapeake Oyster Wars ensued. The oystermen — the tongers and dredgers, known as "drudgers" — battled over rights to oyster beds; tempers ran high, and shots were fired. Maryland authorities, already funding an Oyster Navy to maintain some measure of decorum on the Bay, were angered that Virginia was not so helpful when it came to keeping its watermen within their boundaries whatever exactly they were.

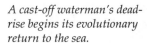

A cast-off waterman's deadrise begins its evolutionary return to the sea.

David Trozzo

The Oyster Wars proved to be the catalyst that finally forced Maryland and Virginia to define their disputed Bay border. Three years of negotiations at the federal bargaining table set the boundary in 1877 about where it is today. The southern shore of the Potomac was always the boundary between the two states, but how far down that shore the river ended and the Bay began, from which point to draw the line east across the Bay was subject to dispute. The two states agreed to draw the line across Smith's Point to Watkins Point on the Eastern Shore's Pocomoke River. Today, the boundary has been further refined: Maryland extends to the low-tide line of the river on the Virginia shore. Present-day Virginians at Colonial Beach accept this arrangement with ingenuity, playing the lottery of their own state in town and betting on their neighbor's jackpot at the end of a long pier — the same device they resorted to decades ago when gambling was legal in southern Maryland.

CHESAPEAKE TOURISM

The late nineteenth century brought the first tourists to the Bay, lured by clever investors who built the first resorts. Vacationers from Baltimore and Philadelphia turned to the Chesapeake, staying at new hotels built at Betterton and Tolchester on Maryland's Eastern Shore. On the Western Shore, Chesapeake Beach, just south of the Anne Arundel-Calvert County line, was carved from the shore by businessmen from the Pennsylvania Railroad. A new train station built there gave easy access to people from Baltimore and Washington, D.C.

Until about 1920, the Bay and tributaries were the region's highways. Ferries connected to railroad lines crisscrossed the network of water and land, and steamships were everywhere. Farming and fishing supported much of the rural Western and Eastern shores in both Maryland and Virginia. Following World War II, the Chesapeake region mirrored the rest of the country, as industry and shipping propelled Baltimore and Norfolk into a new prosperity.

The automobile, too, fueled change, and by the mid-twentieth century the time had come to span the Bay by highway. On October 1, 1949, construction of the Chesapeake Bay Bridge began. Less than three years later, on July 30, 1952, the $112-million, 4.3-mile bridge opened. Over the next thirty years, travelers "discovered" the Eastern Shore as never before. As far south as Salisbury, Maryland, towns saw growth; Talbot and Kent counties in particular became home to many retirees from the cities.

In 1964, the other end of the Bay was spanned. The spectacular Chesapeake Bay Bridge-Tunnel was more than three years in the making, at $200 million, and visitors in 1999 will see its multimillion-dollar twin span erected, allowing four-lane travel for much of the 17.6-mile corridor. Two mile-long tunnels and twelve miles of trestled roadway alternately soar above, then dive beneath the Bay. Four constructed islands serve as supports between bridge and road, as the bridge-tunnel spans the entryway through which early explorers first found the Chesapeake.

What is the future of the Bay area? Apparently, it depends on the self-control of those who live here and of those within the watershed that spreads to upstate New York, whose debris ultimately trickles into the Bay. Annapolis, with ties to Baltimore and Washington, D.C., increasingly is caught in the region's web of urban growth, yet manages to maintain its colonial charm. The Bay area still retains its rural places. Along the Northern Neck of Virginia, there are only a couple of convenience stores. Across the Bay, on the Eastern Shore, the old shipbuilding ports of Oxford and St. Michaels have new lives as quiet, colonial-style villages for people who have opted to escape the city.

The first English settlers, Protestant and Catholic, brought diversity when they came to live among the Native Americans already here. So it is today, as city dwellers and those who fall in love with "the land of pleasant living" move in among the old families whose forebears long ago planted and fished along the Chesapeake Bay.

CHAPTER TWO
Of Ferries & Freeways
TRANSPORTATION

The history of Chesapeake transportation is intimately tied to this vast inland sea, plied in ancient days by dugout canoes, later by indigenous sail craft, and today, by massive steel cargo ships or yachts.

For centuries, native inhabitants, the Susquehannock, Wicomico, and Nanticoke had the Bay to themselves. Then came the Spanish explorers and in 1607, the seventeenth-century Englishmen who settled first at Jamestown, Virginia. Soon after the vessels *Ark* and *Dove* delivered Maryland's first settlers in 1634, commerce drove the development of a ferry system across the Bay's many rivers and creeks.

In the heyday of the Chesapeake steamboats, tourists cruised the Bay aboard such classic vessels as the Dreamland *on their way to Chesapeake Beach (pictured here) and other resort towns.*

By the late 1600s, ferries crossed the South River south of present-day Annapolis to deposit traders at London Town, where they swapped furs for supplies. In 1683, what is said to be the oldest passenger ferry service in the country launched its run between Oxford and Bellevue on Maryland's Eastern Shore — and still makes the crossing.

Next came the steamship era. The *Chesapeake* sailed from Baltimore in 1813, the Patapsco River serving as a nineteenth-century highway connecting the boat's route to now-extinct Frenchtown on the Elk River. Passengers could disembark and cross to the Delaware Bay by stagecoach, then reboard a sailing packet for Philadelphia.

Despite the *Chesapeake's* historic role on the water, it was the Baltimore Steam Packet Company (known more commonly, even lovingly, as the Old

Bay Line) that came to symbolize the Bay's maritime tradition of transportation. The venerable company commenced commerce in 1839 and operated first wooden, then steel, paddle wheel boats and steamships into the 1960s.

Even as boat routes linking small towns spread across the Bay, ambitious plans connected the Chesapeake with the young nation's expanding interior. In 1850, the 184.5-mile Chesapeake and Ohio Canal opened after twenty years of construction. The canal was built alongside the nonnavigable section of the Potomac River above Washington, D.C., which in turn is strategically linked to the Bay via the navigable waters of the lower Potomac. A marvel of modern engineering at the time, the canal was nevertheless cursed by progress. Just about the time it opened, the first rails were laid for the Baltimore & Ohio Railroad.

The B&O was the first railroad to connect Bay country to the "outside," but others soon followed. Working in tandem with packet and steamship lines, railroads dramatically opened up the area. Passenger and freight stations opened deep on the Eastern Shore at places like Crisfield, which boomed from oyster exports in the late nineteenth century.

The 4.3-mile William Preston Lane Memorial Bridge, known locally as the Chesapeake Bay Bridge, frames a familiar seascape for Chesapeake anglers.

David Trozzo

Steamships and ferries, railroads, and small roads all provided transport well into this century. A ferry crossed the Bay near Annapolis, where the 4.3-mile William Preston Lane Memorial Bridge (known locally as the Chesapeake Bay Bridge) now stands, until a single span first connected the isolated Shore to the rest of the world in 1952. Later, a second span was added. Travel to the Shore and to Atlantic beaches by tourists and city dwellers boomed, eventually outgrowing the bridge and roadway system. In 1991, a new bridge replaced an aging drawbridge at Kent Narrows, just east of the Bay Bridge, greatly easing beach-bound traffic over the busy Narrows.

Not long after the Upper Bay was opened to cars, a feat of engineering did the same at the mouth of the Bay. Where Vikings once may have sailed, the Chesapeake Bay Bridge-Tunnel now stands. The massive, 17.6-mile span alternates bridge and tunnel across four constructed islands to Cape Charles from the Virginia mainland and will be joined in midsummer, 1999, by a $197-million twin span headed in the other direction. This means traffic will move through four lanes going north and south, *except* when lanes converge back to a two-lane highway as the road dips beneath the Bay's shipping channels. At that point, traffic will be funneled back into the existing two tunnels.

Travelers can reach the gateway cities to the Chesapeake — Washington, D.C., Baltimore, and Norfolk-Hampton Roads — by air, bus, or train. Keep in mind that mass transportation outside the cities is generally poor, although some connections can be made. To get the most out of your visit, you'll want to rent a car to explore the small towns and back roads of the largely rural, rambling Chesapeake region. For a taste of local adventure, wander back roads and cross tributary creeks and rivers the same way that European forebears did as early as the late 1600s — by ferry.

GETTING TO THE CHESAPEAKE BAY AREA

BY AIR

Four major airports serve the region — one in Baltimore, one in Washington, D.C., another in nearby northern Virginia, and yet another in the Norfolk-Hampton Roads area. In addition, regional airports, located at Salisbury, Maryland, and in the Newport News-Williamsburg, Virginia, area offer commuter service with easy connections to major airports around Washington, D.C. and the MidAtlantic (see From Regional Airports). Check their web sites for key information that could change, such as, ground transport schedules.

Maryland

Baltimore-Washington International Airport (P.O. Box 8766, BWI Airport, MD 21240; 800-435-9294; www.bwiairport.com; 410-859-7111 Baltimore area; 301-261-1000, 301-261-1001 Washington area) BWI lies an easy twenty-five-mile drive north of Annapolis via I-97. Located fewer than fifteen minutes from Baltimore's Inner Harbor, BWI is a major hub for USAirways, but all major airlines fly in and out. Amtrak and light rail serve Baltimore and the region.

Shuttles and limousine services trundle passengers from the airport to nearby cities and towns, generally in the Baltimore-Washington metropolitan area. Cars for hire take passengers farther — to the Eastern Shore, for example — but prices go up accordingly. Make reservations early; check the Yellow Pages or ground transportation pages on the airport's web sites for shuttle companies. Or, catch the *SuperShuttle* (800-BLUEVAN; 410-859-0803) to Baltimore from 5:45 a.m.–11:15 p.m. ($11 one-way; $18 round-trip) and to Annapolis from 7:00 a.m.–11:00 p.m. ($19 one-way; $30 round-trip). The shuttle offers a variety of routes and schedules.

David Trozzo

Baltimore-Washington International Airport is a convenient point of entry to Bay Country.

If you're headed into the Washington, D.C. area, *Airport Connection* (301-441-2345) offers reasonably priced door-to-door service to Prince Georges and Montgomery Counties, northern Virginia, and Washington, D.C. Costs generally range from $18-$25 per person for Prince Georges and Montgomery Counties, but a second person may ride for less.

Washington, D.C. Metropolitan Area

Ronald Reagan Washington National Airport (Ronald Reagan Washington National Airport, Washington, D.C. 20001; 703-417-8000; www.metwashairports.com) At the edge of the city, National opened a spiffy new terminal in recent years, complete with an impressive glass façade and filled with shops, cafés, and food-to-go eateries.

Washington Dulles International Airport (Washington Dulles International Airport, Dulles, VA 20166; 703-572-2700; www.metwashairports.com) Thirty miles to the west in northern Virginia.

If it's ground transportation that you want, check the Yellow Pages, airport web sites, or look to the *Washington Flyer* (Washington Flyer, 15th & K Sts., Washington, D.C. 20001; 888-WASHFLY; 703-685-1400), where you'll find transportation between the two airports, or into downtown Washington, D.C. and its Metrorail subway system, and access to the Baltimore-bound *SuperShuttle*.

If you're not overloaded with luggage, there's another route to Baltimore: from Dulles, get ground transportation to downtown Washington, D.C. and take the Red Line to Union Station, where you can board a MARC train for Baltimore; from National, take the Orange Line to the Metro Center, then transfer to the Red Line to Union Station, where you can board a train for Balitimore (MTA; 410-539-5000, train schedules).

Since the Metro runs daily, you can make it all the way to Annapolis via public commuter transportation. From Dulles, get ground transportation to the Metro Center and take the Orange Line to the New Carrollton's Amtrak-MARC (Maryland Area Rail Commuter) station. From National, get on the Metro's Orange Line to the New Carrollton's Amtrak-MARC (Maryland Area Rail Commuter) station. It's about twenty miles west of Annapolis. Weekday travelers can catch the commuter bus to Annapolis, which also runs from Kent Island or Annapolis into Washington, D.C. Contact: *Dillon Bus Service*; 800-827-3490; 410-647-2321, schedules.

Tidewater Virginia

Norfolk International Airport (2200 Norview Ave., Norfolk, VA 23518; 757-857-3351; 757-857-3200; www.norfolkairport.com) Tidewater's aviation hub. To catch a ride from the airport, try the *Norfolk Airport Shuttle* (757-857-1231), which offers transport throughout the Norfolk-Hampton Roads area, and (for a per-mile fee) will also drive you throughout the region, including the Eastern Shore or villages on the western tidewater peninsulas. Costs vary according to distance and the size of your party.

FROM REGIONAL AIRPORTS

Two strategically placed regional airports offer commuter service via major airlines, while a scattering of smaller local airports supply charters, tie-downs, and other services that you'd seek from a fixed-base operator.

COMMUTER SERVICE

The Newport News-Williamsburg International Airport (900 Bland Blvd., Newport News, VA 23602; 757-877-0221; www.phf-airport.org) Formerly the military's Camp Patrick Henry, this airport hosts service to larger airports in the MidAtlantic area by United/United Express, US Airways and its attendant Express, and AirTran Airlines. For wide-ranging ground transportation throughout the area, contact *Williamsburg Limousine Service* (757-877-0279).

Salisbury-Ocean City; Wicomico Regional Airport (Airport Manager's Office, 5485 Airport Terminal Rd., Unit A, Salisbury, MD 21804; 410-548-4827) Deep into Maryland's Eastern Shore, this airport offers USAirways Express shuttle service (USAirways Express/Piedmont Airlines; 410-742-4190) to Baltimore, Washington, D.C., Philadelphia, and Charlotte. Also, find national car rental offices here.

The area's other airports all offer regular aviation services.

Bay Bridge Airport (202 Airport Rd., Stevensville, MD 21666; 410-643-4364) Flight school, tie-downs, and repairs. Can arrange shuttles.

Easton Municipal Airport (29137 Newnan Rd., Easton, MD 21601; 410-770-8055) Tie-downs, ground support. Charter service based here.

Freeway Airport (3900 Church Rd., Mitchellville, MD 20711; 301-390-6424) Daily, 8:00 a.m. to dark. Tie-downs and maintenance.

Lee Airport (Old Solomons Island Rd./Box 273, Edgewater, MD 21037; 410-956-2114) Tie-downs, no charters. Located two miles south of Annapolis.

BY AIRPORT RENTAL CAR

Three airports clustered in the Baltimore-Washington, D.C. area mean that rental car agencies often let you rent a car at BWI, for example, and return it to National or Dulles without an extra drop-off cost. Generally, you can call any of the major agencies at any of the airports to make arrangements that could take you to another airport. Here's a list of numbers to get you started.

From BWI:
Alamo (800-327-9633).
Avis (410-859-1680).
Budget (410-859-0850).
Dollar (410-684-3316).
Hertz (410-850-7400).
National (410-859-8860).

From Dulles:
Avis (703-661-3500).
Budget (703-437-9373).
Thrifty (703-471-4545; Herndon, VA).

From National:
Alamo (703-684-0086).
Budget (703-419-1021).
Dollar (703-519-8700).
National (202-783-1590).
Thrifty (703-838-6895).

From Norfolk:
Alamo (757-857-0754).
Avis (757-855-1944).
Hertz (757-857-1261).

From Newport News/Williamsburg:
Avis (757-877-0291).
Budget (757-874-5794).
Hertz (757-877-9229).
National (757-877-6486).
Thrifty (757-877-5745).

Toll-Free Numbers:
Alamo (800-327-9633).
Avis (800-331-1212).
Dollar (800-800-4000).
Hertz (800-654-3131).
National (800-227-7368).
Thrifty (800-367-2277).

BY BUS

Travelers with a slim wallet or a sense of adventure may want to reach the Bay area by bus, but be forewarned that service is limited and schedules

CHESAPEAKE BAY AREA ACCESS

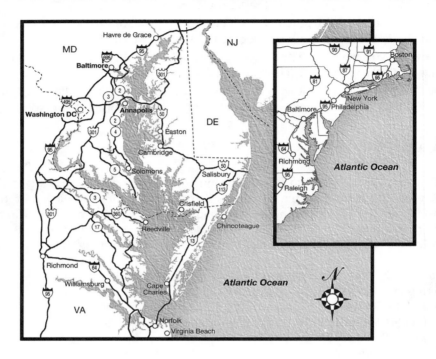

Virginia's less-than-urban interstates post 65 mph speed limits, and Maryland is boosting speeds on some of those roads as well. Given slower driving times on secondary roads, however, we offer you these approximate distances and driving times, calculated at 50 mph, from the following major cities to Annapolis:

City	Miles	Hours
Atlanta	631	12.75
Boston	425	8.5
Chicago	706	14.0
Cincinnati	504	10.25
New York	216	4.5
Norfolk, VA	204	4.25
Philadelphia	120	2.5
Richmond	133	2.5
Raleigh, NC	277	5.5

may change. As always, call ahead. Some routes to the Eastern Shore mean riding Greyhound from Washington, D.C. to Baltimore, then switching to Trailways for the rest of the trip.

Maryland and Washington, D.C.

The Washington Greyhound terminal is located at 1005 1st St. NE. To get from Washington, D.C. to Annapolis, board the Washington Metro at Union Station, ride the Red Line to Metro Center, change to the Orange Line, and head for New Carrollton, MD. During the workweek, you can take the commuter bus into Annapolis. Schedules are available from *Dillon Bus Service* (800-827-3490; 410-647-2321) From Baltimore's bus station at 210 W. Fayette St., find Trailways connections to the Eastern Shore: Baltimore station (410-752-0868); Washington, D.C. station (202-289-5154). Greyhound schedules and fares (800-231-2222 English; 800-531-5332 Spanish; www.greyhound.com).

To get around Annapolis, contact: Department of Public Transportation; 410-263-7964, schedules and fares.

Local stations on the Eastern Shore with twice-a-day service by Trailways to and from Baltimore:

Cambridge (Carolina Trailways, 2903 Ocean Gateway Dr.; 410-228-5825) Located in the Sunburst Mobile.
Easton (Fast Stop Convenience, Rte. 50, Cordova Rd.; 410-822-3333).
Salisbury (350 Cypress St.; 410-749-4121).

Virginia

For municipal service around Virginia's urban tidewater:

Hampton-Newport News (Pentran; 757-723-3344).
Norfolk (Greyhound-Trailways; 757-627-7538) Trailways makes three trips a day from Norfolk to Exmore, on Virginia's eastern Shore, and back again.
Norfolk area (Tidewater Regional Transit (TRT); 757-640-6200).

BY CAR

North

From New York. South from the New Jersey Turnpike, cross the Delaware Memorial Bridge, then take I-95 to 896 S. toward Middletown, then pick up U.S. 301 south through the Delaware Upper Eastern Shore. Head for Annapolis across the 4.3-mile-long William Preston Lane Memorial Bridge, or journey through the Shore on Rte. 50 east. You'll get a good taste of the flat interior of the tidewater landscape.

Travel Tips for Drivers

Circumnavigating Washington, D.C.: For those who live here, Washington's famed **Capital Beltway** is more than a political concept for the pundits. It's the major artery circling the city. Travelers will encounter other names for the elliptical roadway. The eastern half is known as I-95 N. and S. — even as it proceeds east and west. The western half is called I-495, and travelers headed clockwise will find the road referred to as west, north, and east. Locals refer to the clockwise lanes as the Beltway's "inner loop," while the counterclockwise route is known as the "outer loop."

Meanwhile, an anachronism rules the Beltway's southeastern corner — a drawbridge. The **Woodrow Wilson Memorial Bridge** across the Potomac, while offering a spectacular view of the river, opens only occasionally, but travelers weary of the highway may want to avoid the possibility.

Baltimore's Harbor Tunnel can get backed up, especially during rush hour or the weekend rush to the Atlantic beaches. To bypass, take I-695 east to the **Francis Scott Key Bridge.** The trip is a bit longer, but the view is much better. And as long as we're talking summer weekends, consider crossing the William Preston Lane Memorial Bridge (aka the **Bay Bridge**) at Rte. 50 near Annapolis sometime other than eastbound on a Friday in July at 6:00 p.m., or westbound on a Sunday afternoon in August right at 4:00 p.m.

Or, you could take I-95 from Delaware. Cross the head of the Chesapeake at the Susquehanna River near Havre de Grace. (More congested U.S. 40 parallels I-95 for most of the trip between the Maryland line and Baltimore.) Follow I-95 through the Baltimore Harbor Tunnel or the Fort McHenry Tunnel, or take I-695, the Baltimore Beltway, east and south to the Francis Scott Key Bridge over the Patapsco River. The bridge route takes about twenty minutes longer, but the high span provides a spectacular view of the city and its harbor, guarded by Fort McHenry in the fork of the river, to your right.

Either way you traverse Baltimore, take the Beltway (I-695) to I-97 for rapid access to Annapolis and points east and south.

From Harrisburg, Pennsylvania. Take I-83, which crosses through rural Baltimore County to I-695, the Baltimore Beltway. Exit west on the Beltway and eventually you'll reach I-97, a direct connection to U.S. 50 just west of Annapolis.

West

From Pittsburgh. The Pennsylvania Turnpike connects with I-70 at Breezewood, PA, which then drops south to Hancock, MD. This is your quickest route into the region. I-70 splits at Frederick, MD. For a scenic route to Frederick through rolling farmland, take Alternate U.S. 40. Just east of Frederick, the highway diverges. Reach Annapolis and the Eastern Shore by way of either Washington, D.C. or Baltimore.

From Washington, D.C. The quickest way to Washington from the west is via I-270, but avoid it if you're coming into town during rush hour. From I-270, take the Washington Beltway (I-495 E., becoming I-95 S.). Twenty miles after you leave I-270, look for the John Hanson Highway, U.S. 50. Head east to Annapolis and, just beyond the city, you'll reach the dual spans of the William Preston Lane Memorial Bridge, gateway to the Eastern Shore.

From Baltimore. From the west, travel I-70 from Frederick to I-695, the Baltimore Beltway. To reach Annapolis, head south on the Beltway and follow signs for I-97. This is an easy alternative to driving the notoriously traffic-choked Washington Beltway.

From western Virginia and Dulles Airport. Take I-66 east. The road connects with the Washington Beltway seven miles east of Vienna, VA. Take the Beltway's inner loop north to I-95 to Baltimore; take the outer loop south to reach U.S. 50 and Annapolis. Rte. 50 E. crosses the Beltway just north of Cheverly, MD.

South

Coming north on I-95. Which way you go depends on where in the area that you're headed. To go directly to the tip of Virginia's Eastern Shore, pick up U.S. 13 in North Carolina to the Norfolk area and follow the signs for the Chesapeake Bay Bridge-Tunnel. Or, continue on I-95 to Richmond and take I-64 E. down the historic peninsula between the James and York rivers. At the end of the peninsula, the highway tunnels under the mouth of the James River to Norfolk. Pick up the Bridge-Tunnel to the Shore.

If you're headed to the Annapolis area, take I-95 to I-495, the Washington Beltway, and circumnavigate the eastern side of the city. When you reach Rte. 50, turn east toward Annapolis. Since the I-95/I-495 intersection south of the city in northern Virginia often is traffic-choked at rush hour (which can start surprisingly early) consider turning off I-95 thirty miles north of Richmond for a very pleasant scenic ride that's not all that much longer. Follow Va. 207 northeast to Bowling Green and pick up U.S. 301 N. across the Rappahannock River and into Maryland. Expect a twenty-mile stretch of heavy commercial development and stop-and-go traffic around Waldorf. The road merges with U.S. 50 E. twelve miles west of Annapolis.

If you want to visit the Northern Neck, take U.S. 301 until it intersects with Va. Rte. 3. Bear right on U.S. 360 to Reedville or stay on Va. Rte. 3 to Kilmarnock.

Or, back on Rte. 301, cross into Maryland over the only bridge downriver from Washington, D.C. Twenty-four to twenty-six miles later, Md. 234 connects to Md. 5 S. to Leonardtown and St. Marys City, from which you can wend your way up the Bay on Md. Rtes. 235, 4, and 2 past Solomons and Prince Frederick to Annapolis.

BY TRAIN

Amtrak's classic train stations operate in fully renovated pre-World War II-era elegance. Check out Baltimore's Pennsylvania Station (1500 N. Charles St.) and Union Station (Massachusetts & Louisiana Aves.) in Washington, D.C. While waiting for the train, it's fun to explore Union Station's neoclassic interior, filled with an array of shops, restaurants, and cafés.

Amtrak also operates a rail station at BWI Airport, a short ride from the terminal, on the line connecting Washington, D.C. and Baltimore (800-USA-RAIL; www.amtrak.com; schedules and fares).

The Metro subway system (202-637-7000), with a stop at Union Station, offers good service throughout Washington's Maryland and Virginia suburbs every day.

Direct access to the Chesapeake Bay region via Annapolis is available during the workweek from Amtrak's New Carrollton Metro Station (410-539-5000, information). The last commuter bus to Annapolis leaves at 7:50 p.m.

GETTING AROUND THE CHESAPEAKE BAY AREA

We've organized the Chesapeake by five geographic regions. The **HEAD OF THE BAY,** which sprawls across either side of the Susquehanna River, starts north of Aberdeen, circles the top of the Bay, and ends at the Sassafras River. On the western side of the Bay, we've designated the area south of the Magothy River to the Potomac River and west to Rte. 301 as the **ANNAPOLIS/WESTERN SHORE** area. Virginia's **NORTHERN NECK/MIDDLE PENINSULA** region is bordered by the Potomac River and Rte. 301 to the north, Rte. 17 to the west, and the York River to the south. On the eastern side of the Bay, from the Sassafras River south to the Choptank River and east to the Delaware line, visitors find themselves in the **UPPER EASTERN SHORE.** The **LOWER EASTERN SHORE** starts south of the Choptank River and runs to the tip of the Virginia peninsula, with a side trip through Berlin to Assateague Island.

Your best bet for getting around the Chesapeake Bay area is by car. You can take the famous Chesapeake ferries at selected points, but keep in mind that they're small-scale traditions, not bulk mass transport.

BY BUS

Visitors will quickly discover that buses aren't the world's best option for getting around the Bay area, but you can make a few connections (see the heading Getting to the Chesapeake Bay Area, under By Bus).

Maryland

Greyhound offers daily buses from Baltimore (410-752-1393) and Washington, D.C. (202-289-5154) to Easton (Rte. 50 at Cordova Rd.; 410-822-3333), Cambridge (2903 Ocean Gateway Dr.; 410-228-5825), and Salisbury (350 Cypress St.; 410-749-4121). The Baltimore to Salisbury run operates five times a day. Travelers may need to transfer in Stevensville, on Kent Island.

For fare and schedule information on public bus service around Annapolis, contact: Department of Public Transportation; 410-263-7964.

Virginia

Trailways makes three trips a day from Norfolk to Exmore, on Virginia's Eastern Shore, and back again. Contact: Greyhound-Trailways, 701 Monticello Ave., Norfolk, VA 23501; 757-627-7538.

Maps

Once you've got your wheels, put a good map in the glove compartment. Some of the best are the freebies offered by the states of Maryland and Virginia, including maps highlighting scenic routes or historical tidbits. The Maryland Department of Transportation offers not only an excellent highway map, but a scenic routes map. Contact: MD DOT State Hwy. Admin., 707 N. Calvert St., Baltimore, MD 21203; 410-545-8747; fax 410-209-5033. State tourism officials also can help you get ahold of a map. Contact: Maryland Office of Tourism Development, 217 E. Redwood St., Baltimore, MD 21201; 800-543-1036; 410-767-3400.

Virginia's Department of Transportation also gives away a very detailed highway map. Contact: VDOT Admin. Services Division, 1401 E. Broad St., Richmond, VA 23219; 804-786-2801.

For a few well-spent dollars, you can also buy an excellent map of the Chesapeake Bay region that includes historic markers and eliminates the need to switch maps if you cross state lines. The Alexandria Drafting Co., aka ADC Maps, puts out this gem that's available at area convenience stores. You can also buy direct from the company. Contact: ADC Maps, 6440 General Green Way, Alexandria, VA 22312; 800-232-6277; check, credit card.

The American Automobile Association (AAA) offers their members service and TripTiks, their famous route recommendations. Contact: in Maryland-Washington, D.C. area; 800-AAA-HELP emergency roadside service; 800-631-8747 TripTiks; main telephone number for AAA Potomac; 703-222-4200.

For the AAA of Tidewater in Virginia, contact: 757-622-4321 emergency roadside service; 757-622-5634 TripTiks.

BY CAR

To ease confusion for road trippers: U.S. 301 runs north-south from the Potomac River to U.S. 50 at Bowie, Maryland, where it turns east with U.S. 50. The northbound road becomes Md. Rte. 3 to Baltimore. South of the Potomac toll bridge, Rte. 301 traverses Virginia's northern Tidewater area to Richmond. Drive southeast along intersecting Va. Rte. 3 or Rte. 17.

U.S. 50, meanwhile, heads east from Washington, D.C., picking up a Rte. 50/301 designation at Bowie. Soon after crossing onto the Eastern Shore, the road splits. Rte. 50 heads south, providing one of the Shore's major north-south arteries, then east after crossing the Choptank River at Cambridge. North of the split, Rte. 301 goes solo again past the far Upper Eastern Shore. U.S. 13 is the other major north-south highway on the Shore, running all the way up Virginia's Eastern Shore from the Chesapeake Bay Bridge-Tunnel at Kiptopeke, through the middle of Maryland's Lower Shore, and up the Delmarva Peninsula through Delaware.

BY RENTAL CAR

Arrange your rentals before you get to the Northern Neck/Middle Peninsula (see By Airport Rental Car). If you didn't pick up a car at the airport, try these local offices.

ANNAPOLIS/WESTERN SHORE

Budget (2002 West St., Annapolis; 410-266-5030).
Enterprise (1023 Spa Rd., Annapolis; 410-268-7751; 913-A Commerce Rd.,
    Annapolis; 410-224-2940).
Hertz (22711 Three Notch Rd., California; 301-863-0033).

UPPER EASTERN SHORE

Avis (Easton Municipal Airport; 410-822-5040).
Old Reliable (4041 Ocean Gateway Dr., Trappe; 410-476-3055).

LOWER EASTERN SHORE

Avis (Salisbury-Ocean City: Wicomico Regional Airport; 410-742-8566).
Hertz (Salisbury-Ocean City: Wicomico Regional Airport; 410-749-2235).
U-Save (1727 Market St., Pocomoke City; 410-957-1414).

David Trozzo

The Oxford-Bellevue Ferry, said to be the country's oldest, continually operating ferry, also serves as a highlight on a popular Eastern Shore bike ride.

BY FERRY

The 300-year-old ferryboat tradition remains in this region of snaking rivers, creeks, and you-can't-get-there-from-here roadways that support the prevailing Bay-influenced terrain. If you need assistance, check your maps or ask around for exact locations of these fun, charming ferries suited for the slow-going, moseying motorist.

NORTHERN NECK/MIDDLE PENINSULA

Merry Point Ferry (540-899-4093) The Merry Point, in Lancaster County, offers trips across the Corrotoman River. Free. Except for extreme high tides/bad weather, open year-round, Mon.–Sat., 7:00 a.m.–7:00 p.m.

Sunnybank Ferry (540-899-4093) Near Smith Point at the mouth of the Potomac River in Northumberland County, this small ferry crosses the Little Wicomico River at Ophelia. Free. Except for extreme high tides/bad weather, open year-round, Mon.–Sat.,7:00 a.m.–7:00 p.m.

UPPER EASTERN SHORE

Oxford-Bellevue Ferry (410-745-9023) The oldest, continuously operating private ferry in the country was launched on November 20, 1683. Its longevity partially can be explained by its strategic location. Two of Talbot County's most popular and historic towns, Oxford and St. Michaels, aren't situated far apart as the crow flies, but you'll travel a fair piece by road. Open Mar. 1–Nov. (Jun.–Labor Day, Mon.–Fri., 7:00 a.m.–9:00 p.m.; Sat.–Sun., 9:00 a.m.–9:00 p.m.; remaining months, Mon.–Fri., 7:00 a.m.–sunset; Sat.–Sun., 9:00 a.m.–sunset). Car and driver: $5 one-way; $8 round-trip; $.50 each passenger each way. Bicycles: $2 one-way; $3 round-trip. Walk-ons: $1.00. Closed Dec.–Feb.

LOWER EASTERN SHORE

Whitehaven Ferry (410-334-2798) This tiny ferry crosses the scenic Wicomico River about eighteen miles southwest of Salisbury on Rte. 352. Free. Open year-round, 6:00 a.m.–7:30 p.m. in summer; 7:00 a.m.–5:30 p.m. in winter. Also in Wicomico is the **Upper Ferry** (410-334-2798). Free. Open year-round, 6:00 a.m.–7:30 p.m. in summer; 7:00 a.m.–5:30 p.m. in winter.

Several ferries also operate out of Crisfield to Smith and Tangier Islands. Check full listings in Chapter Six, *Recreation* in the heading Boating, under Cruise & Excursion Boats. For year-round service to Smith Island (this is for adventurers only; be sure that you've arranged accommodations in advance if you intend to stay overnight), contact: *Captain Jason I and II* (410-425-4471; 410-425-5931).

CHAPTER THREE
Bed & Breakfast & Boat
LODGING

Chesapeake visitors easily discover an impressive array of accommodations, from upscale waterside resorts offering every amenity of the good life to Victorian inns serving afternoon tea in good china cups. You also find good local motels, where somebody in the office can supply extra ice for weekend fishing parties.

David Trozzo

Lights blaze at the out-of-the-way Virginia Shore lodge, The Garden and The Sea Inn.

Longtime B&B visitors know that these unique lodgings are as different as their owners. Some are cute and cozy; others, elegant and highbrow. Some owners remain at your disposal; others cook breakfast, point you toward attractions, then head off for a day at work. These differences are worth keeping in mind when making reservations.

But other practical considerations also should be weighed when preparing to visit a B&B:

• Are you allergic to pets? Good innkeepers let their visitors know during the reservation process if a dog or cat lives in the house, but anyone can forget once in a while. If animal dander poses a problem for you, be sure to ask. While we're on the subject of pets: it's a rare B&B that accepts your own traveling Fido or Fifi. We've noted those that do, but for the most part, motels and hotels are more inclined to accept your animal companion with prior arrangement.

• It's best to assume that B&Bs ask guests not to smoke in the house.

• Traveling with your children? Many B&Bs discourage children, particularly young children. The reason tends to be the same: these are favored accommodations for couples searching for a private getaway, and a wailing toddler in the night does not a relaxing weekend make. Innkeepers are very good about setting age limits. We've noted those inns that welcome kids.

• Most B&Bs require reservations, although a few take walk-ins. When making reservations, check on a few bookkeeping items. Ask about deposits and refund policies, which can vary widely and could be costly, if you cancel and your reserved room is not rented. Then, check on minimum stays — many inns in popular tourist centers have two-night minimums, especially on busy weekends. Off-season or midweek rates may be discounted, and if you're bunking with a third party, find out about additional per-person costs. Finally, ask about taxes, which in Annapolis can add up to twelve percent.

• Private baths will not be shared, but they could be located down the hall. Innkeepers usually provide robes. If it's an attached bath that you seek, be specific. Also, older houses are hard to rehab; some have individual climate control, and some do not. We have not delved into that issue here, but if window AC units bother you, be sure to ask.

• In our listings, we note whether or not a lodging is handicap accessible. We're considering the comfort of your overnight stay — not simply whether a wheelchair can be lifted through the front door. We hope that we've been accurate.

• Along those same lines, older folks — or anybody with creaky knees or cranky backs — definitely need to find out what floor their room is on. Many older homes have third-floor rooms, and very few have elevators. Ask if the bathroom includes a claw-foot tub; stairs and high-sided tubs can be difficult. Also, elegant high beds are popular in many B&Bs, but these, too, may pose a problem for less-than-nimble guests. Innkeepers are as interested in your comfort as you are, so feel free to ask.

• Finally, make sure that your innkeeper knows if you have food allergies. Most will happily prepare your breakfast accordingly. Keep in mind that most do their grocery shopping mid-to-late week, or at least prior to your Friday afternoon arrival, so it's helpful to let them know in advance.

Not every traveler is a B&B person. For those who prefer the greater privacy of a motel or hotel, we've included a listing of some of those available in the area. And since many Bay visitors road-trip throughout the region, travelers might want to do some camping. Also, the boating public will want to come armed with information about marinas; see Chapter Six, *Recreation*, for information.

LODGING NOTES

Reputable B&B inspection services hold their clients to a high standard of service and can match visitors to B&Bs that suit their tastes. Among those familiar with the region:

Amanda's B&B Reservation Service (1428 Park Ave., Baltimore, MD 21217;

800-899-7533; 410-225-0001) Named for the *Amanda,* a Baltimore ship known for cleanliness. Handles reservations throughout the MidAtlantic. Charge is $5 for successful reservation; no repeat charge.

Annapolis Accommodations (66 Maryland Ave., Annapolis, MD 21401; 800-715-1000; 410-280-0900; www.stayannapolis.com) Matches the person to the property.

RATES

Rates can vary widely according to season; what we offer here is based on high season, generally considered late spring to fall, before taxes. It's often possible to arrange a lower midweek rate, and costs may be lower in colder weather. For the price, two people staying at a B&B can generally expect breakfast (often a full, elaborate meal) and often reduced or free parking. Also, a B&B suite, offering luxuries such as a second room, balcony, or whirlpool bath, is priced higher, thus shifting the full lodging to a higher range. Per-person charges may be made for more than two people. Rates are always subject to change.

Inexpensive	Up to $55
Moderate	$56 to $85
Expensive	$86 to $125
Very Expensive	$126 and above

Credit cards are abbreviated as follows:

AE – American Express	DC – Diner's Club
CB – Carte Blanche	MC – MasterCard
D – Discover	V – Visa

INNS & BED-AND-BREAKFAST LODGINGS

HEAD OF THE BAY

Chesapeake City

INN AT THE CANAL
Innkeepers: Mary & Al
  Ioppolo.
410-885-5995.
www.chesapeakecity.com/
  innatthecanal/inn.htm.

The Victorian inn, replete with elaborate ceiling murals in both the parlor and dining room, is still known locally as the Brady-Rees House, after the Bradys who owned and operated tugboats on the nearby canal. Six rooms reflect their owners' long expe-

104 Bohemia Ave./P.O. Box 187, Chesapeake City, MD 21915.
Price: Moderate to Very Expensive.
Credit Cards: AE, CB, D, DC, MC, V.
Handicap Access: No.

rience in the B&B biz: uncluttered, with easily accessible luggage racks so there's no mystery about where your suitcase is supposed to go. Nice touches include bureaus converted to sinks in the bathrooms and four-poster rice beds. Individually heated with in-room AC, telephones, and TVs, rooms are good-looking without a lot of fuss. Upstairs find a third-floor suite. Breakfast is served at individual tables, and guests will want to visit Inntiques, a store oriented toward antique tools and kitchen implements, located beneath the house in the former milking room.

SHIP WATCH INN
Hosts: Linda & Thomas Vaughan.
410-885-5300.
www.chesapeakecity.com/shpwtch.htm.
401 First St., Chesapeake City, MD 21915.
Price: Expensive to Very Expensive.
Credit Cards: AE, MC, V.
Handicap Access: Yes.

Visitors watching the passing maritime parade along the Chesapeake & Delaware Canal will quickly and no doubt appreciatively discover a pair of binoculars stationed near the window in each guest room. Be it container ship or steel-hulled yacht, "watching the ships" is an entrancing local pastime that the Vaughans clearly kept in mind during their 1996 renovation to this 1920 building. They overhauled everything, including the bathrooms, leaving behind an inn where all eight rooms face the water. Porches run along the three floors, each shared by no more than three rooms. Breakfast may be served here during nice weather. The rooms vary broadly along a design scale that one might call "comfortable elegance," and are nicely detailed and furnished with antiques. A draped "crown" plays headboard to a canopied bed in Room #5, where a lady's secretary, replete with a safe, doubles as a nightstand; the whirlpool bath is just through the attached bathroom door. The Vaughans are descended from one Capt. Firman Layman, once proprietor of a former inn that's now the fine-dining Bayard House. The family tradition continues.

Havre de Grace

LA CLE D'OR GUESTHOUSE
Proprietors: Ron Browning & Bill Kirkpatrick.
888-HUG-GUEST; 410-939-6562; fax 410-939-1833.
226 North Union Ave., Havre de Grace, MD 21078.
Price: Expensive.

La Clé D'or looks sturdily prosperous from the outside, but check out the crystal chandeliers and shiny gold wallpaper in the parlor! The house is surprisingly luxurious, and host Ron Browning knows a thing or two about antiques. Guests staying over for the weekend will find themselves breakfasting on a different set of china each day. The rooms retain the French flair — this is, after all, Havre de Grace, the "Harbor of Grace" named by

Credit Cards: MC, V.
Handicap Access: No.
Restrictions: Smoking allowed only in kitchen.

Lafayette. The Rochambeaux comes with a double bed, and the bath is around the corner. Loofahs join the soaps and other toiletries in the baskets. Next door find the pleasant La Peu, rented only with the Rochambeaux, making a nice accommodation for traveling couples. Then there's the LaFayette Suite, with a queen-sized bed and six friendly windows. Each room comes with TV and VCR. A big hot tub is out back in the gardens. But here's the kicker: you get a bottle from nearby Boordy Vineyards when you check out. Who's paying whom around here? Ron is a schoolteacher and books rooms around his schedule.

SPENCER-SILVER MANSION
Host: Carol Nemeth.
800-780-1485; 410-939-1097.
E-mail: spencersilver@ erols.com.
200 S. Union Ave., Havre de Grace, MD 21078.
Price: Moderate to Very Expensive.
Credit Cards: AE, D, MC, V.
Handicap Access: Yes, in carriage house.
Special Features: Children welcome, including babies.

"J.N. Spencer, 1896" reads the plate by the doorbell. This is authentic Victorian, from the intricate hallway woodwork progressing to the stone carriage house out back, which matches the stone of the house. Four rooms inside the house include details like marble-topped tables or corner cabinets with inset glass. Two rooms share a bath; two have private baths. In one of the private baths, a luxurious two-person whirlpool is approached through French doors with stained glass. The carriage house is cozy enough to spend the winter, with a queen-sized bed, daybed, whirlpool, TV/VCR, and kitchenette. Pine paneling warms up the upstairs bedroom, charming right down to the window seat. TV is available for a small fee in the other rooms. Fresh fruit in the rooms, and well-behaved children are welcome, including babies. Another relative rarity: breakfast is served until 10:30 a.m.

VANDIVER INN
Innkeeper: Suzanne Mottek.
800-245-1655; 410-939-5200; fax 410-939-5202.
www.vandiverinn.com.
301 S. Union Ave., Havre de Grace, MD 21078.
Price: Moderate to Expensive.
Credit Cards: AE, D, MC, V.
Handicap Access: Ramp into building, but claw-foot tubs.

The venerable Vandiver, one-time home to the local mayor and Maryland politician, has been in the hospitality business since 1985. The 1886 Victorian, nine rooms in all, comes with intriguing architectural detail in some rooms, such as twin flues or small tiles artfully placed around the fireplaces. The smallest room retained its antique double bed when last we visited, but the inn was in the process of swapping full-sized for queen-sized beds. Private telephone lines come into each room, and baths may come with claw-foot tubs. Sensible white chenille spreads on each bed lend an aura of the past. There's a new ninth room, which is a very pleasant suite with its own little porch.

ANNAPOLIS/WESTERN SHORE

B&B owners in the crowded historic district of Annapolis, where parking is notoriously difficult, have worked out a deal with the city. Guests of B&Bs belonging to the Annapolis Association of Licensed Bed & Breakfast owners can park in city-operated parking garages for $4 for twenty-four hours. Be aware that you cannot come and go during that period without repaying. (If you plan to stay in town, it's far easier to walk to the historic district restaurants and attractions anyway.) Some of these B&Bs do provide off-street parking.

The B&B association is noted for cooperation among members; if you should find that the inn that you've chosen is full, the member-innkeeper can be very helpful about helping you to book a room elsewhere in town. The city has more B&Bs and lodgings than we've been able to detail here, but those in the association police themselves, and visitors should be comfortable with their recommendations.

Annapolis

ANNAPOLIS MARRIOTT WATERFRONT
General Manager: Colleen Huther.
800-336-0072; 410-268-7555.
80 Compromise St., Annapolis, MD 21401.
Price: Expensive to Very Expensive.
Credit Cards: AE, D, DC, MC, V.
Handicap Access: Yes.
Special Features: Smoking rooms available.

This hotel offers an Annapolis commodity: twenty-four waterside rooms with expansive views. In all, fifty rooms vary but include king or double beds with sitting areas, good-looking bedspreads and window treatments, and niceties like irons, cable TV, hair dryers and coffeemakers. Valet parking costs $12 per night. Visitors also will find a fine location for a cold one at Pusser's Landing (see Chapter Four, *Restaurants & Food Purveyors*), a pub right on the waters of Ego Alley, so named for the parade of boaters showing off their craft, or is it their physiques? Room rates are based on whether or not there's a water view. Suites, king-sized beds, a small on-site fitness room, and concierge service.

CHEZ AMIS
Owners: Don & Mickie Deline.
888-224-6455; 410-263-6631; fax 410-295-7889.
www.chezamis.com.
85 East St., Annapolis, MD 21401.
Price: Expensive to Very Expensive.
Credit Cards: MC, V.

This cute and cozy former corner store comes with a pressed-tin roof downstairs and breakfast at the Stammtisch, named for the German table where family and friends gather. Guests can even use the kitchen. A downstairs suite has a king-sized bed and trundle beds, offering respite to a family. Upstairs, The Capital Room salutes both the Maryland Statehouse visible out the window and the nation's capital, where Mickie was once a

Handicap Access: No.
Restrictions: No children under age 10.

tour guide (husband Don was a longtime Army lawyer). Photos of politicos line the walls, just as they do in the Judge's Chambers — where guests can sleep in a queen-sized sleigh bed. In the smaller red, white, and blue Captain's Quarters, an intriguing collection of chess pieces from around the world adorn one wall. This is the only room with a private bath, requiring a brief trip down the hall, and decorated in a nautical style that even includes an anchor. A kind of nook-and-cranny quality marks the two-toned, rose-colored house, with its collection of bunnies and bears and a handmade quilt hanging from the stairwell wall. Mickie even keeps a stocked umbrella stand next to the front door.

COGGESHALL HOUSE
Owners: Bill & Ruth Coggeshall.
410-263-5068.
198 King George St., Annapolis, MD 21401.
Price: Expensive to Very Expensive.
Credit Cards: No.
Handicap Access: No.
Restrictions: Closed Jan.–Feb.

Gutted and rebuilt in the early 1990s, this 1887 house boasts impressive detail, such as the individually milled wainscoting in the front hallway. Truckloads of dirt were removed from the backyard, making room for a sculpted landscape, featuring brick patios with wrought iron furniture abutting the neighboring U.S. Naval Academy. This must be the best view of the academy chapel dome in town. For such a luxurious, large house, the value couldn't be better. Paintings line the walls, and halls are open and spacious. Guests, who stay on two different floors, no doubt feel that they have plenty of space. On the third floor, a green sleigh bed highlights a Laura Ashley-bedecked suite with a sitting area painted a lighter shade of green. Second-floor guests choose either the room with twin beds covered by Bill's grandmothers' yellow-and-white quilts or a four-poster bed next door. Either way, the bath is located nearby in the secluded corner of the hall, right beside the rooms. Full breakfasts in the formal dining room, short walk to City Dock.

THE DOLLS' HOUSE BED & BREAKFAST
Owners: Barbara & John Dugan.
410-626-2028.
161 Green St., Annapolis, MD 21401.
Price: Expensive.
Credit Cards: No.
Handicap Access: No.

For value, it's hard to go wrong in this classic Victorian, trimmed out in tiger oak and home to innkeeper Barbara Dugan's extensive collection of dolls — which means the frat crowd might want to stay elsewhere. All three attractive rooms are actually suites, two with separate sitting rooms, the third, the Master Suite, an extended room divided by the boxed-in chimney. TVs are in the sitting rooms; queen-sized beds and attached baths accompany each. Great fun is the Victoria Room, featuring Queen Victoria in bureau-top versions and a print on the wall. Upstairs is the ultraeaved

Nutcracker Suite, with two double beds in a large bedroom and a pullout couch in the comfortable sitting room. Add the big bath with its long claw-foot tub and stall shower, and this is one of the city's best options for families with older children (per-person charges for more than two).

The Dugans took over this B&B in 1995 and have done much to update the house, as well as considerable work in the backyard. Landscaped gardens create a delightful getaway, especially since you're only a block from City Dock. Churchill the collie is sociably in residence.

EASTPORT HOUSE BED AND BREAKFAST
Hosts: Barry & Susan Norfolk.
410-295-9710;
fax 410-295-9711.
E-mail: eastporths@toad. net.
101 Severn Ave., Annapolis, MD 21403.
Price: Expensive to Very Expensive.
Credit Cards: No.
Handicap Access: No.
Restrictions: Only children over age 8.

More than a few "Captain's Quarters" dwell among the Bay's B&B accommodations, so it's surprising that nobody else (at least, nobody else we saw) has really done what these transplanted Chicagoans have done. Looking to Orvis or L.L. Bean for inspiration, they've created a really Chesapeakey place with room themes to match: The Fish Room, The Duck (not decoy) Room, The Captain's Quarters, The Sailboat Room, and The Maryland Blue Crab Room. The Captain's Quarters may be the most muted, with white and blue accenting original 1860s floors. The Duck Room comes in green and white, replete with one of those half-canoe shelves, while wooden Costa Rican fish mark their namesake room. The house is recently renovated, so all bathrooms are new. TVs in some rooms, guest refrigerator, private telephone lines, and a nice backyard porch. Breakfast at the oak dining table. One block from the water in a popular local part of town. Streetside parking.

55 EAST
Innkeepers: Tricia & Mat Herban.
410-295-0202;
fax 410-295-0203.
55 East St., Annapolis, MD 21401.
Price: Expensive.
Credit Cards: MC, V.
Handicap Access: No.
Restrictions: Only children over age 12.

"Handsome" leaps to mind to describe the rooms at this tucked-away B&B, which manages to marry worldly aplomb with enough tradition so you'll still know that you're in the cradle of the nation's colonial history. Guests can relax and listen to music or watch TV in two classic, downstairs parlor areas, including one painted the most enviously adventuresome color of blue-green you ever saw. Out French doors stands a treat: a New Orleans-inspired courtyard, with a terra-cotta and brick fountain and big roses blooming in pots. A second-floor balcony overlooks the scene, accessible from two guest rooms. In all, three rooms come with either queen beds or a king that converts to twin, and attached baths — two with an unusual feature, full-body spray showers. The rooms are all uncluttered, with original drawings or Vermont Casting stoves, cedar suit hangers in the closets, and queen- or king-sized beds. Breakfast on toasted pecan and corn waffles in winter or strawberry soup come summer, all served on china and crystal. All in all, sophisticated, upscale taste.

FLAG HOUSE INN
Owners: Charlotte & Bill Schmickle.
410-280-2721.
E-mail: info@flaghouseinn. com
www.flaghouseinn.com
26 Randall St., Annapolis, MD 21401.
Price: Moderate to Very Expensive.
Credit Cards: No, but personal checks accepted.
Handicap Access: No.
Restrictions: No young

Your hosts gave up tenure at a North Carolina college to buy this B&B within a block of the U.S. Naval Academy, where their eldest son is a member of the Class of `99. Their insight into academy life comes out in small ways. During one "Induction Day," the notorious first day when the plebes' hair is unceremoniously — or is that ceremoniously? — shorn as they shift from civilian life, the Schmickles set a photo on the sitting room mantel. It was of them, with their son, taken on his "I-day." A gentle reminder to guests that they know how it is — and that this, too, shall pass.

Large for Annapolis, this B&B offers five straightforward, comfortable rooms: king-sized beds, mini-TVs, AC, and European-style split bathrooms in some. A two-room suite may suit families. Full breakfast is served in the dining room downstairs, where a Russian samovar sits on the sideboard. Bill, a political science professor, found the samovar in a North Carolina antique shop; he also searches out the interesting naval prints that hang in the inns' common rooms. The Flag House Inn encourages 10:00 p.m.–7:00 a.m. "quiet time" due to traveling noise in the old home, says Charlotte. Off-street parking in back.

GEORGIAN HOUSE BED & BREAKFAST
Innkeepers: Dan & Michele Brown.
800-557-2068; 410-263-5618.
E-mail: georgian@erols. com.
www.georgianhouse.com.
170 Duke of Gloucester St., Annapolis, MD 21401.
Price: Expensive to Very Expensive.
Credit Cards: AE, MC, V.
Handicap Access: No.
Restrictions: No children.

Prominent members of the colonial Forensic Society once gathered in this 1747 house, including Annapolitan signers of the Declaration of Independence. Now they remain memorialized by the room names: Thomas Stone, William Paca, Samuel Chase, and one nonsigner with a famous, painterly last name, Charles Willson Peale. Although the formal dining room and parlor reflect that past, only one guest room is clearly of that period, with its 1770 fireplace intact and a small deck outside. Recent renovations to the house bring opportunity for surprisingly updated though classic style to two more rooms and a two-room suite, as well as attached baths. The suite includes a sitting room, with pullout couch, Oriental rugs.

Walls painted a soft yellow-beige prime a cottage-style room, newly renovated with silk screen prints, while upstairs, Irish antiques accent a hideaway room with exposed beams, rustic and very comfortable. On the second floor, guests can watch TV, use the refrigerator, laundry, and microwave, or they can settle in the parlors downstairs. This is a big house first divided a century ago and then remerged, so there's plenty of space.

HISTORIC INNS OF ANNAPOLIS
Asst. Gen. Manager: Alex Bollman.
Owned by Remington Hotels.
800-847-8882; 410-263-2641; fax 410-268-3813.
www.annapolisinns@erols.com.
58 State Circle, Annapolis, MD 21401.
Price: Expensive to Very Expensive.
Credit Cards: AE, DC, MC, V.
Handicap Access: Yes.
Restrictions: No pets.
Special Features: Smoking and nonsmoking rooms available; valet parking; includes the Maryland Inn, Governor Calvert House, Robert Johnson House.

With three inns set on three circles, the historic inns create a unique setup. No matter where you're staying, however, you'll check in at the Governor Calvert House, on State Circle, directly across from the Statehouse. Management does its best to efficiently shepherd guests through the process, down to a valet in a minivan to take you to your room. You may or may not be able to designate which inn you'll be staying in — that depends on the evening's complement of guests. In all, 128 rooms are available, and each room is different. The 1720 **Governor Calvert House** may be the most modern of the three, given an extensive 1983 renovation. Archaeologists discovered a 1730 hypocaust, an eighteenth-century, central heating system originally engineered by the Romans, now preserved in a Plexiglas-covered floor for all to see. The **Robert Johnson House** is probably the quietest of the three, with no conferences and no restaurants, just guests. The **Maryland Inn,** part of which dates to the pre-Revolutionary era, started life as an inn in 1784 and remained so until a post-World War I hiatus as an office/apartment complex. The familiar front desk has been relieved of those duties, so visitors who wander into the lobby will find a concierge to answer questions and to redirect them for check-in.

The Maryland Inn is a sentimental favorite among many Annapolitans and visitors, although the bathrooms may be small, and visitors can expect to see window units and other evidence of this inn's age. Also at the Maryland Inn are the jazz club King of France Tavern and the Treaty of Paris Restaurant (see Chapter Four, *Restaurants & Food Purveyors).* Very much a local institution.

THE INN AT SPA CREEK
Innkeepers: Rick & Jeanne Brown.
410-263-8866.
E-mail: stay@innatspa creek.com.
www.innatspacreek.com.
417 Severn Ave., Annapolis, MD 21403.

There's nothing "ye olde" about this highly contemporary house, with skylights and aluminum bannisters sweeping along like those on the deck of a fancy yacht. It's a terrific addition to the local collection of Georgian, Federal, and Victorian era B&Bs. Three bedrooms and a suite are uncluttered and tend toward classic furniture. The Marina Room comes with a reproduction four-poster king bed; the

Price: Very Expensive.
Credit Cards: AE, MC, V.
Restrictions: Only children age 12 and older.

Garden View Room offers an antique queen-sized bed. Downstairs, the Porthole Room affords versatility, with twin beds made up as a king. New bathrooms are simple and white. Upstairs, a skylight-filled suite with in-room Jacuzzi offers upscale romance, with private deck and fireplace, and a small, bookshelf-lined WC with bidet. Architecturally, this is an interesting home, with a white-and-aqua gourmet kitchen worthy of your envy and open sitting areas. Paddington the friendly dog also lives here, and Jeanne says that he's even filled in for guests' much-missed pups. Off-street parking.

JONAS GREEN HOUSE
Owners: Randy & Dede Brown.
410-263-5892;
    fax 410-263-5895.
E-mail: jghouse@erols.com.
124 Charles St., Annapolis, MD 21401.
Price: Expensive.
Credit Cards: AE, D, MC, V.
Handicap Access: No.
Restrictions: Children and pets allowed with prior notice.

Stand in the nineteenth-century dining room and look back through the eighteenth-century hallway that connects to the seventeenth-century kitchen: this house is the genuine article for visitors seeking colonial accommodations. Widely considered one of the two oldest homes in Annapolis, the Jonas Green House is operated by its namesake's great-great-great-great-great grandson and wife. Green himself was the colony's printer, taught the trade by cousin Ben Franklin. The current owners renovated the old house in the early 1990s and can offer complete tours to architecture buffs. The home's decor is carefully reproduced, with white walls and colonial wainscoting. Three rooms offer antique beds with modern, custom-made mattresses and spare, period accents — like a spinning wheel in one room. There are pine floors and fireplaces in each room. Full breakfasts in the morning. Easygoing, uncluttered atmosphere; off-street parking.

LOEWS ANNAPOLIS HOTEL
General Manager: Terri Ryan.
800-526-2593; 410-263-7777.
126 West St., Annapolis, MD 21401.
Price: Expensive to Very Expensive.
Credit Cards: AE, D, DC, MC, V.
Handicap Access: Yes.
Special Features: Smoking rooms available; pets allowed.

Considered one of the city's finest hotels, Loews provides all of the amenities in a brick courtyard-style hotel. In all, 217 guest rooms and suites offer it all, from basics like queen- or king-sized beds to fax machines in business-class rooms. There's even a scale under the bathroom sink, if you dare, in this city of rich restaurants. Rooms are comfortable and handsome, with coordinated earth tone bedding and window treatments. A wide range of services includes child care, complimentary van service (probably a good idea at night), lounge, and the noted Corinthian Restaurant. Valet parking available; otherwise, $9 and $12 per night. Ideal for visitors seeking straightforward luxury.

MAGNOLIA HOUSE
Owners: John & Mary
     Prehn.
800-293-3477; 410-268-3477.
220 King George St.,
     Annapolis, MD 21401.
Price: Moderate.
Credit Cards: No.
Handicap Access: No.
Special Features: Children
     welcome in third-floor
     suite.

En route to the upper floor of this friendly, historic district B&B, retired Navy Capt. John Prehn stopped to show us his collection of "Lucky Bags." If you know what that is, you may have found your local home away from home. The Prehns, well known in Annapolis, opened up their comfy B&B some years ago, after their five children grew up and moved out. This may be one of the best places in town to take your own kids — a third-floor suite sleeps six. On the second floor, look for the comfortable Peacock Room or the Fireside Room with its shelves of good reading, including some good titles for military history buffs. Breakfast is served in the chandelier-lit dining room during winter and in the brick townhouse patio-garden by the magnolia tree come summer. Oh, and if you don't know, the *Lucky Bag* is the U.S. Naval Academy's yearbook.

TWO-O-ONE
Innkeepers: Graham
     Gardner & Robert A.
     Bryant.
410-268-8053;
     fax 410-263-3007.
E-mail: bbat201@aol.com.
www.201bb.com.
201 Prince George St.,
     Annapolis, MD 21401.
Price: Expensive to Very
     Expensive.
Credit Cards: AE, D, MC, V.
Handicap Access: No.
Restrictions: No children.

The Annapolis B&B scene has diversified mightily in recent years. Parents visiting their kids in college find no-muss-no-fuss lodgings serving ample breakfasts to fuel the busy day; budget-conscious, retiree-history buffs can stay downtown without busting the pension. But if it's a romantic getaway weekend that you're after, other establishments better suit your purpose. Two-O-One falls well into the latter category. Resident parakeets ("budgies" to Scottish co-owner Graham Gardner) chatter away in the antique-filled living room, but the rest of the house whispers only with refinement and comfort. As Gardner explains, "We try to be unobtrusive." That means that you'll find enough towels to last the weekend in your closet, a corkscrew to open the wine, and highball glasses next to the minifridge. Four accommodations include two individual rooms and two suites. Rooms are very tastefully done with Waverly wallpaper or English and American antiques like a "beau brummell" from Pickfair. Expect touches like a hair dryer on the wall of the tailored bathroom, accompanying "The Admiral's Room," named for an elderly friend who formerly owned the house's third dog, Sandy. Whirlpools in the suites; suit hangers in the closets. Full breakfasts are served beneath the dining room's antique crystal chandelier.

**THE WILLIAM PAGE
     INN**
Owner: Robert Zuchelli.

This inn is among the city's most dependable accommodations, with a knowledgeable on-site host, off-street parking, and fresh flowers in

800-364-4160; 410-626-1506.
E-mail:
    wmpageinn@aol.com
www.williampageinn.com.
8 Martin St., Annapolis,
    MD 21401.
Price: Moderate to Very
    Expensive.
Credit Cards: MC, V.
Handicap Access: No.

each room. Five rooms include the Marilyn Suite, which comprises the top floor and boasts a big sitting area and TV. Two rooms share a bath (robes supplied), and two others have their own bath, including one with a whirlpool. While reproductions and antiques add flavor to the turn-of-the-century, cedar-shingled home, they don't clutter. Full breakfasts are offered. Zuchelli, long active in the local B&B industry, knows how to run a classy inn, providing luxury and privacy without a fuss.

Solomons

The Back Creek Inn B&B in Solomons, Maryland, is a civilized retreat for cruisers who want to dock out back and have some "land time."

David Trozzo

BACK CREEK INN B&B
Hosts: Carol Pennock &
    Lin Cochran.
410-326-2022;
    fax 410-326-2946.
www.bbonline.com/md/
    backcreek/.
210 Alexander Lane/P.O.
    Box 520, Solomons, MD
    20688.
Price: Expensive to Very
    Expensive.
Credit Cards: MC, V.
Handicap Access: Yes.
Special Features: Deepwater
    dock (draws 8 ft.).

The gardens may be the first thing that visitors notice at this waterside inn. There's even a goldfish pond, filled by a small stone waterfall. Inside sliding glass doors is a very comfortable common room, with stereo, TV, and the daily newspaper. The pastel rooms are named for herbs, and beds are king- or queen-sized. Seven rooms provide a variety of accommodations to choose from, all with private baths. The stairways and hallways in the 100-year-old section of the former waterman's house tend to slope authentically — certainly no detraction from this comfortable, well-run inn. A full breakfast is served. There is also a bungalow built in 1990. Perhaps best of all are the wonderful waterside lawn and dock, with accompanying deep water where a yachtsperson in need of a shower and a bed can appreciatively anchor.

SOLOMONS VICTORIAN INN
Owners: Helen & Richard Bauer.
410-326-4811.
125 Charles St./P.O. Box 759, Solomons, MD 20688.
www.chesapeake.net/ solomonsvictorianinn/.
Price: Expensive to Very Expensive,
Credit Cards: D, MC, V.
Handicap Access: Yes.
Restrictions: Only children over age 13.

From a sailor's peaked and varnished top-floor suite to a simple bedroom with a bath, this B&B wins the prize for sheer range of available accommodations. The Bauers scouted around before settling on this Solomons mainstay, the 1906 home of the boatbuilding Davis family. They've really put a lot into the place. The Victorian house is home to five rooms with private baths (all but one attached), and all are pleasantly furnished with antiques or reproductions. Upstairs is the spectacular (and yachty) top-floor suite, replete with a blue in-room whirlpool under a skylight and a built-in seating area with matching blue cushions and a small galley. The view of the harbor is enough to make you buy a boat. The new carriage house in back offers two lovely big rooms, including a classy hideaway upstairs with a king-sized bed across from an in-room whirlpool. The Bauers gave up hotels more than a decade ago in favor of B&B travel, and their guest-driven attention to detail shows. Full breakfast is served 8:00 a.m.–10:00 a.m.; the coffee pot is on by 7:30 a.m.

NORTHERN NECK/MIDDLE PENINSULA

Champlain

LINDEN HOUSE BED & BREAKFAST PLANTATION
Hosts: Ken & Sandy Pounsberry.
800-622-1202; 804-443-1170; fax 804-443-0107.
E-mail: lindenhouse@ msn.com
www.inngetaways.com/va /lindenh.html;
www.bbhost.com/linden housebb.
Rte. 17 S./P.O. Box 23, Champlain, VA 22438.
Price: Expensive to Very Expensive.
Credit Cards: AE, D, MC, V.
Handicap Access: Yes.

They're putting in a huge fish pond at Linden House (small lake might be more like it), which we bring to your attention only to point out what industrious folks run Linden House, a 1750 planter's home, eight miles from the crossroads town of Tappahannock. The Pounsberrys found a structurally sound shell when they came here in 1990, and what they've created is inspiring. Licensed catering, you might expect, but beef cows doubling as picturesque — and income — in the vast fields leading to the road? They do a good job here. We stayed in a room over the new carriage house, white with lime-green trim and a bed with good pillows that caused neither husband nor wife to stir during the night. These are the least expensive rooms at the inn, but large and quite comfortable. Upstairs in the old home, the Davis Room exemplifies the accommodations, with a fireplace mantel discovered in the old barn (in pieces) and a whirlpool in the bath just steps from the bedroom door. Everything about this inn seems thoughtful and well considered, from a decision to incorporate the existing columns into a sunroom to the footpaths on the 200-acre spread. Breakfast in the old part of the house was plentiful, and the service was most gracious and warm. A retreat unto itself.

Irvington, Virginia

The stylish Hope and Glory Inn spent a past life as the schoolhouse in Irvington, Virginia.

David Trozzo

THE HOPE AND GLORY INN
Owner: Bill Westbrook.
Manager: Joyce Barber.
800-497-8228; 804-438-6053; fax 804-438-5362.
www.hopeandglory.com.
P.O. Box 425, Irvington, VA 22480.
Price: Expensive to Very Expensive.
Credit Cards: MC, V.
Handicap Access: In one of the cottages.

This inn hits a perfect note of hip whimsey with an outdoor bath — there's even a claw-foot tub. You'll find it after rounding the garden path. The circa 1890 schoolhouse is enormously fun to explore, with unexpected touches and yards of cotton fabric, American flags, and bright folk art pieces, like the lobby's green-and-red prop plane. Seven rooms in all — all different. Among our favorites: a tiny study in white, with a huge gilded mirror. The "bookcase room" means that your bed is built into an alcove, with shelves of books at your feet. An empire-waist wedding gown hangs from the wall of another dreamy accommodation. The bathrooms tend more toward functional than fancy. There's overstuffed furniture and easygoing amenities, like a CD player and TV in a sitting area downstairs. Breakfast is served at a long farm table, which seats fourteen people. There are four cottages in back along the garden path, past the patio umbrellas.

David Trozzo

The Miss Ann *still goes on the Saturday morning "rum run" from the venerable Tides Inn, now part of The Tides Resorts in Irvington, Virginia.*

THE TIDES RESORTS
Tides Inn/Tides Lodge.
Owners: The Stephens
   Family.
800-843-3746; 804-438-5000;
   fax 804-438-5222.
E-mail: the-tides.com.
www.the-tides.com.
King Carter Dr., Irvington,
   VA 22480.
Price: Very Expensive.
Credit Cards: AE, CB, D,
   MC, V.
Handicap Access: Yes.
Restrictions: Pets allowed
   in certain rooms for extra
   charge.

Representing the third generation of this hotelier family, Randy Stephens showed us around the family business one crisp day. He took us from the recently moved children's playground on the grounds of the famed Tides Inn, across Carter's Creek aboard the water shuttle to the Tides Lodge. Long owned by another member of the family, the lodge has now merged officially with the inn to create The Tides Resorts. The inn has 134 rooms compared to the lodge's sixty rooms. In addition to the main building on the inn grounds, there's the Windsor and Lancaster buildings, with larger rooms called "junior suites." Among newer rooms, look for an upscale version of the typical room, with two double or king beds, small TV, coordinated decor that could include an upholstered headboard and double sinks in the bathroom, as well as that all-important coffee pot! A variety of restaurants serves everything from a café lunch to formal fine dining (see Chapter Four, *Restaurants & Food Purveyors*), and the yacht *Miss Ann,* launched as the *Siele* in 1926, is a familiar sight cruising local waterways. Marina dockage is available, and the lodge long has been known for golf.

The price for the inn rooms may strike some as high, but includes absolutely everything but golf and lunch. Lodge rooms are priced in an a la carte fashion, so you'll pay a fee for sailing or bikes. Excellent golf is at the ready, along with tennis, croquet, swimming. The ultimate Chesapeake purveyor of Virginia hospitality.

Lancaster, Virginia

INN AT LEVELFIELDS
Innkeepers: Doris &
  Warren Sadler.
800-238-5578; 804-435-6887;
  fax 804-435-7440.
10155 Mary Ball Rd./P.O.
  Box 216, Lancaster, VA
  22503.
Price: Expensive.
Credit Cards: AE, MC, V.
Handicap Access: No.
Restrictions: Only children
  over age 12.

At an endlessly long lane through a flat tidewater field, this antebellum plantation house was built in 1857 for Thomas Sanford Dunaway, a man of the cloth. Union soldiers bivouacked in the field out back, and, as the story goes, Dunaway sat on the back porch with shotgun in hand and talked them out of burning down the place. The Sadlers have operated it as an inn for some years. Four big guest rooms sit neatly in each corner of the second floor. All have attached baths, ceiling fans, fireplaces, and coordinating antique pieces, complementing the color of the rooms: green, red, blue, and yellow. Particularly nice is the huge blue room, with a pleasant corner sitting/reading area, a balcony, a king-sized, mahogany pencil-post bed, and an Oriental rug. As is common in an old house such as this, air-conditioning comes from window units. Prix fixe dinners for guests and the public, by reservation on Fri. and Sat. nights.

Reedville, Virginia

CEDAR GROVE
Hosts: Susan & Bob Tipton.
804-453-3915.
2743 Fleeton Rd., Reedville,
  VA 22539.
Price: Expensive.
Credit Cards: MC, V.
Handicap Access: No.
Restrictions: Only school-
  aged children.

Located around the point from Reedville at the tiny village of Fleeton ("population 88," reads the sign, "with 17 dogs") Cedar Grove offers a good location for nature lovers. Adirondack-style chairs sit on a small Bayside beach behind the inn, one amenity that's hard to come by given the Bay's famously limited public access. The proprietors have reorganized accommodations in recent years and now offer two suites with sitting room and bath. If you can book it, ask for the very private Lighthouse Suite, with a sunny, water view porch off a cheerful blue room with attached bath. The water views are spectacular, especially in late summer when crape myrtle blooms like crazy in this part of the Bay's world. Susan has been active in local tourism affairs for some years and can easily direct you throughout the region. Formal breakfast. Bikes are available.

The mast of the ship captain, who built The Gables in Reedville, Virginia, runs in the center of its second two stories.

David Trozzo

THE GABLES
Innkeepers: Barbara & Norman Clark.
804-453-5209.
859 Main St./P.O. Box 148, Reedville, VA 22539.
Price: Moderate to Expensive.
Credit Cards: MC, V.
Handicap Access: No.

Built by one Capt. Fisher, former schooner captain and early partner in the booming menhaden industry, which drew New Englanders here and built this town, The Gables is endlessly interesting to architecture buffs. Capt. Fisher incorporated his maritime life into his home, building the house so its gables peak perfectly along the compass rose, erecting one of his schooner's three masts in the center of the third and fourth floors of the house. One bathroom floor is cypress to mimic the feel of a wet shipboard deck after a landlubbin' shower. Two second-floor rooms are big — one even comes with a climb-up, king-sized bed — with private but attached baths. Two terrific sun porches sit at either end of the floor, and Barbara keeps a nice library of local books to satisfy whatever curiosity you've discovered during the day. As of deadline, the Clarks were expanding into their carriage house, which will result in three water view rooms upstairs, another down, and possibly a dining area for guests.

David Trozzo

Built by the baron of the local menhaden fishery, The Morris House in Reedville is a classic Victorian, inside and out.

THE MORRIS HOUSE
Innkeepers: Erin & Heath Dill.
804-453-7016;
fax 804-453-9032.
E-mail: morrishs@ crosslink.net.
www.eaglesnest.net/ morrishouse/.
826 Main St./P.O. Box 163, Reedville, VA 22539.
Price: Moderate to Very Expensive.
Credit Cards: MC, V.
Handicap Access: No.
Restrictions: Discourage young children in main house; children and pets allowed in cottage by prior arrangement.

The new owners of this fine Victorian have gone to considerable lengths to completely redecorate in a stylish update that could easily grace the cover of *Town & Country*. Two rooms, two suites, and a waterside cottage provide a range of accommodations, from the small Hunt Room, with, of course, a hunt-style decor to the cottage, with attention to detail down to the bright tropical fish drawer pulls. Perhaps our favorite is the Balcony Suite, where an arched cutout between two former rooms creates a lovely, airy space, with a huge two-person Jacuzzi in the second room. The Morris House is located right on Cockrell's Creek, and your hosts offer bikes for touring and rent their small row/sailboat for a nominal fee. Boats drawing up to six feet at mean low tide can tie up at the dock. The house was built by an early Reedville menhaden baron, who was in business with his brother-in-law, whose home was The Gables, another local B&B, located right across the street.

Urbanna, Virginia

ATHERSTON HALL
Owner: Phyllis G. Hall.
804-758-2809.
250 Prince George St./P.O.
Box 757, Urbanna, VA
23175.
Price: Moderate.
Credit Cards: No.
Handicap Access: No.
Restrictions: Inquire about
children.

Lots of B&Bs come with antiques — a walnut dresser from here, a mahogany armoire from there — but how many boast a box in the hallway that once was the backpack for a samurai's armor? Four rooms in all, including two rooms sharing one floor and one bath that tend to be rented as a "suite." They're on the second floor of this nineteenth-century home; one with twin beds and one with an antique rice bed, once owned by Gen. John Hunt Morgan of Morgan's Raiders, Lexington, KY. Those in search of more contemporary comfort can take comfort from Phyllis: "All of my mattresses are custom made, because I'm picky about my mattress." In the new section of the house, visitors will find two modern rooms with queen beds and attached baths. Country breakfasts, complimentary bicycles.

HEWICK PLANTATION
Owners: Helen & Ed
Battleson.
804-758-4214;
fax 804-758-4080.
E-mail: hewick@
oasisonline.com
www.hewick.com.
Va. State Hwy. 602/615,
Box 82, Urbanna, VA
23175.
Price: Expensive.
Credit Cards: AE, D, MC, V.
Handicap Access: No.
Special Features: Tours of
the house available by
appt.; $6 adults; $5

Approaching the double front doors of this manor house today must not be so different than it was 300 years ago. Two thick stone steps lead up to the entry; a heavy brass knocker announces a visitor's arrival. Out front, the trees have grown sky-high. Located down a long lane one mile from town, Hewick sits on sixty-six acres and is owned by a direct descendant of Christopher Robinson, who built the manor circa 1678 and served in the Virginia House of Burgesses. Visitors will find one-foot plaster walls and a comfortable elegance that has not been reworked by masters of modern design. Two enormous rooms upstairs house overnight guests, who should be aware of the limits of the ancient house. Ductwork for central heat and air, for instance, does not disturb the integrity of the walls; rather, you'll crank up a Vermont Casting stove, that Helen assures us emanates more than enough heat. The Robinson Room is almost an efficiency, with two twin beds, a double and a queen, with microwave and minifridge. The Beverly Room offers two double beds and three stuffed chairs. Small television sets are in both rooms and clawfoot tubs in both baths, one of which has a handheld shower.

THE INN AT URBANNA
Owners: Lora Rudisill &
Robert Harwell.
888-758-4852; 804-758-4852;
fax 804-758-0516.

Urbanna's midcentury Coca-Cola bottling plant has been a motel for decades now, but Lora and Robert arrived in 1995 and have since put in great effort. In all, thirteen guest rooms are located

250 Virginia St./P.O. Box 861, Urbanna, VA 23175.
Price: Moderate.
Credit Cards: AE, DC, MC, V.
Handicap Access: No.
Special Features: Restaurant, raw bar, outdoor dining in warm weather.

WINDMILL POINT RESORT
Owner: Ron Rickard.
804-435-1166;
fax 804-435-0789.
P.O. Box 368, White Stone, VA 22578.
End of Va. Rte 695.
Price: Moderate to Expensive.
Credit Cards: AE, MC, V.
Handicap Access: Yes.
Special Features: Tennis, pool, 150-slip marina.

in a building behind the fine-dining restaurant and lively raw bar. Designer bedspreads and curtains spruce up what are otherwise relatively ordinary motel/hotel rooms that come with king or double beds. While prices couldn't be more reasonable, expect them to rocket sharply the first weekend in Nov., when thousands crowd tiny Urbanna for the big oyster festival.

What with their vertical blinds, utilitarian bathrooms, and dual queen-sized beds, the rooms at this circa 1960s motel are rather ordinary. But visitors come for the expansive views of the Chesapeake Bay, here at the end of a sandspit at the end of a long, *fin du monde* road that winds through marshland to the sea. A pre-*Miami Vice* palette of Florida colors prevails around the complex, with corals and aquas highlighting the bar known as "Camp Windmill." Two main buildings house most of the sixty-one rooms, although another six rooms sit over the main lodge. Restaurant, golf course, swimming, and croquet.

UPPER EASTERN SHORE

Chestertown

THE BRAMPTON INN
Hosts: Michael & Danielle Hanscom.
410-778-1860;
fax 410-778-1805.
E-mail: innkeeper@ bramptoninn.com.
www.bramptoninn.com.
25227 Chestertown Rd., Chestertown, MD 21620.
1 mi. S.W. of Chestertown on Md. 20.
Price: Expensive to Very Expensive.
Credit Cards: AE, MC, V.
Handicap Access: One room.
Special Features: Children welcome.

You'll feel yourself start to relax as you pull up to this 1860 plantation house, fronted with century-old trees and neatly trimmed boxwoods and set on thirty-five acres just outside Chestertown. Inside, the ceilings are high, the furnishings are a mix of antiques and reproductions, and old wood dominates, from the Georgia pine floors to the three-and-a-half-story walnut and ash central staircase. All ten of the meticulously kept guest rooms have private baths and air-conditioning, eight have working fireplaces, and two (in the Garden Cottage) have Jacuzzis. The second-floor Blue Room, whose windows are in the trees, is particularly lovely in the fall, while the two-story Fairy Hill Suite, once a kitchen topped by slave quarters, is charming. Full breakfast, afternoon tea, and warm, friendly hosts in the business since 1987.

GREAT OAK MANOR B&B

Innkeepers: Don & Dianne
  Cantor.
800-504-3098; 410-778-5943.
E-mail: innkeeper@great
  oak.com
www.greatoak.com.
10568 Cliff Rd.,
  Chestertown, MD 21620.
Price: Expensive to Very
  Expensive.
Credit Cards: MC, V.
Handicap Access: No.
Restrictions: No children.

Great Oak Manor is unusual among the many mansions built along the Eastern Shore in the 1929s and '30s: it is a faithful reproduction of a Georgian house, even to using old brick, which probably was shipped as ballast in Grace Line ships. The detail and carvings are meticulous, and the Cantors have preserved the flavor of the original home in their restoration work; it is formal but not stuffy, classic but homelike. There are eleven guest rooms, many with views of the Chesapeake; all are attractively decorated and furnished, and even the smaller ones are good sized. The old, illegal gambling room on the third floor is high-ceilinged and spacious, with a king bed and sitting area. Five of the inn's nine fireplaces are in guest rooms; guests are given a fire log. The public rooms are varied and interesting, and everywhere is an atmosphere of friendly comfort. Guests have access to the nearby Great Oak Lodge, with a 9-hole golf course, tennis, and swimming. Great Oak Manor has 1,000 feet of private beach on the Bay and hammocks underneath the tall trees. Continental breakfast. Ask for the year-round, midweek discount.

THE INN AT MITCHELL HOUSE

Innkeepers: Jim & Tracy
  Stone.
410-778-6500;
  fax 410-778-2861.
E-mail: innatmitch@
  friend.ly.net.
www.chestertown.com/
  mitchell/.
8796 Maryland Pkwy.,
  Chestertown, MD 21620.
On Md. 21 btw. Md. 20 S. &
  Tolchester.
Price: Expensive.
Credit Cards: MC, V.
Handicap Access: No.
Restrictions: Children
  accepted, by prior
  arrangement.

The Mitchell House has been a bed-and-breakfast for more than a dozen years, but its history of welcoming guests goes back much farther. This is said to be the place where wounded British commander Sir Peter Parker was brought after the nearby Battle of Caulk's Field in 1814. When surgery on the kitchen table failed to save his life, they pickled Peter Parker in a keg of rum and sent him back to England. You'll find your stay here far more pleasant. Mitchell House is in the country but is close to Chestertown, Rock Hall, and the once-bustling, now quiet resort town of Tolchester. The 1743 manor house is situated at the end of a long, tree-lined drive by a pond. Inside are five rooms, all with private baths (a sixth room is rented only as part of a suite) and four with fireplaces (fire logs provided). Four more fireplaces are located in the public areas of the house, whose outdoor motif of mounted waterfowl, marsh grass, and riding hats is a suitable introduction to rural Kent County. A full country breakfast is served in a dining room decorated with china plates and figurines.

THE PARKER HOUSE

Hosts: Marcy & John
  Parker.
410-778-9041;
  fax 410-778-7318.
E-mail: parkerbb@dmv.
  com.
www.chestertown.com/
  parker.
108 Spring Ave.,
  Chestertown, MD 21620.
Price: Expensive.
Credit Cards: No.
Handicap Access: One room.
Special Features: Children
  welcome; pets OK in one
  room, small dogs only.

John Parker loves the B&B trade so much that he's written a manuscript about it, and when regulars said they could no longer come because they had trouble climbing the stairs, the Parkers turned the family room into a spacious first-floor guest room with king-sized bed. That gives you an idea of the warm, gracious welcome that awaits in this circa 1876 Victorian in the heart of Chestertown. The common areas are large and lavishly furnished with antiques. Marcy's popovers, with warm maple syrup and Amish sticky buns, are among the morning delights of the Continental breakfast served in the formal dining room. All three guest rooms have private baths, and the two upstairs rooms have adjoining rooms to create suites with a shared bath when needed; those rooms are otherwise unoccupied.

Once the home of Kent County's first millionaire, it had the first indoor bathroom and electricity in the county. By the mid-1960s, it was vacant and in disrepair; local kids called it the ghost house and dared each other to knock on the door. After restoration and conversion from a home to a B&B, Parker House is now a showcase again.

Colonial accommodations at Chestertown's White Swan Tavern include a bedroom in the old John Lovegrove Kitchen.

David Trozzo

THE WHITE SWAN TAVERN

Manager: Mary Susan
  Maisel.
410-778-2300;
  fax 410-778-4543.
www.chestertown.com/
  whiteswan.
231 High St., Chestertown,
  MD 21620.

Perhaps the most authentic, meticulous colonial restoration on the Eastern Shore, the 1733 White Swan is a time capsule. Check the display cabinet to see artifacts found during the 1978 archaeological dig. This handsome, dignified, eighteenth-century inn on the historic district's main street needs only a collection of folks in waistcoats

Price: Expensive to Very
Expensive.
Credit Cards: MC, V.
Handicap Access: Two
rooms.
Restrictions: Smoking
allowed only in John
Lovegrove Kitchen room.
Special Features: Children
welcome.

and breeches, gathered about in the public rooms, to create a perfect time warp. Guest rooms, however, have modern comforts, with private baths, nonworking fireplaces (the common areas have working fireplaces), and refrigerators with a complimentary bottle of wine. Accommodations range from the John Lovegrove Kitchen, with its massive fireplace and exposed beams dating to 1705 to the winding T.W. Eliason Victorian Suite, complete with parlor. Even if you can't stay here, stop by for afternoon tea, daily 3:00 p.m.–5:00 p.m. Guests also get a full Continental breakfast, which will be brought to your room on request.

Easton

THE BISHOP'S HOUSE
Innkeepers: Diane Laird-
Ippolito & John B.
Ippolito.
800-223-7290; 410-820-7290.
E-mail: bishopshouse
@skipjack.bluecrab.org.
214 Goldsborough St./P.O.
Box 2217, Easton, MD
21601.
Price: Expensive, with
moderately priced rooms
for two-night midweek
stays.
Credit Cards: No.
Handicap Access: No.
Restrictions: Only children
age 12 and older.

This 1880 Victorian served as the home of the bishop of the Diocese of Easton for most of the twentieth century until it was restored and opened as a bed-and-breakfast in 1988. The owners continue to make improvements, but you'll find nothing lacking in this house with its antique furnishings, quaint collection of vintage hats, and wraparound porch. The five guest rooms (a sixth can be rented with a shared bath) all have private baths, two of them whirlpool baths, and one has a fireplace. Some of the bedrooms and the common rooms have airy, fourteen-foot ceilings. Downtown Easton is just a short walk away after a full hot breakfast.

THE TIDEWATER INN
General Manager: Edward
Slavinski.
410-822-1300.
E-mail: info@tidewaterinn.
com
www.tidewaterinn.com.
101 E. Dover St., Easton,
MD 21601.
Price: Expensive to Very
Expensive.
Credit Cards: AE, D, DC,
MC, V.
Handicap Access: Yes.

The gracious Tidewater Inn became an instant landmark when it opened in 1949 facing one of Easton's main intersections and the historic Avalon Theatre. Renovations have improved the details without destroying the Georgian-style ambiance, and the inn has a reputation for friendly service. Famous folks often stay here when they visit Talbot County, and the handsome lobby could make a fine movie set. The 114 guest rooms have been cosmetically improved in recent years and are nicely furnished in period reproductions, although the bathrooms remain small. Suites are available. The restaurant is notable at any time of year, especially

An Easton institution, The Tidewater Inn.

Sun. brunch in the Crystal Room, and don't miss the Decoy Bar, where you can enjoy a beer and a cigar at the copper bar decorated with duck carvings. The inn is convenient to all of downtown Easton's shops, historic sites, and restaurants.

Galena

ROSEHILL FARM B&B
Owner: Marie Jolly.
410-648-5334.
13842 Gregg Neck Rd.,
  Galena, MD 21635.
Price: Moderate.
Credit Cards: No; cash &
  personal checks only.
Handicap Access: Yes, after
  4 steps into house.
Restrictions: Only children
  over age 12.

Rosehill Farm is a homestay rather than a fancy American B&B, but many travelers will appreciate the place for the homey comfort of its four spacious rooms, all with private baths, its setting on a 100-acre farm outside Galena, and its affordable price. In its nearly two decades in operation, the two-story house has attracted people looking to stay close to Galena's antique shops, as well as friends of boaters who need a place to sleep between sails. Two of the rooms have queen beds, and the other two rooms have two doubles. After a deluxe Continental breakfast, you can hit the road or just hit the trail: There is a carved a path from the orchard to the woods, an excellent spot for a stroll, bird-watching, or picnicking by the river.

Georgetown

KITTY KNIGHT HOUSE
Owners: Terry & Louise
  Van Gilder.
800-404-8712; 410-648-5777.

The Kitty Knight House towers over the Georgetown harbor with all of the majesty of its namesake. Kitty Knight was as determined as she

Rte. 213, Georgetown, MD
  21930.
Price: Inexpensive to
  Expensive.
Credit Cards: AE, MC, V.
Handicap Access: No.
Special Features: Smoking
  allowed; children
  welcome.

was beautiful, so the story goes. When the British burned the rest of the town in 1813, she was tending an invalid neighbor and refused to move, so Admiral Sir George Cockburn spared the house and the one next door, which are now joined to make the present inn. A newer section expands the dining room to a deck and gazebo overlooking the Sassafras River and its hundreds of boats. The eleven rooms (with a twelfth room available to make a suite with shared bath) all have private baths, TVs, and telephones. Some have nonworking fireplaces, and many have an enviable view of the harbor. Beds vary widely from a pair of twins to king, so make sure to ask for the size that you want. Decor is attractive, with a few pieces dating back to Kitty Knight's time. A sixty-five-foot charter boat is available for cruises. Guests have a Continental breakfast in the dining room, a series of rooms that seems to go on forever. Nighttime libations are enjoyed in the cozy, first-floor tavern.

Oxford

1876 HOUSE
Owners: Eleanor & Jerry
  Clark.
410-226-5496.
E-mail: oba@tredavon.com.
110 N. Morris St./P.O. Box
  658, Oxford, MD 21654.
Price: Expensive.
Credit Cards: No.
Handicap Access: No.

Fans of quirky old houses will like this one on Oxford's main street. The stairs curve so sharply that there's a handhold to grab as you make your way up to your room. That's in no way a criticism of the house, whose three rooms (one of them actually a two-room suite) are neatly decorated in Queen Anne style; all have private baths, though one is across the hall. A Continental-plus breakfast is served in the formal dining room. Guests who want to avoid driving to their weekend getaway can arrange for a ride from Jerry, who operates a limousine service.

OXFORD INN
Owners: The Schmitt
  Family.
410-226-5220.
P.O. Box 627, Oxford, MD
  21654.
Price: Moderate to Very
  Expensive.
Credit Cards: D, MC, V.
Handicap Access: No.
Special Features: Children
  welcome.

The Oxford Inn is in its third decade of enticing travelers to the head of Town Creek. It does it with a convivial family atmosphere, attractive rooms, and a restaurant with bar on the ground floor that's open to the public. Guests can use the public tennis court across the street or relax in the Harbor View sitting room where afternoon sherry is provided. The inn has eleven rooms, including one suite and two rooms that can either be rented separately or together. There's a real mix of private, semiprivate, and shared baths; the inn will tell you which one that you're getting. Continental-plus breakfast.

David Trozzo

The pre-Revolutionary home of the war's financier serves famous crab cakes, offers lodging, and stands at The Strand in Oxford, Maryland.

ROBERT MORRIS INN
Owners: Wendy & Ken Gibson.
410-226-5111.
www.robertmorrisinn.com.
314 N. Morris St./P.O. Box 70, Oxford, MD 21654.
Price: Expensive to Very Expensive.
Credit Cards: AE, MC, V.
Handicap Access: Yes, one or two rooms.
Restrictions: Only children over age 10.

George Washington may or may not have slept here, but one of his pals owned the place. Robert Morris Jr. helped finance the Revolution, and, besides signing checks, he put his signature on the Declaration of Independence, the Articles of Confederation, and the Constitution. The inn's thirty-five rooms, all with private baths, are split between the mustard-colored clapboard building by the Oxford-Bellevue Ferry landing and the secluded Sandaway nearby, whose rooms provide the most spectacular river views. All the rooms are authentic, romantic, and oozing with historical atmosphere — only fitting given that the inn has stood here since 1710. The inn's restaurant closes in the winter, but the inn's rooms remain open at a reduced rate on some weekends. Continental breakfast year-round.

Rock Hall

THE INN AT OSPREY POINT
Manager: Christine Will.
410-639-2194.
E-mail: innkeeper@osprey point.com
www.ospreypoint.com.
20786 Rock Hall Ave., Rock Hall, MD 21661.
Price: Expensive to Very Expensive.
Credit Cards: D, MC, V.

If the building looks familiar, that's because it is modeled after the Coke-Garrett house in Williamsburg, VA, but it was newly built in 1993. Seven pretty rooms with colonial-style furnishings and decor all have private baths, air-conditioning, cable TV, and other pleasantries of the late twentieth century. The family-friendly rooms are mostly large enough to accommodate a pullout couch or a cot. The house overlooks a marina complex, which has a swimming pool, volleyball, horseshoes,

Handicap Access: No.
Special Features: Children
welcome.

nature trails, and complimentary bicycles for guests; it is more like a small resort than an inn. The management can arrange sailing, fishing, or horseback riding nearby, and the restaurant downstairs serves dinner Thurs.-Mon. Continental breakfast.

SWAN HAVEN
Innkeepers: Diane Oliver &
Harry Newman.
410-639-2527.
www.rockhallmd.com/
swanhaven.
20950 Rock Hall Ave., Rock
Hall, MD 21661.
Price: Expensive.
Credit Cards: AE, MC, V.
Handicap Access: No.
Restrictions: No children
under age 10.

At various times a temporary hospital and a waterman's home, the century-old Swan Haven, a Victorian cottage, is a handy resting place for people in town for sailing, biking, kayaking, or bird-watching. The seven modern rooms, all with private baths and cable TVs, are pretty and comfortable without being overly fancy. Beds are mostly king and queen. The second-floor Cignet Room features a whirlpool tub for two, king-sized bed, and a grand view of Swan Creek and the marina through double doors that open onto a screened-in porch. After a self-serve Continental breakfast, head outside to take advantage of the free bikes (also rented to nonguests, along with kayaks, canoes, small boats, windsurfers, and fishing rods), the sprawling deck, and the pier, a perfect place to watch the boats and waterfowl come and go and to take in the sunset. A half-dozen good restaurants are within walking distance.

St. Michaels

**HARBOURTOWNE GOLF
RESORT &
CONFERENCE CENTER**
General Manager: Harold
Klinger.
800-446-9066; 410-745-9066;
fax 410-745-9124.
www.harbourtowne.com.
P.O. Box 126, St. Michaels,
MD 21663.
On Martingham Dr., just
W. of St. Michaels off
Md. 33.
Price: Very Expensive.
Credit Cards: AE, D, DC,
MC, V.
Handicap Access: Yes.

It looks as if you are driving through a golf course community to get to Harbourtowne, and you are. The 18-hole, Pete Dye-designed course is maintained well, the public areas are especially attractive, and the 111 rooms all have water views and terraces. Twenty-four rooms have wood-burning fireplaces. It's a true resort, so there's a beach on a shallow little inlet from the Miles River, lawn games, tennis, swimming, trails for walking and jogging, biking, softball, volleyball, badminton, horseshoes, and a fitness center. Harbourtowne has two restaurants and three lounges. The water view from most of the resort is spectacular. Check for off-season rates, which begin in the moderate range.

**THE INN AT PERRY
CABIN**
Manager: Stephen Creese.

Absolute luxury carries a hefty tab, but plenty of Fortune 500 companies staging a meeting or couples seeking a romantic getaway are willing to

800-722-2949; 410-745-2200.
www.perrycabin.com.
308 Watkins Lane, St.
  Michaels, MD 21663.
Price: Very Expensive.
Credit Cards: AE, DC, MC,
  V.
Handicap Access: Yes.
Restrictions: No children;
  pets, at management
  discretion.

pay the cost for a first-class stay on the Miles River. This 1820 house was a landmark for years, then Sir Bernard Ashley of the Laura Ashley fabric and fashion empire bought it in 1988. Several million dollars later, this was a showplace for the company's products and a lovely, idealized English country inn. Each of the forty-one rooms comes with a shape and decor all its own. Management strives for perfection here; service is at the highest level, and anything that you want, your hosts will provide. The inn has an indoor heated pool, steam room, health facility, secluded courtyards and porches, and 24-hour room service. Don't pass up the chance to dine in the restaurant, where the food is as good as the inn — and that's very good indeed (see Chapter Four, *Restaurants & Food Purveyors*). If you are aiming to impress for either business or personal reasons, this is the place — perhaps one of the special package deals won't extract so much from the wallet.

KEMP HOUSE INN
Owners: Diane & Steve
  Cooper.
410-745-2243.
412 S. Talbot St./P.O. Box
  638, St. Michaels, MD
  21663.
Price: Moderate to
  Expensive.
Credit Cards: D, MC, V.
Handicap Access: Yes (first
  floor).
Special Features: Children
  and pets welcome.

Flannel nightshirts, a brick floor, and quilts on four-poster beds set a warm, homey tone at this eight-room bed-and-breakfast on St. Michaels' main street. A mix of antiques and reproductions decorate the rooms; some have fireplaces. The back cottage has exposed beams and cathedral ceiling, while the Landing Room has a private terrace. All rooms have private baths, except the two dormer rooms, which share and compensate on price. Sleeping here puts you in good company: A young Robert E. Lee stayed two nights here as Col. Joseph Kemp's guest. You can even stay in the room that he used, identified with his name. Pick up your Continental breakfast from the innkeeper and take it back to your room or onto the patio.

PARSONAGE INN
Owner: Will Workman.
Inkeepers: Walt & Jane
  Johnson.
800-394-5519; 410-745-5519.
www.parsonage-inn.com.
210 N. Talbot St., St.
  Michaels, MD 21663.
Price: Expensive to Very
  Expensive.
Credit Cards: MC, V.
Handicap Access: One room.

Dr. Henry Clay Dodson, pharmacist, postmaster, and businessman, opened the St. Michaels brickyard after two fires devastated the town. He built this place in 1883 as a testament to the permanence of brick. For sixty years, it served the Methodist Church as a parsonage until the present owner purchased it in 1985 and restored it as a B&B. All eight rooms have private baths and king or queen brass beds, except the suite, where a private entrance, porch, and sitting room with TV

Restrictions: No children under age 12.

more than compensate for two double beds. Behind the brick house, a building added with the restoration offers large, ground-level rooms popular for their size and convenience. Three of the inn's premium rooms have wood-burning fireplaces. Breakfast is gourmet, with dishes like the herb waffle with crabmeat and Newberg cheese sauce. Afternoon tea is served for guests who are around to partake. The inn is on the main street in St. Michaels, directly across from the new vehicle entrance to the Chesapeake Bay Maritime Museum, so people tend to be on the go. Bicycles are available if you want to explore the countryside at a leisurely pace.

ST. MICHAELS HARBOUR INN & MARINA

Manager: Renee Minkkinen.
800-955-9001; 410-745-9001.
www.harbourinn.com.
101 North Harbor Rd., St. Michaels, MD 21663.
Price: Expensive to Very Expensive.
Credit Cards: AE, CB, D, DC, MC, V.
Handicap Access: Yes.
Restrictions: Smoking allowed, in some of the rooms.
Special Features: Children welcome.

By far the largest hotel in town, this very modern waterfront resort with inn, conference facilities, and restaurant has its own 56-slip marina. Of the forty-six guest rooms, thirty-eight are suites with extras like a sitting area, sofa bed, desk, kitchenette, patio or balcony, and a king or two queen-sized beds. Five premium suites have Jacuzzis and king beds. Only four rooms in the entire inn lack a water view, and throughout the building, large Palladian windows and decks maximize the view. There's a nice outdoor pool and spa, a workout room, a hot tub, and canoe and bike rentals, all run by a friendly staff. The hotel is not adjacent to the historic sites and the Chesapeake Bay Maritime Museum, but St. Michaels is small enough to walk, and a water taxi operates on the harbor during the summer.

VICTORIANA INN

Owner: Jim Gonden.
410-745-3368.
205 Cherry St./P.O. Box 499, St. Michaels, MD 21663.
Price: Very Expensive.
Credit Cards: MC, V.
Handicap Access: No.
Restrictions: No children under age 12.

This 1865 Victorian manse is on a residential street in the heart of St. Michaels, close to restaurants and the Chesapeake Bay Maritime Museum and overlooking St. Michaels Harbor. Adirondack chairs on the expansive lawn invite guests to take a break, and many do. The inn underwent a recent renovation after a change of ownership, so now all six cozy guest rooms have a private bath. The rooms have queen- or king-sized beds; two have fireplaces. A full country breakfast is served in the dining room, and guests can plan the day's activities in the comfortable, adjacent sunporch.

WADES POINT INN ON THE BAY

Owners: Betsy & John Feiler.

Few places offer the variety of rooms that you'll find at Wades Point Inn, situated on a 1657 land grant on the edge of Eastern Bay. The 1819 main

410-745-2500.
www.wadespoint.com.
P.O. Box 7, St. Michaels, MD 21663.
At the end of Wades Point Rd., 5 mi. W. of St. Michaels off Md. 33.
Price: Expensive to Very Expensive.
Credit Cards: MC, V.
Handicap Access: Yes.
Restrictions: No infants; closed after New Year's–mid-Mar.

house offers three rooms with private baths. Six more rooms share three baths in the 1890 summer wing, but plans are in the works to add more bathrooms. The rooms in this wing are small but bright, with excellent water views. They are also less expensive, because they are not air-conditioned. Rooms in the 1990 addition have all the comforts and are large, elegantly furnished with reproductions and come with either a porch or a balcony by the water. More homey accommodations can be had in the farmhouse, which rents per room or as a whole. Twelve people can sleep comfortably, eighteen if a family rents it and squeezes in children wherever there's space. Only the two first-floor rooms have AC and private baths; upstairs bedrooms share a bath on the first floor. The farmhouse isn't deluxe, but it's comfortable, and the price is right. All guests take Continental breakfast in the pristine, white Bay Room. The inn provides a map of a one-mile nature trail on its 120-acre grounds, and it's just a short drive into St. Michaels.

Stevensville

David Trozzo

Upscale dining and accommodations are featured at the Kent Manor Inn on Kent Island.

KENT MANOR INN
Owners: David Meloy & Alan Michaels.
800-820-4511; 410-643-5757.
500 Kent Manor Dr., Stevensville, MD 21666.

Kent Manor is a faithful restoration of a large plantation house. There's a lovely garden house, a pier on the shallow headwaters of Thompson's Creek, pedalboats, bicycles, and a $1^1/_2$-mile trail winding through the extensive property.

On Kent Island, U.S. 50 to Md. 8 S.
Price: Very Expensive.
Credit Cards: AE, D, MC, V.
Handicap Access: Yes.
Special Features: Children welcome.

All twenty-four rooms are tastefully furnished in period style, some with porches and French marble fireplaces; Chesapeake waterfowl and workboat prints decorate the walls. Ask for a garden view instead of Bay view; the Bay is close, but not close enough to actually see from your room. The restaurant serves fine cuisine in a romantic Victorian setting. A quiet, dignified getaway.

Tilghman

David Trozzo

A hammock, J.J. the black lab, and the Bay. This, too, could be yours at the Black Walnut Point Inn.

BLACK WALNUT POINT INN
Innkeepers: Tom & Brenda Ward.
410-886-2452;
    fax 410-886-2053.
P.O. Box 308, Tilghman, MD 21671.
www.tilghmanisland.com/blackwalnut.
Price: Expensive to Very Expensive.
Credit Cards: MC, V.
Handicap Access: No.

A country retreat rather than a lush resort, Black Walnut Point Inn sits at the very end of Tilghman Island, where the Choptank River meets the Chesapeake Bay. You'll see workboats on the water, the tilting Sharps Point Lighthouse, and perhaps even the bald eagles, great blue herons, and foxes who share this fifty-seven-acre state wildlife sanctuary with the inn. It's a perfect spot for Bay and bird-watching, with a public landing for fishing within walking distance. The main house has four rooms, though no one taller than five-feet-ten-inches is allowed to book the snug Attic Hideaway. Two cottages include one divided into two rooms and the other a solo with sitting room and kitchenette; all rooms have private baths. If you want fancy trimmings or handy nightlife, check in somewhere else, but if you want to get far away from it all, this is the perfect getaway. Continental breakfast.

CHESAPEAKE WOOD DUCK INN
Innkeepers: Dave & Stephanie Feith.
800-956-2070; 410-886-2070.
www.woodduckinn.com.
Gibsontown Rd./P.O. Box 202, Tilghman, MD 21671.
Price: Very Expensive.
Credit Cards: AE, MC, V.
Handicap Access: No.
Restrictions: Only children age 14 and older.

The Wood Duck Inn is an elegant Victorian next to the working harbor, which shelters most of the remaining skipjacks still dredging up oysters from the Bay. The main house, built in 1890 and used over the years as a boardinghouse, a bordello, and a waterman's home, has six impeccably styled rooms with fresh flowers, pine floors, and full or queen beds. The Carriage House suite next door has a sitting room with sleeper sofa, queen four-poster bed, and the inn's only private TV. All rooms have private baths. Guests have full access to the first floor of the house, including the parlor with fireplace. A gourmet breakfast in the dining room showcases in-season seafood, as well as exotica like New Zealand lamb and eggs. A walk of only a few hundred yards puts you at the harbor, where skipjack captains give rides by arrangement.

THE TILGHMAN ISLAND INN
Owners: Jack Redmon & David McCallum.
800-866-2141; 410-886-2141.
www.tilghmanisland.com/tii.
21384 Coopertown Rd./P.O. Box B, Tilghman, MD 21671.
Price: Expensive to Very Expensive.
Credit Cards: AE, CB, D, DC, MC, V.
Handicap Access: Yes.
Restrictions: Children (on first floor); pets ($15 per night cleaning charge).
Special Features: Smoking allowed.

An undistinctive building on the edge of Knapps Narrows from the outside, The Tilghman Island Inn dispels that first impression with the myriad delights inside. The twenty rooms, including two suites, are individually decorated in an attractive modern style. A couple of the rooms have Jacuzzis, and more are being added, as part of the progressive innkeepers' drive to satisfy existing patrons and to attract new ones. You'll find a bar with a fireplace, where there's a piano player on Fri. and Sat. and classical guitar on Sun. The inn's restaurant is highly recommended, and the deck bar is the perfect spot for summer parties. The twenty-two dock slips rent for $1 per foot to guests. For diversion, there's a tennis court, a pool, and a cockatoo named Blanche DuBois to engage in conversation, and management can arrange bicycling, golf, volleyball, and croquet. This is the place to come if you want to have a good time. Continental breakfast on weekdays; full breakfast available on weekends.

LOWER EASTERN SHORE

Berlin

THE ATLANTIC HOTEL
Manager: Gary Weber.
800-814-7672; 410-641-3589;
fax 410-641-4928.
2 N. Main St., Berlin, MD
21811.
Price: Moderate to Very
Expensive.
Credit Cards: AE, MC, V.
Handicap Access: Yes.
Restrictions: Nonsmoking
guest rooms.

It was the renovation of this 1895 hotel that began the vigorous revival of the town of Berlin — residents gained a new pride in their unique surroundings and undertook the restoration of many other buildings. The six deluxe rooms and ten smaller, substantially less-expensive, standard rooms create a nineteenth-century feeling with their rich color schemes and antique furnishings. All rooms have TVs, though you may find yourself more inclined to browse Berlin's boutiques and antique stores or wallow in Ocean City's Boardwalk extravaganza, just five miles away. Breakfast is served downstairs, where you'll find the Drummer's Café, a popular meeting place for locals, and the elegant formal dining room that built The Atlantic Hotel's reputation throughout the East Coast.

MERRY SHERWOOD PLANTATION
Owner: Kirk Burbage.
410-641-2112.
8909 Worcester Hwy. (U.S. 113), Berlin, MD 21811.
Price: Expensive to Very
Expensive.
Credit Cards: MC, V.
Handicap Access: No.
Restrictions: Children
allowed conditionally.

Standing more than fifty feet tall, comprising twenty-seven rooms in over 8,500 square feet, the Merry Sherwood Plantation is as impressive today as when it was completed in 1859. Once a jewel in classic Italianate style, set in 1,200 acres of farmland, Merry Sherwood is now unconscionably close to the highway, though that's not its fault. The grounds, designed by *Southern Living*, are exquisite, almost enough to make you forget the rush of modern life. Inside the house, the rooms are elegant and large, and the antique furnishings honor the affluence that gave the house its start. A gourmet breakfast is served under an enormous chandelier. For a well-rounded visit, be sure to spend time on the sunporch perusing the photo album: It reveals the full marvel of the restoration that readied Merry Sherwood for guests in the mid-1990s.

Cambridge

CAMBRIDGE HOUSE
Innkeeper/Chef: Stuart
Schefers.
410-221-7700.
E-mail: camhausb-b@shore
net.net.

A heart attack persuaded Stuart Schefers to flee his stressful life in the New York City restaurant business, and he settled in Cambridge to open a high-style B&B. The 1847 sea captain's house had

112 High St., Cambridge, MD 21613.
Price: Expensive; corporate discounts.
Credit Cards: AE, MC, V.
Handicap Access: No.
Restrictions: No children under age 8.

become a rundown apartment house, but Schefers lifted away the air of neglect and filled the restored house with niceties like king- and queen-sized beds, other period furnishings, computer hookups, and a telephone and TV in each of the six spacious rooms. Schefers serves a full breakfast and, except in summer when everyone's too busy, afternoon tea in the formal dining room. Historic High St. is right outside the front door, and Long Wharf, a public marina and yacht basin, and downtown restaurants and shops are all within walking distance.

GLASGOW INN B&B
Owners: Louiselee Roche & Martha Ann Rayne.
888-373-7890, reservations; 410-228-0575;
fax 410-221-0297.
E-mail: glasgow@dmv.com.
www.glasgowinn.com.
1500 Hambrooks Blvd., Cambridge, MD 21613.
Price: Moderate to Very Expensive.
Credit Cards: No.
Restrictions: Children allowed conditionally; no smoking or pets.

Glasgow Inn was a private home from its construction around 1760 until Louiselee Roche and Martha Ann Rayne opened it to the public as a B&B more than thirteen years ago. The main house has seven large rooms (four with private baths), and an adjacent building holds three more rooms arranged in colonial fashion around a central fireplace. Third-floor rooms are worth the long walk up the stairs for their cozy window seats, sloping eaves (and floors!), and queen-sized beds, though you'll have to share a bath. Careful development of the land in front of the Glasgow Inn as a modern Williamsburg-style subdivision hasn't hurt the view: You can still see the broad Choptank River from the front guest windows.

SARKE PLANTATION
Owner: Genevieve Finley.
800-814-7020; 410-228-7020.
6033 Todd Point Rd., Cambridge, MD 21613.
Price: Inexpensive to Expensive.
Credit Cards: MC, V.
Handicap Access: No.
Restrictions: No children under age 10; pets can stay in room.
Special Features: Smoking allowed.

Whether you reach this spacious plantation house by car or by shallow-draft boat, you'll understand why its owner decided to go into the hospitality business to stay here. Sarke Plantation is situated in the lovely and usually overlooked Neck District west of Cambridge, an area of slender spits of land bordered by tiny creeks and broad rivers. Many of the rooms come with a water view, as does the breakfast room done up sidewalk café style. Guests often come with canoes to explore the waters off this twenty-seven-acre estate (Oxford is straight across the river). The house, circa 1860, has three bedrooms and a suite, a great room with fireplace, billiard room, and TVs in most rooms.

Princess Anne

**THE WASHINGTON
   HOTEL AND INN**
Owner: Mary Murphey.
410-651-2525.
11784 Somerset Ave. (Rte.
   675), Princess Anne, MD
   21853.
Price: Inexpensive.
Credit Cards: MC, V.; no
   personal checks.
Handicap Access: No.
Special Features: Smoking
   allowed.

Three words sum up the allure of The
     Washington Hotel and Inn: location, history,
and food. Next door to where her son runs the
thriving Washington Hotel restaurant, Mary
Murphey lives in and manages the twelve-room
inn. The Murphey family bought the 1744 building
at auction in 1936 and has run it as an inn ever
since. She'll be happy to point out the double staircase (one for the men, one for the ladies in their
hoop skirts) as she takes you upstairs, but be sure
to come back down and peruse the presidential
and first lady portraits, church plates, and
Confederate memorabilia in the lobby. Rooms are
simple and clean, and though breakfast isn't included in the bill, the restaurant
opens at 6:00 a.m. with its good, affordable food.

**WATERLOO COUNTRY
   INN**
Owners: Theresa & Erwin
   Kraemer.
410-651-0883;
   fax 410-651-5592.
E-mail: innkeeper@
   waterloocountryinn.com.
www.waterloocountryinn.
   com.
28822 Mt. Vernon Rd.,
   Princess Anne, MD
   21853.
Price: Expensive to Very
   Expensive.
Credit Cards: AE, MC, V.
Handicap Access: One
   room.
Restrictions: Closed in Feb.

Theresa and Erwin Kraemer traveled from
     Switzerland a few years ago to visit friends in
Princess Anne. They saw a "For Sale" sign in front
of this 1750 Georgian-style mansion and decided
that they had to stay. You'll be glad that they did as
soon as you check in. The two suites are luxurious,
the three rooms less ornate but still stylish. Outside
there's a pool, miles of country roads to cycle, and
meandering streams to canoe (bicycles and canoe
are complimentary). The inn's restaurant has its
own chef and is open for dinner Thurs.-Sat., but if
you come on another night and chat with the
Kraemers in advance, they'll be sure to have dinner
ready for you. The full breakfast includes freshly
baked breads, eggs, fresh fruit, and, if you're of a
European bent, cheese. The Kraemers may have
settled far from their homeland, but they've
imported a bit of Continental style into the
Somerset County countryside.

Snow Hill

SNOW HILL INN
Innkeepers: Jim & Kathy
   Washington.
410-632-2102.

Ask anyone in this county seat where to get a
     good dinner, and they'll send you to the Snow
Hill Inn, where you can also book one of three

David Trozzo

Is it haunted? This room at the Snow Hill Inn may be home to a resident ghost.

104 E. Market St., Snow Hill, MD 21863.
Price: Inexpensive to Moderate.
Credit Cards: AE, D, MC, V.
Handicap Access: No.

rooms and stay the night. Continental-plus breakfast is served in the dining room; the inn also has a bar and a lovely garden dining room. All guest rooms have period furnishings and private baths, and there's a cozy library/TV room. With sloping floors, the house shows its age (part of it dates to the eighteenth century). The rooms are not overly fancy, but it's affordable and comfortable. It's a great place to stay if you're spending some time in this 300-year-old river town.

Vienna

THE TAVERN HOUSE
Owners: Harvey & Elise Altergott.
410-376-3347.
E-mail: oldgod@shore.intercom.net.
111 Water St./P.O. Box 98, Vienna, MD 21869.
Price: Moderate.
Credit Cards: No.
Handicap Access: No.

Sitting in the second-floor sitting area at The Tavern House, a guest can gaze out on a Nanticoke River marsh scene not much changed from the time that the inn was built in the 1730s. Looking upriver yields a glimpse of cars rushing by on their way to the beach, traffic that blessedly passes Vienna thanks to the new span that replaced the old two-lane drawbridge. In The Tavern House, all is quiet, and there's no particular reason to hurry the day. You can mosey down the country roads, amble about town, or linger over breakfast with your enthusiastic hosts. Upstairs, the faithfully restored rooms are airy and charming, and a backyard garden beckons on a sunny day. "We always tell people that this is a good place to escape the twentieth century," Harvey Altergott says.

Cape Charles, Virginia

NOTTINGHAM RIDGE B&B
Owner: Bonnie Nottingham.
757-331-1010.
28184 Nottingham Ridge Lane, Cape Charles, VA 23310.
Price: Moderate.
Credit Cards: No.
Handicap Access: No.
Restrictions: No children under age 8.

From the private beach in front of Nottingham Ridge, you can see little but the blue Chesapeake and the Chesapeake Bay Bridge-Tunnel in the distance. This secluded home, built in 1974 but decorated like a colonial house in Williamsburg, VA, sits in a pine forest far removed from everyday hassles. It is six miles south of Cape Charles and three miles north of the bridge — the perfect spot to spend the night if you're passing through or to get away from it all for a weekend. The B&B has three rooms and a suite, all with private baths, and a full breakfast is served in-season on the screened porch overlooking the Bay. Delightful!

SEA GATE B&B
Innkeeper: Chris Bannon.
757-331-2206.
E-mail: seagate@pilot.infi.net.
www.bbhost.com/seagate.
Tazewell Ave., Cape Charles, VA 23310.
Price: Moderate.
Credit Cards: No.
Handicap Access: No.
Restrictions: No children under age 7.

"There's no cha-cha, no excitement. It's a place where you come to take your girdle off," says innkeeper Chris Bannon in a phrase that could describe both the town of Cape Charles and Sea Gate. The B&B is less than a block from the beach in a little town with the most period homes in Virginia — ninety percent in the historic district. Town booster Bannon will be more than glad to tell you about Cape Charles' past, present, and future and its recreational and dining possibilities. The inn's four rooms all have a private half-bath or full bath, and two of the rooms share a lovely second-floor porch. A gourmet breakfast is served on a corner porch in all but the coldest months because of Cape Charles' exceptionally mild climate, attested to by the palm tree out front.

Chincoteague, Virginia

CHANNEL BASS INN
Owners: David & Barbara Wiedenheft.
800-249-0818; 800-221-5620;

Operated under the same ownership as Miss Molly's Inn, but more formal in atmosphere, this simple frame building conceals an elegant,

757-336-6148;
fax 757-336-0600.
E-mail: msmolly@shore.
   intercom.net.
www.channelbass-inn.com.
6228 Church St.,
   Chincoteague, VA 23336.
Price: Expensive to Very
   Expensive.
Credit Cards: AE, D, MC, V.
Handicap Access: No.

ISLAND MANOR HOUSE

Innkeepers: Carol &
   Charles Kalmykow.
800-852-1505; 757-336-5436.
E-mail: imh@shore.
   intercom.net.
www.chincoteague.com/
   b-b/imh/html.
4160 Main St.,
   Chincoteague, VA 23336.
Price: Moderate to
   Expensive.
Credit Cards: AE, MC, V.
Handicap Access: No
Restrictions: No children
   under age 12.

MISS MOLLY'S INN

Owners: David & Barbara
   Wiedenheft.
800-221-5620; 757-336-6686;
   fax 757-336-0600.
E-mail: msmolly@shore.
   intercom.net.
www.missmollys-inn.com.
4141 Main St.,
   Chincoteague, VA 23336.
Price: Moderate to Very
   Expensive.
Credit Cards: AE, D, MC, V.
Handicap Access: No.
Restrictions: No children
   under age 6.

quiet decor. There are five rooms, all with private baths and air-conditioning, and most have queen- or king-sized beds; beds are triple sheeted for luxury. Barbara has laid out a pleasant backyard garden, and there's a red hot line telephone to Miss Molly's Inn in case you need anything. Guests of both Wiedenheft inns enjoy a full breakfast in the Channel Bass dining room, which now functions as the island's only tearoom.

Not the usual story: Two brothers built a house in 1848, married two sisters, split the house, and moved half of it next door. Today, the two sections have been connected with a large garden room and redecorated in the Federal style to make a most attractive place to stay. In all, eight rooms include six with private baths and some with water views. The friendly proprietors will be more than happy to share the stories behind their antique furnishings, books, and artwork and to give you guidance on where to find your own treasures as you shop the island. Expect a roaring fire in the winter and breakfast on the secluded brick patio in fair weather. Breakfast is large, and there is an afternoon tea with homemade desserts. Free bicycles and beach towels for guest use.

Miss Molly, daughter of J.T. Rowley, "The Clam King of the World," lived here until age eighty-four, and this 1886 inn has a long-standing and deserved reputation of pleasant accommodations. Marguerite Henry worked out the plot for the children's classic *Misty of Chincoteague* while staying here, and it is still a homelike, friendly place. British Barbara's signature greeting of "good morning, love" has prompted many a guest to leave warm farewells in the guest book, including "I feel loved." Her scones are a local legend, breakfast is substantial, and you'll find a really good pot of tea, too. The place is child friendly — a relative rarity among B&Bs — welcoming children age 6 and older and even the occasional baby. It's very popular with families.

New Church, Virginia

THE GARDEN AND THE SEA INN
Innkeepers: Tom & Sara Baker.
800-824-0672; 757-824-0672.
E-mail: innkeeper@garden andseainn.com.
www.gardenandseainn. com.
4188 Nelson Rd./P.O. Box 275, New Church, VA 23415.
Price: Moderate to Very Expensive.
Credit Cards: AE, D, MC, V.
Handicap Access: One room.
Restrictions: Only children over age 12; pets accepted; closed after Thanksgiving–mid-Mar.

Close enough to Chincoteague to enjoy its attractions, yet far removed from its often congested confines, The Garden and The Sea Inn offers six well-appointed rooms in two Victorian houses. It's easy to relax in the garden, where the air is thick with the scent of mint, or on the screened-in porch of the garden house. Ask about its special arrangement with several other area inns to cater to bicyclists and canoeists and inquire after the Bakers' new deck boat, where for an extra charge, you can join them for a sunset cruise. Breakfast is Continental-plus to avoid filling you up too much before a day at the beach; dinner is first rate. Tom Baker is a Culinary Institute of America graduate who runs the respected dining room, open to guests and locals.

Onancock, Virginia

COLONIAL MANOR INN
Owners: Maphis & Ed Oswald.
757-787-3521;
    fax 757-787-2448.
E-mail: edmanor@shore. intercom.net.
www.onancock.com /inn.htm.
84 Market St., Onancock, VA 23417.
Price: Moderate.
Credit Cards: MC, V.
Handicap Access: Yes.
Special Features: Children welcome.

This 1882 Victorian set back on two acres, off Onanock's main street, has a warm and friendly atmosphere. Children are welcome, with books and toys provided for their enjoyment. Adults often find themselves in the living room, using the inn's piano and guitar for impromptu sing-alongs. There's a gazebo out back for picnics and stargazing. The inn's location makes it convenient to Onancock's attractions, the Tangier Island ferry (tickets available), and beaches and nature preserves thirty minutes north at Chincoteague or south at Kiptopeake. The eight rooms have private or shared baths, comfortable furnishings, and in-room coffee. A full breakfast is served daily.

MOTELS

HEAD OF THE BAY

Havre de Grace

Super 8 (Manager: Angela Garcia; 929 Pulaski Hwy., Havre de Grace, MD 21078; 800-800-8000, reservations; 410-939-1880) Price: Inexpensive to Moderate. AE, CB, D, DC, MC, V. Sixty-three rooms; one handicap access. Small pets and large dogs allowed with permission. Located about ten minutes from I-95 exit.

ANNAPOLIS/WESTERN SHORE

Annapolis

Holiday Inn (General Manager: Dan Cropley; 210 Holiday Court, Annapolis, MD 21401; 800-HOLIDAY, reservations; 410-224-3150) Price: Moderate to Expensive. AE, D, DC, MC, V. Handicap access. 220 rooms, sports bar, outdoor pool, The Regatta Grille and Bar. Free parking. Located at the edge of town off Rte. 50.

Wyndham Garden Hotel (General Manager: William Stoinoff; 173 Jennifer Rd., Annapolis, MD 21401; 800-351-9209, reservations; 410-266-3131) Price: Moderate to Very Expensive. AE, CB, D, DC, MC, V. Handicap access. 197 rooms. Conference facilities, suites. Garden Café restaurant, indoor pool, fitness room, sauna, whirlpool. Located at the edge of town off Rte. 50.

Lexington Park

Days Inn (General Manager: Hans Weisstanner; 21847 Three Notch Rd., Lexington Park, MD 20653; 800-428-2871, reservations; 301-863-6666) Price: Moderate. AE, D, DC, MC, V. 165 rooms, cable TV. Located next to Patuxent Naval Air Station; closest motel to Point Lookout.

Solomons

Comfort Inn/Beacon Marina (General Manager: Darin Miller; Rte. 2-4/255 Lore Rd./P.O. Box 869, Solomons, MD 20688; 410-326-6303) Price: Moderate to Very Expensive. AE, D, DC, MC, V. Sixty rooms. 186-slip marina. Handicap access. Nonsmoking rooms available. Restaurant, outdoor pool.

Holiday Inn (General Manager: Jeff Shepherd; 155 Holiday Dr., Solomons, MD 20688; 800-356-2009; 410-326-6311) Price: Expensive. AE, D, DC, MC, V. 326 rooms. Handicap access. Whirlpool suites, gift shop, waterfront dining, two marinas.

NORTHERN NECK/MIDDLE PENINSULA

Deltaville, Virginia

Deltaville Dockside Inn (Manager: Jane Deagle; Rte. 33/P.O. Box 710, Deltaville, VA 23043; 804-776-9224) Price: Inexpensive to Moderate. MC, V. Twenty-three rooms, handicap access. Most efficiencies with small refrigerators and microwaves in clean accommodations. The only motel around this part of the Middle Peninsula.

White Stone, Virginia

Whispering Pines Motel (Owner: Leslie Morrow; P.O. Box 156, White Stone, VA 22578; 804-435-1101) Price: Inexpensive to Moderate. AE, MC, V. This quiet country motel, nestled in a pleasant wooded setting in Lancaster County, is .5 mi. N. of White Stone on Rte. 3. Twenty-nine rooms, all on one floor, each with TV and telephone. Only lap dogs allowed. Reservations recommended in summer.

UPPER EASTERN SHORE

Chestertown

Foxley Manor Motel (Manager: Reba Postles; 609 Washington Ave., Chestertown, MD 21620; 410-778-3200) Price: Inexpensive to Moderate. AE, D, MC, V. Twenty-five units. A/C, cable TV, swimming pool.

Great Oak Lodge (Managers: Drew & Angelique Litherland; Great Oak Landing Rd., Chestertown, MD 21620; 410-778-2100) Price: Moderate to Very Expensive. AE, D, MC, V. An older motel on a nice marina, with a 9-hole golf course and a pool. Restaurant overlooks the water. Closed mid-Oct.–mid-Apr.

Easton

Days Inn (Manager: Debbie Williams; 7018 Ocean Gateway Dr., Easton, MD 21601; 410-822-4600) Price: Moderate to Expensive. AE, D, DC, MC, V. Eighty rooms. Cable TV, swimming pool. Free continental breakfast.

Econo Lodge (Manager: T.H. Desai; 8175 Ocean Gateway Dr., Easton MD 21601; 410-820-5555) Price: Inexpensive to Expensive. AE, D, MC, V. Forty-eight rooms, some nonsmoking. Refrigerators, microwaves, coffee pots in some rooms. Cable TV.

Grasonville

Comfort Inn Kent Narrows (Manager: Barbara Maniglia; 410-827-6767, 1-800-828-3361; 3101 Main St., Grasonville MD 21638) Price: Moderate to Very

Expensive. All major credit cards. Ninety-seven newly renovated rooms; one handicap accessible room. Water view location next to the Kent Narrows bridge. Indoor pool, hot tub, sauna, exercise room. Continental breakfast.

LOWER EASTERN SHORE

Crisfield

Somers Cove Motel (Manager: Jackie Ward; P.O. Box 387, Crisfield, MD 21817; 800-827-6637; 410-968-1900) Price: Inexpensive to Moderate. MC, V. Forty rooms, with balconies or patios. Operated by the same folks for some years, the motel overlooks the harbor and marina.

Pocomoke City

Quality Inn (Manager: Jacqueline Upshaw; 825 Ocean Hwy., Pocomoke City, MD 21851; 800-228-5151, reservations; 410-957-1300; fax 410-957-9329) Price: Moderate. All major credit cards. Sixty-four rooms, coffee pots, some Jacuzzis and refrigerators, swimming pool. Continental breakfast.

Princess Anne

Econo Lodge (Manager: John Schade; U.S. 13, Princess Anne, MD 21853; 800-615-4653; 410-651-9400) Price: Inexpensive to Moderate. AE, D, DC, MC, V. Fifty rooms. Outdoor pool. Continental breakfast.

Salisbury

Best Western, Salisbury Plaza (Manager: Marjorie Bush; 1735 N. Salisbury Blvd., Salisbury, MD 21801; 410-546-1300) Price: Inexpensive to Expensive. AE, CB, D, DC, MC, V. Handicap access. Some rooms with microwave and data port. Outdoor pool. Continental breakfast.

Econo Lodge, Statesman (Owner: Edward Baker; 712 N. Salisbury Blvd., Salisbury, MD 21801; 800-55-ECONO, reservations; 410-749-7155) Price: Moderate to Expensive. AE, D, DC, MC, V. Ninety-two rooms. Handicap access. Swimming pool. Continental breakfast.

Cape Charles, Virginia

Sunset Beach Inn (Manager: John Maddox; 32246 Lankford Hwy./P.O. Box 472, Cape Charles, VA 23310; 800-899-4SUN; 757-331-4786) Price: Moderate. Eighty-one rooms, one suite, fifty-four RV sites on fifty acres beside the Chesapeake Bay Bridge-Tunnel toll plaza at the tip of the Delmarva Peninsula. Beach, pool, restaurant, lounge, boat ramp, conference center, cable TV.

Chincoteague, Virginia

Assateague Inn (Managers: Gary & Donna Smith; 6570 Coachs Lane/P.O. Box 1038, Chincoteague Island, VA 23336; 757-336-3738; fax 757-336-1179) Price: Moderate to Expensive. AE, D, DC, MC, V. Twenty-six rooms and efficiencies. Condominium complex on edge of marsh.

Birchwood Motel (Owner: Mary Lou Birch; 3650 Main St., Chincoteague Island, VA 23336; 757-336-6133) Price: Moderate to Expensive. AE, D, MC, V. Forty-two rooms. Call ahead Dec. 1 until spring to see if it's open.

Driftwood Motor Lodge (Manager: Scott Chesson; 7105 Maddox Blvd./P.O. Box 575, Chincoteague Island, VA 23336; 800-553-6117; 757-336-6557) Price: Moderate. AE, D, DC, MC, V. Fifty-three rooms.

Island Motor Inn Resort and Spa (Manager: Anna C. Stubbs; 4391 Main St., Chincoteague Island, VA 23336; 757-336-3141) Price: Moderate to Very Expensive. AE, CB, D, DC, MC, V. Probably the best motel on Chincoteague, boasting a splendid sunset view and a full gym with weight-lifting equipment. Sixty waterfront rooms with private balconies, indoor and outdoor pool, hot tub, cable TV. Handicap access.

The Refuge Motor Inn (Manager: Jane Wolffe; 7058 Maddox Blvd./P.O. Box 378, Chincoteague Island, VA 23336; 888-831-0600; 757-336-5511) Price: Moderate to Expensive. AE, D, DC, MC, V. At the entrance to Chincoteague National Wildlife Refuge, seventy-two rooms with patios or balconies look out on loblolly pines. Whirlpool, sauna, exercise room, bike rentals. Fifteen deluxe rooms include sitting areas. Handicap access.

Onley, Virginia

Comfort Inn (Manager: Jay Bundick; Four Corner Plaza, U.S. 13/Box 205, Onley, VA 23418; 800-228-5150, reservations; 757-787-7787) Price: Moderate. Eighty rooms. Complimentary Continental breakfast. Close to Onancock, the "Gateway to Tangier Island."

CHAPTER FOUR
Catch of the Bay
RESTAURANTS & FOOD PURVEYORS

Seafood dominates Chesapeake cuisine, and Chesapeake blue crab dominates local seafood. The word "crab," for instance, appears nearly 200 times in this chapter. That's truly an accurate reflection of this beloved crustacean's dominance, as any menu can attest.

David Trozzo

Chesapeake blue crabs, the Bay's succulent, culinary star.

Picking sweet crabmeat from the hardshell is a time-honored culinary pastime in Bay country. Just witness the crab-picking contests at local seafood festivals. But don't let that messy pile of crab shells fool you. Sophisticated chefs ensure crab shows up in sherried dijon cream sauces topping rockfish or in cilantro sauces over lemon-pepper salmon. Roll it with ricotta and other goodies and sup on an Italian cannelloni, a favorite on one local menu.

Gourmet taste buds won't be disappointed in the range of delicacies found in the region's restaurants, where sea urchin and ostrich have even arrived. Try steak houses of the old-fashioned New York variety or tasteful inns that host the very definition of fine nouvelle cuisine at white linen-topped tables.

Not everyone wants to spend $20 for an entrée, however, in which case we've cased the downtown regulars and the out-of-the-way cafés and fried-oyster watermen's joints. Speaking from a local standpoint, the latter is one of the happiest places of all in which to order seafood: fish sandwiches, oysters in-season, and, of course, crabs — maybe in a crab cake sandwich.

Chesapeake blue crabs are in season during the summer and grown to a tasty size by mid-July and at their fattest from late summer into fall. Demand is high and more than once our spring crab cravings have driven us to local crab houses, where *callinectes sapidus* has been shipped in from the Gulf Coast or South Atlantic states. In the fall, fat Bay crabs are picked, and their meat pasteurized or flash-frozen, ensuring a wintertime supply.

Picking the meat from the shells may be a bit of a problem for the uniniti-ated; the safest course through the formidable task is simple. Ask somebody. A waterman who we once knew taught us how to eat crabs with just a knife alone, now a considerable source of personal Chesapeake pride. And remem-ber: those contest crab pickers may know the fastest route to the meat of the crab, but if seated on a waterside deck with a heaping dozen hard-shell crabs before you, an unhurried pace is the point entirely.

Oysters, subject to their own festival oyster-shucking contests, present a sad Chesapeake story. Once so plentiful that they made tiny, Lower Shore Crisfield rich (and put Solomons Island on the map), their numbers are vastly depleted since then. How the oysters are doing is a common source of Chesapeake conversation come fall, when their "R-month" season begins. But you can find Bay oysters in time for the holidays; remember that the Chincoteagues are salty and considered fine.

Choice Chesapeake eating — striped bass, known hereabouts as rockfish.

David Trozzo

Visitors also should try wild rockfish, so thick and sweet it almost puts other favorite fish to shame. Called striped bass elsewhere, this migratory species suffered a drop in stocks several years back, but have rebounded in the Bay.

As for nonseafood Chesapeake specialties? How about Smithfield ham, cured in that Tidewater town, or even good old fried chicken. Native produce from nearby farms adds endless variety to the local diet from midsummer on: fresh sweet corn (a must with hard-shell crabs), knockout tomatoes, can-taloupes, and peaches. Finally, let us enlighten you on a truly unique local native, one that you're unlikely to find in many restaurants — the Maryland beaten biscuit. You can buy these hard, little floury specimens at the Wye Mills, north of Easton.

More restaurants than we could ever count lie around the Chesapeake Bay. Eleven of us sampled the best and considered a range of tastes and prices for readers in search of either a grand gustatory treat or just a simple café lunch. We've arranged the reviews geographically by region, then alphabetically by town, then by restaurant name. Price ranges are based on the average cost of an appetizer, entrée, and dessert, not including cocktails, wine, beer, tax, or tip.

Inexpensive	Up to $15
Moderate	$16 to $22
Expensive	$23 to $32
Very Expensive	$33 or more

Abbreviations are as follows:

AE – American Express	DC – Diners Club
CB – Carte Blanche	MC – MasterCard
D – Discover	V – Visa

B – Breakfast	D – Dinner
L – Lunch	SB – Sunday Brunch

RESTAURANTS

HEAD OF THE BAY

Chesapeake City

**BAYARD HOUSE
RESTAURANT**
410-885-5040.
www.bayardhouse.com.
11 Bohemia Ave.,
  Chesapeake City, MD
  21915.
Open: Daily.
Price: Expensive to Very
  Expensive.
Cuisine:
  Seafood/Continental.
Serving: L, D.
Credit Cards: AE, D, MC,
  V.
Reservations: Yes, on warm
  weather weekends.
Handicap Access: Limited.
Special Features: C&D
  canal views.

Hunt country sprawls near this end of the Bay, where diners find horse prints, not black-lab-with-duck hunt prints, adorning the walls of this fine-dining inn. In an earlier life, the 1829 brick establishment served the builders of the C&D Canal. Serving on two floors, which includes a dining room with windows wide onto the canal, as well as the downstairs "Hole in the Wall" pub, Bayard's stands near the end of Bohemia Ave., leading to the town wharf.

Plaque after award-winning plaque salute the spicy attributes of the thick vegetable crab soup, where a cupful's broth is drained off a quarter-way into this lively soup. Now, that's impressive, and the judges at the 1998 Maryland Seafood Festival agreed. The night that we visited, the kitchen was serving soft-shell crabs. Soft-shell crabs are definitely an acquired taste. "And it's a taste that I've acquired," as our amiable waitress laughed. Roasted red potatoes and zucchini with winter squash steamed in rosemary rounded out an excellent meal from a fall menu that included such enticing entrées as stuffed Anaheim peppers filled with lobster, lump crab, and shrimp, baked and topped with New Mexican hot green chili salsa and cheddar. Later we learned that the Culinary Institute of America-trained chef has done previous kitchen turns in Santa Fe and Colorado, news that colors the menu's occasional Southwest touches bona fide, not faddish.

SCHAEFER'S CANAL HOUSE
410-885-2200.
Rt. 213, Chesapeake City, MD 21915.
Open: Daily.
Price: Moderate.
Cuisine: Seafood / Continental.
Serving: B, L, D.
Credit Cards: AE, MC, V.
Reservations: Accepted.
Handicap Access: Yes.
Special Features: Public docking.

The Chesapeake and Delaware Canal, linking the upper reaches of the Bay with the Delaware River, virtually cuts Chesapeake City in two. Schaefer's is on the northern bank of the canal, a leisure time complex with lodgings and a marina. Besides serving traditional regional Chesapeake Bay cuisine, Schaefer's reveals a European heritage with several Continental dishes, notably including Wiener schnitzel and piccata Milanese. Soup fanciers can sip three of several homemade soups in miniature crocks, including the exotic Antiguan conch chowder. Many diners review the dessert selections before they choose their main meal to save room for the finale: made-on-premises Austrian pastry. International maritime traffic through the C&D Canal is constant. It's intriguing to watch oceangoing vessels of every size and description from all over the world pass by, seemingly close enough to touch.

Havre de Grace

TIDEWATER GRILLE
410-939-3313.
300 Foot of Franklin St., Havre de Grace, MD 21078.
Open: Daily.
Price: Moderate.
Cuisine: Authentic Regional American Fare.
Serving: L, D.
Credit Cards: AE, DC, MC, V.
Reservations: Recommended on weekends.
Handicap Access: Yes.
Special Features: Water view.

Glass and mirrors dominate the modern dining room of the Tidewater Grille, and for good reason. Aside from having a spectacular view of the Susquehanna River at the head of the Bay, the restaurant sits near what the waitresses describe as one of the busiest railroad bridges in the East. It's true. No fewer than ten trains crossed during a typical Fri. night dinner at the Tidewater. The menu offers a smattering of everything, and the wine list offers several good, inexpensive choices. The restaurant boasts authentic regional fare, but not everything is deep-fried. The stuffed mushroom appetizer is broiled and capped with puffs of hollandaise. The crab wasn't overworked, but very

For dining on the Susquehanna River, try the Tidewater Grille in Havre de Grace.

David Trozzo

lumpy with good texture. The seafood linguine in marinara sauce is spiked with garlic; the mixed seafood grill features tangy skewered shrimp and scallops, and a seafood sausage is set off by a lemon-caper tartar sauce. The menu also features grilled or blackened chicken and steaks, veal dishes, and even more seafood and pasta choices. The desserts are special, too, made in Ocean City and trucked in. The Italian love cake was rich with chocolate, ricotta cheese, and chocolate mousse filling.

A deck is available for outdoor dining. Eye-catching stained-glass panels add to the dining room's warm decor, and the service is friendly and attentive. Even though the restaurant's growing reputation brings in a full dining room, we felt at home.

ANNAPOLIS/WESTERN SHORE

Annapolis

CAFÉ NORMANDIE
410-263-3382.
185 Main St., Annapolis, MD 21401.
Open: Daily.
Price: Moderate to Expensive.
Cuisine: French.
Serving: B, L, D.
Credit Cards: AE, D, MC, V.
Reservations: Recommended on weekends.
Handicap Access: Limited.

Some of the most likeable things about the country-style French restaurant Café Normandie are its contradictions. It's a good-sized place — spread out over two levels, big enough so that they rarely seem to have trouble seating customers — yet strangely cozy, with high-backed booths and small tables centered around a handsome fireplace.

It's a fine-dining establishment where one can feel comfortable in jeans. And while its vast and ever-changing list of entrées can take you into the stratosphere with $20 dishes like duck or croquettes du boeuf, Café Normandie also offers delightful and inexpensive crêpes and omelettes on its everyday menu. Favorite crêpes — apples and cheddar or ratatouille — are perfectly filling alongside the unpretentious house salad, leafy green with a sharp creamy dressing. The tomato bisque with crabmeat is a luncheon meal unto itself, though some sensitive palates may find it unbearably rich. It's also a surprisingly good place for a hearty and simple breakfast. The coffee has a strong cinnamon flavor; while we find it quite tasty, some purists can't stand it. But Café Normandie's ultimate contradiction is depressing — slow, sluggish, and unconcerned service that seems to have grown worse in recent years.

CANTLER'S RIVERSIDE INN
410-757-1467.
458 Forest Beach Rd.,
  Annapolis, MD 21401.
Open: Daily.
Price: Inexpensive to
  Expensive.
Cuisine: Seafood.
Serving: L, D.
Credit Cards: AE, D, DC,
  MC, V.
Reservations: No.
Handicap Access: Yes,
  though not bathrooms.
Special Features: Boat
  access; waterfront porch.

You come to Annapolis in search of crabs, and indeed, if it's soft-shell crab sandwiches or crab cakes that you want, a dozen downtown restaurants can oblige. But if you're looking for the classic hard-shell experience — a mess of freshly steamed, just-caught crustaceans plopped on your table, their tender meat enhanced by butter, Old Bay seasoning, and pitchers of beer — most locals will exhort you to travel beyond the city limits. Specifically, to Jimmy Cantler's place, on the far side of the Severn River.

Call for directions and follow them carefully. Cantler's obscure location, a shady spot on Mill Creek at the end of a winding residential road, is the only thing to relieve its otherwise crushing popularity. You may want to avoid it on a summer weekend, when the wait for a table is nothing compared to the unbelievably long line just to get into the parking lot. Once you're in, you have the choice of the rustic dining room or the waterfront porch — seating at both is along big picnic tables draped with brown paper. Do check out the other seafood items on the menu — a big bucket of mussels makes a great appetizer. But crabs, sizes and prices varying with the season, remain the stars of the show.

CARROL'S CREEK CAFÉ
410-263-8102.
410 Severn Ave.,
  Annapolis, MD 21401.
Open: Daily.
Price: Moderate to
  Expensive.
Cuisine: Seafood/New
  Cuisine.
Serving: L, D, SB.
Credit Cards: AE, D, MC, V.
Reservations:
  Recommended on
  weekends.

Rounding age 35, one starts fretting about pending fuddy-duddyhood. Affording new living room curtains replaces affording endlessly hip nights out, especially since nobody wants to relive all that stuff anyway. Then the old college roommate comes to town — the one with culinary wits honed by years in a New Orleans' thriving food biz. Like Miss Piggy suddenly driven to shed a few pounds, we start paging about in search of whatever foodie find we missed during our love affair with home-decorating magazines. Flipping through the mental Rolodex of Annapolis restaurants, the

Handicap Access: Yes.
Special Features: Waterside deck and view.

savvy local thinks not just about cuisine, but about practicalities, like hassle-free parking and water views. That's when one ends up once again at the ever-dependable Carrol's Creek Café.

Carrol's Creek opened in 1983. Seafood-based dishes are nearly always hits, especially the specials. Of late, elaborate presentation — swirly twirls of potato curls — seems to be rising high above entrées. Rockfish, a beloved Chesapeake staple, is properly cooked, not overdone, and the gingered sweet potatoes still zow when microwaved at home for lunch the next day. The crab soup didn't blow our socks off, but it's easily as good as you're likely to find. Caesar salads are dressed from scratch, tableside. The varied wine and beer selection includes the café's own label. Windows open wide onto Spa Creek from the blond wood dining room, and the deck opens for dining and drinks in good weather. We once stood out there as a hurricane passed offshore and watched the rising tide submerge the lone car left in the underground parking garage. More commonly, folks like to come here to watch the Wed. night sailboat races in the summer.

David Trozzo

They pledge allegiance to the U.S. flag every morning at Chick & Ruth's Delly, an Annapolis institution.

CHICK & RUTH'S DELLY
410-269-6737.
165 Main St., Annapolis, MD 21401.
Open: Daily, 24 hours.
Price: Inexpensive.
Cuisine: Kosher / American.
Serving: B, L, D.
Credit Cards: No.
Reservations: No.
Handicap Access: Limited.

The food is no-frills, the decor decidedly retro. But Chick & Ruth's, a venerable institution in Annapolis, still packs 'em in around the clock. It's a diner, a place for a quick bite that won't break the bank, but only the stodgiest element won't be charmed by the newspaper clippings that crowd the walls, and the sandwiches named for past and present politicos. ("The Al Gore," for example, is chicken salad with lettuce and tomato on wheat, while "The Barbara Mikulski," named for one of Maryland's U.S. senators, is a tuna sandwich with

melted cheese served open-faced on a bagel.) Ted Levitt, son of original owners Chick and Ruth Levitt, makes sure everyone is welcomed warmly and will
even visit with his guests and perform a quick magic trick for the little ones.
You won't find a better milkshake in all of Annapolis, and if all else fails, just
order a BLT and watch the tourists and local luminaries come and go. In a
town that's populated (some would say overpopulated) with saloons and
pubs, Chick & Ruth's provides a welcome slice of twentieth-century
Americana and may be the only spot in town with liver and onions on the
menu.

CIAO
410-267-7912.
51 West St., Annapolis, MD
   21401.
Open: Tues.–Sun.
Price: Moderate to
   Expensive.
Cuisine: Mediterranean/
   American.
Serving: L, D.
Credit Cards: AE, D, DC,
   MC, V.
Reservations:
   Recommended on
   weekends.
Handicap Access: Yes.

In close walking distance but just outside the
tourist district, Ciao thrived for years as a
cheery, gourmet deli-carryout, featuring fancy prosciutto sandwiches and apricot couscous — a more
chic lunchtime option for a business community
bored by burgers and crab cakes. But in 1996,
owner Diane Anderson decided to take the Ciao
ethos upmarket, transforming it into a sleek
nightspot with a Mediterranean-inspired menu.
You can still get a good lunch there, but the atmosphere and the prices may prompt you to wait for a
romantic dinner instead.

With a gleaming tile floor, a retro, mirrored, dark
wood bar, and a swanky attitude, the new Ciao is a
popular happy hour site for the cocktail crowd and
has earned a big following among the state capi-
tal's expense-account set. Its lengthy menu of entrées is ambitious for such a
tiny place, featuring rich and mouthwatering appetizers, such as beef carpac-
cio. Some items miss the mark just ever so slightly — a pork tenderloin, while
deliciously coated in a tangy sauce and crushed pecans, was not quite as tender as it should have been for the money; a paella had surreally plump and
savory mussels along with tasty grilled vegetables, but the saffron rice was
overwhelmed by pepper. Still, Ciao succeeds at bringing a needed dash of
glamour and Continental flair to downtown Annapolis.

**49 WEST WINE BAR AND
   GALLERY**
410-626-9796.
49 West St., Annapolis, MD
   21401.
Open: Daily.
Price: Inexpensive.
Cuisine: Light Café
   Fare/Vegetarian.
Serving: B, L, D.
Credit Cards: AE, MC, V.

For value and style, it's hard to go wrong at this
European-style café-bar, which opened its
doors in 1997 and quickly gathered a local following. Freshly made soups are among the most popular offerings, and the menu also includes a short
but sweet list of salads and appetizers like a cheese
plate with apples and grapes. As for us, a luscious
crab dip and overflowing $5.25 veggie sandwiches
on fresh breads are favorites, although we've sali-

Reservations: For 6 or more.

Handicap Access: Limited.

vated over the occasional special, too. Sandwiches come with salads, which makes for a full plate, indeed. We go for the house salad; you may opt for potato or celery root salad instead. With coffee, two people can enjoy an excellent lunch for less than $16. In addition, the café makes its own pastries, acquires desserts from five different bakeries, and offers a nice choice of by-the-glass wines and coffees. The decor, with its muted colors and current art exhibition hanging from the walls, offers Mediterranean flair along the Chesapeake. With jazz and classical offerings, this may be the city's hottest nightspot for grownups (see the heading Nightlife in Chapter Five, *Culture*).

Dining at Harry Browne's in Annapolis offers a fine view of Maryland's historic statehouse.

David Trozzo

HARRY BROWNE'S
410-263-4332.
66 State Circle, Annapolis, MD 21401.
Open: Daily.
Price: Expensive.
Cuisine: New American.
Serving: L, D, SB.
Credit Cards: AE, D, DC, MC, V.
Reservations: Recommended on weekends.
Handicap Access: Yes.
Special Features: Maryland Statehouse views.

The waitstaff at this twenty-year-old, art nouveau/art deco-trimmed restaurant always seems to be top-notch, even if you're busy making their lives complicated. Witness the day that we arrived fifteen minutes before midday meal service stopped. Our gentle maître d' kindly informed us of the Sunday brunch buffet deadline. "That's OK." — even though our mate was off circling narrow streets in search of a parking spot. Once squired to our table, a waitperson quickly appeared with a menu and departed with drink orders. With seconds to spare, our mate showed up and ordered the all-you-can-eat buffet. "Why don't you order your omelette now?" said our adept server, even as the buffet's omelette maker prepared to strike the weekly set.

She then set the kitchen in motion, returning with a plate of French toast and another of toasty fried potatoes steaming fresh from the pan. As if this already wasn't all he could eat, she then discounted the $12.95 buffet rate by five dollars. Yours truly ordered from the menu: Chesapeake eggs Benedict with fat lumps of crabmeat, which, bravo for the kitchen, was not drowned out by hollandaise. The French toast? "Nine out of ten," pronounced our mate. The bill? About twenty-five dollars, with brunch drinks of mimosa and draft beer included.

Most people consider this institution for fine-dining occasions. With complex specials of venison, beef, or pan-roasted Alaskan halibut in a sea urchin cream, you might, too. Still, that Sunday brunch was quite a treat.

JOSS CAFÉ & SUSHI BAR
410-263-4688.
195 Main St., Annapolis,
   MD 21401.
Open: Daily.
Price: Inexpensive to Very
   Expensive.
Cuisine: Japanese.
Serving: L, D.
Credit Cards: AE, DC, MC,
   V.
Reservations: No.
Handicap Access: Yes.

It's not the only sushi place in town, but the crowds in the postage-stamp-sized foyer and the lines out into the street indicate that raw fish connoisseurs consider Joss to be the best. It's a tiny place, with barely ten tables that give virtually every visitor a window seat onto historic, brick-lined Main St. Each guest also has a direct view of the three sushi chefs who holler a greeting to every newcomer as they painstakingly slice and wrap piles of fish and vegetables behind the bar.

This is the place to take the nervous sushi novice; in fact, it is where this writer became a convert. The sushi is uniformly fresh and tasty, the rice clumps tidy and satisfying. And for the unrepentant sushiphobes in your life, there are delicious nonfish dishes to choose from. A personal favorite is a lunch special of tempura vegetables — hearty slices of carrot, squash, and pepper fried in a light and savory batter. As in most sushi bars, Joss can be expensive, especially if you top off your meal with warm and salty miso soup or a can of Kirin beer. But if you pace yourself, and order your sushi in small batches that don't get ahead of your hunger, you can get out fairly cheaply.

LA PICCOLA ROMA
410-268-7898.
200 Main St., Annapolis,
   MD 21401.
Open: Daily.
Price: Moderate to
   Expensive.
Cuisine: Italian.
Serving: L, D, Mon.–Fri.; D,
   Sat., Sun.
Credit Cards: AE, MC, V.
Reservations:
   Recommended on
   weekends.
Handicap Access: No.

La Piccola Roma has been a hit since the day it opened in 1991, offering authentic Central Italian food both here and, later, at its deli at the edge of town, Giolitti's. The following of regulars has learned to request favorites from the kitchen, even if an entrée has departed the menu. For a real treat, try the cannelloni di pésce, rich with ricotta and other Italian cheeses, touched with crab, scallops, and a whiff of lemon thyme via a cream sauce. It's a knockout. Pastas and fish dishes are always dependable, and as with any good Chesapeakeside kitchen, rockfish is well worth your order. Here, the sweet Bay favorite spends its days refrigerated with fresh herbs. The dining room is simple and sophisticated; black linen napkins top white tablecloths. Individual bas reliefs hang on the far wall. Windows are wide onto the city's Main St. The wine list is well considered, and to top it off, we often find street parking at this end of Main St., or nearby.

**MCGARVEY'S SALOON
& OYSTER BAR**
410-263-5700.
8 Market Space, Annapolis,
    MD 21401.
Open: Daily.
Price: Moderate.
Cuisine: Saloon Fare.
Serving: L, D, SB.
Credit Cards: AE, MC, V.
Reservations: Not on
    weekends.
Handicap Access: No.

From the Tiffany-style lamps to the heavy, dark wood bars dominating both the bar and dining room, McGarvey's is a classic saloon and a City Dock stalwart. You couldn't ask for more selection in a tavern-style menu, which offers reasonably priced, acceptable meals, ranging from spinach artichoke dip to filet bearnaise sandwiches alongside steak and seafood entrées. A smoked bluefish Caesar salad offers a tasty new twist, and the crab cakes win for quantity. Over the years we've reliably found salty Chincoteague oysters in the fall and that's reason enough to belly up to the wellworn wood raw bar. While you're there, try the house ale, Aviator Lager, or an Old Hydraulic Root Beer. But keep in mind that if it's a weekend, the place is likely to be crowded.

MIDDLETON TAVERN
410-263-3323.
2 Market Space, Annapolis,
    MD 21401.
Open: Daily.
Price: Inexpensive to
    Expensive.
Cuisine: Seafood/
    American/Tavern Fare.
Serving: L, D, weekend B.
Credit Cards: AE, D, MC, V.
Reservations: No, but offers
    "priority seating" for
    those who call ahead.
Handicap Access: Limited.

The authentically colonial exterior of this 1740 building belies the surprising versatility of the bar and restaurant within. Despite its quaint decor, Middleton fits several very different kinds of contemporary tastes. There are the prim and cozy dining rooms, just the place to take your visiting older relatives; the smoky and collegial bar, home of the ninety-nine-cent "oyster shooter" (a raw one drenched in cocktail sauce, accompanied by a beer chaser) and live music; and the expansive front porch, possibly the city's premiere venue for people-watching on a warm weekend. The menu, too, is pleasingly diverse. You can go cheap and simple — a healthy meal of black bean soup, laden with raw onions and brown rice, and a side salad will get you out for less than $10. Or you can opt for one of the fine entrées starting in the $20 range — pork medallions or steak Diane — and a nice bottle of wine. But Middleton also has the traditional bar fare that you may crave, burgers and crab dip, reasonably priced. Simple pasta dishes are also well executed, and the half-priced appetizer portions are just big enough for a light dinner.

PUSSER'S LANDING
410-626-0004.
80 Compromise St.,
    Annapolis, MD 21401.
Open: Daily.
Price: Moderate.
Cuisine: American/
    Caribbean.
Serving: B, L, D.
Credit Cards: AE, D, MC, V.
Reservations: No.
Handicap Access: Yes.

Those who resent the arrival of corporate chains like The Gap and Starbucks in downtown Annapolis may turn up their noses at the restaurant in the city's Marriott Waterfront. Yet Pusser's Landing has one thing to put all other Annapolis eateries to shame: location. It's the only place in the waterfront downtown offering actual waterfront dining, as in water lapping directly under your feet, with a porch bordering Annapolis's City Dock — also known as Ego Alley, where yachtsmen cruise as proudly as teenage hot-rodders. Pusser's features a vaguely Caribbean theme, with dark, carved wood fixtures to evoke a Spanish galleon and a menu heavy on things like lime-infused shrimp, Jamaican jambalaya, and fancy rum-based drinks. In all, it does a pretty good job of relieving the competent dullness of most high-end chain hotel restaurants. And it trumps the more authentically Annapolitan restaurants in one impressive way — with a dazzling collection of black-and-white photographs portraying the old Annapolis from back when it was a raffish waterman's village — long before the likes of Marriott came to town.

Brewing beer at the Ram's Head Tavern, the popular Annapolis nightspot.

David Trozzo

RAM'S HEAD TAVERN
410-268-4545.
33 West St., Annapolis, MD
    21401.
Open: Daily.
Price: Inexpensive to
    Moderate.
Cuisine: New American/
    Tavern Fare.
Serving: L, D.

The Ram's Head is the little bar that could. Just a decade ago, it was a tiny basement pub whose specialty was its encyclopedic collection of beers from around the world. But over the past several years, it has relentlessly expanded, adding an upstairs bar, a couple of dining rooms, a sprawling outdoor courtyard, a brewing facility, and finally, a concert hall. But expansion has not diluted its pop-

Credit Cards: AE, D, MC, V.
Reservations:
   Recommended.
Handicap Access: Yes.

ularity. Lively on weekdays, Ram's Head is almost inpenetrable on weekends. It's a slick but comfortable place, with a lustrous, brass rail-and-polished wood decor. Though some scoffed when it became the umpteenth tavern to start brewing its own beer, the stuff turned out to be pretty darn good. The food, too, has proven to be several notches above traditional bar fare, if a couple dollars more expensive. This writer's favorite sandwich is a huge chicken breast topped with slices of apple and a mound of melted Brie, accompanied by an elite class of french fry. The new concert hall is a fairly intimate space that hosts performers in a typically folk-rock vein, many of them fresh from shows at the more famous Birchmere in Alexandria, VA.

RIORDAN'S SALOON
410-263-5449; 301-261-1524.
26 Market Space,
   Annapolis, MD 21401.
Open: Daily.
Price: Moderate to
   Expensive.
Cuisine: American/
   Seafood.
Serving, L, D, SB.
Credit Cards: AE, D, MC, V.
Reservations: Yes, Fri.–Sat.
   only for upstairs dining
   room.
Handicap Access: Yes.

Choosing a spot to eat in downtown Annapolis can be overwhelming, but you really can't go wrong with Riordan's, a favorite among locals and visitors alike. Dark wood, brass, and a healthy smattering of U.S. Naval Academy memorabilia create a warm and inviting atmosphere. If you're parched from navigating the town's history-lined streets, dozens of beers, lagers, ales, and microbrews are on tap, in addition to the usual choices (though Riordan's loses points for charging for soda refills). Appetizers range from well-above-average potato skins to an unforgettable hot crab dip. Riordan's also boasts one of the best burgers in Annapolis, served alongside fries sprinkled with Old Bay seasoning, lest you forget where you are. You can also choose from crab cakes, of course, or overstuffed sandwiches so sizable that you'll need a fork and knife to get started. Entrées and inventive daily specials include a nice variety of beef, chicken, seafood, and pasta dishes that often incorporate the bounty of the Bay in one form or another. All of this great food, combined with a friendly and very attentive staff, keeps Riordan's a cut above the rest.

SAIGON PALACE
410-268-4463.
609 B Taylor Ave.,
   Annapolis, MD 21401.
Open: Mon.–Thurs., 11:00
   a.m.–10:00 p.m.; Fri.–Sat.,
   11:00 a.m.–11:00 p.m.;
   Sun., 5:00 p.m.–9:30 p.m.
Price: Moderate.
Cuisine: Vietnamese.
Serving: L, D.

Saigon Palace is an old favorite, the proprietor, Toi Van Tran, an old-fashioned host who always comes out to say hello to friends and long-time patrons. Over the years, the food never fails, although we've weathered occasional slow service. On our most recent visit, however, a magnificent server pulled out a knife and fork to demonstrate the authentic method for eating Vietnamese-style fish and took pains to ensure that our table under-

Chesapeake's proximity to urbanity brings international cuisine to the Bay, including Vietnamese fare at the Saigon Palace in Annapolis.

David Trozzo

Credit Cards: AE, DC, MC, V.
Reservations: Recommended on weekends.
Handicap Access: Yes.

stood the hows of properly enjoying Vietnamese coffee, the thick, evaporated milk waiting to be properly stirred. A fat serving of duck with seasonal vegetables and the ever-tasty caramel shrimp in pepper sauce rounded out the table's treats. We sipped the house white wine, sampled the big amber bottle of Alsacian Fisher's Ale, and appreciated white tablecloths that center the homey atmosphere of this small restaurant at the city's edge. Especially recommended if you're looking for good cuisine at moderate prices. Located in a shopping center just outside the historic district, so parking is a breeze.

TREATY OF PARIS
410-263-2641.
Church Circle, Main St., Annapolis, MD 21401.
Open: Daily.
Price: Expensive to Very Expensive.
Cuisine: Continental.
Serving: B, L, D, SB.
Credit Cards: AE, D, DC, MC, V.
Reservations: Yes.
Handicap Access: Yes, prior notice requested.
Special Features: Historic building; fireplaces.

For several years, the restaurant in the basement of the landmark Maryland Inn has epitomized Annapolis fine dining in a lushly historic setting, whether it's a romantic dinner or an expense-account splurge. The target of more discerning tour groups, Treaty of Paris is where you can see just-engaged couples enjoying their big night out, as well as the state capital's million-dollar lobbyist holding court and brokering deals at his favorite corner table. Dinner is an extravagance, but you feel as if you get your money's worth in such a plush, candlelit setting, with a roaring fire on the hearth and a solicitous, bow-tied waitstaff. No nouvelle cuisine here — the menu is sumptuously rich, with Continental classics like veal Oscar. Treaty of Paris is also locally renowned for its Sun. brunch buffet — a decadent all-you-can-eat spread, featuring custom-ordered omelettes, Belgian waffles, and an elaborate dessert tray. Bargain hunters are urged to show up for a weekday lunch, where the $8 soup and salad buffet is plenty filling when bolstered by the complimentary basket of famous crisp and fluffy popovers.

Deale

HAPPY HARBOR
410-867-0949; 301-261-5297.
533 Deale Rd., Deale, MD 20751.
Open: Daily.
Price: Inexpensive to Moderate.
Cuisine: Seafood.
Serving: B, L, D.
Credit Cards: D, MC, V.
Reservations: No.
Handicap Access: Partial.

If you're looking for a seafood bacchanal in a genuine waterman's town, have a seat. For sheer local atmosphere, it's hard to go wrong along Rockhold Creek, where in warm weather, the big glassed-in porch is very inviting. The dining room is serviceable but not fancy, which is why everyone asks about the big English sideboard that dominates the front wall. Barbara Sturgell owns and operates the restaurant with daughter Karen, and her family recipe for salty cream of crab soup is among the best that we've ever tried. The crab melt — crab imperial awash in provolone cheese — is so rich that you won't eat for two days after. The vegetable Maryland crab soup was less impressive. Oysters on the half shell had come from Grasonville. Happy hours with specials every night, which means $.25 oysters once a week during the fall season. No summertime hard-shell crabs, though.

PIER 44
410-867-2392.
6029 Herring Bay Rd., Deale, MD 20751.
Open: Daily, Apr.-Nov.
Price: Inexpensive, unless order lots of market-priced crabs.
Cuisine: Crabs/ Hamburgers.
Serving: L, D.
Credit Cards: AE, MC, V.
Reservations: No.
Handicap Access: Yes.

It was a sad early summer day some years back when we stopped at the old Fisher's Wharf to find it forever closed, but now Pier 44 has arrived to close the crab deck chasm on this side of Rockhold Creek. Those who've been wondering where to crack crabs along a waterman's waterfront have found the place, although this is more island parrot-themed than ye olde waterman-themed. Nine pairs of sliding glass doors open from the small bar and indoor restaurant to the porch outside, with eight tables just right for cracking crabs. The rest of the menu is limited to hot dogs, hamburgers, crab cakes, and the like. Manager Gary Broyles says expansion may be in store for the outdoor deck, where servers carefully swap broad table umbrellas for citronella candles as the sun goes down.

Eastport

LEWNES STEAK HOUSE
410-263-1617.

One summer, we must have stopped by Lewnes three or four times in the hopes of getting in

401 Fourth St., Eastport,
  MD 21222.
Open: Daily.
Price: Expensive to Very
  Expensive.
Cuisine: Classic Steak
  House.
Serving: D.
Credit Cards: AE, DC, MC,
  V.
Reservations: Yes.
Handicap Access: Yes.

for a weekend dinner. No luck. Reservations are a must at this intimate steak house, which serves all of the non-PC sides that a steak lover would hope to find, like creamed spinach and lyonnaise potatoes. We finally scored one of the precious few tables late one weekday about 5:00 p.m. and promptly started with six salty raw oysters. Soon came the simple but straightforward stars of the show, a petite filet mignon and a New York strip steak that met every expectation. Elsewhere on the menu, porterhouse, prime rib, and rib eye are joined by chops of veal and lamb, grilled double breast of chicken, and hearty servings of seafood.

The wine list is impressive and lengthy, but pricey. No per-glass of red sold for much below $8 on the night that we dined. That's not to say the pinot noir wasn't excellent, but $28 for three glasses of wine is a commitment. We later learned that the list is a constant work in progress and found a few per-glass prices that had dropped a dollar or so. "Top-quality, sometimes obscure wines are the point entirely," says General Manager Erik Peterson. Two floors seat seventy total; service is attentive. All in all, a classic steak house and, by all accounts, uproariously popular.

O'LEARY'S
410-263-0884.
310 Third St., Eastport, MD
  21222.
Open: Daily.
Price: Expensive.
Cuisine: Seafood.
Serving: D.
Credit Cards: AE, DC, MC,
  V.
Reservations: Yes.
Handicap Access: Yes.
Restrictions: No smoking.

Charlie Bauer was a partner in the Washington, D.C. area's popular Silver Diner chain when he heard that O'Leary's had closed. The former customer of an establishment generally regarded as the best seafood restaurant in town got busy and now commands the kitchen and owns the place along with partner Paul Meyer.

In all, the time lapse between the closing of the old and opening of the new O'Leary's was six months. Some basic similarities remain, but the new owners' efforts to update are welcome and well executed. Gone is the blackboard listing the evening's fish and the ways in which the kitchen would fix them; in its place are menus and, alongside a list of entrées, a new twist. In addition to the usual broiling and grilling are fancier possibilities — have your rockfish or flounder hickory grilled, with sun-dried tomato and caramelized onion compote. We started with a version of oysters Rockefeller. Then came a flounder sautéed with a roasted garlic beurre blanc and pine nuts (one of the pick-your-own options), an exquisite, three-filet serving, and a wild rockfish topped with lump crabmeat and sherry dijon cream. It was swoony. Friendly service, parking, and another welcome change — you now can make reservations.

WILD ORCHID CAFÉ
410-268-8009.
909 Bay Ridge Ave.,
  Eastport, MD 21222.
Open: Daily, except Mon.
Price: Expensive.
Cuisine: New American.
Serving: L, D, SB.
Credit Cards: AE, D, DC,
  MC, V.
Reservations:
  Recommended on
  weekends.
Handicap Access: Yes.

The elegant neighborhood café, formerly known as Café La Mouffe, has moved somewhat upscale since becoming the Wild Orchid a couple years ago. The setting remains charmingly casual — a little house that blends in with the others along Eastport's main street, the interior stripped down airily to its hardwood floors, bare walls, and big windows. The effect is like sitting in a friend's modest but well-appointed living room. The food is far fancier. The house salads are mixed delightfully with slices of strawberry; the freshly baked bread is studded with sun-dried tomatoes. Wild Orchid's specialty seems to be fine-dining standards with a Chesapeake Bay twist. On a recent visit, separate entrées of salmon, New York strip steak, and pork loin all came topped by or stuffed with lump crabmeat. Some of the more ambitious dishes end up being a little heavy on the sauce, but one of the finest is one of the most affordable on the menu — a simple rotisserie-grilled duck coated in a deliciously syrupy soy sauce.

Galesville

**THE INN AT PIRATES
  COVE**
410-867-2300; 410-269-1345;
  301-261-5050.
4817 Riverside Dr.,
  Galesville, MD 20765.
Open: Daily.
Price: Moderate to
  Expensive.
Cuisine: Seafood/
  American.
Serving: L, D, SB.
Credit Cards: AE, DC, MC,
  V.
Reservations: Yes.
Handicap Access: Yes.
Special Features: Waterside
  dining.

Crystal, humid-free days have a way of blowing through sultry Chesapeake just as midsummer wanders past, hinting at the coming fall. Now's the time to hit the tobacco roads south of Annapolis for Galesville, a gentle West River fishing town about an hour's drive east of Washington, D.C. Local Annapolitans widely consider a couple of restaurants there to be off-the-beaten-path gems, and Pirates Cove may be the best. Ask for a table on the deck. The menu is not particularly nouvelle or trendy, but alongside its perfectly acceptable pastas, meat, and chicken dishes comes the seafood saturnalia that you seek. Seafood platters come broiled or fried, and crab imperial, that naughty, creamy Chesapeake classic, actually beckons. Also worth the calories: a cream of crab soup. The house dressing is a tasty mustard-dill — heavier on the dill than mustard the day that we visited, which says something about a kitchen willing to wrestle mustard to a secondary role. Service is prompt. Big Mary's Dock Bar jams next door; for those who would be happier with just the cries of the gulls, ask for a table on the other side of the deck. The indoor dining rooms are relatively simple, but you can catch an excellent West River view from a table inside the roomy bar. Also home to a small inn and a marina with transient slips.

Prince Frederick

Steamers at Stoney's — a Chesapeake treat off the beaten path.

David Trozzo

STONEY'S SEAFOOD HOUSE
410-535-1888.
545 N. Solomons Island Rd., Prince Frederick, MD 20678.
Oyster House Rd., Broomes Island, MD 20615 (closed Nov.–early Feb.).
Open: Daily.
Price: Moderate.
Cuisine: Seafood.
Serving: L, D.
Credit Cards: AE, D, MC, V.
Reservations: No.
Handicap Access: Yes.
Special Features: Full dinner menu available only at Prince Frederick location.

Given the choice between the two locations, we go to the Broomes Island Stoney's. Getting there, down a long and winding tidewater road, is half the adventure, and the broad deck on the water (one of the biggest around) perfects the picture. But sometimes you're on the highway through town, and you don't have time to wander down a back road, or worse, it's the dead of winter and the Broomes Island Stoney's is closed. This is when we go to the Fox Run Shopping Center Stoney's in Prince Frederick, with its clubby Chesapeake waterfowl decor and spacious dining room, as well as a full dinner menu, which you won't find on Broomes Island. Either way, the food's great: peppery crab soup, a humongous "small" crab cake sandwich, which at four ounces seems far fatter than most crab cake sandwiches, comes topped with a juicy, red tomato slice. Service was quick, though we've stopped into the Prince Frederick dining room for takeout before and waited awhile; that was in midwinter. On a 90° day, the shopping center Stoney's was nearly empty. Everybody must be down at the Broomes Island Stoney's, cracking crabs on the waterfront.

Riva

Waterside restaurants like Mike's draw the boating crown in the summer.

David Trozzo

**MIKE'S RESTAURANT &
CRAB HOUSE**
410-956-2784.
3030 Old Riva Rd., Riva,
  MD 21140.
Open: Daily.
Price: Moderate to
  Expensive.
Cuisine: Seafood.
Serving: L, D.
Credit Cards: AE, MC, V.
Reservations: For large
  parties only.
Handicap Access: Yes.
Special Features: Outdoor
  waterside deck.

We like Mike's and have for years. It's located on the outskirts of town, so it's easy to meet incoming friends from Washington, D.C. without explaining how to navigate the city's sometimes confusing historic district. It also comes with parking, overlooks the South River, and serves great hard-shell crabs and big seafood platters. It's a lively scene out on the outdoor deck in midsummer, and a wedding or other celebratory gathering always seems to have taken up residence. Even into Oct., the deck stays open if the weather is good, although service can get a little spotty. Boats dock alongside, mallards paddle in, and with everybody cracking crabs, it's the consummate Chesapeake scene in full glory. The cavernous indoor dining room is as full as the parking lot during summer crab season, but if you come early, during the week, or in the off-season, you should have no problems. The menu's steak and rib entrées should make the beef eaters happy, and a fresh but utilitarian salad bar is offered alongside the bar where bands gather and folks boogie on the small dance floor. A popular place.

Solomons

CD CAFÉ
410-326-3877.
14350 Solomons Island Rd.,
  Solomons, MD 20688.

Although a relative newcomer to Solomons, CD Café, in the Avondale Center, has quickly established itself as one of the best restaurants in the area. Its cozy, eleven-table dining room is

Open: Daily.
Price: Moderately
 Expensive.
Cuisine: Creative Regional.
Serving: B (Continental), L,
 D, SB.
Credit Cards: MC, V.
Reservations: No.
Handicap Access: Yes.

pleasantly subdued, composed of shades of egg-plant, cream, and sage and the most intriguing, Modiglianiesque figures painted into the cupboard doors that run along the bottom of the bar. Despite the main road running outside the first-floor café, the vista to the Patuxent River and the soaring bridge to St. Marys County still begs diners to relax and enjoy. The owners describe their menu as creative cuisine, which features a number of Cajun touches, like red beans and rice with andouille sausage. CD's ever-changing menu also offers regular offerings for vegetarians, including a tempting, roasted vegetable sandwich spilling over with portobello mushrooms, summer squash, and tomatoes marinated and spiced with a mild mustard sauce. Consider a different quesadilla entrée, as well as a fresh seafood dish. If you prefer a little meat in your diet, the curried chicken salad with apples, celery, and almonds in an overstuffed pita is enough for two. Both entrées are presented with a crisp salad of romaine, red onions, mandarin oranges, and almond slivers. Despite the herculean-sized portions, you'd hate yourself in the morning if you passed on dessert. The Mexican chocolate espresso cake, with chocolate sauce, whipped cream, and strawberry garnish, is a showstopper; highly recommended.

DRY DOCK
410-326-4817.
Zahniser's Sailing Center, C
 St., Solomons, MD 20688.
Open: Year-round; closed
 Tues. in winter.
Price: Very Expensive.
Cuisine: Seafood / New
 American.
Serving: D, SB.
Credit Cards: AE, MC, V.
Reservations:
 Recommended for D.
Handicap Access: No.

When it comes to ambiance, the Dry Dock is hard to beat. Candlelight casts an effusive glow over the intimate dining room (only ten tables in the whole place) as yacht club burgees drape down from the ceiling to finish off the very clubby effect. And from nearly every angle, diners are treated to a spectacular view of Solomons' Back Creek through a seemingly endless sea of sailboat masts. Now for the reason you came — the food. The handwritten menu, which can be hard to read, changes daily and includes everything from tenderloin to tilapia, served with seasonal vegetables. For the price — $20 per entrée — a predinner salad would have been a pleasant addition to the meal, particularly considering the long wait that we encountered on a busy weekend evening. Despite this, the tiny kitchen (smaller than some boat galleys) does produce a very good crab cake, as well as a scallop and sausage creation that hovers over angel hair pasta. But save your money when it comes to dessert. Both the chocolate cake and the key lime pie had a mass-produced tinge to them, far less than what you would expect coming from a fine-dining establishment.

NORTHERN NECK/MIDDLE PENINSULA

Irvington, Virginia

THE TIDES INN
804-438-5000.
480 King Carter Dr.,
  Irvington, VA 22480.
Open: Daily, 7:30 a.m.–
  11:00 a.m.; 12:00
  noon–2:00 p.m.; 6:30
  p.m.–9:00 p.m.
Price: Very Expensive.
Cuisine: Continental/
  Seafood.
Serving: B, L, D.
Credit Cards: AE, D, MC, V.
Reservations: Highly
  recommended.
Handicap Access: Yes.
Special Features: Resort
  atmosphere; water view;
  boat access.

The Tides Inn is not for the faint of wallet or credit card. But it's a treat for refined palates and discerning sensibilities. We knew that we were in for elegant dining the moment we stepped into the main dining room — candles glowing among the blue-and-gold place settings, fresh flowers in bud vases, and an army of staff at the ready. The inn is part of a major and pricey waterfront resort, where many guests arrive in expensive cars and motor yachts to play golf or mess about in watercraft. The four main dining rooms are airy, bright, and huge, yet intimate. Every table commands a water view of Carter Creek and the yacht *Miss Ann.*

The prix fixe menu changes daily, but there's always a choice of half a dozen appetizers and soups, entrées, and desserts. Choosing is tough: shrimp and scallop tostada, simmered French onion soup, smoked bay bluefish. And that's just for openers. Entrées included sliced tournedos of beef au poivre, Northern Neck soft-shell crabs, Rappahannock crabmeat imperial, and roasted pork loin with wild mushrooms and crabmeat. For appetizers, we chose "Our Famous Hot Oyster Cocktail" and the Chesapeake vichyssoise blue crab, followed by boneless stuffed quail with wild rice and pan-seared mahimahi with wild Caribbean spices and pineapple salsa. A bottle of Virginia white wine from neighboring Ingleside Winery was accompanied by an apology from Curtis, our wine steward — business had been so brisk that he had run out of ice buckets. Within moments, Curtis, on the run, corrected that with a friendly grin.

Kilmarnock, Virginia

THE CRAB SHACK
804-435-2700.
Rte. 1, Oyster Shell Rd.,
  Kilmarnock, VA 22482.
Open: L, 11:00 a.m.–3:00
  p.m.; D, 5:00 p.m.–9:00
  p.m.; Mem. Day–Labor
  Day, Tues.–Sun.; May
  1–Mem. Day, Labor
  Day–mid-Oct.,
  Thurs.–Sun.

As its name implies, The Crab Shack specializes in crabs, crabmeat, and crab dishes in all forms, but it's certainly not a shack. This is a fine restaurant, right on the water, with tablecloths and fresh flowers on the tables and lemon wedges placed on the water glasses. The menu features seafood, of course, but also includes beef and chicken dishes for landlubbers. In addition to the dining room, which has full-length windows over-

Price: Moderate to
   Expensive.
Cuisine: Seafood.
Serving: L, D.
Credit Cards: AE, D, MC, V.
Reservations: No.
Handicap Access: Yes.
Special Features: Water
   views of Indian Creek
   and Chesapeake Bay;
   quick access by boat from
   Bay; dock.

looking Indian Creek and the Chesapeake Bay, visitors also may dine under umbrellas on the open patio or at picnic tables on the lawn. It's just a brief detour for Bay cruisers to tie up at The Crab Shack's dock for a formal meal or pick up some crabs, crabmeat, or shrimp for cooking aboard. Owner Charles Chase, who also owns Rappahannock Seafood on the same site, said that he was expanding during the 1998-1999 off-season, putting the patio under roof, adding drop-down curtains for bad weather, and building another open patio. This will add about fifty percent to the seating capacity.

Lancaster, Virginia

LANCASTER TAVERN
804-462-5941.
8373 Mary Ball Rd.,
   Lancaster, VA 22503.
Open: Thurs.–Sun., 11:00
   a.m.–2:00 p.m.;
   Thurs.–Sat., 5:00
   p.m.–8:00 p.m.
Price: Inexpensive.
Cuisine: Grandma's Home
   Cooking.
Serving: L, D.
Credit Cards: No; checks
   accepted.
Reservations: Yes.
Handicap Access: No.
Special Features: Authentic
   colonial atmosphere.

Lancaster Tavern has been operating as a restaurant for more than fifteen years. Under new owners since March 1998, the tavern still serves good home cooking like Grandma used to make, except now Grandma has an ABC license to serve wine and ale with your meal. Without the small, painted sign hanging over the front door — Lancaster Tavern 1790 — the weathered, brown clapboard building on the side of the main thoroughfare could be mistaken for the private home it used to be. Most of the 200-year-old building is said to be original, down to the pine plank floors. So Annette Baxter, the new owner, added "Historic" to the name. Inside, up to twenty guests can be seated at four traditional tables and assorted mahogany and pine chairs. Annette also has made the screened porch available for open-air dining.

The tavern features home cooking, served family style (only on Sun.). There is no menu. You just sit down, and the ladies start bringing out the cuisine du jour, from homemade soup, entrées, side dishes, and homemade yeast breads to dessert for one fixed price. Coffee and tea (hot or iced) also are available. Thurs. always bring chicken and dumplings, and other regular specials are featured on other nights. But usually it's anybody's guess. One night it was homemade tomato and vegetable gumbo, pulled pork barbecue, beef and cheddar Yorkshire pie, and a variety of side dishes, including homemade applesauce, peppered mashed potatoes, baked butternut squash, lima beans, yeast bread, and banana pudding. Vegetarians could thrive on the boiled buttered potatoes, green beans, corn, beets, and that wonderful applesauce. Don't worry about leaving the Lancaster Tavern hungry. The platters and bowls keep on coming until you say stop. Then they bring out the dessert.

Mollusk, Virginia

CONRAD'S UPPER DECK RESTAURANT
804-462-7400.
1947 Rocky Neck Rd.,
Mollusk, VA 22503.
Open: Mar.–Nov.; Fri.–Sat.,
5:00 p.m.–9:00 p.m.
Price: Inexpensive to
Moderate.
Cuisine: Seafood.
Serving: D.
Credit Cards: No; checks
accepted.
Reservations: No.
Handicap Access: No.
Special Features: Nautical
atmosphere; sunset view
of Rappahannock River.

Conrad's Upper Deck Restaurant, isolated at the end of a back road on the Rappahannock River and Greenvale Creek, is no secret to Lancaster County residents and regular visitors to the Northern Neck. They flock by car, van, motor home, pickup, and powerboat, parking on the oyster shell lot or tying up at the bulkhead. It's a special treat, since it's open only on Fri. and Sat. nights during the season. Conrad's, which seats 110 in two dining rooms, is especially popular for birthdays. An all-you-can-eat buffet, recommended only if you're starving, includes steamed shrimp, fried scallops, oysters, clams, crab balls, baked fish, ribs, fried chicken, corn on the cob, and hush puppies. The clam chowder, piping hot in a serve-yourself tureen at the salad bar, is excellent. Menu selections are generous and include two vegetables or a trip to the salad bar. Among the popular entrées are the seafood platter, fried flounder stuffed with crabmeat, two pounds of snow crab legs, and the "Pick 3," your choice of three from among oysters, fish, popcorn shrimp, scallops, clam strips, and crab balls. The menu also offers a good selection of beef and chicken entrées and a short selection of favorites of children under age 6 — burgers, fries, and chicken tenders. We never have room for dessert, but we sometimes succumb to a slice of Gale Conrad's homemade German chocolate pie, with two forks.

Conrad's sits atop E.J. Conrad & Sons wholesale seafood, in business since 1935. Milton Conrad bought the business from his father in 1972 and opened the restaurant in the early '80s. It's easy to find from River Rd. (Rte. 354) at Mollusk, a small post office between two "Mollusk" signs. Just turn onto Rocky Neck Rd. and drive two miles to the end. It's worth the trip.

Reedville, Virginia

PEPPERMINTS
804-453-6468.
Main St., Reedville, VA
22539.
Open: Year-round, except 2
weeks before/after
Christmas.

Three tables, four stools at a counter, and, we kid you not, lump crab cakes at least one inch thick in the sandwiches. Slathered with thick slabs of fresh tomato, these rank very high on our list of favorites — and one eats many crab cakes in the

Price: Inexpensive.
Cuisine: Home-style
  Sandwiches/Ice Cream.
Serving: L, D.
Credit Cards: No.
Reservations: No.
Handicap Access: Yes.

course of researching a Bay travel book. Cheerfully pink, Peppermints is a teensy place, and in the summer, the whole town shows up for ice cream with an option to sit on an outside porch with wheelchair ramps. No alcohol. Your proprietress is Patsy Self. Later, we asked her the secret of her crab cakes. "I can't tell you that," she said.

Topping, Virginia

ECKHARD'S
804-758-4060.
Rte. 3, Topping, VA 23169.
One mile south of
  Rappahannock River
  bridge.
Open: Wed.–Sat., 4:30
  p.m.–9:00 p.m.; Sun.,
  11:30 a.m.–9:00 p.m.
Price: Moderate.
Cuisine: German/Fine
  Foods.
Serving: D.
Credit Cards: MC, V.
Reservations:
  Recommended.
Handicap Access: Yes.

What a great find was Eckhard's! Great food — as good or better than many expensive restaurants and resorts — and lots of it, at very reasonable prices. We soon learned to order one entrée and share ($3 extra). After a tasty appetizer (we usually order the lobster and shrimp bisque), salad, breads, side dishes of half a dozen German choices, other vegetables, and pasta, one entrée for two is more than enough. Bruni Thalwitz, co-owner and hostess, explained that her husband and the restaurant's chef, Eckhard, is a big eater, and he expects everyone to have a big appetite. Tastefully appointed Eckhard's features special appetizers and entrées every night, but the menu includes nearly a dozen appetizers and nearly two dozen huge entrées served on colorful oversized platters. German cuisine is most abundant, of course, and the friendly staff is willing and able to translate: Kassler Rippchen is smoked pork loin over mashed potatoes and sauerkraut; hühnerbrustchen Baden-Baden is breast of chicken over apricot-chestnut stuffing with orange sauce. If German isn't to your taste, the left side of the menu includes filet mignon, Long Island duckling Chambord, Atlantic salmon au gratin, and Shenandoah mountain trout. Eckhard's also has an extensive wine list and a full bar, including Rudesheimer (cognac) coffee. Desserts? We rarely get that far, but the sample trays are hard to resist: German apple strudel, white chocolate-mascarpone cheesecake, bread pudding with hot bourbon sauce, etc., etc. Please stop us before we overindulge again!

Urbanna, Virginia

THE INN AT URBANNA
888-758-4852; 804-758-4852.
250 Virginia St./P.O. Box
  861, Urbanna, VA 23175.

Lets start with full disclosure: we didn't actually dine at the inn's dining room. With the World Series underway, we dined beneath the television

Open: Daily; raw bar, 3:00
p.m.–closing; dining
room, Mon.–Sat., 5:00
p.m.–closing; Sun., 11:00
a.m.–3:00 p.m.; 5:00
p.m.–closing.
Price: Moderate to
Expensive.
Cuisine: Seafood/New
Continental.
Serving: D; L on Sun.
Credit Cards: AE, DC, MC,
V.
Reservations: Accepted.
Handicap Access: No.

sets in the jam-packed raw bar in the back of the inn, where we could order from the seasonal specials on the dining room menu. Cornmeal-encrusted rockfish promptly arrived and sent our dining mate into a swoon, its mustard sauce lightening the sweet flavor of this delectable fish. Vegetable and grain sides came sweetly touched as well, by ginger or tarragon. We had to ask for Maryland-style spices on the steamed shrimp, but they arrived also having done time in the steamer with onions and celery. The roomy dining room is a gallery-style space with regional artwork on the walls and linen cloths on the tables. A bar stands off to one side, and the effect is open and easy.

White Stone, Virginia

ROCKET BILLY'S
804-435-7040.
851^1/$_2$ Rappahannock Ave.,
White Stone, VA 22578.
Open: Mon.–Sat., 6:30
a.m.–5:00 p.m.
Price: Inexpensive.
Cuisine: Take-out
Seafood/Hamburgers.
Serving: B, L, early D.
Credit Cards: No.
Reservations: No.
Handicap Access: Yes.

From his kitchen in an 8 x 16-foot Wells Cargo trailer, former Richmond pub owner Billy Ancarrow dispenses one heck of a fried oyster sandwich, and he even makes the rolls from scratch. If that's not recommendation enough, then the curried seafood bisque should cement all culinary opinions. We missed the soft-shell crabs, but we'll make a point of it next time. There are breakfast egg sandwiches in various incarnations for low prices and Black Angus beef in the hamburgers. Everything's takeout.

UPPER EASTERN SHORE

Chestertown

BLUE HERON CAFÉ
410-778-0188.
236 Cannon St.,
Chestertown, MD 21620.
Open: Daily, except Sun.
Price: Moderate to
Expensive.
Cuisine: Creative
American.
Serving: L, D.
Credit Cards: AE, D, MC,
V.

Chestertown's favorite dinner spot had a new name and new owner as of July 1997, but the casual atmosphere and adventurous menu remain the same. Thank goodness. The Ironstone Café (whose owners opened a restaurant closer to home in nearby Kennedyville) was a local institution, and with good reason. The new owner, who trained under the old, knows what customers like and chose to add to the existing menu rather than start anew. You'll still find staples like crab cakes with

Reservations:
  Recommended on
  weekends.
Handicap Access: Yes.

lemon beurre blanc and an oyster fritter appetizer, but you'll also find an expanded array of other entrées and appetizers. Prices are higher at dinner, so if you're skeptical and want to check it out, stop in at lunchtime. Among the midday highlights are a jumbo lump crab frittata loaded with vegetables and topped with a flaky pastry, veal sweetbreads sautéed with lemon and capers, and a hearty chicken potpie. Dinnertime brings pasta delmarva with native chicken, oysters, and ham, pan-seared duck breast, and roasted rack of lamb. Rich desserts are made on premise. You'll be tempted to stay awhile in this comfortable café, with its high ceiling and light instrumental background music, and you'll be more than welcome to do so. It's a meal worth lingering over.

THE FEAST OF REASON

410-778-3828.
203 High St., Chestertown,
  MD 21620.
Open: Tues.–Fri., 10:00
  a.m.–6:00 p.m.; Sat., 10:00
  a.m.–4:00 p.m.
Price: Inexpensive.
Cuisine: Light Fare.
Serving: L; takeout.
Credit Cards: No.
Reservations: No.
Handicap Access: No.

The smell of freshly baked bread greets customers entering this tiny eatery, located just a block and a half off the public landing in Chestertown. Except for a stack of wines against the wall, there's nothing in the appearance to give first-time visitors the least hint of the subtle flavors soon to come. In fact, there are not even waitresses or formal menus. Customers read the chalkboard, place orders, then seat themselves. Homemade is the defining word for this luncheonette, where the fancywork is all saved for the food. Soups, desserts, and breads, such as sunflower seed bread, are made fresh each day. The lunch menu always includes burritos and a quiche. Even the mayonnaise gets an added zest from seasonings before it's generously spread on the bread. And don't expect a handful of chips or fries to fill out the plate. Instead, colorful, pickled carrots are served on the side, and they proved tasty enough to convert the worst junk food lover. Tomato soups have real lumps of tomatoes, and plate-filling turkey sandwiches are dotted with mushrooms. Streams of caramel or chocolate run through the brownies. The temptation is to take something home and, fortunately, you can. When we visited, more than one customer ordered dinner to go before they even finished their lunches. Call a day in advance to order loaves of bread.

HARBOR HOUSE

410-778-0669.
Worton Creek Marina,
  23145 Buck Neck Rd.,
  Chestertown, MD 21620.
Open: Daily, spring-fall;
  closed in winter.
Price: Moderate to
  Expensive.

There was no need to dig through the pasta to find seafood in this crab Alfredo: fifteen fat lumps of crabmeat lay right on top in clear view, evidence that Harbor House lives up to its reputation as a first-class seafood restaurant. There was so much crabmeat that we joked about hiding it away in a napkin to save for a crab cake or two

Cuisine: Chesapeake
   Seafood/American/
   Pasta.
Serving: D, SB, summer
   only.
Credit Cards: AE, MC, V.
Reservations: Yes.
Handicap Access: No.
Special Features: Free
   dockage; water view.

later at home. The quantity of succulent crab, found in a dish that other restaurants would have served with two lumps at best, was only the beginning of the seafood gluttony. We were sure it was too late in the season for soft-shell crabs — no one else had them — but, yes, the waitress assured us that they had this Chesapeake delicacy. But the main course was just part of the culinary experience, which began when we took our seats at a window with a panoramic view of Worton Creek. The restaurant is part of Worton Creek Marina, so diners look down on this favorite boater's anchorage and the busy marina. Then came the tray of homemade breads, made with big lumps of raspberries or nuts and served with the chef's own whipped and flavored butters. Appetizers included bacon-wrapped shrimp, served with a dijon sauce that was worth the long drive out into the boondocks of Kent County. By dessert, we should have been used to the big servings. You should have seen the dish used to serve our Vassar Devil — an ice-cream brownie good enough to die for.

OLD WHARF INN
410-778-3566.
Cannon St., Chestertown,
   MD 21620.
Open: Daily.
Price: Moderate.
Cuisine: American/
   Chesapeake.
Serving: L, D, SB.
Credit Cards: AE, MC, V.
Reservations:
   Recommended on
   weekends.
Handicap Access: Yes.
Special Features: Dock.

For a riverfront town, Chestertown surprisingly has only one restaurant with waterfront dining. Old Wharf Inn makes up for the town's shortfall with a wall of windows that gives every diner a full view of the undeveloped Chester River. Add the dockage out front for cruisers and the occasional home presence of a old wooden skipjack, and it's hard to find a more nostalgic nautical setting. Even the building mimics the "old wharf" red barn style of yesteryear. The menu offers everything from burgers to crab cakes, oysters to catfish, and tacos to salad Niçoise. For those on a short budget or who just want good food without the fancy atmosphere, this is the place to go. The menu is full of mouthwatering sandwiches for under $5 and tempting seafood and chicken salad platters for under $7. Add an appetizer like the homemade Old Wharf cream crab bisque or spicy steamed shrimp, and diners won't miss the expensive, foreign-sounding dishes found at upscale restaurants around the Bay. Besides, the homemade breads, with fruits and nuts, are terrific. With its window on the river, the Old Wharf Inn could have gone upscale and raised prices a long time ago. They've chosen, instead, to keep their prices reasonable so that local families can enjoy the view and a good lunch or dinner out along with the tourists.

Easton

**HILL'S DRUG SODA
  FOUNTAIN**
410-822-9751.
30 E. Dover St., Easton, MD
  21601.
Open: Daily, except Sun.
Price: Inexpensive.
Cuisine: American.
Serving: B, L.
Credit Cards: AE, DC, MC,
  V.
Reservations: No.
Handicap Access: Yes.

There's not a bobby-soxer around, but that's about the only thing missing from this old-fashioned drugstore soda fountain beloved by both young and old for its shakes and burgers. Come through the pharmacy, established in Easton more than seventy years ago and now run by the third generation, and walk through the doorway into a piece of America's past. Gleaming stainless steel soda fountains contrast with the painted pink brick walls, decorated with photos and newspaper stories on local folk; a skylight makes the small room feel more airy. You can grab a table or slide onto one of the high pedestal counter seats to watch your ice-cream soda or shake being made. If a superthick chocolate malt doesn't transport you to the 1950s, nothing will. Hill's doesn't restrict its menu to ice cream, though. Many people come for standard breakfast fare and for lunchtime treats like grilled hot dogs or burgers, served with fries in a plastic basket. It's a simple formula, but sincere, and its loyal customers validate the lunch counter's commitment to turning back the clock — if only long enough to have lunch. You can even have your prescription filled while you're eating.

MASON'S CAFÉ
410-822-3204.
22 S. Harrison St., Easton,
  MD 21601.
Open: Daily, except Sun.
Price: Inexpensive.
Cuisine: Creative
  American.
Serving: L.
Credit Cards: AE, CB, DC,
  MC, V.
Reservations: Yes.
Handicap Access: Park at
  back and enter through
  kitchen.

You won't find a sandwich here like you'd make at home, even though this cozy café is located in a former home. The menu choices range from regional American favorites like Smithfield ham and New York pastrami to international flavors like prosciutto di Parma, liverwurst with sweet onion, and turkey with Brie and apples. Their salads are a treat, whether you get the salada Milanese with tomato, roasted peppers, artichoke hearts, mozzarella, and olives or a more traditional salad topped with shrimp and vinaigrette. The food is excellent, but the service can be slow, so it's best to come when you're ready to sit and relax, perhaps to catch up with an old friend. The best seats are upstairs (not handicap accessible), where brightly painted chairs and old wood tables sit by windows that look out onto the street. There's another seating area on the ground floor. Complementing the café is Mason's specialty store carrying glassware, dishes, and fine foods, from tea to sauces to chocolates.

TIDEWATER INN

410-822-1300.
101 E. Dover St., Easton,
   MD 21601.
Open: Year-round.
Price: Expensive.
Cuisine:
   American/Chesapeake.
Serving: B, L, D, SB.
Credit Cards: AE, D, MC,
   Novus, V.
Reservations:
   Recommended for
   dinner.
Handicap Access: Yes.

From the moment you step through the warm, rich mahogany doors, you're greeted by the glow of candlelight and the welcoming crackle of an open fireplace. Since 1949, this Upper Eastern Shore institution has played host to everyone from camouflage-coated goose hunters to fashionably dressed dinner guests. Once considered *the* place for fine dining on the Shore, the Georgian-style restaurant, appointed with the de rigeur stuffed and mounted waterfowl, has changed hands over the years, and, as a result, some locals believe that the once-great restaurant may now be more style than substance. Having said that, if you go for lunch, be sure to sample the English muffin topped with lump crabmeat and tomato slices draped with hollandaise sauce. It truly is worth the trip. And whether you go for lunch or dinner, partake in the snapper soup. Fashioned from snapping turtle, this rich brown broth is complimented by a generous side of sherry.

Georgetown

KITTY KNIGHT HOUSE

800-404-8712; 410-648-5777.
Rt. 213, Georgetown, MD
   21930.
Open: Daily, 12:00
   noon–10:30 p.m. in-
   season; 12:00 noon–8:30
   p.m. weekdays, 12:00
   noon–9:30 p.m.
   weekends off-season;
   closed Mon.–Tues. off-
   season.
Price: Moderate to
   Expensive.
Cuisine: Seafood/
   American.
Serving: L, D.
Credit Cards: AE, MC, V.
Reservations:
   Recommended on
   weekends.
Handicap Access: To main
   dining room from upper
   parking lot.
Special Features: Water
   view; outside deck;
   gazebo bar.

When Admiral Sir George Cockburn spared Miss Kitty's house during his infamous burning of Georgetown in 1813, he couldn't have projected the legend that he was creating on the high banks of the Sassafras River. Actually, he spared two houses, including that of Miss Kitty Knight's neighbor, and today these two houses are joined in a big, rambling brick house that dominates the landscape. The Kitty Knight House offers diners with discerning tastes everything that they could ask for: culinary taste in an historic setting with a waterfront view. There's room for big family gatherings in the modern sunroom, overlooking the Sassafras or an intimate table for two, scattered in various living rooms. The menu is expansive and enticing, and the servings are big enough to feed two: salmon stuffed with crab imperial, tuna topped with shrimp, and chicken hidden under cashews and cranberries. Perhaps the restaurant's best entrée was among its cheapest: a crab crêpe smothered in a rich white wine sauce. We've never seen so much crabmeat on one plate.

After dinner, patrons who aren't ready to let go

of the historic magic can make their way to the quaint bar where in the winter, they can enjoy a big roaring fire in the kitchen-sized fireplace. There's also lodging upstairs. In the summer, the gazebo bar on the deck overlooking the river creates a perfect setting to while away the evening.

KENT MANOR RESTAURANT
410-643-7716.
Rte. 8, Kent Is.,
  Stevensville, MD 21666.
Open: Daily.
Price: Expensive to Very
  Expensive.
Cuisine: New
  American/Chesapeake.
Serving: Daily; L, 11:30
  a.m.–4:00 p.m. (no lunch
  Sun.); D, 5:00 p.m.–9:00
  p.m.; SB, 10:00 a.m.–2:00
  p.m.
Credit Cards: AE, D, MC, V.
Reservations: Yes, on
  weekends.
Handicap Access: Yes.

Ostrich, buffalo, and wild boar rounds out a menu that reads more like the famed dishes of the now defunct Dominique's in Washington, D.C., than the usual eat-what-you-catch cuisine of the Upper Eastern Shore. The Kent Manor Inn, listed among the Historic Inns of America and unobtrusively set on a farm overlooking Thompson Creek on Kent Island, is just a minute or two from the Bay Bridge and far from the hectic pace of any city. Yet there at the door of this grand 1820 estate was a chauffeur-driven limousine toting a Washington, D.C. license plate, evidence that Washingtonians still miss their exotic dishes.

Dinner is served in various living rooms, still furnished with antiques and working fireplaces that made us feel as if a wealthy landowner oversaw the comfort of his guests. We found ourselves at a table on the cozy, glassed-in back porch overlooking the creek. With such an elegant setting and exotic menu, it was too romantic a moment to do without wine, despite the $50 a bottle price. Appetizers, like bacon-wrapped jumbo shrimp, get a new twist, served with horseradish sauce and vermouth concassé. When we got to the entrées, there was no need to be squeamish about the "wild" in wild boar. Flavorfully marinaded, it arrived with a sun-dried tomato crust, mango chutney on the side, and an unforgettable sweet sauce. Any lingering wild taste was drenched out of our wild boar tenderloin. From the house salad to the main dishes, the chef displayed balance: every sweet sauce was tempered with a peppery or tart side dish of Caribbean slaws or whipped and pancaked potatoes. We usually appreciate the company of old friends for dinner, but for once we were glad to be alone. This is a place to be pampered and to rediscover what it means to enjoy a romantic dinner for two.

Kent Narrows/Grasonville

ANGLER'S
410-827-6717.
3015 S. Kent Narrows Way,
  Grasonville, MD 21638.
Open: Daily.
Price: Inexpensive to
  Moderate.

See that plastic squirt bottle of sherry? It's for your cream of crab soup. If you're sitting at a table with a plastic squirt bottle of sherry aligned with the other condiments (or if they bring it with your soup), you're in a real Chesapeake seafood place — one with local color. We come here for

Cuisine: Chesapeake
  Seafood.
Serving: B, L, D.
Credit Cards: D, MC, V.
Reservations: No.
Handicap Access: Yes.

crab soup or oysters, and any seafood on the menu will be fresh and worthwhile. Breakfasts have become hugely popular, which means the place fills up on summer weekends with beach-bound customers headed through town. But we often find ourselves here on winter evenings, just for a taste of that quiet, gray-sky waterside life. Breakfast served until 11:30 a.m.; no hard-shell crabs.

Crabs, corn, and beer: the Harris Crab House stocks it all for a classic Chesapeake crab feast.

David Trozzo

HARRIS CRAB HOUSE
410-827-9500.
S. Kent Narrows Way,
  Grasonville, MD 21638.
Exit 42 off Rte. 50/301.
Open: Daily.
Price: Moderate.
Cuisine: Seafood.
Serving: L, D.
Credit Cards: MC, V.
Reservations: No.
Handicap Access: Yes
Special Features: Public
  docking.

Kent Narrows, a sliver of a waterway between the eastern edge of Kent Island and the Eastern Shore mainland, is one of the best "boat-watching" spots in the region. Harris Crab House is the Narrows' fun place for food. Diners join others at long picnic tables covered, as is the norm in crab country, with brown packaging paper torn from a giant roll mounted on the wall. Or they may take smaller individual tables upstairs on the inside "upper deck" or on an outside deck, both overlooking the northern end of the Narrows. Fresh steamed crabs (priced according to size: jumbo, x-large, large, or medium), Bay fish, and soft-shell crabs, much of it netted by local anglers,

are the Harris specialty. "For the Rebel," as the menu reads, there is barbecued chicken and ribs (that's "and," not "or") for a veritable feast of half a chicken and half a rack of ribs. On the other end of the scale is the "Kid's Menu." This is Chesapeake Bay food at its most genuine, plentiful, and moderately priced — popular with residents and visitors alike.

THE NARROWS
410-827-8113.
3023 S. Kent Narrows Way,
   Grasonville, MD 21638.
Exit 42 off Rte. 50/301.
Open: Daily.
Price: Moderate.
Cuisine: Seafood/New
   American.
Serving: L, D, SB.
Credit Cards: AE, D, DC,
   MC, V.
Reservations:
   Recommended on
   weekends and holidays.
Handicap Access: Yes.
Special Features: Public
   docking.

Overlooking the southern stretch of Kent Narrows stands the premier restaurant of this growing leisure time area. A sense of style pervades The Narrows, an understated elegance that adds a touch of class to its otherwise informal atmosphere. Even in the warm light of day, a degree of intimacy pervades. The Narrows' dining area seems to thrust out over the water, tall windows on two sides offering a long view toward the southern horizon from even the innermost tables. Its bar is nestled into the corner of those two glass sides, belying its small size. There is also service on the one-table-wide waterside porch. The Narrows calls upon fresh spinach, Gorgonzola cheese, and portobello mushrooms for some of its finer appetizers. Naturally, fish and shellfish dishes are preeminent — crab cakes so lumpy with crab that they barely hold together, grilled loin of peppered tuna — but beef, lamb, and pork are available. For dessert, chocolate bread pudding is a specialty. The Narrows offers premier waterfront dining, perhaps the best experience between Annapolis and St. Michaels.

Oxford

LATITUDE 38
410-226-5303.
26342 Oxford Rd., Oxford,
   MD 21654.
Open: Daily, except Mon.
Price: Moderate to
   Expensive.
Cuisine: Creative Regional.
Serving: L, D.
Credit Cards: AE, MC, V.
Reservations: Accepted.
Handicap Access: Yes.

Latitude 38 can well be described as the Cheers of Oxford. If they don't know your name when you enter, you can be darn sure that they will by the time you leave. A haven for locals and those just sailing on the weekend, Latitude 38 offers the best of both worlds: fine dining, multi-course meals for the sit-down crowd, or inexpensive bar dinners for those who just can't face their own kitchens. For the price and the added camaraderie, you can't beat the latter. Your only difficulty will be finding a place at this incredibly popular bar, which is particularly difficult on Thurs. evenings when prime rib is the featured attraction. For a mere $6.95, you are treated to a hearty slab of the tender beef with whatever starch and vegetable the chef feels like fixing that day. And for an extra dollar, you can get really wild and throw in either a Caesar or a house salad. Bar dinners change every night, while the regular menu varies biweekly, so if something doesn't tickle your fancy come back the next night. You won't be disappointed.

LE ZINC

410-226-5776.
101 Mill St., Oxford, MD
    21654.
Open: Tues.–Sat.
Price: Moderate to
    Expensive.
Cuisine: French Provençal.
Serving: D.
Credit Cards: AE, MC, V.
Reservations:
    Recommended.
Handicap Access: Yes.

Tucked away on one of Oxford's back streets, Le Zinc is most certainly off the beaten path, but well worth the hunt. A cozy French bistro complete with servers in long black aprons and starched white shirts, Le Zinc's ever-changing menu is a fresh feast of the best southern France has to offer. On a typical evening, you can choose from grilled rib steak with a mushroom glacé to fresh tuna or salmon with a citrus beurre blanc. But if you opt to go on a Wed. or Thurs. night, you're in for a special treat — pasta night. Less pricey than the usual menu selections, pasta entrées, such as linguine with mussels or fettuccine Alfredo, also come with a trip to the bar where you can help yourself to freshly baked brown bread, roasted garlic, olives, and olive oil. And while you linger over a sinfully rich dollop of chocolate mousse and sip from your very own single serving of French pressed coffee, let your creative juices flow as you doodle on the table with the arsenal of crayons at your disposal. French this place is, pretentious it is not. When last we spoke, lunch service was being considered. Check to see if they're serving now.

ROBERT MORRIS INN

410-226-5111.
314 N. Morris St./P.O. Box
    70, Oxford, MD 21654.
Open: Daily; closed
    Dec.–Mar.
Price: Moderate to
    Expensive.
Cuisine: Regional
    Seafood/Continental.
Serving: B, L, D.
Credit Cards: MC, V.
Reservations: Yes, only for
    8 or more.
Handicap Access: Yes.

This inn is famed for the crab cakes; we saw no reason to order differently. Indeed, they are excellent, just as James Michener said. Locals tend to agree, and furrow their brows when asked what else should they order here. Light, rich, and full of crabmeat, just as they're supposed to be. The other famous treat that you must try in-season is the strawberry pie. This pre-Revolutionary inn, once home to the father of Robert Morris Jr., "Financier of the Revolution," is a famed Oxford stop. Swept with good taste, this is a grande dame of the Shore. Four enormous murals representing spring, summer, winter, and fall grace the formal front dining room, and it turns out that they're made from 140-year-old wallpaper samples. In back is the brick tavern area, with an open fireplace and a more casual air. Service couldn't have been friendlier. The inn sits along Oxford's Strand, next to the Oxford-Bellevue Ferry, and qualifies as a bona fide stop on any tourist itinerary. See Chapter Three, *Lodgings* for information about staying here.

SCHOONER'S
LLANDING

410-226-0160.
314 Tilghman St., Oxford,
    MD 21654.

After a hard day's sail on the Chesapeake, there's no better place to come ashore and unwind than Schooner's Llanding. But even if

Open: Wed.–Mon., dining room; closed Dec. 28–Feb.; bar and deck, weather permitting.
Price: Moderate.
Cuisine: Seafood.
Serving: L, D, SB.
Credit Cards: MC, V.
Reservations: Recommended.
Handicap Access: Yes.
Special Features: Water view; free dockage for diners.

you're landbound, it's a sure bet for finding good food and a festive atmosphere. An outdoor bar and deck, where they'll serve your entrées, as well as drinks and appetizers, is a favorite in the summer. Indoors, wraparound windows overlook Town Creek where diners can watch the parade of yachts into this Eastern Shore yachting capital. Seafood is the staple here. For us, their popular bread bowl filled with steaming Maryland crab soup or seafood chowder is a must to start our meal. Numerous crab dishes, oysters Rockefeller, clams, and fish round out the entrées. But you can eat light, too. There are plenty of appetizing salads and sandwiches to complement the soup. Of course, there's dockage for boaters (free while you eat) or overnight at the dock for a fee.

Rock Hall

BAY WOLF RESTAURANT
410-639-2000.
21270 Rock Hall Ave., Rock Hall, MD 21661.
Open: Daily, 12:00 noon–9:00 p.m.; summer, 12:00 noon–10:00 p.m.
Price: Moderate.
Cuisine: Austrian/Seafood.
Serving: L, D.
Credit Cards: AE, MC, V.
Reservations: Recommended.
Handicap Access: Yes.

Austrian cuisine in the middle of a waterman's town? It hardly sounds like a plan that would work, but Bay Wolf, owned and operated by an Austrian couple, Larry and Hildegard Sunkler, has carved out a niche for itself. They've done it by combining good German/Austrian food with classic seafood dishes. Set in an old church — stained glass intact — the feel is Old World. Add the wall-sized mural of the owners' hometown, scatter a large collection of beer mugs around, and the setting is complete. We knew we had found something special when we got our soup: lobster bisque, rich and creamy with a hint of sherry, was the best that we've ever had, and the French onion soup was strong and flavorful, obviously homemade. We had to try the Austrian house specials, schweinsbraten mit schnitzel (that's pork, sauerkraut, and dumplings) and Wiener schnitzel, the Teutonic treatment of veal cutlets. But the menu also included seafood dishes, such as lobster, shrimp, and scallops over linguine and drenched in a Parmesan sauce. Chicken Florentine and steak rounded out the menu. The chef likes to serve vegetables and seafood in-season, so the menu changes throughout the year. It's hard to think European cuisine in the middle of rockfish and crab territory, but Bay Wolf has obviously won over the locals; a low-priced daily special helps.

WATERMAN'S CRAB HOUSE

410-639-2261.
Sharp Street Wharf, Rock
Hall, MD 21661.
Open: Daily, Mar.-Nov.,
Feb.
Price: Moderate to
Expensive.
Cuisine: Chesapeake
Seafood/American.
Serving: L, D.
Credit Cards: AE, DC, MC,
V.
Reservations:
Recommended.
Handicap Access: Yes.
Special Features: Water
view; waterfront deck
dining; dock bar; free
dockage; live music
Fri.–Sun.

It's obvious where the locals go in Rock Hall. Live bands on weekends through Sept. help draw in the crowds. But it's the all-you-can-eat crab feasts on Tues. and Thurs. throughout the summer that have made Waterman's, a twenty-year institution on the harbor front, such a favorite among locals and tourists alike. Even without the crab feasts, this is Chesapeake seafood served at its Chesapeake best. With a front row seat on Rock Hall Harbor and the Chesapeake Bay just beyond the breakwaters, it's easy to understand why diners time their dinner with the setting of the sun. A waterman's mural, as long as one room and almost true-to-life, makes it hard to pick anything from the menu but local crabs, fish, and oysters. With free dockage and a dock bar in-season, Waterman's is understandably a favorite among boaters. The restaurant specializes in the locally harvested crabs and rockfish, served every way imaginable. From the creamy mustard crab dip appetizer to the crab imperial-stuffed rockfish and steamed shrimp and crab entrées, it's hard to find a regional restaurant that can beat this one when it comes to serving the bounty of the Chesapeake.

St. Michaels

BISTRO ST. MICHAELS

410-745-9111.
403 S. Talbot St., St.
Michaels, MD 21663.
Open: Thurs.–Tues., in-
season; closed Mon. (L),
Tues., Wed., Nov.–Jan.;
closed Feb.
Price: Expensive.
Cuisine: French Provençal.
Serving: L, D.
Credit Cards: AE, D, DC,
MC, V.
Reservations:
Recommended.
Handicap Access: Yes.

Tucked along the busy main street of St. Michaels, this lively and spirited restaurant is the next best thing to dining in France. Whether you choose to sit indoors or out, the Bistro's art deco furnishings, French theatre posters, and crisp white tablecloths transport you to another place altogether. Although the menu is small (lunch often features no more than five items), don't be deceived. Chef Stein is a master at soups, and his mussels, a standard on each menu, even though it changes seasonally, are fabulous. And if neither of those tickle your fancy, try one of his cleverly designed pizzas — barbecued chicken, pine nuts, and spinach, for example — that differs by the day. True to its French roots, the Bistro's wine selection is extensive. But before you go, you might want to bone up on your language skills. Words like *entrecôte* and *choucroute garni* appear frequently throughout the menu. Luckily, the knowledgeable and courteous staff are happy to lend assistance.

**THE INN AT PERRY
CABIN**
800-722-2949; 410-745-2200.
308 Watkins Lane., St.
 Michaels, MD 21663.
Open: Daily.
Price: Very Expensive.
Cuisine: Continental.
Serving: B, L, D.
Credit Cards: AE, DC, MC,
 V.
Reservations: Yes.
Handicap Access: Yes.

Bring your best manners, a fat wallet, an empty stomach, and no rush for time when you dine at this posh hostelry. Drop "grab-a-bite-to-eat" from your vocabulary and substitute words like sumptuous, elegant, Lucullan. The decor is in Laura Ashley fabrics and wallpapers, no surprise since her heirs own it. The menu is completely prix fixe, which means that you pay $30 for lunch (holidays $35) or $65 for dinner (holidays $69.50). Service is attentive, and the view of the Miles River is superb, but the food is the star of the show. Lunch offers a choice of six appetizers, including a pâté so silky it's like a palate massage. For an entrée, try the onion tart, the breast of Muscovy duck with a sesame rice cake and minted tomato vierge, or braised lamb shank with a honey and tarragon glaze. Eight entrées are listed; take your pick. Dessert follows with any of a half-dozen spectacular and decadent concoctions — chocolate hazelnut torte with coconut sorbet is only one among the temptations. And that's just lunch. Dinner is even more elaborate, with five courses that indulge a taste for fabulous sauces and combinations of flavors with seafood, fowl, lamb, beef, pork, and vegetarian cuisines. This is the ultimate in dining.

**MICHAEL RORK'S
TOWN DOCK
RESTAURANT**
410-745-5577.
125 Mulberry St., St.
 Michaels, MD 21663.
Open: Year-round; closed
 Wed., Jan.–Mar.
Price: Expensive.
Cuisine: Creative Regional
 Seafood.
Serving: L, D, SB.
Credit Cards: AE, D, DC,
 MC, V.
Reservations:
 Recommended.
Handicap Access: Yes.
Special Features: St.
 Michaels harbor view.

Serving up one of the most magnificent panoramas of St. Michaels harbor, Town Dock Restaurant is equally impressive when it comes to food. Owned by Chef Michael Rork, this is home to award-winning creations in a casual, relaxing waterfront setting. Rork now has become a regular at the Beard House in New York. But you can try his creations right here, and you can't go wrong starting with the crab Monterey, a heaping pile of warm, oversized tortilla chips engulfing an overflowing crock of a magical blending of lump crabmeat, fresh tomatoes, and Monterey jack cheese. The portion is so huge that it can easily feed two or three. If soup is more to your liking, the crab bisque is a house speciality. Hearty and rich, the velvety cream base surrounds the lumps of crabmeat, and each bowl is served with its very own minicarafe of sherry to pour on as you see fit.
One of the best features about the Town Dock is that you can choose from the interestingly creative (Fisherman's Crêpe, seafood in a light cream and dill sauce) to the typical Chesapeake selections (crab cakes), and all of it will be prepared to "your complete and utter satisfaction." In addition, Chef Rork is a big proponent of using fresh, local products, from seafood to vegetables. Every

day he features a different fish entrée. But perhaps the best part of dining at Town Dock is the finale. To ease the pain of the bill, everyone is presented with a larger-than-life-sized, chocolate-covered strawberry. You almost won't need dessert at that rate, almost.

208 TALBOT
410-745-3838.
208 N. Talbot St., St.
   Michaels, MD 21663.
Open: Wed.–Sun., 5:00
   p.m.–10:00 p.m., D; 11:00
   a.m.–2:00 p.m., SB.
Price: Expensive to Very
   Expensive.
Cuisine: Innovative
   American.
Serving: D, SB.
Credit Cards: D, MC, V.
Reservations:
   Recommended.
Handicap Access: Yes.

The food here is meant to be remembered. That's why it's not laying flat on the plate like most well-behaved food, but, instead, rises vertically: meat, seafood, and vegetables teetering atop each other in a grand, artistic spire. This chef knows how to grab his patrons' attention. The presentation is a none-too-subtle hint that there's nothing ordinary about this restaurant on the outskirts of St. Michaels. Lodged in an 1871 brick duplex with exposed brick walls and painted ceiling beams, the dining room radiates an intimacy and romance that had us whispering about almost-forgotten memories of good times together over a glass of wine. The towering structure of food eliminated little details for the diner, such as what to eat first. Patrons simply start at the top and work to the bottom. For example, our eight-inch tower of seared salmon was topped with a single fat shrimp. Alternating slices of charred red onion and fish formed the middle, while hardy cheddar cheese grits created the foundation. Mounds of wild mushrooms with a delectably smoked taste topped the only local dish on the menu on the day that we stopped to feast — Chesapeake rockfish. It was almost a relief not to see a single crab cake or imperial among the menu's seven entrées.

In an era when many restaurants rush diners out the door in order to seat more customers, the 208 Talbot servers helped us while away the hours by generously spacing the courses. By the time that we had worked our way through appetizers, salad, dinner, dessert, and coffee, we had squandered almost three hours on the rediscovery of good food and friends. It's not a cheap luxury — almost $50 per person is average — but it's a luxury well worth the investment.

Tilghman

**HARRISON'S
   CHESAPEAKE HOUSE**
410-886-2121.
21551 Chesapeake House
   Dr., Tilghman, MD
   21671.
Open: Year-round.

Harrison's is simply Eastern Shore hospitality at its finest. With more than 110 years of experience behind the fryer, they have become the masters at serving exceptional Shore staples. So, if your style tilts toward waterfront decks with picnic tables that groan under the weight of huge platters

Price: Moderate.
Cuisine: Seafood/Chicken/
    Steaks.
Serving: B, L, D.
Credit Cards: MC, V.
Reservations:
    Recommended.
Handicap Access: Yes.

of hot steamed crabs and sweating pitchers of icy beer and freshlly brewed tea, Harrison's is for you. Or if you prefer to dine indoors in the expansive, multitiered dining room that overlooks the Choptank River and Harrison's fleet of charter fishing boats, the Chesapeake surf and turf is a must entrée. Golden, delicately fried breasts of chicken are paired with crab cakes so thick with lumps of backfin meat that they don't even know the meaning of the word "breading." But be sure to bring your appetite, because the two Eastern Shore delicacies are served with homemade, all-you-can-eat coleslaw, hot rolls, and *four* vegetables served up family style. Harrison's is often described as an old-fashioned Fourth of July picnic that goes on all season long. Here's one party that you won't want to miss.

**TILGHMAN ISLAND
    INN**
410-886-2141.
21384 Coopertown Rd.,
    Tilghman, MD 21671.
Open: Daily, except Wed.,
    D; closed 2 weeks in Jan.;
    call for Feb. hours.
Price: Expensive.
Cuisine:
    Seafood/Continental.
Serving: L, D, SB.
Credit Cards: AE, DC, MC,
    V.
Reservations:
    Recommended.
Handicap Access: Yes.

Overlooking the tranquil marshes of Tilghman Is., home to much of the Bay's dwindling skipjack fleet, the inn features fine dining in an unusually serene milieu. Whether you opt to sit in the main Gallery Dining Room, the bar, or outdoors along the waterfront, you will be surrounded by the inn's ubiquitous avian theme — carved shorebirds on each table, prints on the walls, and even Blanche DuBois, the resident citron-crested cockatoo, who welcomes entering diners. Although the menu changes daily, one standard that has made the inn famous is its black-eyed pea cake. Recently touted in *Gourmet* magazine, it is a heavenly combination of the lowly pea, red peppers, and cornmeal fried to perfection and paired with a spicy salsa. It makes a great starter to the Caesar salad topped with golden oysters, a must for devotees of the Bay's bivalve. Keep in mind, the Tilghman Island Inn is not a dining destination for those constrained by time. Since you're not rushing out the door, your best last-course of action would be to choose something decadent from the dessert menu (the key lime tart with crème anglaise and raspberry coulis is out of this world), sit back, and enjoy the scenery.

LOWER EASTERN SHORE

Berlin

THE ATLANTIC HOTEL
410-641-0189.

One of the Eastern Shore's nicest restaurants, with a dining room menu that draws the

2 N. Main St., Berlin, MD
  21811.
Open: Daily.
Price: Inexpensive to Very
  Expensive.
Cuisine: American.
Serving: D only in dining
  room; L, D, and late bar
  at Drummer's Café.
Credit Cards: AE, MC, V.
Reservations:
  Recommended in dining
  room; not accepted in
  café.
Handicap Access: Yes.

Worcester County elite, as well as visitors to nearby Ocean City in search of something better than beach fare. The dining room is the place to go for special occasions, with its elegant atmosphere and discreet but flawless service. Caesar salad is prepared tableside, and a crab phyllo of sweet crabmeat, creamy cheese, and crispy pastry is delectable. Main dishes include salmon bouillabaisse, the hotel's famous goat cheese-topped rack of lamb, and two large lump crab cakes. All guests are welcome to request variations to the menu to suit their taste. Across the hall in the Drummer's Café, the atmosphere is more relaxed but still special, and the expected menu of sandwiches and appetizers is supplemented with

entrées like Cornish game hens and pecan-crusted catfish. Wherever you sit, be sure to save room for The Atlantic Hotel's desserts, all made on premise.

Crisfield

CAPTAIN'S GALLEY
410-968-3313.
1021 W. Main St., Crisfield,
  MD 21817.
Open: Year-round.
Price: Expensive.
Cuisine: Seafood.
Serving: B, L, D.
Credit Cards: AE, MC, V.
Reservations: Yes.
Handicap Access: Yes.

If Maryland is for crabs, then Crisfield is the self-crowned capital. Virtually perched on the dock that overlooks Tangier Sound, this restaurant offers a spectacular view of life in a small waterman's village. Through its expansive plate glass windows, watch as residents from nearby Smith Island tie up at the neighboring city dock to stock up on supplies. Unabashedly seafood in nature, the menu is a cornucopia of crab concoctions. For the purists, the backfin crab cake is a must. A heaping baseball of a sandwich, it is made solely of the richest lumps of

crabmeat. Then there's always the red crab soup or cream of crab soup, crabmeat cocktail and crab balls (miniature versions of the crab cake), crab pizza bagel, crab imperial, crabmeat au gratin, or seafood Creole — so laden with crab that it could pass for "crab Creole." But if crabs aren't your first choice (blasphemy in Crisfield!), the menu offers an array of tempting fresh oysters, shrimp, chicken, and steak entrées. If you're there at dinnertime, linger as the sun sets over the water and enjoy a hot apple turnover with a cup of coffee; ask for the whipped cream.

**SIDE STREET SEAFOOD
  RESTAURANT**
410-968-2442.
204 S. Tenth St., Crisfield,
  MD 21817.

Long popular and voted one of the best crab houses on the Bay by readers of *Chesapeake Bay Magazine*, Side Street was designed for eating crabs. Massive wooden picnic tables covered with

Open: Daily, Mem.
   Day–Labor Day; Sat.,
   Sun., May and Oct.;
   closed in winter.
Price: Moderate.
Cuisine: Seafood.
Serving: L, D.
Credit Cards: D, MC, V.
Reservations:
   Recommended on
   weekends.
Handicap Access: No.

thick brown paper provide the appropriate setting for hungry folks to dive into a tray of raw oysters, a pitcher of beer, and a dozen ruby red steamed crabs. Beyond the crabs, Side Street's menu is rather run of the mill, but they do fry up a mean hush puppy. Here you have a perennial favorite that unfortunately isn't quite as easy to come by as crab in this shore town. Dragged through a little sugar, these hush puppies could substitute for dessert. Although the restaurant is relatively small in size, diners can choose from indoor, outdoor, or covered deck dining that looks out over the neighborhoods and water views of downtown Crisfield. Perched atop a seafood market, the restaurant also is something of a hike up two flights of outdoor stairs, so come prepared for a workout.

Salisbury

CORBIN'S GOURMET
410-860-6858.
Downtown Plaza,
   Salisbury, MD 21801.
Open: Daily.
Price: Inexpensive.
Cuisine: New American.
Serving: B, L, D.
Credit Cards: MC, V.
Reservations: Accepted.
Handicap Access: Yes.
Restrictions: No smoking.

Corbin's Gourmet accounts for a big part of the classy atmosphere of Salisbury's relatively tiny downtown. This cozy café and coffeehouse, a local favorite, really knows how to create a memorable meal from even a simple take-out lunch order. Fresh deli meats and all manner of toppings — from bean sprouts to Brie — mix with freshly baked breads and homemade soups for the lunch crowd. At night, Corbin's becomes a romantic little spot to experience creative seafood dishes like lemon-pepper salmon with cilantro crab sauce. The bar offers a range of specialty beers, and the coffee menu is also extensive. The best bet for newcomers is to let Corbin's chef choose your meal — they're known for great daily lunch and dinner specials on sandwiches, entrées, coffee, and beer. Corbin's only downside is that it doesn't offer an extensive menu, so it may not suit picky eaters who don't like food that's a little out of the ordinary.

Snow Hill

**SNOW HILL INN &
   RESTAURANT**
410-632-2102.
104 E. Market St., Snow
   Hill, MD 21863.
Open: Daily, in summer;
   Oct.–Mar., Mon.–Sat.

Walk into one of the three cozy dining rooms at the Snow Hill Inn & Restaurant, located off Rte. 50 between Salisbury and Ocean City, and you'll find yourself surrounded by all of the best symbols of the South: magnolia flowers, *Gone with*

Price: Moderate.
Cuisine:
    Seafood/American.
Serving: L, D.
Credit Cards: AE, D, MC, V.
Reservations: Yes.
Handicap Access: Yes.

the Wind memorabilia, timeworn antiques. Our dining room came complete with a set of four town matrons who sipped wine and debated whether men were better at cards. You'll also find wonderful food in generous portions, prepared with care and creativity. We ordered Snow on the Hills, two medallions of filet mignon topped with mounds of lump crabmeat and accompanied by scrumptious green beans and new potatoes. Before our entrée arrived, we savored freshly baked herbal bread and spinach salad topped with a homemade, honey-mustard dressing. The atmosphere, the friendly service, and the special attention to detail — even our iced tea was flavored with a hint of peach — makes guests at the Snow Hill Inn glad to be on the Lower Eastern Shore.

Whitehaven

THE RED ROOST
800-953-5443; 410-546-5443.
2670 Clara Rd.,
    Whitehaven, MD 21856.
Open: Daily, D, Mother's
    Day–Labor Day;
    Wed.–Sun., D, mid-
    Mar.–Mother's Day and
    Labor Day–Nov.1.
Price: Inexpensive to
    Expensive.
Cuisine: Seafood.
Serving: D.
Credit Cards: AE, DC, MC,
    V.
Reservations:
    Recommended for 10 or
    more.
Handicap Access: Yes.

You can reach this remote but popular crab house by riding the Whitehaven car ferry over the Wicomico River or by winding your way through back roads until you reach the shell lane that announces the entrance to — a chicken house?! It's true, The Red Roost was once a riverside chicken house, but former owners had the ingenious idea of clearing it of all its poultry presence and filling it with long picnic tables covered with brown paper and crab mallets so that people could experience a true Eastern Shore seafood experience. Now under new ownership, the place remains popular with locals and with bus trips. Its Wed. night sing-alongs with a ragtime band are legendary. When you order, you can choose from dinners like broiled seafood platter, crab cakes, or fried shrimp, but you're more likely to pick the traditional all-you-can-eat crab special (other specials include steamed shrimp, snow crab legs, fried chicken, and ribs). A word of advice: because those delectable blue crabs will be preceded by fried chicken, hush puppies, fried shrimp, clam strips, corn on the cob, and french fries, come hungry, and eat sparingly of the initial dishes so that you can get both your money's worth and your pleasure's worth out of the crustaceans that are the stars of this show.

Chincoteague, Virginia

AJ'S ON THE CREEK
757-336-5888.

Here in the heart of seafood country stands a casual restaurant with a good heart, courtesy

6585 Maddox Blvd.,
  Chincoteague, VA 23336.
Open: Daily, except Sun.
Price: Inexpensive to
  Moderate.
Cuisine: Seafood.
Serving: L, D.
Credit Cards: AE, D, DC,
  MC, V.
Reservations: No.
Handicap Access: Yes.

of the Stillson sisters who founded it back in 1985. The dining room is imitation elegance with faux wood paneling and black vinyl booths, but white tablecloths, low light, and statues of local birds make it both sincere and comfortable. You can ask for a table outside in the screened porch if the weather is good. The menu is seafood, as well it should be: Chincoteague red clam chowder, oysters on the half shell, clams casino, seafood-smothered flounder, oysters in champagne, and homemade crab cakes. You can also order veal, pasta, and beef dishes. Come here to hear what the locals are saying about life in Chincoteague and to get their tips on where to go.

New Church, Virginia

**THE GARDEN AND THE
SEA INN**
800-824-0672; 757-824-0672.
4188 Nelson Rd./P.O. Box
  275, New Church, VA
  23415.
Off Rte. 13, 2 mi. S. of MD-
  VA line.
Open: Fri.–Sun. most of
  year, plus Thurs. in high
  season; call first. Inn and
  restaurant closed late
  Nov.–mid-Mar.
Price: Expensive to Very
  Expensive.
Cuisine: Seafood/
  American.
Serving: D.
Credit Cards: AE, D, MC, V.
Reservations:
  Recommended.
Handicap Access: Yes.

Tom Baker, trained at the Culinary Institute of America, brings a confident and sometimes adventurous touch to this little corner of the world. In the land where fried seafood is king, Baker dares to be different. His entrées are dishes like grilled and sauced filet mignon or lamb chops, basil-scented shrimp over linguine, and his signature bouillabaisse with shrimp, scallops, and oysters. Fish dishes are "whatever's running, whatever's good," and duck hits the menu in the fall. Desserts vary from crème brûlée and chocolate pecan pie to seasonal fruit dishes like peach Melba, made with succulent local peaches. Two prix fixe menus are available, complete with appetizer or soup, salad, entrée, and dessert for less than $30 or around $40 with wine samples. Tom's wife, Sara, has built an impressive wine list with a wide variety of Virginia whites to highlight the state's booming wine industry. Whether you're an inn guest or just someone in for the evening, their food and hospitality will make you feel good inside.

Painter, Virginia

FORMY'S
757-442-2426.
34446 Lankford Hwy.,
  Painter, VA 23420.

Charles Kuralt stopped here on his way through the Eastern Shore of Virginia, and you should too. It's a surprisingly good restaurant located in

Open: Year-round,
Mon.–Sun.
Price: Inexpensive.
Cuisine: Barbecue.
Serving: L, D.
Credit Cards: No; checks
accepted.
Reservations: No.
Handicap Access: Yes.

the middle of nowhere inside a former day care center. Boston butt pork roasts are slowly cooked right outside the restaurant on a wood grill, where barbecued chicken and ribs are also prepared. Georgia native Jim Formyduval then douses the tender pork pieces with a sauce that combines hot sauce, mustard, spices, and catsup. You can order a plate of barbecue with two side dishes, a barbecue sandwich or a pint to take home. Side dishes include perfectly crisp hush puppies, hand-cut french fries, and turnip greens in the colder months. Hearty Brunswick stew is also available in the fall and winter. Cakes are homemade by local ladies, and you can buy bottles of barbecue sauce and chili vinegar and preserves to take home. This definitely isn't standard roadside food.

FOOD PURVEYORS

There's variety in Bay country, no doubt about that. From Annapolis, Maryland, to Oak Grove, Virginia, special places await food lovers, who can stop in for ice cream or pick through the world's best Silver Queen corn before heading to the seafood market for hard-shell crabs.

Chesapeake crabbers check their pots daily in-season, the better to meet the demand for the Bay's beloved blue crabs.

David Trozzo

As is typical in the region, a dose of history is available — even with your takeout. In a town full of rehabilitated historic buildings, the Annapolis **Market House** stands as one of the city's more enduring phoenixes. Located in the City Dock area at the Market Space, the Market House is heir to a long line of city markets that has stood near here since 1788. (Indeed, shops and markets were first erected near the Statehouse in the eighteenth century.) This particular market was reopened in 1971 following an extensive renovation and is a good place to stop for a quick, take-out lunch. Vendors include the following: **Annapolis Fish Market** (410-269-0490) with a genuine, belly-up-to-the-raw-bar; **Baskin-Robbins** (410-295-6525); **The Big Cheese** (410-263-6915); **Chutney's Gourmet** (410-280-1974); **City Dock Bakery** (410-269-6361); **Kaufman Fancy Fruits and Vegetables** (410-269-0941); **Machoian Poultry** (410-263-5979); **Mann's Sandwiches** (410-263-0644); **Sammy's Deli** (410-263-6883). Open daily, with vendors unshuttering for the day between 7:00 a.m.–9:00 a.m.

If you're down toward the Northern Neck, visit a rare Chesapeake winery. Owned by the Flemer family since the 1890s, the 2,500-acre **Ingleside Plantation and Winery** (Leedstown Rd., Oak Grove, VA; 804-224-8687) dates from 1832. It's been the site of a boys' school and a Civil War garrison for Union troops. In 1969, Carl Flemer planted the first grape vine. Besides wines from a variety of grapes, try their Virginia sparkling wine. Free tours and wine tastings. Located 2½ mi. S. of Oak Grove, VA; near the top of the Northern Neck. Open Mon.–Sat., 10:00 a.m.–5:00 p.m.; Sun., 12:00 noon–5:00 p.m.

COFFEEHOUSES & COFFEE SHOPS

L ike everyone else from Seattle south and west, Chesapeake Country is fully wired — and not necessarily to the Internet. Coffeehouses and coffee shops fuel visitors through the rest of the afternoon in every town around. One such outlet not listed here, the 49 West Wine Bar and Gallery in Annapolis, is so popular that we've listed it under the heading Nightlife in Chapter Five, *Culture* and reviewed it under the heading Restaurants in this chapter. For other jolts of coffee and conversation, see the following:

HEAD OF THE BAY

Java by the Bay (118 N. Washington St., Havre de Grace; 410-939-0227) Nice little café-style coffeehouse that also sells teas and speciality foods. Easy to find in tourist shopping district. Open Mon.–Sat., 7:30 a.m.–6:00 p.m.; Sun., 8:30 a.m.–4:00 p.m.

WESTERN SHORE

City Dock Café (18 Market Space, Annapolis; 410-269-0969) Bright, clean, and often packed. A variety of coffees, sandwiches, fat cookies, and pastry. Front windows offer a fine view of City Dock. Open Sun.–Thurs., 6:30 a.m.–10:00 p.m.; Fri., Sat., 6:30 a.m.–12:00 a.m.

Karen's Kup (84 S. Main St., Kilmarnock, VA) In addition to coffees, also serving smoothies, soups in winter, and a cold plate lunch. Gifts, too. No espresso — a fine statement on laid-back Northern Neck life. Open 8:30 a.m.–6:00 p.m.

Starbucks (124 Dock St., Annapolis; 410-268-6551; Mon.–Thurs., 6:00 a.m.–8:00 p.m.; Fri., 6:00 a.m.–10:30 p.m.; Sat., 7:00 a.m.–11:00 p.m.; Sun., 7:00 a.m.–8:00 p.m.; Annapolis Harbour Center, Annapolis; 410-573-0076; Mon.–Thurs., 6:00 a.m.–10:00 p.m.; Fri., 6:00 a.m.–11:00 p.m.; Sat., 6:30 a.m.–11:00 p.m.; Sun., 7:00 a.m.–9:00 p.m.) The espresso machine operates constantly at these busy branches of the national chain.

EASTERN SHORE

Aesop's Table (124 N. Division St., Salisbury; 410-546-4471) Coffee bar with breakfast and lunch menus, less than a block off Rte. 50. Reproductions, gifts, cards, candy, jewelry, and other specialty items. Open Mon.–Fri., 8:00 a.m.–5:00 p.m.; Sat., 10:00 a.m.–5:00 p.m.; closed Sun.

Allegro (11775 Somerset Ave., Princess Anne; 410-651-4520) Good coffee, pastries, sandwiches, and soups, with tables so you can rest awhile and a nice selection of gifts. Open Mon.–Fri., 9:30 a.m.–6:00 p.m.; closed weekends.

America's Cup (5745 Main St., Rock Hall; 410-639-7361) Coffee bar, visitor center, lunch and dinner spot, and used bookstore — all under one roof. Open Sun.–Thurs., 7:00 a.m.–7:00 p.m.; Fri.–Sat., 7:00 a.m.–9:00 p.m.

Globe Theatre's Café (12 Broad St., Berlin; 410-641-0784) Coffee bar and deli inside a historic theater that offers live concerts, local and regional art, gourmet food items, books, cards, and gifts. Open Mon.–Fri., 8:00 a.m.–6:00 p.m.; Sat., 10:00 a.m.–6:00 p.m.; Sun., 10:00 a.m.–5:00 p.m.; coffee served until closing, deli closes thirty minutes early.

Play It Again Sam (108 S. Cross St., Chestertown; 410-778-2688) Coffee bar with baked goods and a few sandwiches inside an old store with a wood floor and pressed-tin ceiling. Open Mon.–Sat., 7:00 a.m.–5:30 p.m.; Sun., 9:00 a.m.–4:00 p.m.

CRAB, SEAFOOD & FISH MARKETS

HEAD OF THE BAY

Price's Seafood Restaurant (654 Water St., Havre de Grace; 410-939-2782) This is where Havre de Grace cracks crabs. Open Apr.–Nov.

The Tap Room (201 Bohemia Ave., Chesapeake City; 410-885-9873; 410-885-2344) OK, so it's not a market, but it's where Chesapeake City goes for hard-shell crabs. No credit cards.

WESTERN SHORE

Annapolis Seafood Market (Forest Dr. & Tyler Ave., Annapolis; 410-269-5380) Longtime, popular local seafood market, beautifully organized from in-season white corn to the line at the crab and spiced shrimp counter to the excellent take-out sandwiches for folks on the go. All kinds of good and fresh seafood.

Cap'n Tom's Seafood (60 Wood Rd., Lancaster, VA; 804-462-5507) Some of the fanciest restaurants in Richmond have discovered Cap'n Tom's, and now you can, too. If you're in the area, drop by and pick up a pound tub of some of the best fat lump crabmeat around.

An oysterman hoists the Bay's treasures to market.

David Trozzo

Captain's Choice Fresh and Frozen Seafood (839 Rappahannock Dr./P.O. Box 13, White Stone, VA; 804-435-6750) A good place to look first for local seafood, located right before (or after) you cross the Rappahannock River between the Northern Neck and Middle Peninsula. If we hadn't stopped, we'd have never found Rocket Billy's next door (see the heading Restaurants). And that would have been a shame. Rocket Billy's buys those plump oysters in its famous fried oyster sandwiches at this market.

Cockrell's Creek Seafood (Fleeton Rd., Reedville, VA; 804-453-6326) Crab cakes to go and a variety of other fresh seafood at this quiet point outside Reedville. Closed mid-Jan.–early Mar.

J&W Seafood (Rte 33 E./Box 549, Deltaville, VA; 804-776-6400) Stop in for fresh seafood in this outpost fishing and sailing town. Peeler tanks in back. Fishing and hunting licenses. Open seven days, except Jan.–Apr., when they're closed on Sun.

McNasby's (723 2nd St., Eastport; 800-4MD-CRAB; 410-280-CRAB) A crab deck out on the creek for take-out customers makes this one of the most scenic crab-pickin' places around. In addition, customers find loads of fresh seafood in the market, from rockfish to soft crabs to mussels. Anything that they sell, you can get cooked for takeout, says the manager.

Winter Harbor Seafood (3706 King's Hwy., Oak Grove, VA; 804-224-7779) Crabs, locally caught fish, fishing and hunting licenses. Open daily.

EASTERN SHORE

Big Al's Market (302 N. Talbot St., St. Michaels; 410-745-3151) Where St. Michaels buys its hard-shell crabs for summer crab feasts. Grocery, deli, beer, wine, and liquor.

Captain's Ketch Seafood Market and Carry-Out (316 Glebe Rd., Easton; 410-820-7177) Picked crabmeat, lobster, and fish, including orange roughy, catfish, and smoked bluefish are available at this thriving place, along with a good take-out business.

Chesapeake Landing Seafood Market and Restaurant (Rte. 33, McDaniel; 410-745-9600) People drive all the way from Easton to get seafood at this spot between St. Michaels and Tilghman Island. It has its own picking plant, soft-shell crab shedding tanks, oysters, crabs, and more. Once a wholesale business, it's now a thriving retail market, a restaurant, and a takeout with good prices. Located 2½ mi. W. of St. Michaels.

David W. Wehrs Seafood (1819 Little Creek Rd., Chester; 410-643-5778) Wehrs is the place on Kent Island to get fresh crabmeat, live or steamed crabs, and clams right off the boats. A high deck over the water offers dining with a view. Great crab cakes and steamed crabs — the real thing. Take exit 39-B (Dominion Rd.) from Rte. 50, 2 mi. to right at the T onto Little Creek Rd., go to end.

J&J Seafood (21083 Chesapeake Ave., Rock Hall; 410-639-2325) Steamed hard-shell crabs and live soft-shell crabs, rockfish, perch, and oysters, along with bait and ice.

Kool Ice and Seafood Co. (110 Washington St., Cambridge; 800-437-2417; 410-228-2300) Dorchester-caught crabs and a fine selection of oysters, clams, and lobsters. Buy it here to take home or have it shipped anywhere. Kool Ice is (surprise!) an ice dealer, too.

S.T. Moore & Co. (Rte. 50, Hebron; 410-546-9385) Seafood, fish, and seasonal delicacies like muskrat, plus takeout. Check for specials.

Susan's Seafood (Rte. 13, New Church, VA; 757-824-5545) The oysters that made Chincoteague famous, clams, scallops, crabs, fish, shrimp, and lobsters. Shipping available.

HEALTH & WHOLE FOODS GROCERIES & SHOPS

WESTERN SHORE

Country Sunshine Market (115 Annapolis St., Annapolis; 410-268-6996) Bright veggie-oriented grocery with take-out kitchen for sandwiches and soups. Licensed nutritionist in the house; parking. Open Mon.–Fri., 9:00 a.m.–7:00 p.m.; Sat., 10:00 a.m.–4:00 p.m.

Fresh Fields (Annapolis Harbour Center, 2504 Solomons Island Rd., Annapolis; 410-573-1800) Not that the whole foods giant needs a plug from us, but the locals fill the aisles here. Favorites: focàccia topped pizza-style with artichokes; Coleman's antibiotic-free beef, Arctic char most any time of the year, and the best buffalo mozzarella around. Good takeout if you're off for a day on the Bay. Open Mon.–Sat., 9:;00 a.m.–9:00 p.m.; Sun., 9:00 a.m.–8:00 p.m.; Jun.-Sept., 8:00 a.m.–9:00 p.m.

Sun and Earth Natural Foods (1933 West St., Annapolis; 410-266-6862) Beloved old health and whole foods shop stocks all of the necessities, including Green Goddess sandwiches. Open Mon.–Sat., 9:30 a.m.–6:30 p.m.; Sun., 12:00 noon–4:00 p.m.

EASTERN SHORE

Chestertown Natural Foods (214 Cannon St., Chestertown; 410-778-1677) Natural foods, organic produce, vitamins and supplements, bath products, and snacks. Open Mon.–Fri., 10:00 a.m.–6:00 p.m.; Sat., 9:00 a.m.–5:00 p.m.; Sun., 12:00 noon–4:00 p.m.

Healthful Habits (720 E. College Ave., Ste. 7, Salisbury; 410-749-1997) Organic and natural foods, vitamins, supplements, herbs, and specialty items, for example, for people with food allergies. Open Mon.–Thurs., 10:00 a.m.–8:00 p.m.; Fri., 10:00 a.m.–4:00 p.m.; Sun., 12:00 noon–5:00 p.m.; closed Sat.

The Railway Market (108 Marlboro Rd., Easton; 410-822-4852) Where healthy gourmets on the Shore shop. Originally located in Easton's old-time railway depot, the store moved to a strip mall and is now bigger than ever. Organic and natural groceries, takeout and café, health and beauty products, books. Open Mon.–Fri., 9:00 a.m.–7:00 p.m.; Sat., 9:00 a.m.–6:00 p.m.; Sun., 10:00 a.m.–5:00 p.m.

ICE CREAM

WESTERN SHORE

Storm Brothers Ice Cream Factory (130 Dock St., Annapolis; 410-263-3376) Longtime resident of the City Dock area draws its devotees. Large selection of ice cream, five selections of sherbet. Open daily, 11:30 a.m.–10:00 p.m.

EASTERN SHORE

Dairy Queen (320 Sunburst Hwy., Cambridge; 410-228-1680) A local hangout where you'll always find a line on the weekends. Burgers, fries, and all kinds of ice-cream treats for takeout only, since it has no seating. Open daily, 10:00 a.m.–9:30 p.m.

Durding's Store (5742 Main St., Rock Hall; 410-778-7957) An old-fashioned soda fountain sits amid old-fashioned pharmacy equipment — and lots of luscious ice-cream flavors. Open daily.

Muller's Old Fashioned Ice Cream Parlor (4034 Main St., Chincoteague, VA; 757-336-5894) Fresh fruit sundaes, malts, ice-cream sodas, frozen yogurt, and yes, ice-cream cones, in an 1875 house with authentic Victorian atmosphere. Open 11:00 a.m.–11:00 p.m. in summer.

Scoops! (1147 S. Salisbury Blvd., Salisbury; 410-548-9889) Good ice cream on cones or on sundaes named for local luminaries, plus ice-cream cakes and a full line of coffee drinks. Open weekdays, 7:00 a.m.–10:00 p.m.; Sat., 10:00 a.m.–11:00 p.m.; Sun., 12:00 noon–10:00 p.m.

PRODUCE MARKETS

What we're not listing: each and every farm stand that you're sure to see as you travel Chesapeake highways. Starting with strawberries in late spring and moving through the seasons of Silver Queen corn, the world's best tomatoes, cantaloupes, peaches, squash, and pumpkins, this is prime agricultural territory. Local farms set up their own stands, which you might find operating from the back of a pickup, or set out, gourmet style, beneath a white canopy. You'll be awed by the selection in the late summer and early fall. Make a point of stopping.

Anne Arundel County Farmers' Market, Inc (Harry S. Truman Pkwy., Annapolis; 410-280-0751) A big variety of farmers and vendors spread their wares here during the longer summer markets or the shorter "fall" and "Christmas" markets. Always open on weekends, but call for hours, especially if you're interested in attending the summer market midweek.

How Sweet It Is (southbound Rte. 13 at Somerset Wicomico county line, Eden; 410-742-8600) Open daily from the late spring until late Oct. for local strawberries, super sweet white corn, giant pumpkins, and other kinds of produce.

Jack's Market (westbound Rte. 50 near Hebron; 410-749-1889) Produce, preserves, candy, flags, country crafts, and an impressive array of lawn ornaments. Open daily 8:00 a.m.–8:00 p.m. in summer; shorter hours rest of year; closed Jan.–Feb.

SPECIALTY GOURMET SHOPS & MARKETS

HEAD OF THE BAY

Bomboy's Home Made Candy (322 Market St., Havre de Grace; 410-939-2924) Family-owned business a block from the water brings you chocolates and candies, ranging from butter creams to Havre de Mints. Open Tues-Sat., 10:00 a.m.–6:00 p.m.; Sun., 12:00 noon–5:00 p.m.; closed Mon.

WESTERN SHORE

Giolitti Delicatessen (2068 Somerville Rd., Annapolis; 410-266-8600) Fine Italian bakery and gourmet shop at the edge of town in Parole. Sandwiches and focàccia, pastas and cheese, tiramisu and wine. Small café, catering. Open Mon.–Fri., 10:00 a.m.–7:00 p.m.; Sat., 9:00 a.m.–6:00 p.m.; Sun., 12:00 noon–5:00 p.m.

Pennsylvania Dutch Farmers' Market (2472 Solomons Island Rd., Annapolis Harbour Center, Annapolis; 410-573-0770) Operating weekends in its huge space. Stalls filled with everything from subs to fresh produce. Quilt shop, restaurant. Open Thurs.–Sat.

River Market (#1 Rappahannock Blvd., White Stone, VA; 804-435-1725) A lot of prepared foods, plus they bake their own bread. Microbrews, some wines. Call for hours.

White Stone Wine and Cheese Co. (572 Rappahannock Dr., White Stone, VA; 804-435-2000) Smart market in upscale Northern Neck town stocks imported cheeses, good meats, imported wines, fresh breads, and cookies. Open Mon.–Sat., 8:30 a.m.–5:00 p.m.; Fri., 8:30 a.m.–6:00 p.m.

Woodburns of Solomons (13920 Solomons Island Rd. S., Patuxent Plaza, Solomons; 410-326-3284) Solomons is changing for sure when the local grocery goes upscale and stocks California rolls, packaged for takeout in the deli section. Locals appear to be thrilled. Open daily.

EASTERN SHORE

Blue Crab Bay Co. (29368 Atlantic Dr., Melfa, VA; 800-221-2722; 757-787-3602) A phenomenally successful, specialty food maker with a worldwide mail-order business and a retail shop, featuring its clam sauce for pasta, Sting Ray Bloody Mary mix, herb blends, gift baskets, and gifts. Blue Crab recently moved to a new industrial park building to have enough space. Open Mon.–Fri., 9:00 a.m.–5:00 p.m.; Sat., 10:00 a.m.–4:00 p.m. (seasonal).

Chesapeake Gourmet (189 Outlet Center Dr., Prime Outlets, Queenstown; 410-827-8686) A well-supplied shop with dishes, kitchenware, coffee and tea, wines, microbrew beers, and specialty food products. Deli counter. Open summer Mon.–Sat., 10:00 a.m.–8:00 p.m.; Sun., 11:00 a.m.–7:00 p.m.; Jan., Feb., Mon.–Thurs., 10:00 a.m.–6:00 p.m.; Fri.–Sat., 10:00 a.m.–8:00 p.m.; Sun., 11:00 a.m.–6:00 p.m.

Flamingo Flats (100 Talbot St., St. Michaels; 410-745-2053) Owner Robert Deppe has the world's second-largest collection of hot sauces, and you'll find many of his discoveries here along with cookbooks, jewelry, flamingo stuff, gourmet condiments and sauces. Hot sauce tasting bar in summer. Open daily 10:00 a.m.–5:00 p.m.; longer hours in summer; closed Tues.–Wed., Jan.–Mar.

Pony Tails (7011 Maddox Blvd., Chincoteague, VA; 757-336-6688) OK, so gourmet might be stretching it, but this is one delicacy that visitors feel that they have to take home. Saltwater taffy playfully named for the famous ponies is made daily in-season in an antique cutting and wrapping machine that you can see in operation. Open weekdays 9:00 a.m.–5:00 p.m.; Sat., 9:00 a.m.–6:00 p.m.; closed Sun.

Wye River (5201 Ocean Gateway Dr., Queenstown; 410-643-2666) An outlet for this specialty maker of soups, snacks, and spices. Full take-out menu. Open weekdays 9:30 a.m.–5:30 p.m.; weekends 9:00 a.m.–6:00 p.m.

CHAPTER FIVE
The Best of the Bay
CULTURE

Chesapeake culture combines well-preserved vestiges of early colonial life with southern graciousness and pieces of city living imported by refugees from nearby metropolitan centers. Add to that the abundant traditions and influence of the Bay, and you get a varied mix that ranges from free waterside concerts by the U.S. Naval Academy Band to tours of colonial-era homes to folk festivals celebrating duck decoys and oysters. Whatever the medium, the emphasis is on the Bay and the region's abundant heritage.

The performing arts scene in the smaller

David Trozzo

The U.S. Sailboat Show, the biggest boat show anywhere and beloved by sailors near and far, is held on Columbus Day weekend.

cities and towns is a miniature replica of that found in the big city, with an emphasis on classics appropriate to the cradle of U.S. history. That means, for example, that you'll easily find classical symphonic or chamber music; if you're in the mood, for example, for improvisational jazz, you may have to look a little harder.

Visually, expect to see what the locals jokingly refer to as "art ducko." The grand duck-hunting tradition here is depicted in small galleries scattered from Havre de Grace to Cape Charles, with concentrations in Annapolis and Easton. Hanging alongside this art, though, are lots of maritime watercolors and prints. Stop by the St. John's College Elizabeth Myers Mitchell Gallery in Annapolis for a dose of Henry Moore or Picasso; Maryland Hall for the

Creative Arts in Annapolis or the Academy of the Arts in Easton show exhibitions of contemporary regional artists.

Take advantage of the region's vast history. Tour the manor home of a seventeeth-century Virginia Burgess or visit the exemplary Annapolis homes of four signers of the Declaration of Independence. Archaeological digs are abundant, their finds well preserved.

Here is your guide to what to see and to do around the Bay. For details on events, schedules, or seasonal offerings, check area newspapers and magazines (see Chapter Eight, *Information*, for a list of publications).

CINEMA

A vant-garde cinema is not a great strength here, probably for the same reasons so few other forms of experimental culture thrive — booming Washington, D.C. and Baltimore are just up the Maryland road from urban Annapolis, and the rest of the region is relatively rural.

Still, local institutions of higher learning can always be counted upon to fill the cultural void. If you're searching for noncommercial films in the **ANNAPOLIS/WESTERN SHORE** area, St. John's College offers the Saturday night gem during the school year. Movies by masters like Bergman and Kurosawa start at 8:15 p.m., cost $3, and the **FSK Auditorium theater** (410-263-2371) is rarely overcrowded. **Crown Cinemas** (410-224-1145) operates the *Annapolis* commercial movie houses, which include **The Annapolis Harbour Center IX,** the **Crown Annapolis Mall IV,** and the **Crown Eastport Cinemas II.**

First-run fare on the **UPPER EASTERN SHORE** is screened at the new **Chester 5 Theatres** (410-778-2227) at Washington Square on Rte. 213 in *Chestertown* and in *Easton* at **Tred Avon Movies 4** (410-822-5566) in Tred Avon Square on Marlboro Rd. Washington College in *Chestertown* offers a free weekly film series that brings high-quality movies and foreign films to campus on the weekends, during the school year in the **Norman James Theatre** (410-778-2800) on campus: Fri., 7:30 p.m., 9:30 p.m.; Sun., 3:00 p.m., 7:30 p.m.; Mon., 7:30 p.m. On the **LOWER EASTERN SHORE, Cambridge Premiere Cinemas** (410-221-8688) in Dorchester Square in *Cambridge* offer first-run films. Down *Salisbury* way, movies play at **Hoyts Cinema 10** (410-543-0902; 410-543-0905) in the Centre At Salisbury and **Hoyts Cinema 6** (410-546-4700) at 317 E. Main St. Call the Hoyts box office (410-546-1776). *Chincoteague Island's* Roxy (757-336-6301) at 4074 Main St. shows *Misty of Chincoteague* twice daily during Pony Penning for free; you can see Misty's hoofprints in the concrete outside. During the summer, the theater has nightly movies, four nights a week in the winter.

DANCE

ANNAPOLIS/WESTERN SHORE

Annapolis

BALLET THEATRE OF ANNAPOLIS
410-263-2909, tickets;
410-263-8289,
information.
Maryland Hall for the
Creative Arts, 801 Chase
St., Annapolis, MD
21401.
Season: Oct., Dec., Apr.
Tickets: $10 children; $17
seniors; $20 adults.

The Western Shore's proximity to Baltimore and Washington, D.C. means that most denizens head there for their dance fixes. One notable exception is the Ballet Theatre of Annapolis, with its own principal dancers, including those formerly with the Bolshoi and the National Ballet of China, and school. Four major productions each year at Maryland Hall generally include a modern production and a pure classic, such as the second act of *Swan Lake*. The annual *Nutcracker* is a holiday sell-out (matinee tickets go first).

LOWER EASTERN SHORE

Salisbury

SALISBURY STATE UNIVERSITY DANCE COMPANY
410-543-6353.
SSU, 1101 Camden Ave.,
Salisbury, MD 21801.
Season: mid-Nov.–end
Apr., 8:00 p.m.
Tickets: $8 general
admission adults; $6
seniors and teens; free 12
and under.

A professionally-run company at Salisbury State University presents diverse styles and forms of dance. Performances in Holloway Hall Auditorium feature student choreography in the Fall Showcase, while the Spring Concert highlights faculty, selected student works, and notable guest choreographers.

GALLERIES

The visual arts scene in Annapolis revolves around Maryland Hall and the historic district's commercial galleries. Watercolors of local scenes and marine prints are more likely to hang than cutting-edge abstracts, although interesting work can be found at these noncommercial galleries (see Chapter Seven, *Shopping*, for commercial galleries.)

ANNAPOLIS/WESTERN SHORE

Annapolis

ELIZABETH MYERS MITCHELL ART GALLERY
410-626-2556.
St. John's College, Mellon Hall, Annapolis, MD 21401.
Attached to the Francis Scott Key auditorium lobby.
Open: Tues.–Sun., 12:00 noon–5:00 p.m.; Fri., 7:00 p.m.–8:00 p.m. during school year; hours may vary in summer.

This is your best chance in Annapolis to see major works by major artists. Visiting shows often are curated elsewhere by groups like the Smithsonian Institution's Traveling Exhibition Service or the American Federation of Art in New York. Recent exhibitions: Lasting Impressions: Drawings by Thomas Hart Benton, Picasso Ceramics, and Reflections on Nature: Small Paintings by Arthur Dove. Lectures, gallery talks, and group tours are held in conjunction with exhibits.

MARYLAND FEDERATION OF ART GALLERY ON THE CIRCLE
410-268-4566.
www.annearundelcounty.com/art/circle.htm.
18 State Circle, Annapolis, MD 21401.
Open: Tues.–Sun., 11:00 a.m.–5:00 p.m.

A fun space. Originally built in the mid-1800s as a storage loft for the Jones and Franklin General Store, the building's exposed brick walls serve as backdrop for changing shows. Paintings, sculpture, wearable art, and photographs by artists in the 300-member roster. Two gallery rooms host monthly exhibitions, which often feature small group shows of artists operating in different media. A good place to look for a well-priced piece from an unknown artist.

An artist at the easel at the Maryland Hall for the Creative Arts in Annapolis.

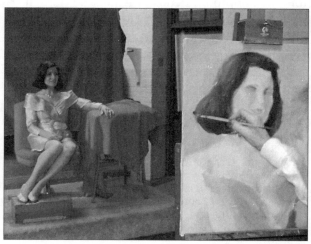

David Trozzo

MARYLAND HALL FOR THE CREATIVE ARTS
410-263-5544.
www.mdhallarts.org.
801 Chase St., Annapolis, MD 21401.
Open: Mon.–Fri., 9:00 a.m.–5:00 p.m.; Thurs., 9:00 a.m.–8:30 p.m.; Sat., 10:00 a.m.–1:00 p.m.

The city's performing and visual arts center and school houses two distinct galleries showing a variety of work. The **Cardinal Gallery** hosts contemporary works in a variety of media by MidAtlantic artists, with changing exhibitions, while the **A.I.R. Gallery** ("Artist in Residence") offers the work of Maryland Hall's thirteen artists-in-residence, as well as students and others. While you're in the building, wander upstairs and see if any of the artists are working in their studios located on the top floor of the former Annapolis High School building.

Solomons

ANNMARIE GARDEN
410-326-4640.
13480 Dowell Rd., Solomons, MD 20688.
Mailing Address: 175 Main St., Prince Frederick, MD 20678.
Open: Daily, 10:00 a.m.–4:00 p.m.

Before you reach the turnoff to Solomons, hang a left down Dowell Rd. and keep an eye out for a pair of colorful ceramic gates to your left, topped by the sculpted echo of waves. Turn in to discover one of Chesapeake's least expected delights: a sculpture garden-in-progress. A bronzed oyster tonger (an oysterman using "tongs," a cross between scissors and a pair of long-handled rakes) greets visitors soon after entering. Park and explore the well-land-scaped woods to find pieces like The Council Ring, quietly inviting reflection. The county-owned garden is graced by commissioned works from artists throughout the country, paid for by fund-raising from the nonprofit Friends of Annmarie Garden. The annual ArtsFest falls the third weekend in Sept., with a juried visual and performing arts scene.

UPPER EASTERN SHORE

Chestertown

CHESTER RIVER CRAFT AND ART SCHOOLS
410-778-5954.
www.chesterriver.com/.
105 S. Cross St., Chestertown, MD 21620.
Open: Classes year-round; call for schedule and prices.

Artisans and craftspeople are the teachers in this unique new school, whose aim is to create opportunities for hands-on learning of the Upper Eastern Shore's artistic heritage. The school has classes in crafts, visual and fine arts, performing arts, shipbuilding, and culinary arts, so you can build a canoe, make furniture, learn butchering or bread-making skills, or try your hand at watercolor, bookbinding, or photography. Geared to "learning vacations" for adults and children. Of particular interest right now is its construction of a reproduction of the eighteenth-century schooner *Sultana*. The project will take up to three years, during which people can pitch in to make her seaworthy. Once built, *Sultana* will once again patrol the Chester River, this time as a living classroom.

CHESTERTOWN ARTS LEAGUE
410-778-5789.
204 Cannon St./P.O. Box 656, Chestertown, MD 21620.
Open: Call for hours.

Chestertown's promoters of the local arts scene offer a variety of classes and gallery exhibits year-round, featuring works by members and guests. The Arts League hosts an annual juried art show in the spring and an Art in the Park Festival.

CONSTANCE STUART LARRABEE ARTS CENTER
800-422-1782, ext. 7849; 410-778-2800.
Washington College, Gibson Fine Arts Center, 300 Washington Ave., Chestertown, MD 21620.
Open: Tues.–Sun., 1:00 p.m.–5:00 p.m. during school year.

This large studio-and-exhibitions space was once the school's boiler plant. Thanks to the building's rebirth, the college's fine arts department has expanded studio space for painting, drawing, pottery, sculpture, printmaking, and photography. While largely academic space, the center also shows student artwork. Chestertown resident, Larrabee, on assignment for a South African newspaper, was one of the first women photojournalists in World War II, and her work has been exhibited at the Smithsonian and Corcoran galleries in Washington, D.C. Also on campus is the gallery of the Gibson Performing Arts Center.

Easton

ACADEMY OF THE ARTS
410-822-0455.
106 South St., Easton, MD 21601.
Open: Mon.–Sat., 10:00 a.m.–4:00 p.m.; Wed., 10:00 a.m.–9:00 p.m., fall–spring.

Long the gathering place for the area's artists, the academy, a white clapboard former schoolhouse, provides 24,000-square feet of studios and gallery space. Looking like what you'd expect to find in the middle of a cosmopolitan city, the academy supports a growing membership, changing exhibits, popular classes, a growing permanent collection, and periodic performances and lectures. The spirit is democratic, with exhibited artworks ranging from small, traditional still lifes to the large, vibrant seascapes of the late Herman Maril.

David Trozzo

The Academy of the Arts in Easton is the hub of Shore culture.

Stevensville

**KENT ISLAND
FEDERATION OF ART**
410-643-7424.
405 Main St., Stevensville,
MD 21666.
Open: Wed.–Fri., Sun., 1:00
p.m.–4:00 p.m.; Sat., 10:00
a.m.–4:00 p.m.

Local and regional artists in various media, including oils, watercolors, pastels, and acrylics exhibit works in this fine Victorian at the edge of historic Stevensville. Monthly exhibits have featured everything from quilting to pottery; a separate member gallery changes its exhibit every two months.

LOWER EASTERN SHORE

Cambridge

**DORCHESTER ARTS
CENTER**
410-228-7782.
120 High St., Cambridge,
MD 21613.
Open: Mon.–Sat., 10:00
a.m.–2:00 p.m.

Housed in a pretty house on Cambridge's historic High St., the center showcases area artists and offers classes, weekend fine arts workshops, and performances. Its gallery exhibit changes monthly. Every fall, usually on the last Sun. in Sept., the center puts on the Dorchester Showcase, a street festival with entertainment, juried fine arts and crafts show, and food the length of High St.

Salisbury

**ART INSTITUTE &
  GALLERY**
410-546-4748.
212 W. Main St., Salisbury,
  MD 21801.
Open: Mon.–Sat., 12:00
  noon–4:00 p.m.

The beautifully renovated former Woolworth's store on the Downtown Plaza in Salisbury is now called The Gallery Building, and among its fine tenants is The Art Institute & Gallery. The AI&G exhibits works by local, MidAtlantic, and national artists in all media, with a national juried show, member shows for professional and emerging artists, and solo shows. Look for the fine gift shop.

UNIVERSITY GALLERY
410-543-6271.
SSU, Fulton Hall, Salisbury,
  MD 21801.
Open: Tues.–Fri., 10:00
  a.m.–5:00 p.m.; Sat., Sun.,
  12:00 noon–4:00 p.m.,
  during school year;
  otherwise, call ahead.

The works of Joan Miró, Ansel Adams, Edward Hopper, and Yousuf Karsh have hung in this small but ambitious college gallery in SSU's fine arts building. You'll also find student and faculty works and pieces by regional folk crafters and artists. The Atrium Gallery, in the Guerrieri University Center, houses smaller exhibits and a gift shop; open Tues.–Fri., 11:00 a.m.–4:00 p.m.; Sat.–Sun., 12:00 noon–4:00 p.m.

HISTORIC BUILDINGS & SITES

HEAD OF THE BAY

Cecilton

**MOUNT HARMON
  PLANTATION**
410-275-8819.
Grove Neck Rd., Cecilton,
  MD 21913.
Off Rte. 282, about 1 mi.
  S.W. of Rtes. 282 & 213
  intersection at Cecilton.
Open: May–Oct. and by
  appt.
Admission: $5 docent-
  guided tours.

In colonial days, when "King Tobacco" was the main moneymaker in these parts, Tidewater gentry set themselves up in sprawling plantations. Mount Harmon now represents these shoreside fiefdoms that ruled the river-laced frontier. The restored Georgian manor house, built in 1730, has been reopened to the public after a five-year hiatus. One can tour more than 200 acres of preserve along the Sassafras River until the gates close at dusk. Owned and operated by the nonprofit Friends of Mount Harmon, the site is a nature preserve featuring rare and endangered plant species like the American lotus.

Havre de Grace

David Trozzo

The distinctive Concord Point Lighhouse at Havre de Grace.

CONCORD POINT LIGHTHOUSE
410-939-1498.
Lafayette & Concord Sts.,
  Havre de Grace, MD
  21078.
Open: Apr.–Oct., Sat., Sun.,
  1:00 p.m.–5:00 p.m.

The Susquehanna River, prehistoric precursor to the Chesapeake, flows into the Bay at Havre de Grace. Perhaps the best view — though only during weekends from spring to fall — is from the Concord Point Lighthouse. Visitors to the 1827 lighthouse will notice the boardwalk that ends here. One-half mile long, the promenade rounds the point along the Susquehanna, affording an exhilarating view. Lots of locals stroll the boardwalk or take in the view from one of many benches placed alongside.

ANNAPOLIS/WESTERN SHORE

Annapolis

CHARLES CARROLL HOUSE
410-269-1737.
107 Duke of Gloucester St.,
  Annapolis, MD 21401.
Open: Fri., Sun., 12:00
  noon–4:00 p.m.; Sat.,
  10:00 a.m.–2:00 p.m.
Admission: $5 adults; $4
  seniors; $2 students.

Four Marylanders signed the Declaration of Independence; all of them, at least for a time, owned homes in Annapolis. This was the birthplace and boyhood home of Charles Carroll of Annapolis, the only Roman Catholic to sign the Declaration. His home, now located on the grounds of St. Mary's Church, housed a chapel in which Catholics worshiped during the mid-eigh-

(12–17); free 11 and younger. Group prices available.
Handicap Access: Yes.

teenth century, when the religion was forced underground. Restoration has been underway for some years, beginning with archaeological digs in the formal gardens that turned up artifacts, likely from a tavern that once operated on the property. Construction of the original house began in 1721; Carroll of Annapolis added a story, an A-frame room, and a three-story wing in 1770. His chapel was the precursor of **St. Mary's Church** (410-263-2396), which stands in front on the same property. It's worth a peek inside the century-old church to see the magnificent altar. Public activities at the Carroll House include teas and architectural history programs. Call for specific information.

CHASE-LLOYD HOUSE
410-263-2723.
22 Maryland Ave.,
    Annapolis, MD 21401.
Open: Mon.–Sat., 2:00
    p.m.–4:00 p.m.; closed in
    Jan.–Feb.
Admission: $2.

Samuel Chase, yet another Annapolitan to sign the Declaration, started this house in 1769 — before he became one of the new nation's first Supreme Court justices. Later, Chase sold the home, unfinished, to Edward Lloyd IV, member of a prominent Maryland political dynasty. Inside, the brick mansion is most noted for the spectacular "flying" stairway, which has no visible means of support.

GOVERNMENT HOUSE
410-974-3531.
State & Church Circles,
    Annapolis, MD 21401.
Open: By appt. only,
    Tues.–Thurs., 10:00
    a.m.–2:00 p.m.; during
    legislative session,
    Jan.–mid-Apr., only
    Tues., Thurs.

Maryland's latest governor came to town and promptly restored the old name — "Government House" — to what the previous administration had called the "Governor's Mansion." Built in 1868, the Georgian-style home is filled with Maryland arts and antiques. Arrange tours by appt.

HAMMOND-HARWOOD HOUSE
410-269-1714.
19 Maryland Ave.,
    Annapolis, MD 21401.
Open: Mon.–Sat., 10:00
    a.m.–4:00 p.m.; Sun.,
    12:00 noon–4:00 p.m.;
    tours on the hour, last
    tour at 3:00 p.m.
Admission: Small
    admission fee.

Widely considered one of the nation's finest remaining examples of Georgian architecture, this 1770s center-block house boasts two wings connected by two hyphens, a style known as a five-point Maryland house (a Palladian varietal that turned up only in colonial Maryland). Preserved as a museum since 1926, intricately carved ribbons and roses mark the front entrance. The symmetry is meticulous: false doors balance actual entrances. Inside hang portraits by one-time Annapolitan Charles Willson Peale and furniture by noted Annapolis coffin maker-turned-cabinetmaker John Shaw. Besides the gift shop, also visit

The circa 1774 Hammon-Harwood House, designed by noted architect William Buckland, was built by a young lawyer when he became engaged, but alas, his intended apparently left him, and he never lived there.

the gallery, which shows exhibitions related to the home. Discount tour tickets are available for those who also visit the nearby William Paca House.

MARYLAND STATEHOUSE
410-974-3400.
State Circle, Annapolis, MD 21401.
Open: Mon.–Fri., 9:00 a.m.–5:00 p.m.; Mon.–Fri. tours, 11:00 a.m., 3:00 p.m.; Sat.–Sun. tours, 10:00 a.m., 4:00 p.m.

The first statehouse was built on this hill in 1699; the present building is the third. Fire, the scourge of so many colonial-era buildings, destroyed the first building, but it was replaced in 1705. The second statehouse lasted until 1766, when the government decided to build a more architecturally distinguished capitol building. Marylanders now boast that theirs is the country's oldest state capitol building in continuous use. And, from Nov. 26, 1783-Aug. 13, 1784, the building then standing served as the capitol to a new nation. The Old Senate Chamber where George Washington resigned his commission in the Continental Army in 1783 remains, the legislators' chairs lined up in rows. The Treaty of Paris officially ending the Revolution was ratified here in 1784. Visitors also will see Charles Willson Peale's portrait of Gen. Washington with Marylander Tench Tilghman and the Marquis de Lafayette. (Peale lived in Annapolis for a time). During Maryland's annual, ninety-day legislative session, the General Assembly convenes here. Abundant state travel information is available in the visitor center.

ST. ANNE'S EPISCOPAL CHURCH

410-267-9333 (Parish House; 199 Duke of Gloucester St.)
Church Circle, Annapolis, MD 21401.
Open: Daily; tours by appt.

This is the third church built on this hallowed Annapolis site. Fire destroyed much of the second (1792-1858), but parts of the old building were incorporated when the new church went up in 1859. Many graves in the old churchyard were moved when Church Circle was widened years ago, but the graves of Annapolis's first mayor, Amos Garret, and Maryland's last colonial governor, Sir Robert Eden, remain. Inside is a silver communion service given by King William III, dating from the 1690s.

WILLIAM PACA HOUSE AND GARDEN

410-263-5553, house; 410-267-6656, garden.
186 Prince George St., Annapolis, MD 21401.
Open: Mon.–Sat., 10:00 a.m.–5:00 p.m.; Sun., 12:00 noon–5:00 p.m.; closed Thanksgiving, Christmas Eve, Christmas; winter hours: Fri., Sat., 10:00 a.m.–4:00 p.m.; Sun., 12:00 noon–4:00 p.m.
Admission: Admission fee.

William Paca, three-time colonial governor of Maryland and signer of the Declaration of Independence, built his magnificent Georgian mansion between 1763-1765. Here he entertained during the era known as Annapolis's golden age.

Preservationists always say that they've meticulously restored their buildings, but what they've done here really is amazing. During renovations in the 1960s and 1970s, X rays revealed that two architectural styles found in the main staircase dated to the same era, a mixing and matching apparently chosen by Mr. Paca himself. First-floor antiques date to Paca's residency here, with a few more liberties taken on the second floor, like a nineteenth-century spinet. Early in the twentieth century, the house became the Carvel Hall Hotel. In 1965, high-rise apartments were slated to replace the building. Historic Annapolis, Inc. bought the house and in six weeks' time, convinced the Maryland General Assembly to buy the two-acre garden site in back. Archaeologists set about reconstructing the gardens and knew that they had hit pay dirt when they uncovered an original pond — it promptly refilled from a spring beneath. A must-see for any gardener, the formal, terraced Paca Gardens boast a reconstructed pavilion and Chinese-style bridge. Avid gardeners will want to keep an eye out for the spring and fall plant sales and the opportunity to purchase intriguing species. A discount package is available to those touring the Hammond-Harwood House.

Edgewater

LONDON TOWN HOUSE AND GARDENS

410-222-1919.

Take time to cross the South River Bridge south of Annapolis to visit this old tavern on the

David Trozzo

Sifting for architectural gold at London Town, the former town south of Annapolis where volunteers can work the open digs.

839 Londontown Rd., Edgewater, MD 21037.
S. on Rte. 2 from Annapolis; 1 mi. past South River Bridge, left on Mayo Rd. (Md. 253), 1 mi. to left on Londontown Rd.
Open: Mon.–Sat., 10:00 a.m.–4:00 p.m.; Sun., 12:00 noon–4:00 p.m.; Jan., Feb., Sat., 10:00 a.m.–4:00 p.m.; Sun., 12:00 noon–4:00 p.m.
Admission: $6 adults; $4 seniors; $3 children 7–12; free 6 and under.

banks of the South River and the site of a once booming town. Knowledgeable docents in colonial garb give complete tours of traveling-class life in the eighteenth century. Men of limited means shared beds upstairs; traveling gentleman professionals — an itinerant dentist, for example — had their own rooms while they stayed in town to do business. Notice the clay pipes stored in a box by the hearth in the main drinking room. A pipe was communal property; the smoker merely broke off the end and returned the pipe to the box at the end of the evening. Monthly luncheons and teas; volunteers help with archaeology digs on Sat. during nice weather to help unearth the story of this former colonial port. There are self-guided tours of eight acres of gardens and the largest archaeological dig in the state.

Hollywood

SOTTERLEY PLANTATION
800-681-0850; 301-373-2280.
www.sotterley.com.
9 mi. E. of Leonardtown on Rte. 245, Hollywood, MD 20636

Gaslights flicker at night at this private working plantation on the Patuxent River, where they still raise sheep and up to six acres of crops on the grounds, which include 1.3 miles of trails. An orchard, smokehouse, and slave cabin stand near the manor house, which has been the focus of

Open: Grounds, year-round, Tues.–Sun., 10:00 a.m.–4:00 p.m.; manor house, May–Oct., Tues.–Sun., 10:00 a.m.–4:00 p.m.
Admission: $7 adults; $5 children 6–16; ground fee, $2; group tour rates.

extensive efforts to upgrade in recent years. Begun as a manorial grant issued in 1650 by Lord Baltimore to Thomas Cornwallis, Sotterley's first house was built in 1717 by a wealthy Englishman named James Bowles. The sixth governor of Maryland made the home into the mansion that it is today. Indentured servant Richard Boulton's construction work here so impressed George Washington that the father of our country asked him to help build Mount Vernon. Annual public events include Family Heritage Day in the spring, a celebration of African-American life, and an annual Christmas celebration.

St. Mary's City

Costumed interpreters prepare food at Farthing's Ordinary, St. Mary's City.

David Trozzo

HISTORIC ST. MARY'S CITY
800-SMC-1634;
    301-862-0960.
www.webgraphic.com/
    hsmc.
Rte. 5/P.O. Box, St. Mary's City, MD 20686.
Open: Late Mar.–Nov., Wed.–Sun., 10:00 a.m.–5:00 p.m.
Admission: $7.50 adults; $6 seniors and students; $3.50 children 6-12.

In 1634, newly arrived settlers created Maryland's first capital here. By 1720, the city was gone. Now, researchers unearth tantalizing discoveries about seventeenth-century colonial life — like the find a few years back, when archaeologists exhumed three lead coffins. Given their cost in the late 1600s, surely the coffins belonged to a family of means. Were these the remains of Calvert family members, from Maryland's founding family? In came experts from all disciplines, including NASA scientists who tested to see if seventeenth-century air was trapped inside. Alas, it was not. In the end, the team concluded — "99.9 percent" as one insider said — that the bodies were those of Philip Calvert, the colony's first chancellor; his first wife, Anne Wolsey Calvert; and a six-month-old child whose identity remains unknown, but might have been Philip's child from a second marriage. Archaeology digs are ongoing.

Also at St. Mary's City: Godiah Spray's re-created, seventeenth-century tobacco plantation (complete with a 300-year-old species of pigs called Ossabaws), the 100-acre town green **Governor's Field, Farthing's Ordinary,** a seventeenth-century inn exhibit, the reconstructed **1676 Statehouse,** the *Maryland Dove,* a replica of the type of square-rigged boat that brought supplies for the first colonists, and the **Woodland Indian Hamlet,** with two longhouses (thatched houses on bentwood frames that housed families). Takeout is available at the Farthing's Kitchen. Also, there is the Brome-Howard Country Inn and Restaurant, a circa 1840 house with guest rooms and fine dining. St. Mary's City is wrapped around portions of the **St. Mary's College** campus (see the heading Historic Schools).

NORTHERN NECK/MIDDLE PENINSULA

Westmoreland County, Virginia

Along Pope's Creek stands the George Washington Birthplace National Monument and a re-created house honoring the site near where his father's house once stood.

David Trozzo

GEORGE WASHINGTON BIRTHPLACE NATIONAL MONUMENT
804-224-1732.
Rte. 3 to Rte. 204, 38 mi. E. of Fredericksburg.

It didn't all start at Mount Vernon, as visitors here will soon discover. Colonial history and the Washington family headline the Pope's Creek Plantation complex on Pope's Creek off the Potomac River. The home where Washington was born burned in 1779, but archaeologists have outlined the footprint of the U-shaped house in oyster

Open: Daily, 9:00 a.m.–5:00 p.m.

Admission: $2; free children 16 and under.

shells. The brick Memorial House here was built in the early 1930s. A colonial garden stands alongside, amid a gorgeous stand of cedars. The park, on a creek off the Potomac River, has hiking trails, one of the most delightful waterside picnic areas around (replete with more huge cedars), and a visitor center showing a film about the plantation. Look for special holiday events, such as the Christmas celebration and George Washington's birthday celebration.

STRATFORD HALL PLANTATION
804-493-8038; 804-493-8371, weekends and holidays.
www.stratfordhall.org.
45 mi. E. of Fredericksburg, Rte. 214, Stratford, VA 22558.
Open: Museum, daily, 9:00 a.m.–4:30 p.m.
Admission: $7 adults; $6 seniors; $3 children.

"Light Horse Harry" begat Robert E., the best-known member of the illustrious Lee family. Their historic home features a 1,670-acre working plantation and Great House (circa 1738) and is considered one of the finest museum houses in America. It was built in 1738 by an ancestral Lee named Thomas, one-time acting governor of the colony and father to eight children, including six sons, almost all of whom went on to distinguished careers. Two, Richard Henry Lee and Francis Lightfoot Lee, were the only brothers to sign the Declaration of Independence. "Light Horse Harry," their cousin, was a friend to George Washington and lived here for more than twenty years. Built of brick made on-site and timber hewn nearby, the H-shaped manor house features the twenty-nine-square-foot Great Hall, renowned as one of the finest colonial rooms still in existence. Visitors can see the crib where the Confederate general slept as an infant in 1808. More than three miles of trails lead through the working farm, and at a reconstructed mill, the millstones still grind barley, wheat, and corn, which are sold at the Plantation store. Confederate Gen. Robert E. Lee's birthday is celebrated every Jan. 19. Students of U.S. history will be fascinated to find that the George Washington and Robert E. Lee birthplaces are practically next-door — at least as far as roundabout, country road travel allows.

UPPER EASTERN SHORE

Chestertown

GEDDES-PIPER HOUSE
410-778-3499.
101 Church Alley, Chestertown, MD 21620.
Open: May–Oct., Sat., Sun., 1:00 p.m.–4:00 p.m.
Admission: $2 donation requested.

This three-and-a-half story brick townhouse designed in the "Philadelphia style" was built in the early 1700s. Now the museum headquarters of the Historical Society of Kent County, the home was owned by a series of merchants, including William Geddes, customs collector for the Port of

Chestertown. Geddes claims a notorious local fame — his was the brigantine ravaged during the 1774 Chestertown Tea Party, which is still celebrated (see the heading Seasonal Events & Festivals). Geddes sold the house to merchant James Piper. It now features eighteenth- and nineteenth-century furnishings, maps, china, and library. Private tours can be arranged.

Easton

HISTORICAL SOCIETY OF TALBOT COUNTY
410-822-0773.
25 S. Washington St., Easton, MD 21601.
Open: Tues.–Fri., 11:00 a.m.–3:00 p.m.; Sat., 10:00 a.m.–4:00 p.m.; call for Sun. hours; tours 11:30 a.m., 1:30 p.m.; Jan.–Feb., by appt.
Admission: $3–$5.

The Historical Society of Talbot County collects and exhibits objects and images that tell the story of Talbot County, Md. Of interest in the main building's conference room: photographs capturing Talbot's rural and maritime history. On the grounds stand historic structures representing different periods of local history. Joseph's Cottage (1795) tells the story of an Easton cabinetmaker. The James Neall House (1810), an excellent example of Federal architecture, shows how life changed for the affluent cabinetmaker and his Quaker family after success in the early nineteenth century. The Society's buildings surround a stunning garden based on an eighteenth-century design.

THIRD HAVEN FRIENDS MEETING HOUSE
410-822-0293.
405 S. Washington St., Easton, MD 21601.
Open: Daily, 9:00 a.m.–5:00 p.m.; services Sun., 10:00 a.m.; Wed., 5:30 p.m.

Built from 1682-1684, this Quaker Meeting House is believed to be the oldest frame building in the country continuously used for religious purposes; it is the oldest building in Maryland. Originally located in virgin timber (Easton was not founded until twenty-five years later), the Meeting House is now neatly tucked into a residential street on a sizable seven-acre parcel. Visitors come to stroll through the peaceful grounds and to admire a simple, venerable building that is still in use three centuries after Pennsylvania founder and Quaker William Penn preached here.

Tilghman Island

Skipjack sails once numbered in the hundreds in the Chesapeake Bay, so it's a bittersweet pleasure to spot the distinctive outlines of one of the few remaining ladies that plied the Bay in search of oysters.

Fewer than a dozen skipjacks still work the water, and most of those dock in Tilghman's Dogwood Harbor. (You'll also find a couple of working skipjacks on Deal Island, and several continue to "work" the Bay as ecotour boats.) Get a

Visit the working veterans: skipjacks moor at Dogwood Harbor, Tilghman Island.

David Trozzo

sense of life aboard a skipjack, learn the lore, and "drudge" for oysters by taking a cruise on either its oldest member, the 1886 *Rebecca T. Ruark* (Capt. Wade H. Murphy Jr., 410-886-2176) or its youngest, the 1955 *H.M. Krentz* (Capt. Ed Farley, 410-745-6080), both docked at Dogwood Harbor. Follow Rte. 33 through St. Michaels and over the Tilghman Island drawbridge, then turn left after a bit to reach the harbor.

Wye Mills

WYE GRIST MILL
410-827-6909.
Box 277, Wye Mills, MD 21679.
Rte. 662 off Rte. 50, N. of Easton.
Open: Mid-Apr.–mid-Nov., Mon.–Fri., 10:00 a.m.–1:00 p.m.; Sat., Sun., 10:00 a.m.–4:00 p.m.
Admission: $2 donation suggested.

A gristmill has been grinding cornmeal and flour on this site since 1671, and you can still see the great stone turn by water power on the first and third Sat. of every month. Nonprofit Preservation Maryland and Friends of Wye Mill operate the mill. You can buy a bag of freshly ground meal as a souvenir, with *The Wye Millers Grind*, a 100-recipe cookbook, as a good accompaniment. An exhibit focuses on the glory days of Wye Mill, from 1790-1830, when wheat brought prosperity to the Upper Eastern Shore. Wye Mill is a hotbed of historic sites, all within a few hundred yards of each other. Look for the restored, early

Episcopal Old Wye Church, circa 1717, and Maryland's official state tree, the Wye Oak, now more than 400 years old — mature when Europeans first explored the upper reaches of the Chesapeake Bay! Call 888-400-RSVP for information on any of these sites.

But wait, that's not all. Orrell's Maryland Beaten Biscuits (410-820-8090), the world's only commercial beaten biscuit company, makes the small local delights the old-fashioned way — by beating the dough for thirty to forty-five minutes with a hammer to incorporate air. The result, surprisingly, is flaky and chewy and certainly worth trying. You'll find the flour flying and can take a tour Tues. and Wed., 7:00 a.m.–2:00 p.m., and other days around the busy winter holidays.

LOWER EASTERN SHORE

Cambridge

MEREDITH HOUSE & NEIL MUSEUM
410-228-7953.
902 LaGrange Ave./P.O. Box 361, Cambridge, MD 21613.
Turn E. off U.S. 50 at Maryland Ave., right on Crusader Rd.
Open: Thurs.–Sat., 10:00 a.m.–4:00 p.m.; large groups and bus tours call ahead for appt.
Admission: Free to individuals; large groups and bus tours $2 per person.

This circa 1760 Georgian house with Greek Revival ornamentation is noted for Flemish bond brickwork and its devotion to county history — particularly the local contribution to the governor's mansion. Seven Maryland governors resided in Dorchester County, including Thomas Holiday Hicks, who managed to suppress the state's strong secessionist element to maintain Maryland's Union status. The Neil Museum stands on the grounds, displaying the sickles, scythes, and yokes of the Lower Shore's yeoman class, as well as maritime tools used in oystering and crabbing. Look also — believe it or not — for memorabilia from one-time Cambridge resident Annie Oakley. The Goldsborough Stable (circa 1790), moved from a nearby site, houses a transportation exhibit, and a colonial-style herb garden stands near the Neil Museum.

Lloyds

SPOCOTT WINDMILL
410-228-7090.
Rte. 343, Lloyds, MD 21613.
Open: Daily, 10:00 a.m.–5:00 p.m.
Admission: Donations accepted.

One of the region's most enduring residents, the great boatbuilder James B. "Mr. Jim" Richardson took it upon himself to build this reproduction of a windmill destroyed here during the blizzard of 1888. "Mr. Jim," who passed away in 1989, kept his master builder's wooden boat workshop at his LeCompte Creek boatyard. His windmill, the only post windmill in Maryland, commemorates the eighteen post windmills that once towered over the marshy countryside. Also open to the public are a colonial tenant house (circa 1800) and the 1870 one-room schoolhouse called Castle Haven. Lloyd's County Store Museum has been created as a new addition, open only occasionally.

Princess Anne

TEACKLE MANSION
410-651-2238.
Mansion St., Princess Anne, MD 21853.
Open: Mid-Mar.–mid-Dec., Wed., Sat., Sun., 1:00 p.m.–3:00 p.m.; Dec.–mid-Mar., Sun., 1:00 p.m.–3:00 p.m.; call for appt. at other times.
Admission: $3; children under 12 free.

Back before the Manokin River became so shallow, its deep water encouraged ships to travel upriver. Plantations and ports thrived along its banks, and Teackle Mansion is a well-preserved holdover from that era. Probably the best example of neoclassical architecture on the Lower Eastern Shore, the 1801 Teackle Mansion dominates the town with its 200 feet of pink brick and stylish symmetry. Built by Littleton Dennis Teackle, who moved up from the Eastern Shore of Virginia with his wife, the house boasts his and her dressing rooms on either side of a central high ceiling, multiple stairways, and entrances by river or land. Outside are beautiful gardens. Teackle fell onto hard times and lost nearly everything in the depression of 1821, but his mansion still stands as testament to his one-time wealth.

Salisbury

PEMBERTON HISTORICAL PARK
410-742-1741, Pemberton Hall; 410-860-0447, Wicomico Heritage Centre.
Pemberton Dr., Salisbury, MD 21801.
About 2 mi. S.W. of Rte. 349 & U.S. 50.
Open: Pemberton Hall: Apr.–Oct., Thurs., Sat., 1:00 p.m.–3:00 p.m. and by appt.; Wicomico Heritage Centre: May–Sept., Tues.–Fri., 10:00 a.m.–2:00 p.m.
Admission: Donations accepted.

One of the oldest brick gambrel-roofed houses in Maryland, Pemberton Hall was built in 1741 for Col. Isaac Handy, a plantation owner and shipping magnate who helped found what would become the city of Salisbury. Col. Handy's home is the centerpiece of a museum complex operated by a handful of groups that includes nearby Wicomico Heritage Centre, which was designed to resemble a colonial tobacco barn. It is also the headquarters for the Wicomico Historical Society, with a permanent collection of local history memorabilia and rotating exhibits. Don't skip Pemberton just because you come when the museums are closed. The park features several miles of nature trails through woods and along the Wicomico River, where you may spot a bald eagle or grazing deer. Lovely picnic area. The park hosts the Pemberton Colonial Fair on the last Sat. in Sept.

Snow Hill

**FURNACE TOWN
HISTORIC SITE**
410-632-2032.
3816 Old Furnace Rd.,
Snow Hill, MD 21863.
Off Rte. 12 (Snow Hill Rd.).
Open: Apr. 1–Oct. 31,
Mon.–Sun., 11:00
a.m.–5:00 p.m.
Admission: $3 adults; $2.75
over 60; $1.50 for 18
mos.–high school; does
not include entry to
special events held at
Furnace Town.

The imposing Nassawango Iron Furnace looms over a swamp, a forest, and a small collection of buildings at this quiet echo of the bustling nineteenth-century village that once stood here. From 1832-1847, thousands of people lived and worked around the thirty-five-foot-high hot blast furnace in the forest, digging up bog ore and smelting it into pig iron. Around the remaining furnace stand re-creations of the old ways, including broom making, printing, blacksmithing, weaving, and gardening. There are a museum, a gift shop, a picnic area, exhibit buildings, and many nature trails and boardwalks over the Nassawango Cypress Swamp. Come midweek to have the place almost to yourself, or visit Furnace Town when it's hosting one of many festivals, including the Worcester County Fair in Aug. and the Chesapeake Celtic Festival in Oct.

Onancock, Virginia

KERR PLACE
757-787-8012.
P.O. Box 193, Onancock,
VA 23417.
On Onancock's Main St.,
turn W. off U.S. 13.
Open: Tues.–Sat., 10:00
a.m.–4:00 p.m.; closed
Jan.–Feb.
Admission: $3; children
free.

Prosperous merchant John Shepherd Her (original spelling) had the Kerr Place built in 1799 in the port town of Onancock. The elegant Federal house has been restored as a museum and the home of the Eastern Shore of Virginia Historical Society. Through period decorative arts, furnishings, and exhibits, Kerr Place enables visitors to catch a glimpse of eighteenth-century Virginia plantation life. Bus tours welcome; call ahead.

HISTORIC SCHOOLS

ANNAPOLIS/WESTERN SHORE

Annapolis

The "Johnnies," as students at **St. John's College** are called, study only the Great Books during their years here, where intellect is greatly valued and humor tends toward plays on Greek or Latin phrases. The college, descended from King William's School in 1696, claims to be the nation's third oldest. On campus, look for the centuries-old Liberty Tree, where the Sons of Liberty met to dispel any hint of closed-door politics. The oldest building on campus, McDowell Hall, houses the venerable Great Hall, where contemporary college students hold waltz parties (and the students really do waltz), a banquet was tossed for the aging General Lafayette in 1824, and a hospital was set up during the Civil War. The 1934 Maryland Archives building now houses the college library. While visitors are welcome to walk around the campus, those interested in learning more about the school's history are best advised to take a tour with one of the organized tour groups. Contact: St. John's College, 60 College Ave., Annapolis, MD 21401; 410-263-2371; www.sjca.edu.

The yin and yang of Annapolitan collegiality, at the annual croquet match between St. John's College and the U.S. Naval Academy.

David Trozzo

For many in the U.S., "Annapolis" and "U.S. Naval Academy" are synonyms. Although the locals would beg to differ, none would disagree that the **U.S. Naval Academy** has had great influence on the city. Founded in 1845 at old Fort Severn, the Academy's long history includes its notable move from Annapolis to Newport, RI, during the Civil War, prompted by the Maryland city's overwhelming southern sympathies. During the war, both the Academy and St. John's College up the street became military hospitals. Upon their return, naval officers found the campus in great need of military spit-shine. "It was quite a mess," said Academy museum curator Jim Cheevers. "The cavalry horses had eaten the leaves off the willow trees, and in the superintendent's quarters were beer bottles and pool tables. So commenced plans for a "new Academy," the collection of Beaux Arts buildings designed by architect Ernest Flagg and constructed between 1899–1908.

Inside the **Academy Chapel,** begun in 1904, is the final resting place of "Father of the U.S. Navy," John Paul Jones. Jones was finally entombed in 1913 after a fantastic journey. He was buried in Paris in 1792, but his grave was lost in the turmoil of the French Revolution as the cemetery, owned by the House of Bourbon, was seized, sold by the Revolutionary government, and later developed. After a concerted search, Jones's tomb was rediscovered 100 years later. Following much politicking, it was determined that the admiral should be laid to rest in the Academy Chapel — then still under construction. The casket arrived at the Academy in 1906. "The midshipmen carried the casket into the newly finished Bancroft Hall, put it under the grand staircase that leads to Memorial Hall, and there the casket sat . . . for seven years," said Cheevers. Visitors won't want to miss the admiral's spectacular marble sarcophagus downstairs. Enter from the outside, beneath the chapel, and look for the names of the seven ships that Jones commanded, which are inscribed in the floor circling the tomb. Open Mon.–Sun., 9:00 a.m.–4:00 p.m.; closed Thanksgiving, Christmas, New Year's Day, weddings, funerals, military events.

David Trozzo

The Blue Angels fly over Annapolis in honor of the U.S. Naval Academy commencement each spring.

Visitors also might want to catch a glimpse of the brigade at full military attention. Noon meal formations are held Mon.–Fri., 12:05 p.m.; Thurs., 12:15 p.m. in front of Bancroft Hall (the nation's largest college dormitory) from Mar.–Oct., as long as it's not a holiday, exam time, or other special event. Dress parades are held on Worden Field in the spring and fall. For times and dates, contact: 410-263-6933.

Visitors enter the academy grounds at Gate 1, at the foot of King George St., then head to the Armel-Leftwich Visitor Center, next to the Halsey Field House (52 King George St., Annapolis, MD 21402). Highlights on the grounds include **Bancroft Hall,** where the rotunda looks out on one of the best Bay views in town, and the **Academy Museum** in Preble Hall, home to the notable Henry Huddleston Rogers Ship Model Collection, 108 models of British and French sailing ships built from 1650-1850. Also, the Beverly Robinson Collection of naval prints includes 5,000 images of every naval engagement from the thirteenth century to the Spanish-American War. Academy tours daily, contact: 410-293-6933. Call the Academy Museum (410-293-2108; www.usna.navy.mil; Mon.–Sat., 9:00 a.m.–5:00 p.m.; Sun., 11:00 a.m.–5:00 p.m.) and ask for their new visitor's guide, which provides a broad range of information, including historical thumbnails of the buildings, as well as practical information regarding rules inside "The Yard."

St. Mary's City

St. Mary's College was established at St. Mary's City in 1840 to commemorate the legacy of the colonial achievements of Maryland's first settlers. The small liberal arts institution is one of two public honors colleges in the country and is set on a beautiful Potomac riverside campus on the grounds of Maryland's first settlement and capital. Its reputation as a well-kept secret may be out, however, because national magazines have discovered it in their various rankings. The campus includes a number of historic buildings and gardens. Contact: St. Mary's College, St. Mary's City, MD 20686; 301-862-0380; www.smcm.edu.

UPPER EASTERN SHORE

Chestertown

The father of our country gave express permission for use of his name, contributed fifty guineas to its 1782 founding, and served six years on the Board of Visitors and Governors of **Washington College.** This small liberal arts college is known for its creative writing program and the Sophie Kerr Prize (at $40,000 in 1999, the largest undergraduate literary prize in the country). Beautiful grounds and an active Chestertown resident. Contact: Washington College, 300 Washington Ave., Chestertown, MD 21620; 410-778-2800.

LIBRARIES

ANNAPOLIS/WESTERN SHORE

Interested in learning more about the Chesapeake or maybe your family's genealogical past? In *Annapolis,* visit the **Maryland State Archives** (350

Rowe Blvd.; 410-974-3914) to peruse 7,509 different series of records, from vital statistics to church registers, including many from the Roman Catholic Archdiocese in Baltimore. Here author Alex Halley of *Roots* fame found his African ancestor, the slave Kunta Kinte, after local historian and longtime archivist Phoebe Jacobsen figured out how to use manumissions and other documents of slaveholders to help African-Americans trace their pasts. Tues.–Fri., 8:00 a.m.–4:30 p.m.; Sat., 8:30 a.m.–12:00 noon, 1:00 p.m.–4:30 p.m.; call for registration information. Also, visit the **Anne Arundel County Public Library** (1410 West St.; 410-222-1750) for its excellent section of books on Maryland and Chesapeake history, including many works by local writers. Mon.–Thurs., 9:00 a.m.–9:00 p.m.; Fri.–Sat., 9:00 a.m.–5:00 p.m.; Sun., 1:00 p.m.–5:00 p.m.

NORTHERN NECK/MIDDLE PENINSULA

The long-settled Northern Neck offers a couple of good places to spend time on historical research. In *Heathsville, Virginia,* the **Northumberland County Historical Society** (Rte. 360/P.O. Box 221; 804-580-8581) offers a collection of genealogical and historical documents. Tues.–Thurs., 9:00 a.m.–4:00 p.m.; Sat., by appt. Also, the **Mary Ball Washington Museum and Library** (8346 Mary Ball Rd./P.O. Box 97; 804-462-7280) in *Lancaster, Virginia,* offers a historical lending collection, genealogical sources, and research facilities, including an extensive collection of Lancaster County records dating to 1651. Named for the mother of our country's father, this complex also offers five buildings that host changing shows about the lower Northern Neck. Wed.-Fri., 10:00 a.m.–5:00 p.m.; Sat., 10:00 a.m.–3:00 p.m. or by appt.

UPPER EASTERN SHORE

The **Kent County Public Library** (410-778-3636) has a main branch in *Chestertown.* The **Historical Society of Kent County** headquarters (410-778-3499; call ahead) are at the Geddes-Piper House, also in Chestertown, with a library that contains historic site surveys, genealogical records, and documents.

The **Queen Annes County Free Libraries** in *Centreville* (410-758-0980) and *Kent Island* (410-643-8161) have a good reputation when it comes to helping users with research questions.

The **Talbot County Free Library** (410-822-1626) in *Easton* houses the Maryland Room, a research facility filled with books and periodicals (some on microfiche) about the area. Talbot also has a library branch (410-745-5877) in *St. Michaels.* Also in St. Michaels, the **Chesapeake Bay Maritime Museum** maintains the **Chapelle Memorial Library** (410-745-2916; call ahead), devoted to maritime and Chesapeake writings and named for the famed naval architect and historian.

LOWER EASTERN SHORE

The **Dorchester County Library's** Maryland Room, in its main branch in *Cambridge* (410 228-7331) offers reference works on regional and state history. In *Salisbury,* the **Edward H. Nabb Research Center** (410-543-6312; call ahead) for Delmarva History and Culture at Salisbury State University, in the Power Professional Building, is a gold mine of documents, maps, and archives going way back. Here also is the Dryden Collection of genealogical records of the Lower Eastern Shore and research into Native American and colonial life. The **Wicomico County Free Library** (410-749-3612) in Salisbury also has a large Maryland Room.

The main branch of the **Somerset County Library** (410-651-0852) in the little town of *Princess Anne* has genealogy on Somerset. Maryland and regional history, as well as genealogical data, can be researched in the Worcester Room of the **Worcester County Library** (410-632-2600) in *Snow Hill.* The **Eastern Shore Public Library** (757-787-3400) in *Accomac, Virginia,* has a genealogy room with historical materials. The microfilm is available on a first-come, first-served basis, so you can use it all day once you have it. Open Mon.–Sat.; genealogy room closed Fri.

MUSEUMS

HEAD OF THE BAY

Chesapeake City

C&D CANAL MUSEUM
410-885-5621.
815 Bethel Rd., Chesapeake City, MD 21915.
Open: Year-round, Mon.–Sat., 8:00 a.m.–4:00 p.m.
Admission: Free.

The fourteen-mile-long Chesapeake and Delaware Canal severs the top of the Delmarva Peninsula from the mainland, linking the Upper Chesapeake Bay with the Delaware River. In so doing, the grand old C&D shaves 300 miles off an otherwise round-about journey from Philadelphia to Baltimore by way of Norfolk and the Virginia capes. The canal was discussed for 150 years before it finally was dug by 2,600 men in the 1820s, a project that then cost a whopping $2.5 million. The canal opened in 1829. Photos, models, maps, and a thirty-eight-foot, nineteenth-century waterwheel, at the time considered a marvel of engineering, are on display at the tiny museum — the former pump house for the old locks. Interactive exhibits and a TV monitor let you track the location of ships headed through the canal. Run by the U.S. Army Corps of Engineers, who operate the canal.

Havre de Grace

Famed decoy carver Capt. Harry R. Jobes lives on at the Havre de Grace Decoy Museum.

David Trozzo

**HAVRE DE GRACE
   DECOY MUSEUM**
410-939-3739.
www.decoymuseum.com.
Giles & Market Sts., Havre
   de Grace, MD 21078.
Open: Daily, 11:00
   a.m.–4:00 p.m.; closed
   holidays.
Admission: $4 adults;
   $2 seniors and students
   9–18.
Handicap Access: Yes.

So you want to know about decoy carving? You've come to the right place, where visitors immediately discover a proud piece of the past of this growing little tourist/sailing town. The museum is dedicated to preserving the Bay's old "gunning" tradition, the art of hunting with decoys. Works by noted carvers R. Madison Mitchell, Bob McGaw, Paul Gibson, and Charlies Joiner and Bryant are exhibited here, as well as tools of the trade and displays, recalling the early twentieth-century days when they gathered around the stove. Perhaps most intriguing is a peek into why conservation measures have become so important: the sinkbox. This clever contraption was outlawed in the mid-1930s — "because it was too effective," — chuckled a longtime Chesapeake outdoor enthusiast. Shaped like a bathtub with square wings weighted down with flat-bottomed decoys, the sinkbox held a hunter who climbed inside and took to the duck hunt at the Susquehanna Flats. The Flats were famous in drawing the rich and famous from Baltimore, Washington, D.C., and Philadelphia. But in the 1940s, the river's wild rice and wild celery disappeared — and so did the Flats. Now, Mitchell's actual carving shop has become an exhibition, and, in a separate museum workshop, carvers demonstrate their craft and the modern evolution of this old tradition. Nice book/gift shop features duck and decoy books. On the first weekend in May, enjoy the Annual Decoy, Wildlife Art, and Sportsman Festival.

ANNAPOLIS/WESTERN SHORE

Annapolis

**BANNEKER-DOUGLASS
MUSEUM OF
AFRICAN-AMERICAN
LIFE AND HISTORY**
410-974-2893.
84 Franklin St., Annapolis,
MD 21401.
Open: Tues.–Fri., 10:00
a.m.–3:00 p.m.; Sat., 12:00
noon–4:00 p.m.
Admission: Free.

Victorian Mount Moriah African Methodist Episcopal Church, built in 1874, stood amid what was the historic district's black neighborhood going back to the mid-nineteenth century. Now named for two prominent black Marylanders, Frederick Douglass and Benjamin Banneker, it's Maryland's African-American museum. A range of exhibitions includes a recent exhibition on the pre-civil rights era. Annual celebrations include Kwanza and Juneteenth.

Solomons

**CALVERT MARINE
MUSEUM**
410-326-2042.
Rte. 2/P.O. Box 97,
Solomons, MD 20688.
Open: Daily, 10:00
a.m.–5:00 p.m.
Admission: $5 adults;
$4 seniors; $2 children
5–12.
Handicap Access: Yes.

The tale of the Patuxent River and Chesapeake marine life is told in all its chapters here, from the recently historic to the prehistoric — down to crocodile jaws and the teeth of mastodons and other fossilized Miocene era creatures dug from nearby Calvert Cliffs. Visitors take a spin through the post-war recreational industry and see boats built by Solomons' M.M. Davis & Sons Shipyard or harken back to the days of tobacco. Learn also about the estuarine life of the river, and see river otters in their tank. Behind the museum stands the **Drum Point Lighthouse,** one of only three remaining screw-pile lighthouses. Forty-three of these distinctly Chesapeake-designed sentinels once stood in the soft bottom of the Bay, warning mariners off dangerous shoals. When threatened by wreckers in 1975, the lighthouse was moved to the museum from Drum Point, a few miles north. Visitors can see the cozily re-created lighthouse keeper's home or go aboard the *William B. Tennison,* an 1899 sailing "bugeye," a classic Chesapeake workboat (May–Oct., Wed.-Sun., $5 adults; $3 children).

Down the street, the 1934 J.C. Lore Oyster House shows visitors how oysters moved from tongers' boats to gourmets' plates. Watch for family events and good concerts, featuring talent like Nils Lofgren or the Neville Brothers.

NORTHERN NECK/MIDDLE PENINSULA

Reedville, Virginia

REEDVILLE FISHERMEN'S MUSEUM
804-453-6529.
504 Main St., Reedville, VA 22539.
Open: Daily, 10:30 a.m.–4:30 p.m. in summer; call for winter hours.
Admission: $2; children under 12 free.
Handicap Access: Yes.

Reedville is still a little fishing village, where a menhaden plant emits what old-timers call "the smell of money." Stop in at this little museum and gift shop, originally culled from neighborhood attics and homesteads, to view a photographic explanation of purse seining for menhaden or to see the restored 1922 "buyboat," as the boats that went around purchasing oysters from skipjacks were called. Appropriately enough, visitors have been known to arrive here by water, rowing or motoring in by dinghy to the museum dock.

UPPER EASTERN SHORE

Kennedyville

KENT FARM MUSEUM
410-348-5721.
Turner's Creek Rd., Kennedyville, MD 21645.
Open: Mid-May–mid-Oct., 1st & 3rd Sat., 10:00 a.m.–3:00 p.m.; tours by appt.
Admission: Free.

Explore the working past of this largely agricultural area at the Kent Farm Museum, which houses antiques, old agricultural machinery, and other artifacts of rural life. Special programs like rug making and threshing are occasionally offered. You'll find bucolic countryside, with walking trails and abundant wildlife thanks to the nearby 147-acre Turner's Creek Park and the 1,000-acre Sassafras Natural Resource Management Area (open dawn–dusk year-round). For information on Turner's Creek Park, contact: 410-778-1948; on Sassafras Natural RMA, contact: 410-820-1668.

Rock Hall

ROCK HALL MUSEUM
410-778-1399.
S. Main St., Rock Hall, MD 21661.
Open: Daily, Apr.–Oct.; mostly weekend hours at other times of year, call ahead.
Admission: Free.

Schoolteacher Audrey Johnson, formally known as "Miss Audrey," decided back in 1957 that Rock Hall ought to have a museum showcasing its life and culture. She took anything people would donate — old waterman's gear, agate ware, boat models, and more than 2,000 Indian artifacts (many of which she found herself) — and turned it into a collection. Once located in the town's municipal building, the Rock Hall Museum recently moved to the Shoppes at Oyster Court. Miss Audrey, well into her eighties, may even show you around, and she'll open the museum for you if she's not busy.

ROCK HALL WATERMAN'S MUSEUM
410-778-6697.
20880 Rock Hall Ave.,
Haven Harbour Marina,
Rock Hall, MD 21661.
Open: Daily, 10:00
a.m.–4:30 p.m. (honor
system: pick up key at
The Ditty Bag store).
Admission: Free.

Many visitors know Rock Hall as a sailing and boating center, but its real roots as a watermen's community are celebrated at this charming museum in an old waterman's shanty. Inside you'll find tools of the trade for oystering, crabbing, and fishing, photographs, local carvings, and boats. The museum has ambitious expansion plans, so in the coming years, you'll see more authentic workboats at its pier.

St. Michaels

Preserving the past: Richard Scofield, the Chesapeake Bay Maritime Museum's assistant boat shop manager, applies a coat of varnish to the mast of the classic, log-hull bugeye Edna E. Lockwood, *built in 1889. The Hoopers Straight Lighthouse, an 1879 screw-pile light, stands sentinel in the background.*

David Trozzo

CHESAPEAKE BAY MARITIME MUSEUM
410-745-2916.

The world's largest fleet of indigenous Bay workboats tells the story of the watermen's his-

www.cbmm.org.
Mill St., Navy Point, St.
   Michaels, MD 21663.
Open: Year-round, daily,
   summer 9:00 a.m.–6:00
   p.m.; spring/fall 9:00
   a.m.–5:00 p.m.; winter
   9:00 a.m.–4:00 p.m.
Admission: $7.50 adults;
   $6.50 seniors; $3 children
   6–17.

tory — and indeed of the Chesapeake Bay itself. Among the eighty-five vessels are the *Rosie Parks,* a famous skipjack; the *Edna E. Lockwood,* the last log-hull bugeye still plying the Bay; and the *Old Point,* a crab dredger from Virginia. The eighteen-acre complex on the shores of Navy Point comprises twenty-three buildings, nine of them devoted to exhibits on the bay's geological, social, economic, and maritime history, from the age of sail and steamboats to the advent of gas and diesel engines.

Find everything from a Native American dugout to a five-log, oyster tonger in the Small Boat Shed or craftspeople demonstrations in the Boat Shop. The screw-pile Hooper Strait Lighthouse moved here in 1966. Inside, the lighthouse keeper's late nineteenth-century life is re-created, and everyone stops for the prime view of the Miles River. Also displayed are the massive punt guns used by the market gunners, as well as a huge collection of the decoys used by all waterfowl hunters. There's the waterman's work life exhibit in warm weather, Tolchester Beach Bandstand with summer concerts, including sea chanty men, and many boat-related festivities (see the heading Seasonal Events & Festivals). Also, the gift shop offers a range of nautical items, as well as maritime and Chesapeake books.

The new vehicle entrance on Talbot St. incorporates another Bay artifact: the Knapps Narrows drawbridge, which served as the gateway to Tilghman Island for sixty-four years until 1998. The bridge was moved to St. Michaels and positioned partially open so that motorists could see the same view that boaters saw during the bridge's many years of service.

LOWER EASTERN SHORE

Cambridge

**RICHARDSON
   MARITIME MUSEUM**
410-221-1871.
401 High St., Cambridge,
   MD 21613.
Open: Apr.–Oct., Wed.,
   Sat., Sun., 1:00 p.m.–4:00
   p.m.; or by appt.
Admission: Donations
   accepted.

Dorchester County's maritime history and the accomplishments of Capt. Jim Richardson are celebrated in this museum, located in a former bank. Richardson built the Spocott Windmill and *The Dove,* floating at St. Marys City, and his craft is highlighted here. You'll also find a waterman's dock exhibit, examples of Bay boats, and a photo history on the building of a new skipjack, the *Nathan of Dorchester.* Folks in the museum are knowledgeable and eager to educate visitors.

Crisfield

J. MILLARD TAWES MUSEUM
410-968-2501.
Somers Cove Marina,
Crisfield, MD 21817.
Open: Mon.–Fri., 9:00
a.m.–4:30 p.m.; Mem.
Day–Labor Day, Sat.,
Sun., 10:00 a.m.–3:00 p.m.
Admission: $2.50.

Crisfield has a wealth of history, from a Maryland governor to watermen's ways to the most famous pair of decoy carvers that the world has ever known. All are featured at the J. Millard Tawes Museum, named for the Crisfielder who ascended to the statehouse in the '60s. You'll find Native American artifacts, cultural and natural history of the Tangier Sound area, crabbing and oystering tools, and plenty on Lem and Steve Ward. The famed carvers lived and worked at a house "Down Neck" on Sackertown Road, which was recently restored and turned into a museum. Gov. Tawes' birthplace, in the middle of town, is a modest museum, library, and archive.

Hudson's Corner

EARLY AMERICANA MUSEUM
410-623-8324.
30195 Rehobeth Rd.,
Marion Station,
Hudson's Corner, MD
21853.
Southbound on U.S. 13 out
of Salisbury, go right on
Md. 413 and then left on
Old Westover Rd. to
Hudson's Corner.
Open: Apr. 1–Oct. 31; call
for appt.
Admission: Donations
accepted.

Lawrence Burgess is in his nineties now so he doesn't open his personal museum of twentieth-century life as much as he used to, but you'll still find him here nearly every afternoon from spring to fall. This museum is the ultimate attic exploration, which even the Smithsonian has been to see, housed in a collection of ex-chicken houses. What at first seems overwhelming becomes a delight when a visitor recognizes a toy or book from childhood. There's also lots of farm equipment and household junk.

Salisbury

WARD MUSEUM OF WILDFOWL ART
410-742-4988.
909 S. Schumaker Dr.,
Salisbury, MD 21801.
Open: Mon.–Sat., 10:00
a.m.–5:00 p.m.; Sun.,
12:00 noon–5:00 p.m.
Admission: $7 adults; $5
seniors; $3 students; $17
family; Sun. discounts,
$8.50 family.

The legendary Ward brothers, Lem and Steve, elevated the pragmatic craft of decoy carving to artistry, and their name symbolizes the decoy-as-art-form around here. This may be the region's most extensive public collection of antique decoys. The evolution of decoys is traced from the Native American's functional, twisted-reed renderings to the latest lifelike wooden sculpture. View the personal collection of the Ward brothers, including their own favorites among their earliest and latest efforts. The Ward Foundation was established in 1968 and holds the annual World Championship Carving Competition and a wildlife art exhibition and sale. The building and gift shop are on a four-acre site, over-looking a pond.

Snow Hill

JULIA A. PURNELL MUSEUM
410-632-0515.
208 W. Market St., Snow Hill, MD 21863.
Open: Apr.–Oct., Tues.–Sat., 10:00 a.m.–4:00 p.m.; tours by appt. in off-season.
Admission: $2 adults; $.50 children.

At the age of eighty-five, Snow Hill native Julia A. Purnell (1843-1943) fell and broke her hip. In place of her former active lifestyle, she completed more than 2,000 needlepoint pieces, documenting Worcester County's homes, churches, and gardens. Her son, William, was so proud that he opened a museum of her work one year before her death. The place is informally known as "the attic of Worcester County" for all of the everyday items and artifacts that it holds. About five percent of what is on display is the lady's original work.

Parksley, Virginia

EASTERN SHORE RAILWAY MUSEUM
757-665-RAIL.
18468 Dunne Ave./P.O. Box 135, Parksley, VA 23421.
Turn W. off U.S. 13 onto Rte. 176, turn right before railroad tracks.
Open: Mon.–Sat., 10:00 a.m.–4:00 p.m.; Sun., 1:00 p.m.–4:00 p.m.; closed Wed. Nov.-Mar.
Admission: $2 adults; children free.

Before the Chesapeake Bay Bridge in the west and the Chesapeake Bay Bridge-Tunnel in the south opened the peninsula for travelers coming by car, most people and goods came to Delmarva from the north by train. The Eastern Shore Railway Museum celebrates the area's rail heritage with model trains, railcars, and railway artifacts, including a turn-of-the-century, crossing guard shanty.

MUSIC

From chamber concert series to opera to jazz, any music lover will hear fine performances. See also the heading Performing Arts & Theater for information about additional happenings.

ANNAPOLIS/WESTERN SHORE

Annapolis

ANNAPOLIS CHORALE
410-263-1906.
Maryland Hall for the
  Creative Arts, 801 Chase
  St., Ste. 304, Annapolis,
  MD 21401.
Tickets: $20–$30.

The 150-voice chorale, which has performed at Carnegie Hall, includes the smaller Chamber Chorus and the Annapolis Chamber Orchestra. Several performances are given each year, with programs ranging from classical, including baroque, to pops ("Mozart, Motown, and More"). A local favorite is the annual Christmas performance, where a high-profile celebrity, thriller author Tom Clancy, a local, for example, narrates a performance. Concerts are held at Maryland Hall and occasionally at St. Anne's Episcopal Church — always home to the annual *Messiah*. Conductor J. Ernest Green has been with this group for some years now.

ANNAPOLIS OPERA
410-267-8135.
Maryland Hall for the
  Creative Arts, 801 Chase
  St., Ste. 304, Annapolis,
  MD 21401.
Tickets: $35 and $40 for
  major productions.

The Opera stages one major performance, such as *Tosca,* plus an annual vocal competition. In addition, aria lovers can catch such performances as "Mozart by Candlelight" at the historic Carroll House in Dec., or an al fresco performance at the annual spring opening of Quiet Waters Park in Annapolis. There are family operas, too.

**ANNAPOLIS SYMPHONY
  ORCHESTRA**
410-263-0907, tickets; 410-
  269-1132, administration.
Maryland Hall for the
  Creative Arts, 801 Chase
  St., Ste. 304, Annapolis,
  MD 21401.
Season: Sept.–May.
Tickets: $20–$29; $7
  students; family concerts:
  $6 children; $10 adults.

A five-concert symphonic series and holiday pops concert mark the annual calendar of this venerable orchestra, which recently acquired a new musical director, Leslie B. Dunner. Alternating conductors direct pieces ranging from Brahms First Piano Concerto to Rossini's Overture to *L'Italiana in Algeri.* Occasional al fresco performances are given in local parks. Sat. tickets usually are given to subscription holders, so call early if you hope to attend that night. Popular, annual children's concert series.

**NAVAL ACADEMY
  MUSICAL
  PERFORMANCES**
800-US-4-NAVY; 410-268-
  6060, tickets; 410-293-
  2439, information.
U.S. Naval Academy, Music
  Dept., Alumni Hall,
  Annapolis, MD 21401.
Tickets: $6–$25.

Whatever you do, don't pass up a chance to hear a performance in the exquisite Naval Academy Chapel. Now in the hands of Julliard-trained organist Monte Maxwell, these are not your grandma's organ recitals. In addition, the **Distinguished Artist Series** brings in about four productions a year offered by traveling groups, such as the London City Opera or the St. Petersburg (Russia) State Symphony, plus a choral concert by the academy's Glee Club performing with the Annapolis Symphony. Performances are held in the Bob Hope Performing Arts Center in Alumni Hall, where an acoustic shell is lowered into the basketball arena. Visitors hoping to attend a performance, take note: the series is heavily subscribed and is aimed at the Brigade of Midshipmen. Public tickets go on sale two weeks prior to show time.

The academy Glee Club is famous for its annual *Messiah,* performed with the Hood College Choir and soloists from the New York Metropolitan Opera. Also, the Masqueraders theatrical club is known for an annual winter musical, such as *1776* or *A Few Good Men.*

The Naval Academy provides another very popular offering: the **Summer Serenade Concert Series** (Tues., 7:30 p.m. in the summer). It's fun, casual, and free. Folks bring chairs and blankets to the City Dock, settle in, and listen to the USNA band perform everything from Broadway to the blues. In addition, the **U.S. Naval Academy Band** offers its own concerts, such as a Chamber Music Series. Free and open to the public. Contact: 410-293-0263; 410-293-1262.

NORTHERN NECK/MIDDLE PENINSULA

Gloucester, Virginia

CONCERTS ON THE GREEN
804-693-2355.
Gloucester County Parks and Recreation Dept., Gloucester, VA 23061.
Season: Jun., Jul., Aug.

Summer evenings in Gloucester bring Concerts on the Green at the Courthouse Green. Bring a chair or blanket and enjoy jazz or big band, performed by groups like the traveling Army and Navy bands.

Kilmarnock, Virginia

RAPPAHANNOCK FOUNDATION FOR THE ARTS
804-435-0292.
P.O. Box 459, Kilmarnock, VA 22482.
Tickets: $75 for subscription in 1998–1999 season; about $20 per individual performance.

The community's arts supporters — bringing programs to the schools and supporting visual artists — also bring a six-performance series featuring professional artists to the Northern Neck from fall to spring. Recent shows have included Gershwin music from a trio from the south of France. There is also an annual concert by the Virginia Symphony, dance, and other performances, too. Because the series is virtually fully subscribed, call for ticket cancellations, which are often available, or call for a schedule in the spring if you're planning to be in the area. Performances held at the Lancaster County Middle School (191 School St.).

Mathews, Virginia

DONK'S THEATER
804-725-7760.
P.O. Box 284, Mathews, VA 23109.
Located at the intersection of Rtes 198 & 223 in Hudgins.
Tickets: $10; $2 children under 12.

Home of Virginia's "Li'l Ole Opry," this is Tidewater's capital of country music. Hometown musicians and stars alike show up on stage. "We've had the big ones," says Harriet Smith Farmer, one of the many Smith family who lease the place. "We had Dolly. She was here in 1977." The former movie theater is an appropriate venue for families (no alcohol sold), who may want to check out the Smith Family Christmas Show the first week of Dec. Number of musical Smiths? "It's a bunch," says Harriet. Shows every other Sat. night.

UPPER EASTERN SHORE

Centreville

QUEEN ANNES COUNTY ARTS COUNCIL
410-758-2520.
206 S. Commerce St./P.O. Box 218, Centreville, MD 21617.
Season: Year-round.

The Arts Council sponsors a variety of regional events at various locations, including summer Concerts in the Park, featuring top-grade regional talent (Jun.–Aug., Thurs., 7:00 p.m.). Also, check out the Commerce Street Coffee House at the council headquarters (Oct.–Apr., Thurs., 7:00 p.m.; $5 adults; $3 students under 18).

Chestertown

WASHINGTON COLLEGE CONCERT SERIES
410-778-7849.
300 Washington Ave., Chestertown, MD 21620.
Season: Sept.–early May.
Tickets: Call for ticket prices and schedule.

The popular Washington College Concert Series is pushing the half-century mark. The annual five-concert series features such performers as Peter Schickele (aka P.D.Q. Bach), The American Boychoir, and the madrigal group Chanticleer, appearing in the Gibson Performing Arts Center.

Easton

EASTERN SHORE CHAMBER MUSIC FESTIVAL
410-819-0380.

Since 1986, J. Lawrie Bloom, principal clarinetist with the Chicago Symphony Orchestra, has brought in a host of top young names on the inter-

P.O. Box 461, Easton, MD 21601.
Season: Two consecutive weekends in mid-Jun.
Tickets: $12–$25; subscription packages available.

national concert circuit for a week of performances at various Talbot County locations. For audiences, it's a week of chamber music at its finest. For the musicians, including Bloom, whose parents live here, it's a busman's holiday of sorts. The Mendelssohn String Quartet are regulars, and the rest of the talent roster is always equally impressive. Performances are usually held at the Avalon, Wye Plantation, and a private estate on the Miles River.

LOWER EASTERN SHORE

Salisbury

SALISBURY SYMPHONY ORCHESTRA
410-543-ARTS; 410-548-5587.
SSU, Dept. of Music, Salisbury, MD 21801.
Season: Winter and spring concerts; occasional special events.
Tickets: Prices vary; call for information.

Based at Salisbury State University and funded by both the Salisbury Wicomico Arts Council and the MD State Arts Council, the Salisbury Symphony Orchestra performs two major concerts a year in Holloway Hall Auditorium, including a special holiday performance in Dec. and a spring concert in May. The SSO membership includes faculty, students, professionals, and community players and enjoys enthusiastic regional support.

NIGHTLIFE

HEAD OF THE BAY

Chesapeake City has always enjoyed an interesting paradox. It's small and seemingly remote, but ships from all corners of the globe pass by on the bustling C&D Canal. Applaud the Caribbean flavor brought by calypso combos that play from Mother's Day to Labor Day at the dockside terrace of **Schaefer's Canal House** (off Rte. 213 on the north side of the canal; 410-885-2200). The owner of Schaefer's, we're told, travels to the Islands to book talent for his popular, summertime Caribbean fiestas.

ANNAPOLIS/WESTERN SHORE

Nighttime in *Annapolis* means folks head for City Dock, where places that are quaint colonial taverns at lunchtime open their doors to the music and tourist scene at night. Summer weekends can be mobbed, but even locals try to slip in one night down there to soak up the warm breezes off the water. Over the Spa Creek Bridge is Eastport, a hotbed of sailors and some good places to grab a drink.

The hottest local ticket may be the **Ram's Head Tavern** (33 West St.; 410-268-4545), home to the **Fordham Brewing Co.** microbrewery, and also host to the biggest name bands in town, like Eddie from Ohio, Fairport Convention, and Tony Rice & Peter Rowan (see Chapter Four, *Restaurants & Food Purveyors*). Also in this block is **49 West Wine Bar and Gallery** (49 West St.; 410-626-9796), a European coffee-bar-style café gaining popularity with its regular art openings, poetry readings, and range of jazz or classical music (see Chapter Four, *Restaurants & Food Purveyors*).

A favorite cozy brick pub located downstairs at the Maryland Inn is the tiny **Drummer's Lot,** a terrific spot for a quiet drink, next to the **King of France Tavern** (410-216-6340), a jazz club where local favorite Charlie Byrd still plays. Free blues on Sunday nights.

One of the best places for a romantic drink is the waterside bar at the **Chart House** (300 2nd St.; 410-268-7166) in *Eastport.* Big windows onto the water give a great view of Annapolis Harbor, and a copper-topped fireplace dominates the room. Also in Eastport is the bar at **Carrol's Creek Cafe** (410 Severn Ave.; 410-263-8102), with lots of local comraderie. Go for drinks on the patio in the summer.

Pubs ring City Dock, and many offer live music. **Armadillos** (132 Dock St.; 410-268-6680) brings weekend bands. Just up the street **Acme Bar and Grill** (163 Main St.; 410-280-6486) now has mostly acoustic music, primarily during the week. **Middleton Tavern** (2 Market Space; 410-263-3323), an eighteenth-century watering hole, apparently drew `em in then the way it does now. The patio overlooking the City Dock scene is the best summer people-watching spot in town; acoustic music most nights, piano bar upstairs. **McGarvey's Saloon** (8 Market Space; 410-263-5700) brings an uptown saloon flavor, with mirrors backing heavily polished, dark wood bars and often crowded weekends; serves until 1:00 a.m. Both McGarvey's and Middleton's serve their own house lagers. Also nearby is **Riordan's Saloon** (26 Market Space; 410-263-5449), still claimed by the locals. Everyone loves the burgers. Full menu until 1:00 a.m. on weekends; midnight during the week (see Chapter Four, *Restaurants & Food Purveyors*). Also at City Dock are **Griffins** (22-24 Market Space; 410-268-2576) and **O'Brien's Oyster Bar & Restaurant** (113 Main St.; 410-268-6288).

UPPER EASTERN SHORE

Around *Chestertown,* you'll find fifty-cent-draft establishments for the college crowd, as well as rough-and-tumble roadside saloons. The best destination for the discerning nightlifer is **Andy's** (337 1/2 W. High St.; 410-778-6779), a small, friendly, popular club that regularly hosts live music: jazz, bluegrass, rock, blues.

Kent Narrows, where Kent Island and the Queen Annes County mainland meet, has undergone a real growth spurt in recent years that's spawned its own dock bar night scene, particularly on summer nights when the boating set ties up here. **Red Eye's Dock Bar** (Mears Point Marina; 410-827-3937) brings in rock bands and DJs and generally gets wild and crazy on the weekends (and on some weeknights) during the busy season; serves its own house beer. **The Jetty** (Wells Cove Rd.; 410-827-8225) joins the decibel competition. By comparison, the hometown waterfront bar at **Angler's** (410-827-6717) seems tame. If the watermen (look for white boots) there are wearing T-shirts with a beer logo, the summer crabs are in; if they're wearing plaid flannel, it's oyster season.

In *Easton,* the **Washington Street Pub** (20 N. Washington St.; 410-822-9011) can get pretty packed, especially ThursDay–Saturday nights, and even more especially when a DJ or local band plays. At the **Avalon Theatre** (42 E. Dover St.; 410-822-0345), you'll find **Legal Spirits** (410-820-0033), a small bar done up in cozy lawyer's-office green and dark polished wood. If you feel like dancing, **Yesteryears** (Easton Plaza; 410-822-2433) offers a live band on Thursday and a DJ every Friday, and the dance floor is always packed. The crowd is a bit on the young side, and a singles-bar atmosphere pervades on Friday. **Time Out Tap and Grill** (219 Marlboro Ave.; 410-820-0433) gives Talbot Countians billiard tables and sports-oriented television year-round.

Oxford offers a few good spots to stop and have a drink. **Latitude 38** (26342 Oxford Rd.; 410-226-5303) is out on the road and also is a good place for dinner. **Schooner's Llanding** (314 Tilghman St.; 410-226-0160; closed Tues.) on Town Creek has a deck bar in-season, a restaurant, and a lounge. **Pope's Tavern** (510 S. Morris St.; 410-226-5005), a beloved local stalwart for food and drink, is located at the Oxford Inn on Town Creek.

PERFORMING ARTS & THEATER

ANNAPOLIS/WESTERN SHORE

Annapolis

ANNAPOLIS SUMMER GARDEN THEATRE
410-268-0809, information.
143 Compromise St.,
Annapolis, MD 21401.
Season: Mem. Day–Labor Day.
Tickets: $10 or less.

This blacksmith shop near City Dock dates from 1696 and may even have housed George Washington's horses out back — right where the audience sits today. The Annapolis Summer Garden Theatre, established in 1966, offers light musicals and comedies under the stars.

CHESAPEAKE MUSIC HALL
800-406-0306; 410-626-7515.
339 Busch's Frontage Rd.,
   Annapolis, MD 21401.
Season: Fri.–Sun.; some
   Wed. matinees.

Weekend dinner theater (Fri.–Sun.) for Annapolis has included weekend performances such as *Sugar Babies* and *Anything Goes*. In addition, there is a children's theater production on weekends, such as *Aesop's Fables*. While dinner theater is the mainstay, jazz lovers will want to check local entertainment listings for tributes to such greats as Gene Krupa and Benny Goodman. Call for ticket prices and schedules.

COLONIAL PLAYERS
410-268-7373.
108 East St., Annapolis, MD
   21401.
Season: Thurs.–Sun. (run
   opens on Fri.)/five-week
   run.
Tickets: regular seats: $8
   Thurs., Sun; $11 Fri., Sat.;
   seniors and students: $6
   Thurs., Sun.
Handicap Access: Yes.

A book has been published on the fifty years of this venerable theater company, which hit the half-century mark with the 1998-1999 season. Known for its breadth, plus bargain-priced tickets, Colonial Players does everything from comedies to classics. For the big 5-0, for instance, the schedule was based on reruns of productions from previous decades: *Jacques Brel is Alive and Well and Living in Paris, The Rainmaker, On Golden Pond*, and *Barefoot in the Park*. There is an annual musical and an annual Christmas Carol production.

MARYLAND HALL FOR THE CREATIVE ARTS, INC.
410-263-5544; 410-269-1087;
   301-261-1553.
www.mdhallarts.org.
801 Chase St., Annapolis,
   MD 21401.

Popular Maryland Hall serves as the center for the city's arts scene, headquarters to the major performing arts companies and classes, offering everything from children's programs to music lessons with teachers from Baltimore's prestigious Peabody Conservatory. Performances include a summer concert series, musicians like the David Grisman Quartet, or other performing groups, such as dance troupes.

UPPER EASTERN SHORE

Chestertown

WASHINGTON COLLEGE
410-778-7849, Special
   Events Office.
300 Washington Ave.,
   Chestertown, MD 21620.

Drama majors at Washington College fulfill their "senior obligation" by staging a full dramatic production in Tawes Theatre. Their obligation is your evening entertainment. Various student musical ensembles, from the Concert Band and Jazz Band to the Early Music Consort, perform throughout the year. For a monthly listing of performance events and prices, contact: Special Events Office; 410-778-7849.

Church Hill

CHURCH HILL THEATRE
410-758-1331.
P.O. Box 91, Church Hill, MD 21623.
Md. 19/103 Walnut St. off Md. 213 bet. Centreville & Chestertown.
Tickets: Prices vary.

This 1929 building has gone full circle, from town hall to movie theater to decline and, finally, rescue. Now restored with its 1944 Art Deco theater interior, the Church Hill Players' home maintains a lively performance schedule that has included *Steel Magnolias, Nicholas Nickleby,* and *Into the Woods.* A range of touring performers and an active Young People's Series offer theater, magic, and puppetry.

Easton

AVALON THEATRE
410-822-0345.
www.stardem.com/avalon.
40 E. Dover St., Easton, MD 21601.
Season: Year-round.
Tickets: Prices vary; call 410-481-SEAT.

This beautifully restored and renovated 1920s Art Deco theater is a showplace for all of the performing arts in this part of the Upper Eastern Shore. The calendar is packed with classic film screenings, children's theater, performances by the MidAtlantic Symphony Orchestra, a variety radio show, and regional and national folk, Celtic, jazz, and classical musicians. All of the seats in this intimate theater are good, but come early to enjoy the architecture and to capture a prime spot on the main floor in front of the stage.

Oxford

TRED AVON PLAYERS
410-226-0061.
P.O. Box 444, Oxford, MD 21654.
Season: Oct., Nov., Feb., Apr., Aug.
Tickets: $8 plays; $10 musicals; $6, $8 matinees.

An established community theater approaching its twentieth season stages musicals, contemporary comedies, and classical dramas with thespians from around Talbot County. It's worthwhile to book a ticket for this first-rate troupe if you're going to be in town. Performances take place at the Oxford Community Center (200 Oxford Rd.; 410-226-5904), which also hosts a winter chamber concert and occasional visiting concerts.

LOWER EASTERN SHORE

Salisbury

COMMUNITY PLAYERS OF SALISBURY
410-543-ARTS.

Noteworthy among the Lower Eastern Shore's community troupes, the Players, at over sixty

c/o Salisbury Wicomico Arts Council, 104-A Poplar Hill Ave./P.O. Box 884, Salisbury, MD 21803.
Tickets: Prices vary.

SALISBURY STATE UNIVERSITY
410-543-6030.
1101 Camden Ave., Salisbury, MD 21801.
Tickets: Prices vary.

years, is the oldest continually running, community theater organization. Performances at locations in and around Salisbury usually include a musical, a drama, and a comedy per year.

The theatre stage in Fulton Hall hosts drama, comedy, and musical productions, put on by faculty and students, throughout the school year. Call for schedule.

SEASONAL EVENTS & FESTIVALS

David Trozzo

A frosty good time is had by all who come to watch the Parade of Lights on Spa Creek, Annapolis.

A couple of easy rules: oysters in the "R" months and crabs all summer long. Keep an eye peeled for the many festivals, church suppers, and volunteer firemen's association events that include a chance to chow down on these Chesapeake delicacies. For current information about food-theme festivities and other happenings, pick up a copy of *Maryland Celebrates*, an annual calendar of festivals and events, at area visitor centers. Or contact: Maryland

Office of Tourism Development; 800-543-1036; 410-767-3400; www.mdisfun. org. In Virginia, contact: The Virginia Tourism Corporation; 800-VISITVA; 804-786-4484; www.VIRGINIA.org.

ANNAPOLIS/WESTERN SHORE

Annapolis

If the thought of a gut-busting, all-you-can-eat seafood session leaves you salivating, move the **Annapolis Rotary Crabfeast** to the top of your summer must-do list. *National Geographic* has even covered this event. Generally held the first Fri. of Aug., the feast leaves the hammered shards of 375 bushels of big blue crab shells scattered across the tables. Held at the Navy-Marine Corps Memorial Stadium. Contact: 410-841-2841.

Thousands show up for the annual **Chesapeake Bay Bridge Walk,** an early May event that goes hand-in-hand with the early morning **Governor's Bay Bridge Run** that fills up far in advance. Shuttles take bridge walkers from the Navy-Marine Corps Memorial Stadium and from other locations. Contact: 410-288-8405. Whatever you do, don't plan a drive across the Bay that day. One-half of the bridge is open, but you don't want to deal with the human bottleneck.

Celebrate Maryland's African-American history at the **Kunta Kinte Festival,** named for author Alex Haley's African forebear in *Roots,* who stepped off a slave ship at Annapolis City Dock. Regional entertainment includes dance troupes and steel drum bands, crafts, food, and more. Second weekend in Aug. on St. John's College lower field. Contact: 410-349-0338.

The **Maryland Seafood Festival** features big-name entertainment and lots of seafood, from the "crab dog" to coconut shrimp to oyster shooters. Live music. Held in Sept. at Sandy Point State Park. Handicap access. Contact: 410-268-7682.

A critical Chesapeake taste test: the "Best Crab Soup" Cook-off at the Maryland Seafood Festival.

David Trozzo

Every mariner for miles around attends the Columbus Day weekend's **U.S. Sailboat Show,** Annapolis City Dock. The very latest in sailboat designs, from racing to cruising vessels, can be found in the water along with every imaginable service or sailing gimmick. Parking will be a nightmare, but expect bargains, deals, and celebrations among the restaurants and bars. Admission. Contact: 410-268-8828.

U.S. Powerboat Show, Annapolis City Dock. The weekend after the Columbus Day weekend U.S. Sailboat Show. Here's your chance to see the newest workboats and play boats in the water, from yachts to inflatables. Admission. Contact: 410-268-8828.

Crownsville

Preparing to participate in the state sport at the Maryland Renaissance Festival in Crownsville.

David Trozzo

From its start on the weekend before Labor Day, sixteenth-century England is the order of nine consecutive weekends at the **Maryland Renaissance Festival,** held just west of Annapolis in Crownsville. Bearded men wrestle in the mud, and lovely ladies work the crowd. A roving band of jesters, crafters, jugglers, magicians, and minstrels. Admission. Contact: 410-266-7304.

Davidsonville

Spectators bring family crystal to their picnics at the **Marlborough Hunt Races,** also known as the Roedown. Held since 1975 at the private Roedown

David Trozzo

Equestrians run for the Roedown Cup every spring at Davidsonville, Maryland.

Farm, southwest of Annapolis, the event draws hundreds to watch the thoroughbred point-to-point timber race. Held the beginning of Apr. Contact: Annapolis & Anne Arundel Co. Conference and Visitors Bureau; 410-280-0445.

Port Republic

Maryland's official state sport, believe it or not, is jousting, and the Calvert County Jousting Tournament, south of Annapolis, now is well into its second century. Knights engage in mock battle, and a bazaar is set up. Held the last Sat. of Aug. at Christ Episcopal Church on 3100 Broome's Island Rd. Admission; handicap access. Contact: 410-586-0565.

NORTHERN NECK/MIDDLE PENINSULA

Gloucester County, Virginia

The **Daffodil Festival and Show** celebrates the annual daffodil harvest with tours of the many daffodil plantations in Gloucester County and includes a parade, arts and crafts show, 5K- and 1-mile run, historical exhibits, live entertainment, food, children's games, and rides. Held the first Sat. in Apr. Contact: Gloucester County Parks and Recreation Dept.; 804-693-2355.

Urbanna, Virginia

People come by road and water (and the thousands) to attend the annual **Urbanna Oyster Festival,** which essentially is an excuse to eat oysters served in every way possible, be they frittered or on the half shell. Also, there are crafts, live music, and tall ships, which you can board. Enter the town by Rte. 227, off Rte. 33 or Rte. 602, off Rte. 17. Either way, expect to walk. Held each year on the first Fri. and Sat. in Nov. Contact: Urbanna Oyster Festival Foundation; 804-758-0368.

UPPER EASTERN SHORE

Chestertown

Chestertown's contribution to pre-Revolutionary War radical politics is commemorated on the Sat. of Mem. Day weekend in the **Chestertown Tea Party Festival.** The townwide celebration features colonial parades, music, festivities, historical reenactments, boat rides for children, and food recalling the 1774 Chestertown Tea Party, where the townspeople rose up against Port Collector William Geddes, whose brigantine *Geddes* was plundered, Boston-style, by the locals. (Maybe it's apocryphal, but some say that they saved the same shipment's rum.) Free admission; handicap access. Also check out **Chestertown's Candlelight Walking Tour** on the third weekend in Sept. and the **Christmas House Tour** through this delightfully old-fashioned town. Contact: 410-778-0416.

Easton

During the **Waterfowl Festival**, Easton undergoes an amazing transformation on the second weekend in Nov. — and what small town wouldn't, if 20,000 visitors showed up? This internationally known, three-day event features more than 450 of the world's finest decoy carvers and wildlife painters. Since its founding in 1971, the Waterfowl Festival has raised millions for conservation organizations devoted to preserving waterfowl. Exhibits spread across town at the "Gallery at Tidewater Inn" and "Gallery at the Elks," (i.e., the Elks Lodge), showcasing paintings in a variety of price ranges. The exquisite decoy art, housed in two areas, ranges from classic traditional pieces to uncannily lifelike decoratives. Antique decoys are vied for at the Sat. afternoon auction. It's lively and not for the shallow pocketed. Other Festival events include retriever demonstrations, the Federal Duck Stamp exhibit, fly-fishing demonstrations, master classes with artists, a sporting clay tournament, and, always a hit, the World Championship Goose-Calling Contest. A fleet of shuttle buses provides free transportation from the parking areas to the exhibit locations. Admission; handicap access. Contact: 410-822-4567.

Decoy carver David Wallace of Havre de Grace keeps alive the old art.

David Trozzo

Grasonville

The **Queen Annes County Waterman's Festival** at Kent Narrows is unique. Where else can you see an anchor-throwing contest, a rowing race, and a docking competition for Bay workboats, while listening to country music and munching food? An easygoing, friendly event that's growing. Held on the first Sun. in Jun., 11:00 a.m.–6:00 p.m. at Wells Cove Public Landing. $3 admission; handicap access. Contact: Queen Annes County Office of Tourism, 425 Piney Narrows Rd., Chester, MD 21619; 888-400-7787; 410-604-2100.

Rock Hall

Blues, bluegrass, and Irish folk music are featured at the **Rock Hall FallFest** in early Oct., a celebration of music and mariners. Artists, children's theater, food, and regional favorites like oysters shucked before your eyes and Maryland beaten biscuits. Most activities center on Oyster Court in downtown Rock Hall. Contact: 410-778-0416.

St. Michaels

The **Mid-Atlantic Maritime Arts Festival** is Talbot County's rite of spring, a three-day affair on the third weekend in May, with maritime paintings, prints, photography, waterfowl and fish carvings, ship models, and seafood, spilling out of the buildings and into the streets.

But that's just one Chesapeake Bay Maritime Museum fest — the **Antique & Classic Boat Festival** in mid-June features more than 100 classic boats and automobiles. While crab lovers should catch **Crab Days** on the first weekend

Examining the sweep of a Bay-built boat's hand-laid curves at the Chesapeake Bay Maritime Museum in St. Michaels.

David Trozzo

in Aug., **Oyster Fest** comes in the first weekend in Nov. Free with museum admission. Contact: 410-745-2916; www.cbmm.org.

Tilghman Island

The annual **Tilghman Island Day** celebration combines demonstrations of the watermen's way of life with a heaping helping of what that way of life yields: seafood. Crab and oyster aficionados come from afar on the third Sat. of Oct. Watermen's tricks like boat maneuvering and oyster tonging are shown off in folklife demonstrations and high-spirited contests. But the big event is the skipjack races — it's great to see them under sail. The celebration benefits the Tilghman Volunteer Fire Company. Contact: Bud Harrison, Harrison's Country Inn; 410-886-2121.

LOWER EASTERN SHORE

Cambridge

You'll find no more hard-core celebration of Lower Eastern Shore country living than the **National Outdoor Show** deep in Dorchester County's marshland. You can compete in the muskrat-cooking contest if you bring your own 'rat, but stand back and watch the natives vie for honors in the muskrat-skinning contest. Come Fri. night to watch the crowning of Miss Outdoors; Sat. brings exhibits, food, and log-sawing races. The Outdoor Show is held the last full weekend in Feb. at the school in Golden Hill; take Rte. 16 S. from Cambridge and follow signs to nearby Blackwater National Wildlife Refuge. Contact: 800-522-TOUR; 410-397-3533.

Crisfield

In the late 1800s, Crisfield was a noisy strip of brothels and saloons and street-brawl recklessness. The harbor was thick with watermen's vessels, and people were getting rich on oysters. The oyster boom faded a century ago, but Crisfield remains an active, working watermen's port that ships soft-shell crabs as far as Japan everyday. The town has just cause to call itself the "Crab Capital of the World," and for more than fifty years has hosted the **National Hard Crab Derby & Fair.** The highlight of the Labor Day Weekend bash is the annual Governor's Cup Race — a crab race, with entrants from as far away as Hawaii. There's also a crab-picking contest, a crab-cooking contest, the "Miss Crustacean" beauty contest, a boat-docking contest, a carnival, a fair, a 10K race, a parade, fireworks, live entertainment, and, of course, plenty of excellent eating. Handicap access. Contact: 800-782 3913; 410-968-2500.

Deal Island

Hundreds of sloop-rigged skipjacks dredged for Bay oysters back in the 1890s, the dawn of the fleet's now-endangered work life as the last commercial sailing fleet in the country. In honor of these graceful veterans, the Deal Island-Chance Lions Club hosts the annual **Skipjack Races** on Tangier Sound each Labor Day weekend. Most of the remaining skipjacks call this watermen's community home, and the races start in Deal Island Harbor. Spectators can watch from shore (bring the binoculars) and also catch the boat-docking contests and the food and crafts. Those who want to get a little closer to the skipjack action can board a spectators' cruise boat motoring out to watch. The races are held Mon. and the "land festival" Sun. and Mon. Very worthwhile for those interested in authentic Chesapeake. Contact: 800-521-9189.

Cape Charles, Virginia

Hawks, songbirds, and other migratory birds cruising down the eastern seaboard on their way to the tropics converge on the Delmarva Peninsula's southern tip every fall, an annual event now celebrated by the **Eastern Shore Birding Festival.** In one recent year, alert birders spotted 175 different species at Kiptopeke State Park, Sunset Beach, and other sites in and around Cape Charles. The festival in early Oct. features tours, presentations, exhibits, and workshops. Contact: 757-787-2460.

Chincoteague, Virginia

According to legend, the wild ponies of Assateague Island, on the Maryland-Virginia border, descended from Spanish horses who swam ashore following a long-forgotten shipwreck. Scientists, always ready to dispel a good story, suggest that they descended from the ponies grazed on the outpost island in centuries past. Whatever the case, the annual **Pony Penning** in Chincoteague is an event to see. Always held the last Wed. and Thurs. of July, it starts when members of the sponsoring Chincoteague Volunteer Fire Co. corral the ponies and send them swimming across the channel from Chincoteague National Wildlife Refuge to town. The swim attracts tens of thousands of visitors; for a more intimate experience, preview the ponies in a corral on Assateague Island on Tues. or stick around for the return swim on Fri. The pony sale, held on Thurs., is a long tradition to raise funds for the fire company, who officially own the ponies in Virginia. A firemen's festival lasts for a couple of weeks leading up to Pony Penning. Contact: Chincoteague Chamber of Commerce, 6733 Maddox Blvd./Box 258, Chincoteague Island, VA 23336; 757-336-6161.

David Trozzo

The time-honored art of oyster shucking at the popular Chincoteague Oyster Festival.

The **Chincoteague Oyster Festival,** held annually on the Sat. of Columbus Day weekend, is one of the hottest tickets around, so be sure to buy well in advance. The Bay hosts lots of oyster festivals, but this one is designed for serious oyster lovers. Famous Chincoteague oysters are slightly salty and considered by many to be the Bay's best. Tales are told of folks who get all the way to Chincoteague on festival weekend only to find it sold out back in midsummer, so call the island's Chamber of Commerce (757-336-3131) to get your advance tickets. Held at the Maddox Family Campground.

TOURS

From tour companies to brochure-style walking tours produced by local tourism centers, here's a great way to learn about a town. The tour companies know about events like Halloween ghost tours and Christmas candlelight tours, and walking tour brochures are generally found in shops, B&Bs, or restaurants. For maritime tours, see the heading Boating in Chapter Six, *Recreation.*

HEAD OF THE BAY

Chesapeake Horse Country Tours offers a private, narrated walking tour of *Chesapeake City,* a little town with a historic district, featuring early nineteenth-century homes that prospered with the nearby C&D Canal. A van takes visitors on a tour to see private horse farms nearby. $20, three hours; reservations. Contact: Uniglobe Hill Travel, 200 Bohemia Ave., Chesapeake City, MD 21915; 800-466-1402; 410-885-2797.

ANNAPOLIS/WESTERN SHORE

Tour *Annapolis* with Walter Cronkite. The **Historic Annapolis Foundation** has prevailed upon the avid Chesapeake sailor to narrate two intriguing tours of this 300-year-old city. The famed newsman tells of the city's colonial or African-American heritage via "Acoustiguide" recordings. Reserve an hour for the African-American history walk; ninety minutes for colonial history. Tapes rented at the Historic Annapolis Foundation's Welcome Center and Museum Store, at City Dock. Open daily, $5 per person. Contact: 410-268-5576.

From **Three Centuries Tours,** guides in colonial dress lead groups through the streets of Annapolis, point out the highlights, and disclose insider stories that you'd otherwise miss. Included are the City Dock. U.S. Naval Academy, and the Statehouse areas. Group tours, garden tours, tavern suppers, candlelight tours, and excursions to the Eastern Shore are also offered from Apr. 1–Oct. 31; tours leave twice a day. The first tour departs from the city's visitor center at 26 West St. at 10:30 a.m., or catch up with the 1:30 p.m. tour at the City Dock information booth. From Nov. 1–Mar. 31, a 2:30 p.m. tour leaves every Sat. from Gibson's Lodgings. Prices for regular tours: $9 adults; $3 students. Contact: Three Centuries Tours, 48 Maryland Ave., Annapolis, MD 21404; 410-263-5401; 410-263-5357; www.annapolis-tours.com.

Discover Annapolis takes visitors for one-hour bus rides through the city's sights, departing the city's visitor center at 26 West St. $10 adults; $3 children 12 and under; no credit cards. Contact: 410-626-6000.

UPPER EASTERN SHORE

In *Chestertown,* learn a blend of architectural, local, and national history on a Sunday morning **Historic Chestertown & Kent County Tour** (410-778-2829). Tour led by area historian. Meet at the fountain in Fountain Park, High & Cross Sts., at 11:00 a.m.; $5; about 1½ hours; Mar.–Nov. Call to check in the off-season and to arrange special group tours, which can also take in *Rock Hall.*

Brochure-style, individual walking tours include the **Walking Tour of Old Chester Town,** a twenty-eight-stop tour, stretching from the entrance riverfront through this picture book, colonial maritime town. With the exception of the Geddes-Piper House, these are largely private residences and closed to the public. Also pick up a "Driving Tour of Kent County, Maryland" for county and town maps and explanations of places. Contact: Kent County Chamber of Commerce, 400 S. Cross St., Chestertown, MD 21620; 410-778-0416.

LOWER EASTERN SHORE

The "Moses of her people," Harriet Tubman led more than 300 slaves north to freedom along the Underground Railroad. See her birthplace and take a tour through Dorchester County's rich African-American history. Also visit the Underground Railroad Gift Shop, 424 Race St., *Cambridge,* and **Home-Towne Tours,** operated by the Harriet Tubman Organization, Inc.

If you're interested in the architecture of these little Lower Eastern Shore towns, don't overlook their **walking tour brochures;** most are easily available at local businesses or tourist bureaus (see Chapter Eight, *Information*). Hidden well behind the dull commercial strip along U.S. 50 stands *Cambridge,* with abundant history, beautiful waterfront, and fine old buildings. The Nanticoke River town of *Vienna* also is worth a ramble to see the town's cemeteries, homes, and churches. Stroll through *Snow Hill,* a peaceful town of brick sidewalks on the banks of the Pocomoke River known for its numerous historic houses. None are open to the public, but you can admire the architecture from the street. Contact: Julia A. Purnell Museum; 410-632-0515. Historic *Princess Anne,* established in 1733 and named in honor of the twenty-four-year-old daughter of King George II, is distinguished by many Federal-style and mid-to-late Victorian houses and commercial structures from the turn of the century. Note the oldest dwelling in the town, the circa 1755 William Geddes House, and the circa 1850 Boxwood Garden on Somerset Avenue. At the southern tip of the Eastern Shore stands *Cape Charles, Virginia,* laid out around 1883 as the southern terminus of a new railroad line that soon linked this remote town with New York and Philadelphia. Most of the once-thriving town, devastated by the Depression and the end of ferry and steamer service, now is a historic district. The fine homes of its heyday remain intact.

CHAPTER SIX
Water, Water Everywhere
RECREATION

The Chesapeake is a huge playground, where those who are so inclined can sail out onto her waters, drop fishing or crabbing lines deep, or sit on a pier and admire the view. Trails wander through the surrounding woods and shoreline, drawing hikers and bird-watchers, and in-season, hunters. Woodland or marsh, look for all the diversity of creatures who are drawn to the water's edge just like the rest of us.

David Trozzo

Sailboats battle for the lead during the popular Wednesday night boat races in Annapolis Harbor.

Boating enthusiasts will be duly impressed not only by the wide variety of watery worlds available for exploring, but also by the tremendous recreational industry that has grown up around the pursuit. No one should have any problem figuring out how to get on the Bay. Although summer sailing winds on Chesapeake waters can be unreliable and dangerous, as fast-moving, late-afternoon thunderstorm squalls roll in, Bay sailors enjoy a long season, lots of organized racing, and thousands of beautiful protected creeks and coves for secluded overnight anchorage. Most folks take rod and reel onboard and enjoy some of the best fishing anywhere.

This chapter covers everything from baseball to windsurfing. Because so many partake of so many activities at parks and wildlife refuges, we also offer a quick-glance reference to some of the best (see the section Parks & Wildlife Areas).

Besides the information provided here, for more details, maps, and advice, including information about both saltwater and freshwater fishing, contact: Maryland Department of Natural Resources, Tawes State Office Bldg., Annapolis, MD 21401; 800-688-FINS; www.dnr.state.md.us. For information about parks in Virginia, contact: Department of Conservation and Recreation,

Virginia State Parks Reservation Center, 203 Governor St., Ste. 306, Richmond, VA 23219; 800-933-7275; 804-225-3867; www.state.va.us/~dcr/. Sports persons should contact: Virginia Department of Game and Inland Fisheries, 4010 W. Broad St., Richmond, VA 23230; 804-367-1000; www.dgif.state.va.us/.

BASEBALL

America's favorite pastime is happily ensconced on both Bay shores, a hometown luxury for those who aren't prepared to navigate their way to Baltimore's Oriole Park at Camden Yards. (Although there is much to recommend the widely praised ballpark, for more information, see Chapter Nine, *Baltimore & Nearby Attractions.)*

Home for the minor league AA league **Bowie Baysox** is Prince George's Stadium, located just south of the intersection of Rtes. 50 and 301 on Rte. 301. Besides the regular season, replete with fireworks at every Saturday night home game, see the annual Congressional Baseball Game. Contact: 301-805-6000; 301-805-2233, tickets.

The **Delmarva Shorebirds** play at Arthur W. Perdue Stadium (named for poultry magnate Frank Perdue's father) at 6400 Hobbs Road, just east of the intersection of Rte. 50 and the Rte. 13 bypass in Salisbury. The low Class-A team draws league-leading crowds, particularly for Saturday fireworks in the summertime. Contact: 410-219-3112, tickets.

BICYCLING

Low-lying coastal plains meet rolling farmlands along the Bay and tributaries, where wide shoulders stretch alongside many main roads. The most famous local route sends cyclists out across the Eastern Shore road from St. Michaels to Oxford, across the Tred Avon River on the Oxford-Bellevue Ferry. (All Bay-area ferries allow bicycles — some for a fee.) You can't cross the William Preston Lane Jr. Memorial Bridge (aka the Bay Bridge) and a few other major bridges in the region, but you can arrange a ride. Call the Bay Bridge for a referral (410-757-6000). Cyclists should remember that many roads are heavily traveled by motorists, but nearby, designated bike paths are safe and enjoyable for casual rides.

Both Maryland and Virginia offer clearinghouses for cyclists. In Maryland, contact: Maryland Department of Transportation's **Bicycle Information Hot Line**; 800-252-8776, or **Bicycle and Pedestrian Team,** 707 N. Calvert St., C-502/P.O. Box 717, Baltimore, MD 21203; E-mail: bikes@sha.state.md.us; www.sha.state.md.us. In Virginia, contact: Dept. of Transportation's **Bicycle Coordinator,** 1401 E. Broad St., Richmond, VA 23219; 800-835-1203; E-mail: vabiking@vdot.state.va.us.

Serious cyclists should mark their calendars for early October, when the 100-mile **Sea Gull Century** takes more than 6,200 riders from Salisbury to the ocean and back in the largest century in the East. Call months ahead for a registration packet (410-548-2772).

ANNAPOLIS/WESTERN SHORE

*A*nnapolis offers some good in-town riding, but remember that streets are narrow, and weekend motorists are plentiful. (Helmets are required by Maryland state law on all roads for cyclists under age 16.) A favorite local ride traverses the U.S. Naval Academy grounds (helmets required), starting at Gate 1 and departing through Gate 8. Bear right on Md. 450 N. across the Severn River, via the academy bridge. Downriver, the academy grounds stretch along the banks to Spa Creek, the town's central harbor. Upriver, mansions and the former Catholic retreat house, Manresa, nest on the high banks of the Severn. When you get to the far side of the bridge, go straight to the 13.3-mile-long Baltimore-Annapolis Trail on your left, built for cyclists along the old railroad bed. The trail goes from Annapolis to Glen Burnie, and you'll share it with in-line skaters and walkers. Some complain that the trail has become over-crowded, not too bad south of Severna Park Trail. For information or maps, contact: 410-222-6244.

Quiet Waters Park (south of town on Hillsmere Dr.) is a favorite local destination for family cyclists and in-line skaters. Just under six miles total, the paved trails wind through woods and open parkland and end at an overlook on the banks of the South River. Contact: 410-222-1777; closed Tues.

Bike Doctor (150 Jennifer Rd. Annapolis, MD 21401; 410-266-7383).

Capitol Bicycle Center (1 Parole Plaza, Annapolis, MD 21401; 410-266-5510) A
　big store with a certain following.

If you're down around ***Solomons,*** another good ride will take you deep into one of the great, uncrowded corners of the Chesapeake. Cross the Patuxent River at the Thomas Johnson Bridge to reach rural St. Marys County. Get off Rte. 4 at Md. 5, Indian Bridge Rd., a lightly traveled highway with a wide shoulder. It's a fourteen-mile ride south to waterside St. Marys College and historic St. Marys City. A little more than twelve miles farther south on Rte. 5, you'll reach Point Lookout State Park. A nice day trip.

UPPER EASTERN SHORE

*T*he Shore's user-friendly topography moves from pleasantly rolling hills at its upper extreme to sprawling flatland further south, giving cyclists a mix of riding conditions on lightly traveled roads through great coastal scenery. In ***Kent County,*** the tourism office offers a booklet detailing bike-tour options.

Distance and difficulty levels range from the eleven-mile "Pomona Warm-Up" to the eighty-one-mile "Pump House Primer," which takes in Chesapeake City and Cecil County's rolling horse country. The Baltimore Bicycling Club developed the routes. For a copy of *The Kent County Bicycle Tour,* contact: Kent County Tourism Office, 100 N. Cross St., Chestertown, MD 21620; 410-778-0416; www.kentcounty.com.

In *Talbot County* the thirty-one-mile Easton-to-St. Michaels and ten-mile Easton-to-Oxford runs are popular bicycling jaunts. Many cyclists make a point of riding the Oxford-Bellevue Ferry. For a map of the best cycling routes, developed by the Oxford Mews Bike Boutique, contact: the boutique (information below) or the Talbot County Chamber of Commerce, P.O. Box 1366, Easton, MD 21601; 410-822-4653; E-mail: info@talbotchamber.org.

Bikework (208 S. Cross St., Chestertown, MD 21620; 410-778-6940) Mon.–Fri., 9:00 a.m.–5:00 p.m.; Sat., 9:00 a.m.–1:00 p.m.

Easton Cycle & Sport (723 Goldsborough St., Easton, MD 21601; 410-822-7433).

Oxford Mews Bike Boutique (103 S. Morris St., Oxford, MD 21654; 410-820-8222).

St. Michaels Town Dock Marina (305 Mulberry St., St. Michaels, MD 21663; 800-678-8980; 410-745-2400) Bike rentals, helmets, maps.

Swan Haven Rentals (20950 Rock Hall Ave., Rock Hall, MD 21661; 410-639-2527) Bicycles, boats, and fishing gear.

LOWER EASTERN SHORE

In *Dorchester County,* the **Blackwater National Wildlife Refuge** is a favored cyclists' destination. For a map of the region's recommended cycling trails, contact: Dorchester Tourism, 203 Sunburst Hwy., Cambridge, MD 21613; 800-522-TOUR.

In *Worcester County,* relatively light traffic makes for some good riding on the main roads. (Beware the overcast day, however; heavy traffic often heads inland from the Atlantic beaches.) A good ride starts in *Berlin,* a historic town with some interesting shops and a couple of worthy cafés, then heads down Evans Road. Wander off to the west along Bethards Road to Patey Woods Road, then pedal down Basket Switch Road to Taylor Road. This route is about nineteen miles and brings you to a good choice of destinations: go left and head to Chincoteague Bay, or travel another four miles west to little *Snow Hill,* a pretty, historic town.

The Bikesmith (1053 N. Salisbury Blvd., Salisbury, MD 21801; 410-749-2453).

BikeSport (1013 S. Salisbury Blvd., Salisbury, MD 21801; 410-543-BIKE).

Salisbury Schwinn Cyclery & Fitness Center (1404 S. Salisbury Blvd., Salisbury, MD 21801; 410-546-4747).

David Trozzo

Biking the wildlife loop in Chincoteague National Wildlife Refuge in Virginia.

BIRD-WATCHING

A vian enthusiasts will find no shortage of hot spots to visit in Chesapeake country, whether you tote a worn and crumpled life list, or you've just learned to distinguish a robin from an osprey.

Train your binoculars on the Bay's many channel markers, and you'll quite likely discover an osprey nest, constructed with kindling-sized sticks. During the mating and child-rearing season, its inhabitants likely have not wandered far. From woodlands to shore, the region's geographical diversity creates interesting habitat for all types of birds, ranging from passerines and peregrines to the occasional winter phalarope or spring plover.

Blackwater National Wildlife Refuge in Maryland's Dorchester County carries the Chesapeake's blue-ribbon birding reputation, especially if you want to see an ever-growing population of bald eagles. Two golden eagles arrived with the bald eagles during January's northern migration and brown pelicans are finding their way to the Bay's southern, summer shores. The end-of-the-road peninsulas, like **Point Lookout** in southern Maryland, where the Potomac River flows into the Bay, create interesting migratory viewing spots. **The Virginia capes,** where the bay flows into the Atlantic Ocean, offer prime migratory viewing.

Along the Upper Bay, look for a bountiful collection of wintering migratory birds (and wildlife, including the endangered Delmarva fox squirrel) and the threatened bald eagle at **Eastern Neck Wildlife Refuge,** a favored birding ground where the Chester River meets the Bay. Over by the ocean is Assateague Island, home of **Assateague Island National Seashore.** The location draws abundant shorebirds and waterfowl, including nesting species like black skimmers. The island straddles the state border, becoming **Chincoteague National Wildlife Refuge** in Virginia. The "Virginia end" of the island generally is considered to be the superior birding spot. Piping plovers scratch their near-invisible nests in the sand, and manmade lagoons offer a natural stopover on the MidAtlantic Flyway for skimmers and coots. At the very tip of the Shore peninsula is the 651-acre **Eastern Shore of Virginia National Wildlife Refuge,** where you may see the resurgent brown pelican and bald eagle and endangered peregrine falcons. Located at the intersection of Bay and ocean, it's a terrific fall migration staging spot for many avian species. **Kiptopeke State Park,** a few miles north, also is a prime birding spot and is home to the Eastern Shore Birding Festival each October (see the heading Seasonal Events & Festivals in Chapter Five, *Culture*).

For more information about these sites, see the section Parks & Wildlife Areas. Visitors who combine canoeing or kayaking with their love of birding will find opportunities listed, but also see the heading Canoeing & Kayaking for more possibilities.

Got your binoculars? You might also want to pick up these publications:

Meanley, Brooke. *Birds and Marshes of the Chesapeake Bay Country.* Centreville, MD: Tidewater Publishers. With its black-and-white photos, it's a better home reference than a field guide.

Wilds, Claudia. *Finding Birds in the National Capitol Area.* Washington, D.C.: Smithsonian Institution Press. Just about the best field guide to birding around the Bay.

ANNAPOLIS/WESTERN SHORE

Sandy Point State Park (100 E. College Pkwy., Annapolis, MD 21401; 410-974-2149), located at the base of the Bay Bridge on the western shore in *Annapolis,* sits along the Atlantic Flyway and offers many viewing opportunities, especially during migrations.

Like the Bay itself, **Jug Bay** is a single ecosystem with bureaucratic boundaries. The former colonial, deepwater harbor offers the range of marsh species. On the Anne Arundel County side in *Lothian,* the **Jug Bay Wetlands Sanctuary** (1361 Wrighton Rd., Lothian, MD 20711; 410-741-9330; open Wed., weekends; closed Sun., Dec.-Feb.) offers trails, including a nice one overlooking the water. Access is controlled by reservation, call before heading out; small fee. Occasional birding excursions and canoe trips.

Across the river in Prince George's County, in *Upper Marlboro*, **Jug Bay Natural Area** (Patuxent River Park, Jug Bay Natural Area, 16000 Croom Airport Rd., Upper Marlboro, MD 20772; 301-627-6074) sprawls across 2,000 acres and eight miles of trails. They have boat ramps and wonderful canoeing; canoe trips are available.

A quarter-mile boardwalk runs through the spookily beautiful, 100-acre sanctuary **Battle Creek Cypress Swamp** (Grays Rd., Prince Frederick, MD 20678; 410-535-5327; off Rte. 506 in Calvert County) in *Prince Frederick.* Go in the off-season, where you may find yourself alone to look for birds in the northernmost stand of bald cypress trees. You may even spot a wild turkey.

UPPER EASTERN SHORE

On *Kent Island,* Terrapin Park includes the **Terrapin Beach Nature Area** (410-643-8170; 410-758-2928), which offers a nature trail with excellent bird-watching for birds of prey, migratory birds, and waterfowl. It has two pondside observation blinds, a one-mile trail, and beach access over a board-walk. Take the first exit east of the Bay Bridge, go north on Md. 8, and turn left into the business park; continue until you reach the nature area. To reach **Wye Island Natural Resource Management Area** (Carmichael Rd., Queenstown, MD 21658; 410-827-7577), take Carmichael Road west from U.S. 50 near Wye Mills and cross the little wooden bridge to the island. Look for waterfowl. The state manages 2,550 acres on the island, privately owned by early Maryland settlers for 300 years before the state took it over in the mid-1970s. Goose sanctuary, managed hunting, and nature programs.

In *Grasonville,* another good spot, especially for beginners, is **Horsehead Wetlands Center** (600 Discovery Lane, Grasonville, MD 21638; 800-CANVAS-BACK; 410-827-6694; off Rte. 18 E. of Kent Narrows), operated by the Wildfowl

A wood duck quietly glides across the water at the Horsehead Wetlands Center in Grasonville.

David Trozzo

Trust of North America. Five hundred acres of wetland habitat, trails, observation blinds, a useful nature center, and towers (exhibit areas for observing wildlife and waterfowl).

Millington Wildlife Management Area in upper _Kent County_ has nature trails and ponds. Operated by the Maryland Department of Natural Resources (410-928-3650).

In _Rock Hall,_ the **Eastern Neck National Wildlife Refuge** (Rock Hall, MD 21661; 410-639-7056) is a favorite Upper Bay destination, nestled at the end of the peninsula where the Chester River meets the Bay. A handy brochure details the island's story since prehistoric times.

Between Rock Hall and Chestertown, you'll find the **Chesapeake Farms Wildlife Habitat** (7319 Remington Dr., Chestertown, MD 21620; 410-778-8400), which features a free driving tour through its 3,000 acres of wildlife and agricultural management demonstration area. The drive is open in March or April–October 10 (call in the spring). Privately owned.

LOWER EASTERN SHORE

In _Dorchester County,_ the 24,000-acre **Blackwater National Wildlife Refuge** (2145 Key Wallace Dr., Cambridge, MD 21613; 410-228-2677) hosts all manner of species in its lowlands and forests, including, at fifty year-round residents, the largest nesting population of bald eagles north of Florida. As many as 135 bald eagles came in during a recent migration. Depending on the season, you might see yellow-billed cukoos, bewick's wrens, and even northern goshawks down toward Hooper's Island. Other inhabitants include 15,000 ducks, 35,000 wintering geese, and hawks by the dozen: red shouldered and Cooper's hawks, and marsh harriers. You might even glimpse the Chesapeake's endangered Delmarva fox squirrel, its territory reduced to just four counties. Take the six-mile driving loop, which costs $3 per car and $1 for pedestrians and bicyclists. Good nature center.

The 30,000-acre **Fishing Bay Wildlife Management Area** (410-376-3236), fourteen miles south of _Cambridge,_ is southeast of the better-known Blackwater National Wildlife Refuge. The park offers canoeing, boating, hunting, bird-watching, and boat ramps.

Deal Island and the vast _Somerset County_ marshes nearby are wild spaces (go to Princess Anne, then take Md. 363 through Monde and Chance to Deal Island). The **Chesapeake Bay Natural Estuaries Research Reserve** and the **Deal Island Wildlife Management Area** are here. Also, take the nifty, free Whitehaven Ferry across the Wicomico River to the **Ellis Bay Management Area.**

In _Accomack County, Virginia,_ just south of the state line, is the **Saxis Wildlife Refuge** (turn west off U.S. 13 at Temperanceville). In _Northampton County, Virginia,_ prime flyway viewing is located at **Kiptopeke State Park**

(757-331-2267), three miles north from the Bay Bridge Tunnel on the Eastern Shore, off U.S. Rte. 13, west on Rte. 704 to the park.

BOATING

Sailors say you can spend a lifetime exploring the Chesapeake coastline and never see it all. The nation's largest estuary stretches 200 miles and is fed by 150 rivers. The surface of the Bay spans nearly 2,500 square miles, and its tributaries add as much again. Cross the Bay Bridge on a breezy, clear day between April and November, and you'll see schools of sails heading both north and south, as well as the white wakes of powerboats.

In addition to the sheer volume of water and coastline available to explorers, the Bay offers a soft bottom more forgiving than that along the Atlantic coast. High summer brings flat calm, and the water is filled with boaters seeking refuge from the humidity onshore. That leaves some of the year's best sailing in April, May, September, and October, when predictable breezes blow.

Annapolis calls itself America's Sailing Capital. Deck shoes are *de rigueur*, masts fill Spa Creek in the middle of town, and everybody can talk a little boat talk. On Wednesday nights in the summer, the business suits do a mad dash from their Washington, D.C. or Baltimore offices to make the Annapolis Yacht Club races on Spa Creek — starting gun, approximately 6:00 p.m. To watch, stake out a spot at the Eastport Bridge or the U.S. Naval Academy seawall and cheer the spinnakers pounding to the finish.

Elsewhere, the snaking Bay coastline offers endless opportunity for "gunkholing," a pastime perhaps best defined as the leisurely sport of moseying about a body of water. On Maryland's Upper Eastern Shore, Talbot County lays claim to more than 600 miles of shoreline — said to be the most of any county in the continental U.S.

Sailors rave about the Bay, but it is also ideal for powerboating, especially during the summer calms. With leisure time short and working hours long, many people find that the only practical way that they can enjoy the water is with a motorboat; zip across to St. Michaels or Kent Narrows for dinner and still be home on schedule. Kent Narrows, which lies between Kent Island and the Upper Eastern Shore, has become a powerboat mecca, with races and marinas that cater to the sport.

BOATING OPTIONS

What the heck is a "bareboat" charter? If you don't know, you'll definitely need to take a course to learn. Bareboating is one of many ways to get out on the water. Your options include the following:

Charter boats are what you want if you plan to sail (or power) for a day or longer. You'll do so with a captain or by yourself (aka bareboating). Charter agencies will want to see your sailing résumé and to check references, while local boating schools offer courses to get you certified to handle someone else's prized vessel. Keep in mind that "chartering" means a range of things: you can charter the fifty-foot yacht that you're thinking of buying and take yourself to the Caribbean, or you can charter a weekend sailboat with skipper and relax on deck. Many outfits set two-day minimums that can start at about $250 per day, and that's a bare minimum, for a relatively small boat. According to a couple of local charter operators, a family of four on a thirty- to thirty-eight-foot boat can expect to pay something closer to $850. Also, you can usually rent or charter boats through the boating schools, who will also want to see your sailing résumé.

Cruise and excursion boats take folks out for a ride, and your vessel may be anything from an authentic Chesapeake skipjack to a reproduction schooner to the equivalent of a waterborne bus. They're good get-acquainted options, perfect for an afternoon outing, and your crew often narrates the history (either natural or manmade) of the passing shoreline. See Cruise & Excursion Boats below for listings. Water taxis can stand in for an excursion boat, providing fun (and usually cheap) rides across the harbor to a good restaurant or other destination.

Boating schools supply all that you'll need to learn to handle a jib, navigate by the stars, or take a safe spin through crowded waters aboard a powerboat. Some folks plan vacations around weeklong sailing lessons.

Rent a daysailer, skiff, windsurfer, jet ski, rowboat, canoe, or kayak! Your outfitter is in charge of how much experience that you'll need to take the boat out and will ask all the necessary questions. You can go out for as little as an hour. See the heading Canoeing & Kayaking to find out how to rent those craft or take a trip with a guide. Many marinas charter boats or host vendors who rent various craft.

For those who have their own boats, volumes have been written about Chesapeake Bay sailing and powerboating. Check our marina listings, as well as a few helpful books.

CHARTERS & BOAT RENTALS

This section covers a wide range of options — and craft. Boat rentals tend to be straightforward transactions; you want to go fishing or sailing, you rent a boat for a few hours. Charters mean leasing somebody else's boat or perhaps even a boat that a yacht broker hopes to sell, for a cruise of a day or week. You'll often find both at marinas, and you also may find this to be a service available one year at a particular marina/yacht broker/wharf, but not the next. Just ask. If you're interested in checking out a particular craft, check with the yacht broker who sells that particular type of boat. Most of the sailing schools also offer rentals and are a good, dependable bet, so check their listings, too.

ANNAPOLIS/WESTERN SHORE

Annapolis

Annapolis Bay Charters (7310 Edgewood Rd./P.O. Box 4604, Annapolis, MD 21403; 800-292-1119; 410-269-1776; E-mail: abcinc@erols.com; www.erols.com/abcinc) Charter fleet, since 1980, of thirty or more boats, up to eighty-six feet, sail or power, captained or bareboat. Charters also available out of Solomons.

AYS Charters & Sailing School (7416 Edgewood Rd., Annapolis, MD 21403; 800-382-8181; 410-267-9151) All-sail fleet of twenty-eight- to forty-six-foot vessels, and three catamarans. Offers three charter certification courses, including a three-day class on bareboat chartering. Longtime business.

Destination Paradise (7074 Bembe Beach Rd., Annapolis, MD 21403; 800-391-6560; 410-268-9330) Specializing in captained sailboats and powerboats, thirty to sixty feet, and larger.

Edgewater

Suntime Rentals (2820 Solomons Island Rd., Edgewater, MD 21037; 410-266-6020) Powerboats (nineteen-footers), jet skis, waterskiing equipment, wakeboards. Two-hour minimum; daily rates available. May 1–Oct. 1.

Galesville

Hartge Chesapeake Charters (4880 Church Lane, Galesville, MD 20765; 410-867-7240; www.hartge.com) Charter fleet of fourteen sailing vessels, twenty-eight to forty-four feet, all bareboat.

Solomons

Baileywick Sailboat Leasing (P.O. Box 710, Solomons, MD 20688; 410-326-3115; www.erols.com/baileywick) Sail a twenty-four-foot daysailer or lease a thirty-five-foot Niagara.

Solomons Boat Rental (Rte. 2 & A St., Solomons, MD 20688; 800-535-BOAT; 410-326-4060) Powerboats from fifteen to twenty feet, 5 hp to 120 hp. Fish, cruise, or water-ski.

Information about Chesapeake Waters

Cruising the Chesapeake: A Gunkholer's Guide. William H. Shellenberger. International Marine/McGraw-Hill. (800-822-8158) The Bay is known as gunkholing paradise, where sailors can meander among secluded anchorages. $34.95.

Guide to Cruising Chesapeake Bay. Published annually by *Chesapeake Bay Magazine* (1819 Bay Ridge Ave., Annapolis, MD 21403; 410-263-2662), it is comprehensive, even to suggesting cruises to fill a week. $34.50.

Life in the Chesapeake Bay. 2nd Ed. by Robert and Alice Lippson. Johns Hopkins Univ. Press, 1997. The title says it all. Nature lovers will want to check out this book.

Maryland Cruising Guide. (William & Heintz Map Corp., 8119 Central Ave., Capitol Heights, MD 20743; 800-338-6228; 301-336-1144) This is a popular chart book that shows you the upper part of the Chesapeake. $20.

Public Boat Access Areas. (Virginia Dept. of Game and Inland Fisheries, 4010 W. Broad St., Richmond, VA 23230; 804-367-9369).

Also see the heading Bibliography in Chapter Eight, *Information,* for those all-important field guides. Look for the free *PortBook,* for its wealth of information about boating services. It is published twice a year and is available at marine stores or newsstands.

NORTHERN NECK/MIDDLE PENINSULA

Deltaville, Virginia

Deltaville Yachts Charter (P.O. Box 775, Deltaville, VA 23043; 804-776-7575; E-mail: charter@deltavilleyachts.com; www.deltavilleyachts.com) Sailboat charters, twenty-eight to forty foot. Beneteaus only. Captain service available if necessary. Day, weekend, and more. Located at corner of Rte. 33 and 631.

UPPER EASTERN SHORE

Easton

Little Boat Rentals (846 Port St., Easton, MD 21601; 800-221-1523; 410-819-0881) Wide range of small craft, from daysailers and crab skiffs for $15 an hour to pontoon boats for $25 an hour (prices may change, call first). Canoes, too. Two-hour minimum; reservations preferred. Rentals also available by the week. Your best bet for renting a small boat. Daily, May 1–Oct. 31.

Grasonville

C&C Charters (506 Kent Narrows Way N., Grasonville, MD 21638; 800-733-SAIL; 410-827-7888) Bareboat or captained charters; choice of fifteen to twenty powerboats and sailing vessels, ranging in size from thirty-one- to sixty-foot powerboats or twenty-eight- to fifty-foot sailboats. One of the area's better-known companies.

Oxford

Tred Avon Yacht Sales and Charters (26106 Bachelor Harbor Dr., Oxford, MD 21654; 410-226-5000) Captained or bareboat, sail or power.

Rock Hall

Gratitude Yachting Center (5924 Lawton Ave., Rock Hall, MD 21661; 410-639-7111) Charter island packets; captained or bareboat.

St. Michaels

St. Michaels Town Dock Marina (305 Mulberry St., St. Michaels, MD 21663; 800-678-8980; 410-745-2400) Take vessels, including the twenty-one-foot *Osprey* or the eighteen-foot *Cygnet*, for sunset cruises and excursions by hourly, half-day, and daily rates.

Tilghman

All Aboard Charters (Rte. 33, Knapps Narrows Marina, Tilghman, MD 21671; mailing address: 9340 Macks Lane, McDaniel, MD 21647; 410-745-6022) Charter the *Nancy Ellen* for fishing trips or nature tours. A "Bay boat," the *Nancy Ellen* is a workboat built here and finished to yachting standards.

CRUISE & EXCURSION BOATS

Listings reflect the main interest of the business noted, but many are multi-service. For example, marinas and sailing schools often offer charters. A sailing charter outfit may offer fishing trips, and vice versa. Remember that weather may dictate your day.

HEAD OF THE BAY

Chesapeake City

Miss Clare (64 Front St., Chesapeake City, MD 21915; 410-885-5088) The classic

Chesapeake deadrise — a crab boat design — started life in Cambridge and did duty as a charter fishing boat in the charming Atlantic town of Lewes, Del., before Capt. Ralph H. Hazel brought her back to the family hometown to do history tours of the C&D canal, where his great-grandfather ran wooden steam tugboats from Chesapeake City to Havre de Grace. Hour-long cruise, May–Oct. or Nov., maybe even Dec. Depart the dock at Chesapeake City. $10 adults; $5 children.

Havre de Grace

Martha Lewis (Chesapeake Heritage Conservancy, 121 N. Union Ave., Havre de Grace, MD 21078; 800-406-0766; www.newmc.com/martha_lewis) This skipjack, restored in 1994, offers public cruises in the summer and oyster cruises in the fall and winter. Public cruises depart Lighthouse Pier in Havre de Grace; Sat., Sun., 2:00 p.m., 4:00 p.m.; $10 per person. Daylong oyster cruises show the public how it's done and cost $150. Call for departure and other information.

ANNAPOLIS/WESTERN SHORE

Beginagain (1056 Eaglewood Rd., Apt. TD, Annapolis, MD 21403; 800-295-1422; 410-626-1422; E-mail: captpaul@erols.com) This thirty-six-foot sloop operates three-hour trips, three times a day. May 1–Sept. 30; $55 per person, plus tax; maximum six passengers.

Chesapeake Marine Tours and Charters (Slip 20, Annapolis City Dock, P.O. Box 3350, Annapolis, MD 21403; 410-268-7600; E-mail: boattours@aol.com; www.member.aol.com/boattours/cmt.html) Longtime operators offer forty- and ninety-minute tours out of Annapolis Harbor and Severn River or excursions across the Bay to St. Michaels aboard vessels, ranging from the 297-passenger *Harbor Queen* to the twenty-four-passenger *Miss Anne.* Also look for their City Dock-based Jiffy Water Taxis for a quick ride across Spa Creek.

Liberte, The Schooner (222 Severn Ave., Annapolis, MD 21401; 410-263-8234; E-mail: Liberte@maritime-online.com; www.maritime-online.com/Liberte/) Classic replica of 1750 pinky schooner. Call for information.

Schooner *Woodwind* (Annapolis Marriott Waterfront Dock, 80 Compromise St., Annapolis, MD 21401; 410-263-7837; E-mail: woodwind@pipeline.com; www.schooner-woodwind.com) Twin seventy-four-foot wooden ***Woodwinds: I and II*** now ply Annapolis Harbor. The original ***Woodwind*** takes the tourists. On Fri. sunset sails, catch the popular locals, "Them Eastport Oyster Boys," performing their own brand of Bay music. Sails daily; call for schedule.

Stanley Norman (162 Prince George St., Annapolis, MD 21401; 410-268-8816) The famed skipjack belongs to the Chesapeake Bay Foundation, and you must be a member to take a trip aboard. For $25 for an annual membership, what the heck, eh? Fall and spring member trips may include an oyster dredging trip out of the Severn River into the Bay, or perhaps farther.

Wm. B. Tennison (Calvert Marine Museum, 14200 Solomons Island Rd, Solomons, MD 20688; 410-326-2042) Restored 1899 bugeye sloop, her chunk-built hull constructed of nine logs at Crab Island, Md., offers hour-long trips around Solomons Harbor. She spent her early-to-midcentury career as a powered oyster buyboat. Sails May–Oct., Wed.–Sun.; $5 adults; $3 children 5–12.

Smith Island Cruises (Capt. Alan Tyler, 4065 Smith Island Rd., Ewell, MD 21824; 410-425-2771) Sail the *Chelsea Lane Tyler* from Point Lookout State Park in St. Marys County to Smith Island. The same outfit also operates the sixty-five-foot catamaran *Capt. Tyler I* out of Crisfield (see Lower Eastern Shore below) Wed.–Sun., Mem. Day–Labor Day. $22 per person, $12.50 for lunch.

Annapolis Marriott Waterfront (80 Compromise St., Annapolis, MD 21401; 410-263-8994) Home to both the Schooner *Woodwind* and rental concessions for both small sail and powerboats.

NORTHERN NECK/MIDDLE PENINSULA

Capt. Billy's Charters (Ingram Bay Marina, Wicomico Church, VA 22579; 545 Harvey's Neck Rd., Heathsville, VA 22473; 804-580-7292) Sail out of Ingram Bay aboard *Liquid Assets*, a forty-foot vessel designed for fishing parties and sight-seeing. Personalized service and instruction in fishing and cruising. Reservations required.

Smith Island and Chesapeake Bay Cruises (382 Campground Rd., Reedville, VA 22539; 804-453-3430) A native Smith Islander, Capt. Gordon Evans once oystered aboard the skipjack *Ruby Ford*. He knows his way through the inland waterways, creeks, and canals that lace the cluster of islands collectively known as Smith Island, and now he's shown the way to his son, Capt. Greg Evans. Depart on the ninety-minute trip from the family's KOA Campground and Resort in Reedville to dock at Ewell, the largest of this island's three fishing villages. En route, you might even get a glimpse of the old Evans family place at Rhodes Point as the boat cruises past. Island tours are offered. Visitors can bring picnics, but many like to stop at one of a couple of island eateries. (Mrs. Evans, a Georgian, says Islanders tend to drop by Ruke's Seafood Deck.) Remember that weather conditions may dictate your trip. No credit cards. Departs 10:00 a.m., returns 3:45 p.m., May–Oct.; $19.50 adults; $9.75 children 3–12. Reservations requested, not required.

Tangier and Rappahannock River Cruises (Rte 1, Box 1332, Reedville, VA 22539; 800-598-2628; 804-453-2628) Day trips to windswept Tangier Is. Also ask about day cruises of the Rappahannock River — known hereabouts as "The Rivah." May–Oct. Reservations required.

UPPER EASTERN SHORE

Dream Weaver (Sassafras Harbor Marina, 1 George St., Georgetown, MD 21930; 800-757-7171) Sassafras River tours aboard a classic Chesapeake Bay-designed deadrise, a wooden workboat built in Cambridge. Tours last four to seven hours; some take in the one-time resort town of Betterton. Call ahead for itinerary, times, and prices.

Patriot Cruises Inc. (P.O. Box 1206, St. Michaels, MD 21663; 410-745-3100) Perennially popular cruise of the Miles River, with narration on local history. The 170-capacity *Patriot* departs daily 11:00 a.m., 12:30 p.m., 2:30 p.m., 4:00 p.m., Apr.–Oct. from a dock near the Chesapeake Bay Maritime Museum. During the peak summer tourist months, prepare to wait in line. $9 adults; $4 children under 12. Special lunch cruises and evening charters are available.

Rebecca T. Ruark (Capt. Wade H. Murphy Jr., 21308 Phillips Rd., Tilghman, MD 21617; 410-886-2176) The oldest, prettiest, and fastest skipjack in the Bay's dwindling oyster fleet, captained by a man who has shown a talent for harvesting oysters and talking about the trade with visitors. Two-hour tours; $30 per person, for up to six passengers. Longer cruises can be arranged.

Southern Cross Charters (Great Oak Landing Marina Resort, P.O. Box 426, Chestertown, MD 21620; 410-778-4460) Day, sunset, and overnight cruises on the Chesapeake Bay in a forty-one-foot Morgan Out Island ketch-rigged sail yacht, with food service on all cruises. Overnight cruises go to Baltimore's Inner Harbor, Rock Hall, Annapolis, and Georgetown.

LOWER EASTERN SHORE

Capt. Jason & Capt. Jason II to Smith Island (Capts. Terry Laird and Larry Laird; 410-425-4471; 410-425-5931) For a no-frills taste of island life, use the boats that the island people board — year-round. After the prescriptions and grocery orders are loaded (and boxes of soft crabs have been lifted off the deck), settle in for the twelve-mile ride to Ewell or Tylerton on Smith Island. Boats leave Crisfield 12:30 p.m., return 4:40 p.m.; the captains make a return trip to their island homes, so you can also return to Crisfield at 7:00 a.m. If you decide to stay the night, $15 round-trip, under age 12 free. Accommodations on the island can be limited; be sure that you know in advance where you're staying before you commit to overnight.

The Nathan of Dorchester (Dorchester Skipjack Committee, 526 Poplar St., Cambridge, MD 21613; 410-228-7141) Sail on the Shore's newest skipjack, built a few years ago to promote the area's nautical heritage and to preserve the craft of wooden boat building. Sat. sunset cruises ($15), Sun. afternoon cruises ($10 adults), and skipjack races ($25) from Long Wharf in Cambridge. Operates mostly in summer. Reservations required.

The Osprey (Purchase tickets at The Refuge Motor Inn, 7058 Maddox Blvd., Chincoteague Island, VA 23336; 757-336-5511) Ninety-minute guided tours of the Chincoteague/Assateague area. Mem. Day–Oct., daily, mid-Jun.–Sept.; $20 adults; $10 children. Reservations recommended.

Smith & Tangier Islands

Imagine a place so close to the water that the stone vaults of shallow graves lie exposed in front yards, constant reminders of forebears who came here three centuries ago.

Some still say there's a touch of Old English in the speech of these remote Islanders, who harvest the sea and place morals before money. With all of its glitz, Hollywood found this out the hard way when the town council firmly rejected plans to film a movie here.

Such is Tangier Island, which, along with neighboring Smith Island, comprise the remaining vestiges of a remote island life once commonplace on the Chesapeake Bay. Over time, bridges spanned shorter distances or inhabitants departed remote, erosion-gnawed spits of land, leaving only the 1,200 or so hardy souls of Smith and Tangier to cling, twelve miles from the mainland, to the Islanders' self-sufficient lifestyle. This is a place where every view is a panoramic seascape. Thick marshes pulse with fluttering songbirds and leggy herons. Brackish water fingers its way inland, forming a network of shallow creeks known as guts. Narrow paths serve as the roads leading across them, over wooden, hump-backed bridges just high enough to let Islanders in their skiffs pass beneath — under and out to the double-edged life of working the Bay. Freedom, yes, but hard, hard work.

Despite powerful nor'westers that frequently push high tides up to their doorsteps, the Islanders stick to their way of life as if there were no other. "Our lives are geared to the water, and the water is demanding," said Jennings Evans, an eleventh-generation Smith Islander, who also has relatives on Tangier. "We can't even think about mainland clocks. That's the difference in an Islander."

A trip to these islands may provide visitors with the most authentic taste of Chesapeake life left on the Bay, but it is one best undertaken aboard one of the tour boats that comes here for a day visit. The more adventurous who want to stay overnight should carefully plan and make reservations. Once here, don't expect to find a chain motel with the "vacancy" sign lit. Consider how hard it is to simply import everyday goods — the Islanders' biggest obstacle. It may be easy enough, for example, to use a forklift or crane to put a load of lumber on a boat or barge in Crisfield on Maryland's Lower Eastern Shore, "But once it gets here, we have to handle it piece by piece," Evans said. Home construction and repair is a slow process.

Part of a chain of shifting, sinking, eroding islands, Tangier and Smith lie only three feet above sea level — and sometimes far less. On tiny Tangier Island, only half of the three-mile island is livable; the rest is tidal marsh. Smith Island, far larger at eight-by-four miles, hosts thousands of acres of marshland, teeming with birds and fish. But just a tiny silver here and there offers the upland compatible with three communities of humans. At one of them, Rhodes Point, residents routinely slosh through water several inches deep on a very high tide.

Despite popular legend, Smith Island is not named for the great explorer, John Smith, who first charted Chesapeake Bay, but for the wealthy Englishman Henry Smith, who acquired the lower half of the island in 1667. (As early as the 1630s, one Robert Cager kept 100 head of cattle here.) When Smith fell into financial ruin and began to sell off lots, families named Evans and Tyler bought large parcels to farm. Today, these are common island names; indeed, folks around the Bay know them to be synonymous with Smith Island. Although they were farmers well into the 1800s, the Islanders inevitably augmented their food supply with fish, oysters, and crabs. By 1900, the land had become too marshy or salty for crops, and residents turned to the Bay.

From the Big Thorofare, a two-mile highway of water that cuts through the marshes of Smith Island and connects to Tangier Sound on the east and Chesapeake Bay on the west, Ewell, Smith's largest town, appears as a portrait of life frozen in time. Crab pots are piled high around the waterfront, and the narrow harbor is needled with rickety wharves that lead to weathered crabbing shanties over water. Today, many of these shanties are abandoned, but they once housed the island's main seafood industry: soft-shell sloughing operations. In recent years, the crab sheds have been moved ashore and modernized, and the women of the island help their husbands with the twenty-four-hour job of monitoring the delicate peelers during the summer months. These are soft-shell crabs that must be nabbed and packed on ice within two hours after sloughing their hard shells, or they form a paper shell that is neither edible nor marketable. In the winter, women take on an even more important role, running households and tending to business when the men ship out for months at a time to work menhaden boats out of Cape Charles or to fish for conch out of Wachapreague on the Atlantic Ocean.

Ewell is a village of white picket fences, surrounding two-story frame houses. Cars are in abundance, though none of the 300 or so residents bother with license tags. Ewell is connected to Rhode Point by a long road through the marshes, but Smith's third community, Tylerton, is cut off from the rest of the island by a large gut. Bicycles are the main mode of transportation in Tylerton.

Unlike Smith Islanders, the watermen of Tangier Island never brought their crab shedding operations ashore, mainly due to the lack of land. Consequently, the approach to Tangier leads through rows of well-kept crabbing sheds on stilts, which stand as symbols of the people's independence. To visitors, these 10 x 14-foot sheds seem impractical places to do business, but they are easy for watermen to reach in their forty-foot workboats. Here, they not only run crab-shedding operations, which require lots of saltwater, but they also store heavy equipment, like crab pots and scrapes, once used to dredge oysters, but now more commonly dragged along a shallow bottom to harvest crabs.

Tangier is a place to stroll and take in the beauty of the residents' close-knit relationship with nature. Old skiffs lie dying in shallow guts and gleaming white workboats are pulled up to backdoor wharves. Life here is more primitive than on Smith. With only sixteen cars and a half-dozen trucks among 750 inhabitants, most residents travel across the island on golf carts, bicycles, motorized scooters, or by foot. This is just as well, since all roads, except the main road, are only four or five feet wide.

From the water, church steeples and water towers distinguish the two inhabited

(Continued)

islands from the many uninhabited clumps of earth that dot the horizon. Outsiders can glimpse life as it once was in a Chesapeake waterman's community from May through October when cruise boats run daily from Crisfield, Maryland, and Onancock, Virginia, on the Eastern Shore, and from Reedville, Virginia, on the western shore. Both islands have a few restaurants and gift shops (some of which sell crafts, such as carvings, made by the Islanders). A couple of inns and B&Bs are run by locals who can give visitors the names of Islanders who charter fishing trips or possibly arrange tours of soft-shell shanties or crab-picking houses.

At Ewell, the new Smith Island Center houses exhibits on the history of the island — good preparation for absorbing the islands' living history. If you buck the Smith Island tour boat tide and take the *Capt. Jason* to Tylerton instead, you can visit the Chesapeake Bay Foundation and view its operation there. Tylerton is also home to the Women's Crab Picking Co-op, which welcomes visitors. A note to those who like an evening cocktail: the islands are dry, and restaurants close early. For nightly entertainment, there's the setting sun over Chesapeake Bay.

SMITH ISLAND

Accommodations

Ewell Tide Inn (Ewell; 410-425-2141) Seasonal, opens Apr. 1. Reservations.
Inn of Silent Music (Tylerton; 410-425-3541) Waterfront, canoes, and bikes; break-
    fast, evening seafood meal. Host Sharryl Lindberg arranges tours of soft-shell
    crab shanties and crab-picking co-op. Open year-round.
Smith Island Motel (410-425-3321) Apr.–Sept. Reservations.

Restaurants

Bayside Inn Restaurant (Ewell) Open Mem. Day–Oct.; daily, 11:00 a.m.–4:00 p.m.;
    buffet, family-style, or a la carte.
Ruke's (410-425-2311) The only sandwich shop. Waterfront deck. Open in-season,
    daily, 11:00 a.m.–8:00 p.m.; off-season, daily, 11:00 a.m.–4:00 p.m., except Sun.

TANGIER ISLAND

Hilda Crockett's Chesapeake House (757-891-2331) Family-style seating, 11:30
    a.m.–6:00 p.m. Lodging, daily, Apr. 15-Oct. 15. Also breakfast. Take the tour boat
    or call to arrange a ride over with a Tangier waterman.
Shirley's Bay View Inn (757-891-2396) Private tours, AC, cable, four new cottages.
    Walking distance to gift shops, beach, and airport.

by Pat Vojtech

Smith Island Cruises (Capt. Alan Tyler, 4065 Solomons Island Rd., Ewell, MD 21824; 410-425-2771) Sail from Crisfield's Somers Cove Marina into Smith Island daily during the tourist season, which lasts through Oct. Departs Crisfield 12:30 p.m., returns 5:15 p.m.; $20 adults; add $12.50 for dinner.

Tangier Island Cruises (1001 W. Main St., Crisfield, MD 21817; 410-968-2338) The cruise boat *Steven Thomas* takes tourists across Tangier Sound to Tangier Island, the classic waterman's community. One of the more venerable of the island boat businesses. Runs May 15–Oct., daily, departs 12:30 p.m., returns about 5:15 p.m.; $18 adults; children 12 and under free. Tangier Island cruises also operates *Capt. Rudy Thomas,* which takes overnight cruises to Norfolk and Portsmouth May–Oct. Reservations required.

Tangier-Onancock Cruises (16458 W. Ridge Rd., Tangier, VA 23440; 757-891-2240) Leave daily from Onancock's historic Hopkins & Bro. General Store, aboard the sixty-five-foot *Capt. Eulice* at 10:00 a.m.. After a narrated, 1-hr., 45-min.-cruise, passengers meet a guide at the Tangier dock, who takes them through the narrow streets of this tiny fishing village. Gift shops feature locally made crafts, such as dolls; dining features a family-style dinner at the well-liked Hilda Crockett's Chesapeake House, or picnic lunches. Runs Mem. Day weekend–Oct. 15; $18 adults; children under 12 free. Reservations required for groups only.

MARINAS

Many marinas line the Bay shores; they vary in size and quality, and we do our best to list those that are reported back to us as reliable. These generally are "full service" marinas, with electrical hookups, holding tank pump-out facilities, fresh water, and sometimes, other amenities such as laundry, showers, and groceries. Others include recreation, such as tennis or swimming. For specifics, call ahead. In high season, reservations may be necessary for "transient" slips. Also, consider these marinas a resource for finding charters for sailing, powerboating, or fishing.

HEAD OF THE BAY

Chesapeake City

Bohemia Bay Yacht Harbor (1026 Town Point Rd., Chesapeake City, MD 21915; 410-885-2601) Full service, transients. 299 slips.

Havre de Grace

Penn's Beach Marina (411 Concord St., Havre de Grace, MD 21078; 410-939-2060) 146 slips.

Tidewater Marina (Bourbon St., Havre de Grace, MD; 410-939-0950) Nice facility. 160 slips.

ANNAPOLIS/WESTERN SHORE

Annapolis

Annapolis City Marina (410 Severn Ave., Annapolis, MD 21403; 410-268-0660) Right in the midst of the bustle. Transient dockage for boats drawing up to ten feet. Groceries, laundry, showers, fuel, and pump-out station. 87 slips.

Annapolis Landing Marina (980 Awald Dr., Annapolis, MD 21403; 410-263-0090) Transients, fuel, showers, laundry, café, pump-out station, and swimming pool. Transients. 120 slips.

Annapolis Yacht Basin (2 Compromise St., Annapolis, MD 21401; 410-263-3544) Transients, fuel, ice, showers, laundry. 107 slips (about 40 slips for transients).

Bert Jabin's Yacht Yard, Inc. (7310 Edgewood Rd., Annapolis, MD 21403; 410-268-9667; www.bjyy.com) One of the biggest marinas in the area, with about 400 slips and a huge yard with all services. Transients. Also in Eastport (726 Second St.; 410-268-9667) section of Annapolis.

Chesapeake Harbour Marina (2030 Chesapeake Harbour Dr. E., Annapolis, MD 21403; 410-268-1969; www.ChesapeakeHarbour.com) Transients, water taxi to City Dock area. Pool, tennis court. 200 slips.

Bailing the boat, an occupational hazard after a shower passes through.

David Trozzo

Mears Marina (519 Chester Ave., Annapolis, MD 21403; 410-268-8282; 301-261-1234; www.mearsmarinas.com) Transient slips fluctuate among the 236 slips, including a few that accommodate boats up to eighty feet. Pool, tennis courts. Call in advance. Headquarters of Severn River Yacht Club.

Petrini Inc. (1 Walton Lane, Annapolis, MD 21403; 410-263-4278) Range of services on Spa Creek. Biggest Travelift in Annapolis. Since 1946. About 45 slips; transients can find space.

Port Annapolis (7074 Bembe Beach Rd., Annapolis, MD 21403; 410-269-1990; www.portannapolis.com) Bikes, rental cars. No fuel. 281 slips.

Galesville

Hartge Yacht Yard (4880 Church Lane, Galesville, MD 20765; 410-867-2188; 301-261-5141) A favored area marina that's been there forever — since 1865. All services. 280 slips; usually slips available for transients.

Ridge

Point Lookout Marina (16244 Miller's Wharf Rd., Ridge, MD 20680; 800-246-6274; 301-872-5145; E-mail: plm@us.hsanet.net; www.mtam.org/members/plm.htm) Transient dockage for years. 160 slips.

Severna Park

Magothy Marina (360 Magothy Rd., Severna Park, MD 21146; 410-647-2356; E-mail: magothymar@aol.com) Marina services, swimming pool. Deep-draft slips, 182 total, including some off the seventeen-foot channel. Located on the Magothy River, just north of the Bay Bridge.

Solomons

Hospitality Harbor (205 Holiday Dr./P.O. Box 382, Solomons, MD 20688; 410-326-1052; E-mail: novatech@radix.net.) Pool, tennis courts, weight room — all of the amenities from the Holiday Inn next door. About 80 slips, roughly 30–35 slips available for transients.

Spring Cove Marina (455 Lore Rd./P.O. Box 160, Solomons, MD 20688; 410-326-2161) Fuel, laundry, Naughty Gull restaurant. Approximately 250 slips, 40 for transients. Popular dockage for transients.

Zahniser's Yachting Center (245 C St., Solomons, MD 20688; 410-326-2166; www.zahnisers.com) Pump-out station, pool, restaurant, sail loft, yacht brokerage. Reservations recommended. Over 300 slips; transient slips available.

Tall Timbers

Tall Timbers Marina (Herring Creek Rd./P.O. Box 9, Tall Timbers, MD 20690; 301-994-1508) Restaurant, pool, and nearly one mile of beach. Fuel, laundry, no pump-out station. About 120 slips, about 30 slips for transients. Located twelve miles from Point Lookout.

NORTHERN NECK/MIDDLE PENINSULA

Coles Point, Virginia

Coles Point Plantation (307 Plantation Dr./P.O. Box 77, Coles Point, VA 22442; 804-472-3955; E-mail: colespoint@3n.net) Fuel dock, boat ramp, beach, seafood restaurant, 110-site campground, and a 575-ft. fishing pier, available to the public for a nominal fee. 132 slips; transients welcome. Located near prime Chesapeake Bay fishing grounds, up the Potomac River.

Deltaville, Virginia

Fishing Bay Harbor Marina (P.O. Box 459, Deltaville, VA 23043; 804-776-6800; www.fishingbay.com) Pump-out station, gas, café, and pool. About 10 transient slips among the 110 available on Fishing Bay Harbor. Located on Rte. 1104.

J&M Marina (P.O. Box 646, Deltaville, VA 23043; 804-776-9860) Slips for both powerboats and sailboats, and transients. Located on Rte. 33 through Deltaville to Dockside Inn; left on Rte. 1112, at end of road.

Kilmarnock, Virginia

Chesapeake Boat Basin, Inc. (1686 Waverly Ave., Kilmarnock, VA 22482; 804-435-3110) Ship's store, ice, showers, fresh water, transient slips. Located on Indian Creek, just above the Rappahannock.

Kinsale, Virginia

Kinsale Harbour Yacht Club (Rte. 203 at Kinsale Bridge, Kinsale, VA 22488; 804-472-2514) Fuel, fresh water, pool, tennis courts, showers, laundry, launching ramp, and restaurant. 99 slips; transient slips available. Located on the Yeocomico River.

Lancaster, Virginia

Yankee Point Marina (1303 Oak Hill Rd., Lancaster, VA 22503; 804-462-7018;

E-mail: bsayankeepoint@rivnet.net) Charters, a sailing school, and a good reputation for repairs and restoration. 95 slips. Located on the Corrotoman River.

Lottsburg, Virginia

Olverson's Lodge Creek Marina (1161 Melrose Rd., Lottsburg, VA 22511; mailing address: P.O. Box D, Callao, VA 22435; 800-529-5071; 804-529-6868; www.port-starboard.com/marina) Fuel dock, pump-out station, boat ramp, pool, showers. Open year-round. 160 open and covered slips; about 30 transients. Located off the Yeocomico and Potomac Rivers.

UPPER EASTERN SHORE

Chester

Castle Harbour Marina (301 Tackle Circle, Chester, MD 21619; 410-643-5599) Restaurant nearby. 314 slips, open and covered. Located on the Chester River.

Piney Narrows Yacht Haven (500 Piney Narrows Rd., Chester, MD 21619; 410-643-6600) 279 slips, open and covered. Located on Kent Narrows.

Chestertown

Chestertown Marina (211 Front St., Chestertown, MD 21620; 410-778-3616) Mechanic on premises, fuel. 54 slips; transients welcome. Located on the Chester River.

Georgetown

Georgetown Yacht Basin (14020 Augustine Herman Hwy./P.O. Box 8, Georgetown, MD 21930; 410-648-5112) More than 300 open and 100 covered slips at this location; 156 more slips at Granary Marina directly across the river.

Skipjack Cove Yachting Resort (150 Skipjack Cove Rd., Georgetown, MD 21930; 410-275-2122) Tennis courts, Olympic-sized pool. Thirty-three moorings, fourteen lifts. 360 slips.

Grasonville

Lippincott Marine (3420 Main St., Grasonville, MD 21638; 410-827-9300) 200 slips; transient slips available.

Mears Point Marina Kent Narrows (428 Kent Narrows Way N., Grasonville,

MD 21638; 410-827-8888) Seven restaurants within walking distance, plus the happenin' Red Eye Dock Bar. An impressive 600 slips; many powerboats live here.

Oxford

Crockett Brothers Boatyard (202 Banks St., Oxford, MD 21654; 410-226-5113) Pool, pump-out station, laundry. 74 slips. Located in center of town.
Oxford Boatyard (402 E. Strand, Oxford, MD 21654; 410-226-5101) Year-round. 76 slips.

Rock Hall

Gratitude Yachting Center (5924 Lawton Ave., Rock Hall, MD 21661; 410-639-7011) 50 slips, although not for boats drawing more than five feet or with more than fourteen-foot beam.
Osprey Point Marina (20786 Rock Hall Ave., Rock Hall, MD 21661; 410-639-2663) Floating docks, bathhouse, pool. 150 slips. Situated beside full-service restaurant and seven-room inn.
Rock Hall Landing (5681 Hawthorne Ave., Rock Hall, MD 21661; 410-639-2224) Pool. Closest marina to town. 77 slips. Open Apr. 15–Nov. 15.
Sailing Emporium (21144 Green Lane, Rock Hall, MD 21661; 410-778-1342) Laundry, lending library with liberal policy: give a book, take a book; almost 300 volumes. 150 slips.

St. Michaels

St. Michaels Harbour Inn & Marina (101 N. Harbor Rd., St. Michaels, MD 21663; 410-745-9001) Open dawn to dusk, May–Oct., mostly serving transients. Adjacent hotel renovated 1997. 60 slips.
St. Michaels Town Dock Marina (305 Mulberry St., St. Michaels, MD 21663; 800-678-8980; 410-745-2400) Boat and bike rentals. More than 50 transient slips.

Stevensville

Bay Bridge Marina (357 Pier One Rd., Stevensville, MD 21666; 410-643-3162) Restaurant and small airport adjacent; shopping nearby. 310 slips. Located next to Bay Bridge on Kent Is.

Tilghman

Knapp's Narrows Marina (6176 Tilghman Island Rd./P.O. Box 277, Tilghman, MD 21671; 410-886-2720; www.knappsnarrowsmarina.com) Swimming pool, laundry, showers, restaurants on site and within walking distance. Deep-water harbor can accommodate boats up to eighty feet. 130 slips.

LOWER EASTERN SHORE

Cambridge

Cambridge Municipal Yacht Basin (Mills & Water Sts., Cambridge, MD 21613; 410-228-4031) City-run docks at Port of Cambridge. Next to historic district. Borrow a bicycle to get around ashore. 196 slips.

Crisfield

Somers Cove Marina (Broadway & Water Sts./P.O. Box 67, Crisfield, MD 21817; 800-967-3474; 410 968-0925) Municipal marina right in the town. 450 slips.

Salisbury

Port of Salisbury Marina (506 W. Main St., Salisbury, MD 21801; 410-548-3176) Full-service marina; free bike use. 112 slips. Located downtown, on the Wicomico River.

SAILING & POWERBOAT SCHOOLS

Taking a few sailing lessons is a good way to spend a Chesapeake-area vacation, especially with kids. Like chartering, learning to handle a boat is not an inexpensive proposition, but the money is well spent for those who really want to know how, and you'll learn proper, safe technique. Some marinas also offer instruction, including the Gratitude Yachting Center (5990 Lawton Ave., Rock Hall, MD 21661; 410-639-7111).

HEAD OF THE BAY

Havre de Grace

BaySail School and Yacht Charters (Tidewater Marina, Bourbon St., Havre de Grace, MD 21078; 410-939-2869; fax 410-939-3779; www.baysail.net) In 1998, Kim Richards took over this sailing school, which teaches American Sailing Association-certified courses. Beginner to advanced, also private instruction aboard your own boat for an hourly rate. Charters Hunters and Catalinas, bareboat or captained.

ANNAPOLIS/WESTERN SHORE

Annapolis

Annapolis Sailing School (601 6th St., Annapolis, MD 21403; 800-638-9192; 410-267-7205) Classes offered by a venerable, reputable school. Experienced instructors teach classes from "Become a Sailor in One Weekend" to "Bareboat Cruising." Sail the waters off Annapolis, between the Chesapeake Bay Bridge and Tolly Point, and up the Severn River, popular with local sailors. Rentals of twenty-four-foot Rainbow daysailers are available. Also home to KidShip, where sailors as young as age 5 learn to tack. Holder 12s and Americas and Barnetts, and the **Annapolis Power Boat School**, with five- and two-day courses.

Chesapeake Sailing School (7074 Bembe Beach Rd., Annapolis, MD 21403; 800-966-0032; 410-269-1594; 301-261-2810; E-mail: chessail@annapolis.net) Well-established school offers a wide range of sailing courses, as well as half-day to weeklong charters on vessels ranging from eight-foot Optis for beginning kids to Tanzer 22s for older folks. The Kids on Boats family program means you and yours can learn to sail together. Also home to the Tiller Club, an option where sailors can pay a yearly fee to take out Tanzer 22s. Rentals on boats ranging from twenty-two to thirty-eight feet.

J World (213 Eastern Ave., Annapolis, MD 21403; 410-280-2040) Begun in Annapolis in the early 1990s, the J-boat-oriented, sailing school offers weekend programs for any level. Also, weeklong schools.

Womanship (137 Conduit St., Annapolis, MD 21401; 800-342-9295; 410-267-6661) Womanship sailors wear T-shirts that say, "Nobody Yells," and many women who've been one half of a boating couple can appreciate the laugh. This reputable school was started by women for women and now has spread to fifteen locations, hosting seven-, five-, and three-day comprehensive classes, including mother-daughter classes and beyond. Daytime classes in Annapolis.

CAMPING

BACKCOUNTRY CAMPING

The only true backcountry camping in Chesapeake territory is at the **Assateague Island National Seashore** (7206 National Seashore Lane, Berlin, MD 21811; 410-641-3030). The seashore governs for thirteen miles, protecting a spectacularly wild beach where you can see bottlenose dolphin offshore during the summer. Shellfishing and crabbing are allowed in island waters, as is canoeing. Hike down the beach (stay off those coastal dunes) or

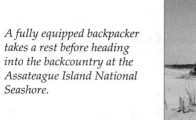

A fully equipped backpacker takes a rest before heading into the backcountry at the Assateague Island National Seashore.

David Trozzo

move slightly to the interior along miles of hiking trails to explore each aspect of the barrier-island ecosystem. Inland grow myrtle brush, loblolly pine, and some hardwoods.

A word about the famous wild ponies here: expect to run into them, especially in the less-crowded spring or fall seasons. They're mild-tempered and will leave you alone if you leave them alone. Explanations of their origin are mixed (and your belief therein seems to depend on whether you're a romantic or a pragmatist). They may have descended from Spanish mustangs that swam ashore after a shipwreck or from the animals owned by seventeenth-century settlers who grazed them here. At the Maryland-Virginia line, you'll run into the fence where management changes to the **Chincoteague National Wildlife Refuge.** While you're not allowed to camp, you can access the Maryland park from here as long as you obtain a permit for overnight parking. On the refuge,

The famed wild ponies of Assateague.

David Trozzo

you might spot the intriguing Sika deer, an animal that's actually part of the elk family and no larger than a big ol' dog.

If you camp at Assateague, stop in at the ranger station by midafternoon for a $5 backcountry permit (a flat charge no matter how many nights or people in the party), but get permits by 12:00 noon if you need time to walk to the two farthest sites. Carry your own fresh water or do without. Be forewarned that the mosquitoes are world-class. The bay side of the island is seldom visited in the summer because of this pest. More than one wag has christened them Virginia's state bird.

CANOEING & KAYAKING

Canoeing in the Lower Shore's swampland, home to plenty of bugs. Bring repellent.

David Trozzo

Water-skiers zipped past as we unloaded our trusty aluminum Grumman canoe at Selby Landing, an obscure access known mostly to locals along the Patuxent River's Jug Bay. Wild rice grows with midsummer abandon at this suburban outpost landing. But three centuries ago, this was the deepwater harbor where the schooner *Peggy Stuart* departed with her last load of southern Maryland tobacco. Upon her return to Annapolis, her cargo filled with British goods sparked the Chesapeake's own Boston Tea Party.

This is also the site of a late nineteenth-century industrialist's dream. If all had gone as planned, the western shore town of Chesapeake Beach, south of Annapolis, might today be a Bayside version of Virginia Beach or Ocean City, Maryland. The Chesapeake Beach Railroad from Washington, D.C. to the southern Calvert County resort bearing its name ran for the last time in 1935, a year after a mighty hurricane blew through. Along with harbor siltation dating back two centuries, the railroad track bed has left Jug Bay a quiet, marshmallow-studded paradise beloved by late twentieth-century nature enthusiasts.

We put in at the landing, paddled a few hundred yards, then hung a right into silent Mattaponi Creek, home to kingbirds, territorial red-winged blackbirds, and the kind of quiet canoeing that makes the Chesapeake's tributaries no less than paddlers' nirvana.

From the quiet of a canoe or kayak, the region's abundant wildlife is easily seen. Paddlers may spot silent barn owls or discover great blue herons living in nearby marshes. The exception to typical Bay area flatwater is Tuckahoe Creek, south of the dam at the lower end of Crouse Mill Lake, which, after heavy spring rains, is roughly equivalent to Class 3 whitewater.

While both types of craft allow quiet encounters with wildlife, canoeing and kayaking are different sports in many ways. "Canoeing is more of a pulling stroke; kayaking is more of a pushing stroke," says Mary Greene, who has run Island Kayak/Chesapeake Bay Kayaks from Tilghman for some years. In general, canoes are best suited to protected waterways. Kayaks can go into more adventurous waters, but for safety's sake, inexperienced kayakers should take some instruction first. Greene points out that instruction will not only show kayaking newcomers how to paddle to conserve energy — "You've got to know your own strength" — but also safety techniques that will be critical if you capsize, especially if the wind comes up.

Paddlers will find dozens of tributaries well worth exploring here in Bay Country and dozens of local park landings at which to put in. (Addresses and telephone numbers are offered in the Parks & Wildlife section.) Folks in search of rentals will find reliable outfitters to offer both canoes and kayaks. If you want to get out on the water but aren't comfortable going alone, consider joining an outfitters' group trip.

SUGGESTED TRIPS, OUTFITTERS & RENTALS

ANNAPOLIS/WESTERN SHORE

The **Jug Bay Natural Area** (16000 Croom Airport Rd., Upper Marlboro, MD 20772; 301-627-6074; 301-699-2544, TDD) is uncrowded and rents both canoes and kayaks. The river's marshy, western shore in _**Prince George's County, Maryland**_ is but one side of the bureaucratically divided body of water. This is a tidal river, which means you don't want to be caught downstream on a windy day with the sun sinking low. Two landings and some good canoeing in the creeks off the river. Fish for largemouth bass or perch when they're running. You'll need a nominally priced permit to paddle and a fishing license to cast. Check for canoe trips, even pontoon boat trips. Canoe and kayak rentals: $15 for nonresidents of Montgomery or Prince George's County; $12 for those county residents. Part of the Patuxent River Park, managed by the Maryland National Capital Park and Planning Commission.

Across the river, in _**Anne Arundel County,**_ lies the **Jug Bay Wetlands Sanctuary** (Lothian, MD 20711; 410-741-9330), which offers guided canoe trips from time to time. Together, the two areas are part of a research cooperative known as the **Chesapeake Bay National Estuarine Research Reserve.** Call in advance for access on Wednesdays and weekends.

Based in _Annapolis,_ **Amphibious Horizons** (600 Quiet Waters Park Rd., Annapolis, MD 21403; 888-I-LUV-SUN; 410-267-8742; www.amphibioushorizons.com) operates out of the **Quiet Waters Park** from April to October. Primarily a sea kayaking outfit, the business rents singles, doubles, and sit-on-top kayaks, plus canoes and pedalboats to folks who venture to the park. All but the most experienced kayakers will be restricted to Harness Creek, since the South River, a quarter-mile away, is known for its heavy powerboat traffic and the attendant mighty wakes that these craft kick up. Ask about kayaking classes. No canoe trips, but folks interested in broader Bay exploration may want to try kayaking trips in waters from Havre de Grace to Smith Island, from one day to one week. The **Springriver Corp.** (311 Third St., Annapolis, MD 21403; 410-263-2303) has reasonably priced rentals by the hour or day, from $25–$40 for a half day. Call by Thursday for weekend reservations. Located on Spa Creek.

NORTHERN NECK/MIDDLE PENINSULA

Reedville, Virginia

Belle Isle State Park (Rte. 683, Reedville, VA 22539; 804-462-5030) This is a relatively new Virginia state park and runs along seven miles of the Rappahannock River. The park remains under development, but is open daily sunup to sundown. Rent canoes for a nominal fee, as well as bikes and motorboats, and check in to find out about guided tours. Take Rte. 3 to Rte. 354, then Rte. 683 near Litwalton to the park.

UPPER EASTERN SHORE

The **Choptank River,** the largest of the Shore's twenty or so rivers, is fed into by **King's Creek,** a worthwhile canoeing territory. Put in at Kingston Landing, accessible via Rte. 328 and Kingston Landing Road. A meandering tidal waterway, King's Creek runs past The Nature Conservancy's **Choptank Wetlands Preserve** and some of the most pristine marshes on the East Coast. Plenty of wildlife and blessedly few boats.

Tuckahoe Creek, which runs through **Tuckahoe State Park** in _Caroline County_ before reaching the Choptank, is one of the Shore's more popular canoeing spots. At the park, Tuckahoe Creek runs into **Crouse Mill Lake,** which has a dam at its lower end, after which the Tuckahoe continues its journey to the Choptank. The lake and the section of the creek north of it are freshwater; it's a good area for less experienced canoeists. Below the dam, the Tuckahoe is tidal, with different vegetation from the freshwater upper reaches.

From the dam to the landing in **Hillsboro** are six miles of pleasurable canoeing, with great fishing for bass, pickerel, and bluegill. (*Warning:* Do *not* run the dam!)

Watts Creek, entering the Choptank at **Martinak State Park** near *Denton,* makes for a pleasant two-hour paddle up and back. Go at high tide; it's a bit muddy at low tide.

In *Queen Annes County,* put in at the **Corsica River** at *Centreville* and poke around upstream or downstream on a pretty stretch of water. **Turner's Creek,** which flows northwest into the **Sassafras River** in *Kent County,* affords some scenic canoeing past stunning sixty- to seventy-foot-high bluffs. While development has crept in on the north side, the south side remains unspoiled.

The **Nanticoke River,** which defies our neat Upper/Lower Shore boundary, is too broad and busy for canoeing; its tributaries, though fine for paddling, are generally hard to get to. The exception is **Marshyhope Creek;** put in at Federalsburg and canoe downstream for some sunny open tripping or upstream, ducking the brush on your way toward **Idylwild Wildlife Management Area.** Mary Greene, owner of Island Kayak/Chesapeake Bay Kayaks, suggests putting in at the public landing in *Whitman.* Stay on the peninsula side, running alongside Rte. 33, to enjoy beautiful farmland habitat, especially in the fall. From **Cummings Creek** into **Harris Creek,** there are some nice beaches along the way, and you'll pass through *Sherwood,* a neat little town. Follow the shoreline.

Chester River Kayak Adventures (5758 Main St., Rock Hall, MD 21661; 410-639-2001; 410-639-2061) Kayak rentals and sales, group and individual tours are available. No experience necessary; all tours begin with fifteen minutes of instruction.

Island Kayak/Chesapeake Bay Kayaks (21536 Mission Rd./P.O. Box 357, Tilghman, MD 21671; 410-886-2083) Highly recommended up and down the Eastern Shore, Mary Greene leads kayak trips from Tilghman Island. Consider a three-hour paddle, a sunset tour, or call to see if Mary is running an overnight trip farther south on the Shore in a spot such as Virginia's Kiptopeke State Park, where you'll see pelicans and oystercatchers.

LOWER EASTERN SHORE

Assateague Island National Seashore (7206 National Seashore Lane, Berlin, MD 21811; 410-641-3030) A good place to canoe in the marshes and interior bays, although wildlife protection regulations must be followed. Canoe rentals.

Pocomoke River Canoe Co. (312 N. Washington St., Snow Hill, MD 218631; 410-632-3971) Knowledgeable outfitter rents canoes and kayaks every day, Apr.–Dec. Well worth contacting even if you're going out with your own canoe. Company will drive you and your rented canoe to a put-in point so that you can canoe back to Snow Hill.

Survival Products (1116 N. Salisbury Blvd., Salisbury, MD 21801; 410-543-1244) Canoe and kayak rentals from knowledgeable people who cruise area waterways. Cartop rack kit included in cost of rental. Will transport groups using more than six canoes; call ahead.

FAMILY FUN

Visiting with the whole family? The region offers many opportunities for kids and their parents. Be sure to check out the local state parks, as well as the maritime museums, listed in Chapter Five, *Culture*. The extensive waterman's exhibitions at the Chesapeake Bay Maritime Museum, for instance, are sure to capture the fancy of a budding angler or sailor.

WESTERN SHORE

It's a few miles west of the area covered by this book, in *Upper Marlboro, Maryland,* but **Merkle Wildlife Sanctuary** (11704 Fenno Rd., Upper Marlboro, MD 20772; 301-888-1410) is well worth a detour for neophyte birders. The 1,600-acre sanctuary on the Patuxent River offers limited access to the river in deference to the fantastic numbers of Canada geese who have ruled their grassy winter roosts here for up to 5,000 years.

The visitor center is laid out for learning. Downstairs, a glass wall looks out to two ponds and fields; a counter runs alongside. A couple of telescopes are set up for viewing the vast landscape, and photo albums, filled with pictures and descriptions of birds, are available to help with identification. Specimens of birds native to the area, such as cedar waxwings, Eastern bluebirds, or the Eastern screech owl, are behind glass. But best of all for the kids is the Nature Discovery Room, where they can color a picture of a bluebird to the soothing sounds of the water-filling aquaria or learn about local critters, such as the rare and endangered tiger salamander that lives in local habitats. After your "discovery," hike trails from three-quarter-mile to three miles. Ask directions to the blue heron rookery and be sure to stay on the trail.

The **Jefferson Patterson Park and Museum** (10515 Mackall Rd., St. Leonard, MD 20685; 410-586-8500; open Wed.–Sun., 10:00 a.m.–5:00 p.m.) in *St. Leonard* may be one of the best-kept family secrets around. Easy trails through fields and along the Patuxent River pass archaeological digs of colonial times past. The old barn has been transformed into a broad picnic pavilion. Consider visiting during the mid-April–mid-October season, especially on weekends when school's in session. We visited on an 80+° Saturday in September and had the place to ourselves. About 500 acres.

Groups from local schools and day care centers make it a point to visit **Westmoreland Berry Farm and Orchard** (Rte. 637/Box 1121, Oak Grove, VA 22443; 800-997-BERRY; www.westmoreland-berry.com) in *Oak Grove, Virginia,* and if you're in the area with a backseat full of kids, you should, too. Overheard from an employee, "I can handle the eighteen four-year-olds." Need we say more?

Located along the Rappahannock River, the farm boasts historic, European-invasion roots dating to 1641. In all, 800 acres at the berry farm, another 800 acres in an adjoining nature preserve. Farm managers Chuck and Anne Geyer come with impressive berry credentials rooted in their work at the University of Maryland. Their carefully planned, seasonal wave of harvests would make any gardener green with envy; strawberries arrive in May, followed by cherries, black and red raspberries, blueberries, and peaches. By October, kids are picking apples on their allotted plots of trees.

Parents will quickly note the boundaries here. Everyone is given a particular plot upon which to pick berries. Charts in the main building explain the harvest: gala apples, for example, yellow with red blush, ripen by late August. Others come later. Pay for the berries by the bucketful, with raspberries costing the most. There's a kid-friendly food stand in the market area and a broad veranda with picnic tables. Best berry months: Jun.–mid-Jul. Best days to pick: Tues.–Thurs. The river runs alongside down a steep slope, and there's a pier. Open daily in-season, because as Anne says, "Fruit knows no holidays."

EASTERN SHORE

A bunch of science and math-loving kids who grew up to be engineers and scientists started the **Excel Interactive Science Museum** (2300 N. Salisbury Blvd., Centre at Salisbury, Salisbury, MD 21801; 410-546-2168) in their spare time to interest a new generation of children in topics like rocketry, physics, and electronics. The museum in the Centre at Salisbury is filled with fun and educational, interactive exhibits. Classes are held at the same site. Call for class schedule. Open Fri., 5:00 p.m.–9:00 p.m.; Sat., 12:00 noon–9:00 p.m.; Sun., 11:00 a.m.–5:00 p.m.

An outpost of the **NASA Goddard Space Flight Center,** the **NASA Wallops Flight Center** (NASA Wallops Flight Center Visitor Center, Rte. 175, Chincoteague, VA 23336; 757-824-2298) at *Wallops Island, Virginia,* is a beehive of scientific activity, but is closed to the public. You can get a glimpse, however, at the goings-on in the visitor center, which features programs like model rocket launches and exhibits on spaceflight past, present, and future. Gift shop, picnic area. Free. Open Mar.–Jun., Sept.–Nov., Thurs.–Mon., 10:00 a.m.–4:00 p.m.; Jul. 4–Labor Day, daily, 10:00 a.m.–4:00 p.m. Open in the winter for group tours by appt.

Hailed as one of America's finest small zoos, the **Salisbury Zoological Park**

(410-548-3188) has distinctive and well-conceived animal exhibits. Free, but donations welcome. Picnicking area and concessions outside zoo. Open year-round. Located E. of Rte. 13 and S. of U.S. 50.

FISHING

From marshy creeks to wide open water, the Chesapeake and its tributaries comprise one of the greatest anglers' destinations anywhere. With the Bay the focus of so much environmental concern, catch-and-release fishing is becoming much more popular, and fly-fishing also has caught on.

CHESAPEAKE FISH SPECIES

Anglers pursue the Bay's seventeen species of recreational finfish.

David Trozzo

Seventeen species of game fish live in the Bay, and fishers pursue them from riverbanks, piers, skiffs, head boats, and charter boats. Bait your hook and go in search of bluefish, sea trout, white and yellow perch, spot, rockfish (striped bass), catfish, summer flounder, channel bass (red drum), and hard-head (croaker), to name a few.

"I start fishing about May 8; we chum for stripers up until about June 30," says Gene Pittman, a longtime charter boat skipper based in Heathsville, Virginia. "Then we start bottom fishing for trout, croaker, and spot until about mid-September. Then we go back to chumming for striped bass again until about Christmas." Pittman fishes from the broad midbay region with its deep channel. From July to September, look for bluefish and Spanish mackerel in the mid and south part of the Bay. But with fresh water pumping in from the Susquehanna River up north, black bass fishing up that way is so good that the Twenty-first Annual BASS Masters Classic was held there in the early 1990s.

The upper reaches also host white perch, catfish, and rockfish, says

Annapolis fisherman Ed Kalb. Though not legal to catch, shad are on the way back and even a sturgeon or two have inadvertently been caught.

Closer to Annapolis — from Annapolis south — big chopper blues (six-to-twenty-pound fighters) offer thrills until the summer. Then just as ferocious tailer blues come in. The big rockfish trophy season starts in late April, picking up with the blues in late May, says Kalb, a former officer with the Maryland Saltwater Sportfisherman's Association. Bluefish school into November. Bottom fishing picks up by June when the weather warms up and continues into the fall. Serious fishers look for black drum, which made for exceptional fishing up Annapolis way in 1998.

Shellfish include clams, crabs, and oysters (depleted because of disease; though not harmful to humans, people with health problems are routinely cautioned against eating raw oysters). Most recreational shellfishermen are after crabs, and any local tackle shop (see the heading Sporting Goods & Camping Supply Stores) can help you gear up and find a good local pier.

CRABBING

Callinectes sapidus, better known as Maryland blue crabs, are hugely popular and have encountered up-and-down populations during the 1990s. Some

This is how it's done — "chicken necking" for Chesapeake blue crabs.

David Trozzo

blame overharvesting of these ultratasty and stratospherically popular critters. Some cite other possible problems, including the natural up-and-down life cycle of any species, loss of their grass bed habitat, and predation by finfish whose populations have recovered. Whatever the reason, be kind and resist the urge to catch a couple dozen for yourself alone. Some people think that it would be a good idea not to catch females, which have rounded, U-shaped aprons, unlike the pointed aprons of the males.

Catch a crab by tying chicken necks or eels in the bottom of a crab trap (widely available at hardware, fishing, or sporting goods stores) and drop the trap into the water. You can also partake of the fine art of "chicken necking." Tie a chicken neck to a string, tie the string to a piling, and when it tenses up, slowly ease the bait up into sight, a crab or two hanging on to feed, and scoop with a long-handled dip net. Just as Bay folks like to show newcomers how to eat — or pick — crabs, they'll also show you how to catch them. Ask at any tackle shop.

Unless you're planning to catch more than two bushels, you probably don't need a license to go about your recreational crabbing. The size restriction for hard-shell crabs is five inches across from point to point. But both Maryland and Virginia regulate the spring-to-fall season, and regulations are updated frequently. Check at a tackle shop for the latest regulations or contact the state fisheries (see the section The Best Fishing Guide).

ROCKFISH

The premiere Chesapeake game fish, Maryland's Official State Fish, is striped bass, known locally as rockfish. Of North America's stripers, ninety percent spawn in the Bay. Concern was high when the fish declined dramatically from the 1970s-1980s, forcing a rockfish moratorium. The rockfish has made a terrific comeback, and charter boat captains now look for schools of them when out with fishing parties. Fly-fishing for rockfish also has caught on in the Bay in the last few years. If you're interested, check with charter operations.

Since rockfish is a migratory fish up and down the East Coast, each state is granted a quota by an interstate fisheries management commission. Regulations change seasonally, so be sure to check sporting goods stores and tackle shops for up-to-date information.

FISHING LICENSES

Fishing licenses are widely available at fishing and sporting foods stores and not required if you are under age 16. A saltwater fishing license issued by either state is good in Maryland or Virginia, although there are some limits when it comes to fishing certain tributaries. If you're fishing from a chartered boat, you won't need a license. Nor do you need one if you are fishing as a nonpaying guest from private property. In addition, there are a number of Maryland-designated Free Fishing Areas; contact: Maryland Department of Natural Resources (see above) for locations. In Maryland, you'll need a striped bass permit. Ask about nonresident licenses for consecutive days of fishing — probably a bargain if you're visiting the region. Generally prices are reduced for fishers over age 65.

THE BEST FISHING GUIDE

A complete county-by-county list of public boat ramps can be found in a booklet that no one coming to fish in Chesapeake country should be without, *A Fisherman's Guide to Maryland Piers and Boat Ramps.* It provides license details, creel limits, and seasonal limits for each species, maps highlighting the prime fishing grounds, and showing every ramp in the state. Contact: Maryland Department of Natural Resources, Fisheries Service, 580 Taylor Ave., Annapolis MD 21401; 800-688-FINA; www.dnr.state.md.us. For information on Virginia freshwater fishing, contact: Department of Game and Inland Fisheries, 4010 W. Broad St./P.O. Box 11104, Richmond, VA 23230; 804-367-1000; www.dgif.state. va.us/. Virginia saltwater anglers, contact: Marine Resources Commission, 2600 Washington Ave./P.O. Box 756, Newport News, VA 23607; 757-247-2200.

BOAT RAMPS

The following are some easy launch points:

HEAD OF THE BAY

In *Cecil County,* try the Fredericktown boat launch on the Sassafras River; call Cecil County Parks and Recreation (410-392-4537) or Elk Neck State Park (410-287-5333). Easy-to-find ramps in downtown *Havre de Grace* include the ramp at Jean Roberts Memorial Park (410-939-9448) on the Susquehanna River and at the end of town at the city yacht basin at Tydings Park (410-939-9448; nominal fee), where you're on the Upper Bay.

ANNAPOLIS/WESTERN SHORE

In *Annapolis,* Sandy Point State Park (410-974-2149; nominal park entry fee) will get you right onto the Bay. A grand total of twenty boat ramps launch boaters into Mezick Pond, a little inlet on the Chesapeake. Very popular and reasonable. Spa Creek access is at Truxtun Park (410-263-7958; fee in summer, Mem. Day–Labor Day; $2 on weekends to launch, no park fee) in the middle of town. In *Solomons,* use the Solomons Boat Ramp (410-535-1600 weekdays; fee). Down in *St. Mary's County,* try the Point Lookout State Park (301-872-5688; fee).

UPPER EASTERN SHORE

In *Queen Annes County* (410-758-0835), there's a nominal, one-day permit fee for both residents and visitors. Try the ramps at Kent Narrows, Little Creek, Thompson Creek, Shipping Creek, Goodhand Creek (all on Kent Island), and Southeast Creek, Centreville, Crumpton, and Deep Landing (in the northern part of the county).

LOWER EASTERN SHORE

Access includes Choptank River Boat Ramps, the Fishing Bay Wildlife Management Area (410-376-3236), the Taylors Island Wildlife Management Area (410-376-3236), Janes Island State Park (410-968-1565), and Taylors Island Boat Ramp (410-221-2911).

CHARTER BOATS & HEAD BOATS

Charter boat captains can be counted on to supply anglers with a rod, reel, and bait, but plan on bringing lunch. You also may find that this is a fluid business — somebody who's running a boat this season may not be doing so next season. Contact the Maryland Charter Boat Association; 410-639-2906.

Head boats are so named because they carry so many "heads" (thirty or more) out to the fishing grounds. Reservations may or may not be necessary, depending on the height of the season. Anglers generally pay a fee for use of the rod and reel; bait may or may not be included. Fishing is confined to bottom fishing, which isn't as exciting as the sport of casting. But off southern Maryland, expect to catch white perch, Norfolk spot, and croaker. If the boat specializes in "chumming," you can catch bluefish and summer flounder. Some folks aren't in love with this fishing method, because crowded boats can mean tangled lines, although bottom fishing is designed to minimize this aggravating problem.

Fishing boats often operate out of marinas, so also check the section Marinas under the heading Boating.

HEAD OF THE BAY

Havre de Grace

Penn's Beach Marina (411 Concord St., Havre de Grace, MD 21078; 410-939-2060) Rent fifteen-foot fiberglass boats with little 9.9 engines and go look for everything from rockfish to catfish. $50 for the day.

ANNAPOLIS/WESTERN SHORE

Chesapeake Beach

Rod `n' Reel Marina (Rte. 261 & Mears Ave., Chesapeake Beach, MD 20732; 301-855-8351) Sportfishing May–Nov. Half-day and full-day trips on twenty-eight-boat fleet of Coast Guard-licensed captains. Per-person rates also available for head boat fishing. Helping fishers find everything from spot to flounder to trophy rock since 1949.

Edgewater

Sportfishing on the Chesapeake Bay, Inc. (P.O. Box 53, Edgewater, MD 21037; 800-638-7871; 301-261-4207; www.belindagail.com) Capt. Jerry Lastfogel, former officer for the Maryland Charterboat Assoc., has been running charter boat fishing expeditions for years. Fish aboard the forty-two-foot *Belinda Gail III.* Half-day and full-day trips out of Collins Marine Railway on Rockhold Creek in Deale, MD.

Ridge

Scheible's Fishing Center (48342 Wynne Rd., Ridge, MD 20680; 301-872-5185) Charter and head boats comprise the twelve-boat fleet. Head boats run full-day trips; otherwise, half-day or full-day trips in-season, where fishers can go after striped bass or bluefish.

Solomons

Fishing the Patuxent River, off Solomons Island.

David Trozzo

Bunky's Charter Boats, Inc. (14448 Solomons Island Rd. S./P.O. Box 379, Solomons, MD 20688; 410-326-3241; fax 410-326-9322; E-mail: bunkys@ chesapeake.net; www.solomonsisland.com/bunkys) Long the center for Solomons' sportfishing, Bunky's offers the full range of opportunities to get out on the water. Charter boats are available for half-day and full-day trips; head boats for groups. Also, sixteen-foot fiberglass skiffs are available for rent. Fishing, Apr.–Nov.; bait and tackle shop open year-round.

Solomons Charter Captains Association (P.O. Box 831, Solomons, MD 20688; 888-591-7222; 410-326-2670) Year-round charter boat fishing offered aboard more than thirty vessels, all operated by U.S. Coast Guard-licensed captains.

NORTHERN NECK/MIDDLE PENINSULA

Heathsville, Virginia

Crabbe's Charter Fishing (51 Railway Rd., Heathsville, VA 22473; 804-453-3251) Capt. Danny Crabbe's family has been tying up here for eighty years and says that rockfishing has never been better around Smith Point. Fish for rockfish until Dec. 31. The _KIT II_ is licensed for twenty-six passengers.

Reedville, Virginia

Betty Jane (Buzzard's Point Marina, Reedville, VA 22539; mailing address: 227 Crosshills Rd., Heathsville, VA 22473; 804-580-5904; E-mail: charters@rivnet. net; www.christopher-family.com/charters) Capt. E. Wayson Christoper has been at it for years. Licensed for six passengers.

Pittman's Charters Inc. (2998 Fairport Rd., Reedville, VA 22539; 804-453-3643) Head out aboard the forty-six-foot _Mystic Lady II_. May–mid-Dec.; $55 per person; $385 minimum. Night trips vary; call for prices.

Wicomico Church, Virginia

Capt. Billy's Charters (Ingram Bay Marina, Wicomico Church, VA 22579; mailing address: 545 Harveys Neck Rd., Heathsville, VA 22473; 804-580-7292) Sail out of Ingram Bay aboard _Liquid Assets_, a forty-foot vessel designed for fishing parties and sight-seeing. Personalized service and instruction in fishing and cruising. Reservations required.

Jimmick Jr. III (95 Long Cove Lane/P.O. Box 38, Wicomico Church, VA 22579; 804-580-7744) Everything-supplied fishing and catered cruises for up to twenty-five passengers. Full-timer since 1986, Capt. Jim Deibler. Reservations required.

Reeling in a rockfish near Smith Point.

David Trozzo

UPPER EASTERN SHORE

Rock Hall

The Kent County Office of Tourism (Rock Hall, MD 21661; 410-778-0416) lists fishing charters in its visitor's guide. Contact: Capt. Walter Fithian, *Wife's Mercedes* (410-639-7850); Capt. Greg Jetton, *Miss Gayle* and *Oneida* (410-639-7127); Capt. Bob Gibson, *Daddy's Girl* (410-778-9424); and Capt. Larry Simns, *Dawn II* (410-639-2966).

Tilghman

Harrison's Sport Fishing Center (21551 Chesapeake House Dr./P.O. Box 310, Tilghman, MD 21671; 410-886-2121) Sportfishing central on the Bay, by an inn open since the last century's last decade. Sportfishers have been coming here since the late 1930s. Fourteen-boat fleet, plus a phalanx of on-call captains; charter boats and "make-up" boats, meaning you and a buddy might end up on board with a few others who "make up" a full load. Charters cost about $480 for six passengers. Boat rentals, marina, and crab deck.

LOWER EASTERN SHORE

Chincoteague, Virginia

The Chincoteague Island Charterboat Association publishes a brochure listing licensed professional charterboats. Contact: Chincoteague Chamber of Commerce, P.O. Box 258, Chincoteague, VA 23336; 757-336-6161.

Chincoteague Hunting & Fishing Center (3801 Main St., Chincoteague, VA 23336; 888-231-4868; 757-336-3474) One charter vessel, equipped for offshore angling, along with a bait and tackle shop. The bays behind Virginia's barrier islands offer good fishing. In-season, catch spot, flounder, and other edible species in sheltered waters; offshore, albacore, tuna, and shark are among the favorites. Guided waterfowl hunting is also available. Capt. Pete Wallace.

Wachapreague, Virginia

Wachapreague Hotel & Marina (17 Atlantic Ave./P.O. Box 360, Wachapreague, VA 23480; 757-789-3222) Bottom and deep-sea fishing from a choice of several charter craft. They also rent small boats that you can take out yourself. The Island House Restaurant is located by the marina.

GOLF

What to do if you're not out on the Chesapeake waters? Golf is a fine alternative, with widely distributed courses on both of the Bay's shores. It's a longish season, too, given the mild MidAtlantic climate. Spring and fall may offer the most pleasant days on the links, if the Chesapeake summer's humidity is not to your liking. Most clubs have equipment for rent. Be sure to call ahead for tee times at the public courses. Semiprivate clubs give first dibs to their members.

Although *The Chesapeake Bay Book* only touches on the *Williamsburg, Virginia* area, serious golfers will want to check out this golfing paradise. The **Kingsmill Resorts** offers three courses, including the Pete Dye-designed River Course, an Arnold Palmer-designed course, and a third from Curtis Strange. Not far away is the **Golden Horseshoe,** designed by Robert Trent Jones. If that isn't enough, *Golf Digest* has been bestowing awards throughout the region, naming the **Royal New Kent** Best New Course in America in 1997 — a year after the nearby **Legends at Stonehouse** won the same. And those are just the marquee courses. Contact: 804-786-1919; www.VIRGINIA.org; ask for the annual *Virginia Golf Guide.*

HEAD OF THE BAY

Brantwood Golf Club (1190 Augustine Herman Hwy., Elkton, MD 21921; 410-398-8848) 18 holes; semiprivate. Located on Rte. 213.
Bulle Rock (320 Blenheim Lane, Havre de Grace, MD 21078; 888-285-5375; www.bullerock.com) Voted "Best New Upscale Golf Course" for 1998 by

Golf Digest. Public, full-time locker room attendant, fine-dining restaurant, Bay views.

ANNAPOLIS/WESTERN SHORE

Annapolis Golf Club (2638 Carrollton Rd., Annapolis, MD 21403; 410-263-6771) 9 holes. Nice, local course; semiprivate. Located in the Annapolis Roads community.

Bay Hills Golf Club (545 Bay Hills Dr., Arnold, MD 21012; 410-974-0669) 18 holes; semiprivate. Located north of Annapolis.

Dwight D. Eisenhower Golf Course (Generals Hwy., Crownsville, MD 21032; 410-571-0973) 18 holes. This popular public course was taken over by Billy Casper Management in the summer of 1998. Interesting environmental features remain along the busy course. Located just outside Annapolis.

South River Golf Links (3451 Solomons Island Rd., Edgewater, MD, 21037; 800-SO-River; 410-798-5865; www.mdgolf.com) 18 holes. Challenging public course. Driving range, putting green. Earned $3^1/_2$ stars in *Golf Digest* 1998-1999 "Places to Play." Brought to you by the same folks who brought you Queenstown Harbor Golf Links.

Swan Point Golf Club (11550 Swan Point Blvd., Issue, MD 20645; 301-259-0047; 301-870-2951) 12 holes on the water. Where the serious players go. Turn off Rte. 301, east onto Rte. 257, and head back eight miles.

Twin Shields Golf Club (2425 Roarty Rd., Dunkirk, MD 20754; 410-257-7800) 18 holes; semiprivate. A local golf pro says that he'd head here first among these Western Shore courses. Located on Rte. 260.

NORTHERN NECK/MIDDLE PENINSULA

Bushfield Golf Club (P.O. Box 157, Mount Holly, VA 22524; 804-472-2602) 9 holes; par 72. Golf carts, driving range, pro shop, snack bar. Located at the historic Bushfield Plantation.

Gloucester Country Club (Golf Club Rd., Gloucester, VA 23061; 804-693-2662) 9 holes; public. Good for beginners. Located twelve miles north of York River Bridge.

Golden Eagle Golf Course (P.O. Box 480, Irvington, VA 22480; 800-843-3746; 804-438-5501) 18 holes; championship course. A par 3 for guests. Part of The Tides Resorts. Restaurant, professional instruction, and driving range. $85 high-season greens fees for nonguests, but that includes lunch.

Tartan Golf Course of the Tides (480 King Carter Dr., Irvington, VA 22480; 800-843-3746; 804-438-6200) 18 holes. At an upscale resort, pro shop, game room, snack bar, restaurant. The Tides Lodge and Tides Inn are now under the same ownership; guests at either resort can use facilities at the other. Reservations required.

The Village Green Golf Club (17390 Northumberland Hwy., Callao, VA 22435; 804-529-6332) 9 holes; public. Pro shop and restaurant year-round.

UPPER EASTERN SHORE

The Easton Club (28449 Clubhouse Dr., Easton, MD 21601; 800-277-9800; 410-820-9800) 18 holes. Championship golf course in a waterfront community. Restaurant.

Hog Neck Golf Course (10142 Old Cordova Rd., Easton, MD 21601; 800-280-1790; 410-822-6079) 27 holes, with both 18-hole championship course, 9-hole executive course. Golf pros, pro shop, snack bar. Ranked by some golf experts as one of the top twenty-five public golf courses in the U.S.

Mears Great Oak Landing Resort and Conference Center (Great Oak Landing Rd., Chestertown, MD 21620; 800-LANDING; 410-778-5007) 9 holes; executive course. Open to the public.

Queenstown Harbor Golf Links (310 Links Lane, Queenstown, MD 21658; 800-827-5257; 410-827-6611) 36 holes. Very busy. Rated best public golf course in Maryland by *Golf Digest* in 1997. A beautiful setting on the Chester River.

The Sports Trappe (P.O. Box 408, Trappe, MD 21673; 410-822-7345) A driving practice range, heated and covered. Also batting cages, miniature golf, and equipment. Located nine miles south of Easton.

LOWER EASTERN SHORE

Captain's Cove Golf and Yacht Club (3370 Captain's Corridor, Greenbackville, VA 23356; 757-824-3465) 9 holes; public. Open water on 4 holes.

Eastern Shore Yacht and Country Club (14421 Country Club Rd., Melfa, VA 23410; 757-787-1525) 18 holes. Private club available to visitors by reciprocal agreement with other clubs. Reservations required. Open year-round.

Nassawango Country Club (3940 Nassawango Rd., Snow Hill, MD 21863; 410-632-3114; 410-957-2262) 18 holes; semiprivate championship course. Pro shop.

Northampton Country Club (P.O. Box 267, Cape Charles, VA 23310; 757-331-8423) 18 holes; public.

Nutters Crossing Golf Course & Driving Range (30287 Southampton Bridge Rd., Salisbury, MD 21801; 410-860-4653) 18 holes; semiprivate.

Winter Quarters Golf Course (355 Winter Quarters Dr., Pocomoke City, MD 21851; 410-957-1171) Public. Two separate sets of tees to make a "front nine" and a "back nine."

HIKING

The beauty of the Chesapeake region is its diversity, and hikers will find an intriguing range of habitat to explore. Cypress swamps stand on both sides of the Bay, not far from forests of loblolly pine. Explorers from Maryland's **Calvert Cliffs State Park** to Virginia's **Westmoreland State Park** may discover washed-up sharks' teeth, vestiges of life from an ancient, Miocene sea. (*Warning:* Do *not* dig in the cliffs!)

The vista stretches out from atop the Assateague Lighthouse at the Chincoteague National Wildlife Refuge.

David Trozzo

Over 100 miles to the east of the Bay is the Atlantic Ocean and **Assateague Island,** home to forty-four different mammal species. Look out to the ocean in the summer, and you may see bottlenose dolphins. The flat beaches there are the southernmost point at which gray seals are born. Less than twenty miles west of the Bay is the Patuxent River, home to Jug Bay, where wild rice and water hyacinths grow in the summer. If you're very quiet and even more lucky, you might see the river otters who live here.

Virtually all of the region's state parks, refuges, and wildlife management areas offer tidewater trails worth exploring. You'll find more details under the heading Bird-Watching and in the section Parks & Wildlife Areas. The observant naturalist may spot such rare species as the Delmarva fox squirrel or catch a memorable eyeful when a bald eagle's immense wingspan glides over the cattails.

Parks & Wildlife Areas

Here's a quick compendium of some of the region's favorite state, federal, and local parks, refuges, and natural areas arranged in geographical order for quick reference. All of these wild areas offer an abundance of fishing, hiking, birding, or boating opportunities, and you've seen most listed elsewhere in the chapter under those headings.

HEAD OF THE BAY

Elk Neck State Park (4395 Turkey Point Rd., North East, MD 21901; 410-287-5333) 2,188 acres. Located on Rte. 272, 9 mi. S. of North East.

Susquehanna State Park (3318 Rocks Chrome Hill Rd., Jarrettsville, MD 21084; 410-557-7994) 2,639 acres.

ANNAPOLIS/WESTERN SHORE

Calvert Cliffs State Park (Point Lookout State Park; P.O. Box 48, Scotland, MD 20687; 301-872-5688) 1,313 acres. N. of Solomons, on Rte. 2/4.

Helen Avalynne Tawes Garden (Tawes State Office Bldg., 580 Taylor Ave., Annapolis, MD 21401; 410-260-8189) Handicap access on six-acre garden designed to be touched.

Jug Bay Wetlands Sanctuary (1361 Wrighton Rd., Lothian, MD 20711; 410-741-9330) Seven miles of trails; uncrowded; limited hours.

Point Lookout State Park (P.O. Box 48, Scotland, MD 20687; 301-872-5688) 1,045 acres. Located at the confluence of the Potomac River and the Chesapeake Bay.

St. Marys River State Park (St. Marys City, MD 20686; 301-872-5688) 2,176 acres, on a lake created from a flood-controlled dam. Located off Rte. 5.

Sandy Point State Park (1100 E. College Pkwy., Annapolis, MD 21401; 410-974-2149) 786 acres. Located on Rte. 50, near the last exit 32 before the Bay Bridge. Ask about access to the 2,500-acre **Severn Run Natural Environmental Area,** at the headwaters of the Severn River.

NORTHERN NECK/MIDDLE PENINSULA

Belle Isle State Park (1632 Belle Isle Rd., Lancaster, VA 22503; 804-462-5030) Seven miles on the Rappahannock River. Located off Rte. 354 on Rte. 683.

Westmoreland State Park (State Park Rd., Montross, VA 22520; 804-493-8821) Almost 1,300 acres along almost two miles of the Potomac River. Located off Rte. 3, E. outside Montross.

UPPER EASTERN SHORE

Eastern Neck National Wildlife Refuge (1730 Eastern Neck Rd., Rock Hall, MD 21661; 410-639-7056) 2,300 acres of island.

Idylwild Wildlife Management Area (Houston Branch Rd., Federalsburg, MD 21632; 410-376-3236) 3,000 acres.

Martinak State Park (c/o Tuckahoe State Park, 13070 Crouse Mill Rd., Queen Anne, MD 21657; 410-479-1619) 107 acres. Located off Rte. 404, 2 mi. S. of Denton.

Tuckahoe State Park (13070 Crouse Mill Rd., Queen Anne, MD 21657; 410-820 1668) 3,800 acres.

Wildfowl Trust of North America (Horsehead Wetlands Center, 600 Discovery Lane, Grasonville, MD 21638; 410-827-6694) 500 acres.

Wye Island Natural Resources Management Area (632 Wye Island Rd., Queenstown, MD 21658; 410-827-7577) 2,550 acres.

LOWER EASTERN SHORE

Assateague Island National Seashore (7206 National Seashore Lane, Berlin, MD 21811; 410-641-3030) Thirteen miles of barrier island. **Assateague State Park** (7307 Stephen Decatur Hwy., Berlin, MD 21811; 410-641-2120) Two miles of oceanfront.

Blackwater National Wildlife Refuge (2145 Key Wallace Dr., Cambridge, MD 21613; 410-228-2677) 24,000 acres. Located south of Church Creek.

Chincoteague National Wildlife Refuge (P.O. Box 62, Chincoteague, VA 23336; 757-336-6122) Ten miles of beach.

Deal Island Wildlife Management Area (Contact: Salisbury's state DNR office; 410-543-8223).

Eastern Shore of Virginia National Wildlife Refuge (5003 Hallett Circle, Cape Charles, VA 23310; 757-331-2760) 750 acres.

Ellis Bay Wildlife Management Area (Contact: Salisbury's state DNR office: 410-543-8223).

Janes Island State Park (26280 Alfred Lawson Dr., Crisfield, MD 21817; 410-968-1565) About 3,000 acres, 2,800 on the island.

Kiptopeke State Park (3540 Kiptopeke Dr., Cape Charles, VA 23310; 757-331-2267). Located off Rte. 13, 3 mi. N. of the Bay Bridge Tunnel.

Pocomoke River State Park (3461 Worcester Hwy., Snow Hill, MD 21863; 410-632-2566) Over 900 acres at two sites. Located on Rte. 12 and on Rte. 113.

HEAD OF THE BAY

Elk Neck State Park (4395 Turkey Point Rd., North East, MD 21901; 410-287-5333) Five different hiking trails, the most of any Maryland park east of the Bay. Traverse steep bluffs, forests, marshland, and beaches.

Susquehanna State Park (3318 Rocks Chrome Hill Rd., Jarretsville, MD 21084; 410-836-6735; 410-557-7994) Gently rolling hills are a departure from much of the flatlands that mark the Bay region. Spectacular spot along the river.

ANNAPOLIS/WESTERN SHORE

Calvert Cliffs State Park (Rte. 765, Lusby, MD 20657; 301-872-5688) A great spot. This Bayside park offers thirteen miles of hiking trails with a bonus above and beyond the birds offshore: fossils dating fifteen to twenty million years back to the Miocene Era may be collected by hikers if they've been uncovered by nature (no digging in the cliffs!). You have to hike back a couple of miles to the beach. Open sunrise to sunset. Contact: Point Lookout State Park, P.O. Box 48, Scotland, MD 20687; 301-872-5688.

Jug Bay Wetlands Sanctuary (1361 Wrighton Rd., Lothian, MD 20711; 410-741-9330) Seven miles of nature study and hiking trails. Pause along the Patuxent River, and if you're lucky, you might — and we mean *might* — catch a glimpse of the elusive river otter. A terrific, serene spot that is not overcrowded. Open Wed. and weekends in warm weather; small entrance fee. Call for reservations and winter hours.

Point Lookout State Park (P.O. Box 48, Scotland, MD 20687; 301-872-5688) Hike back along the beach to the ruins of the Civil War's Fort Lincoln. Located at the end of Rte. 5.

Severn Run Natural Environmental Area (Sandy Point State Park, 100 E. College Pkwy., Annapolis, MD 21401; 410-974-2149) Here the state has bought 2,500 acres along the Severn River. Located at the headwaters of the Severn, this is one of the few wild places near Annapolis. Closed to the general public, but may be accessed by contacting Sandy Point State Park.

NORTHERN NECK/MIDDLE PENINSULA

Chesapeake Nature Trail (W. of Kilmarnock, VA, on the south side of Rte. 3) A 1.6-mile trail that passes the west branch of the Corrotoman River.

UPPER EASTERN SHORE

Eastern Neck National Wildlife Refuge (Rock Hall, MD 21661; 410-639-7056) Nearly 2,300 acres of pristine wilds, only a portion of which is open to visitors. Among the plentiful wildlife is the Delmarva fox squirrel, an endangered species found nowhere on the planet but on the Eastern Shore. Open daily, sunrise to sunset. Go past Rock Hall until the road ends. Located at the mouth of the Chester River in Kent County.

Horsehead Wetlands Center (Grasonville, MD 21638; 410-827-6694) Operated by the Wildfowl Trust of North America. A trail winds through part of the 500-acre center, complete with blinds and towers to observe wildlife, as well as a boardwalk over the marsh. Public programs. Handicap access; no pets; small fee; closed Christmas. Located east of Kent Narrows.

Idylwild Wildlife Management Area (Houston Branch Rd., Federalsburg, MD 21632; 410-376-3236) 2,994 acres of serenity and beauty.

Martinak State Park (Deep Shore Rd., Denton, MD 21629; 410-479-1619) On old, Native American territory and stamping grounds. Located off Rte. 404, 2 mi. S. of Denton.

Tuckahoe State Park (Rte. 480, Queen Anne, MD 21657; 410-820-1668) A pretty lake and lots of woods, including a marked fitness trail with exercises at each station. Located on Rte. 480, off Rte. 404, 6 mi. N. of Queen Anne.

LOWER EASTERN SHORE

Blackwater National Wildlife Refuge (2145 Key Wallace Dr., Cambridge, MD 21613; 410-228-2677) A couple of fairly short nature trails take visitors back into this bird-watchers' paradise, where in the fall, you'll see flocks of Canada geese and other waterfowl passing through. One of the last bastions of the Delmarva fox squirrel. Located south of Cambridge.

Pocomoke State Forest and Park (Rte. 12, Snow Hill, MD 21863; 410-632-2566) Winding forest roads cut by long-ago loggers go for some ninety miles. Used for hunting in-season.

HUNTING

Not every quarry is fowl or afoot — **sporting clays** are growing in popularity on the Shore, and there are a number of places where you can catch the flying clays in your sights. In Kent County, try **Alexander Sporting Farms** (13503 Alexander Rd., Golts, MD 21635; 410-928-3549) or **Hopkins Game Farm** (Rte. 298/P.O. Box 218, Kennedyville, MD 21645; 410-348-5287), which also has quail, pheasant, chukar, Hungarian partridge, mallard, deer, and 3-D archery. Queen Annes County offers **Pintail Point** (511 Pintail Point Farm Lane, Queenstown, MD 21658; 410-827-7029), a 1,000-acre "recreation destination" with sporting clays, preserve hunting, charter boat fishing, and two B&Bs.

Still, Native Americans and turn-of-the-century gentleman gunners alike pursued a sport synonymous with the Eastern Shore and Virginia's Tidewater: waterfowling.

Seasons are complicated, but hunters in the Bay region typically are on the lookout for **ducks** (mallard, black duck, pintail, redhead, and wood duck) and for fast-flying **sea ducks** that make good sport and are hunted from charter boats. **Snow geese** fly through Chesapeake in growing flocks these days, and their wiliness (they're harder to attract with decoys) and flavorfulness make them a pleasing challenge for waterfowlers. **Dove** hunting is quite popular on the Shore and the Northern Neck. The mourning dove, with its small size and zigzagging flight, is a challenge: the national average is one dove per five shells spent.

There are some good waterfowl hunting guides on the Chesapeake Shore. Among the best known are Floyd Price (410-778-6412) of Kennedyville, with his sizable operation, and Dutch Swonger (410-643-2766) on Kent Island. If these fellows are unavailable, maybe they'll recommend others. Guides' fees vary, but expect to pay something in the neighborhood of $100/day per person in your hunting party. You also might want to check with the sporting goods stores listed under the heading Sporting Goods & Camping Supply Stores.

Beyond Chesapeake waterfowling, the **whitetail deer** hunting here is some of the best around. Quite a few Pope and Young Club record-book bucks have come out of the Shore, including a Kent County buck that held the national size record for two years. An exotic expatriot, the **Sika deer,** was brought to the area years ago from its native Japan by wealthy landowners who wanted unusual pets to roam their grounds. The Sikas escaped into the wild. Today, they're prolific, especially in Dorchester County. The Sika deer season often runs concurrent with the whitetail deer season. A small species, the Sika makes for excellent table game. Incidentally, the Sika is actually a member of the elk family, and they make better eating, Dutch Swonga says.

Both Virginia and Maryland enforce extensive hunting regulations, set annually, regarding seasons, bag limits, and licensing — not to mention violations. In Maryland, contact: Maryland Department of Natural Resources, Wildlife and Heritage Division, 580 Taylor Ave., E-1, Annapolis, MD 21401; 410-260-8540. In Virginia, contact: Department of Game and Inland Fisheries, 4010 W. Broad St./P.O. Box 11104, Richmond, VA 23230; 804-367-1000; www.dgif.state.va.us/.

SPORTING GOODS & CAMPING SUPPLY STORES

Forgot your tent's sand stakes? Need a spare Styrofoam cooler? No sweat. Sporting and outdoor goods stores are your local repositories of information about where the fish are biting, how to obtain a hunting license, and other important details about recreation, indoor or outdoors.

HEAD OF THE BAY

Penn's Beach Marina (411 Concord St., Havre de Grace, MD 21078; 410-939-2060) Everything for the angler. Tackle store, boat motors, but no fishing licenses.

ANNAPOLIS/WESTERN SHORE

Angler's Sport Center (1456 Whitehall Rd., Annapolis, MD 21401; 410-757-3442) Hunting and fishing licenses, fishing gear, decoys, outdoor clothing. The dean of local fishing supply stores. Located on Rte. 50, between Annapolis and Bay Bridge, exit 30 off Rte. 50, E. of Cape St. Claire.

Marty's Sporting Goods (95 Mayo Rd., Edgewater, MD 21037; 410-956-2238) Everything for fishing.

Tyler's Tackle Shop (8210 Bayside Rd; Chesapeake Beach, MD 20732; 410-257-6610) A neat little place, with rods, reels, and whatever you need for fishing. Also, takeout, featuring crabs and shrimp.

NORTHERN NECK/MIDDLE PENINSULA

Winter Harbor Seafood (Rte. 3, Oak Grove, VA 22443; 804-224-7779) This may be a seafood market, but it's also the place to get hunting and fishing gear and licenses. Game checking.

UPPER EASTERN SHORE

Albright's Gun Shop (36 E. Dover St., Easton, MD 21601; 410-820-8811) Fishing and hunting gear; Orvis dealer.

Bear's Den (851 High St., Chestertown, MD 21620; 410-778-0087).

Shore Sportsman (6184 Ocean Gateway Dr., Trappe, MD 21673; 800-263-2027; 410-820-5599) Hunting, fishing, bait, and tackle.

Sportsman Service Center (112 Piney Creek Rd., Chester, MD 21619; 800-342-3123 in Md. only; 410-643-4545).

Toy's Outdoor Store (6274 Rock Hall Rd., Rock Hall, MD 21661; 410-778-2561).

LOWER EASTERN SHORE

Assateague Market (Stephen Decatur Hwy./Rte. 611, Berlin, MD 21811; 410-641-3380) From doughnuts to kitchen magnets to camping supplies.

Buck's Place (11848 Assateague Rd., Berlin, MD 21811; 410-641-4177) Groceries, bait and tackle, souvenirs, take-out subs and seafood.

Dave's Sport Shop (23701 Nanticoke Rd., Quantico, MD 21856; 410-742-2454)
Everything that you need for the hunting season, deep in the heart of
Wicomico's best hunting territory.

Tommy's Sporting Goods (U.S. 50, 300 Sunburst Hwy., Cambridge, MD
21613; 800-236-0295; 410-228 3658) Serving hunters and fishers for more than
forty years.

SWIMMING

The Bay's limited public access combines with a natural nuisance to create
limited beach swimming. Sea nettles, stinging critters that like the saltier
regions of the bay, show up after the cooler waters of early summer pass.
These not-so-welcome visitors arrive in July or August in proportions inverse
to the preceding spring's wetness. Lots of fresh rainwater discourages their
growth, while a dry spring increases the saltiness of the Bay waters where they
thrive. Betterton Beach, on the Upper Eastern Shore, is beloved because it has
no stinging nettles. Let us also get in a word about Bay water quality: it's generally good, but occasionally unpleasant or unacceptable. Before diving ran-
domly off your boat, use common sense: stay out of the water in heavily developed creeks around Baltimore or Hampton Roads; enjoy it in tributaries of the
Choptauk or Rappahannock.

HEAD OF THE BAY

North East Beach (Rte. 272, North East; 410-287-5333) Lifeguard, picnicking,
bathhouse. $2 per carload. Along the North East River.

ANNAPOLIS/WESTERN SHORE

Arundel Olympic Swim Center (2690 Riva Rd., Annapolis; 410-222-7933; 301-
970-2216) Where you go for a good workout. Olympic-sized pool. Operated
by the Anne Arundel County Recreation Parks Dept. Nominal entrance fees.
Open Mon.–Fri., 6:00 a.m.–10:00 p.m.; Sat., 8:00 a.m.–8:00 p.m.; Sun., 10:00
a.m.–6:00 p.m.; closed Easter, Thanksgiving, Christmas, New Year's Day.

Breezy Point (5 mi. S. of Chesapeake Beach in Calvert County; 410-535-0259)
The county took over this formerly private Bayside enclave. Nets off the
beach help protect swimmers from sea nettles. Also, fishing and crabbing. $4
fee. Open Mem. Day–Labor Day, 6:00 a.m.–6:00 p.m.

Chesapeake Beach Water Park (4079 Creekside Dr., Chesapeake Beach; 410-
257-1404) Town-owned waterworld includes eight slides, a "dreamland
river," where you can tube or swim, and a variety of other activities, includ-

ing a separate "diaper" pool. Height and residence (locals pay less) factor into the price; discounts in the evening. Open Mem. Day–Labor Day.

Point Lookout State Park (P.O. Box 48, Scotland; 301-872-5688) The beach is nice for sunning, but there's also a beach for surf casting. Swim in designated areas. Located on Rte. 5, Point Lookout.

Sandy Point State Park (1100 E. College Pkwy., Annapolis; 410-974-2149) One of the few sandy beaches on the Bay. It's fun to hang out here and watch what goes on out on the Bay — from the massive, coal-filled colliers headed for port in Baltimore to the crisp white sails of the yachting set in the summer. You'll have an up close and personal view of the Bay Bridge. Prices vary from $1–$3 per person. Over age 62 and kids in car seats, free. On Rte. 50, take the last exit before the Bay Bridge.

NORTHERN NECK/MIDDLE PENINSULA

Gloucester Point Beach Park (Rte. 17, on the York River next to Coleman Bridge/York River Bridge, Gloucester, VA; 804-642-9474) Fishing pier, picnic area, horseshoe and volleyball courts, and swimming. Concession stand, rest rooms open seasonally.

Westmoreland State Park (State Park Rd., Montross, VA; 804-493-8821) Olympic-sized pool at this park on the Potomac River. Located 5 mi. W. of Montross, off Rte. 3 E.

UPPER EASTERN SHORE

Betterton Beach (Rte. 292, Betterton, Kent County; contact Parks and Recreation; 410-778-1948) Deep in the Upper Bay, where freshwater, not saltwater, dominates, Betterton is noted for reliable swimming conditions devoid of stinging nettles. Picnicking, fishing jetty, bathhouse, beach. Free. Lifeguard only on Sat., Sun.; Mem. Day–Labor Day. Picnic pavilion available for group rental.

Rock Hall Public Beach (Beach Rd., Rock Hall; 410-639-7611) From this small, quiet beach you can watch the giant container ships make their way from the Bay Bridge up to Baltimore. You won't find a lifeguard at this no-frills beach run by the town of Rock Hall, but it's free, and you can't beat the view.

LOWER EASTERN SHORE

Assateague State Park (7307 Stephen Decatur Hwy., Berlin; 410-641-2120) Ocean swimming and beachcombing. Also check the Assateague Island National Seashore next door (410-641-3030).

Dorchester County Pool (106 Virginia Ave., Cambridge) Where the locals go, especially after the sea nettles arrive in the Bay. $2 adults; $1 students. Open daily, Mem. Day–Labor Day.

Great Marsh (Somerset Ave., Cambridge; contact Dorchester County Tourism; 410-228-1000) Boat ramp, picnicking, pier, and playground. Swim in early summer, before the sea nettles arrive.

TENNIS

With a long, warm season, Chesapeake is ideal outdoor tennis country. Chasing the ball is a great antidote for stiffened sea legs or for birdwatchers who've spent the day crouched in a blind. Or maybe you are simply cut from the same cloth as the author's great, late, grandfather, who played tennis for eighty-five years and always said that it helped him to focus and to forget his cares. Public courts abound throughout the Bay area. For locations, contact the recreation departments of the county where you're staying. For county Chamber of Commerce telephone numbers, see the heading Tourist Information in Chapter Eight, *Information.*

ANNAPOLIS/WESTERN SHORE

In Anne Arundel County, forty-five county parks have tennis courts; eight have lights for nighttime play. Visitors to Annapolis, where court time is harder to find, may want to use courts in nearby towns in less-congested central or rural south county. Contact: Anne Arundel County Department of Recreation and Parks; 410-222-7300.

UPPER EASTERN SHORE

Cross Court Athletic Club (1180 S. Washington St., Easton; 410-822-1515).

LOWER EASTERN SHORE

Salisbury City Park (E. Main St. & S. Park Dr., Salisbury; 410-548-3188) A few public courts are located in a tree-shaded park, which features a bandstand for summer Sun. concerts, a playground, paddleboats, and walking trails along the river.

WINDSURFING

You'd expect the Bay's vast shoreline to breed lots of windsurfing — aka boardsailing — and it does, if you have your own board. You'll also need some help finding a way onto the water from the famously limited public access to the shoreline surrounding this estuary. The Annapolis windsurfing gurus hang out at **East of Maui** (Festival at Riva Shopping Center, 2303 Forest Dr., Annapolis, MD 21401; 410-573-9463), the only place around town where you can rent a board. They also host lessons and offer rentals (Saturday and Sunday only) at **Kentmoor Marina,** located at the base of the Bay Bridge on Kent Island.

Your other major outlet works out of the **Gunpowder State Park's Hammerman Area,** a Bayside corner of this enormous park that stretches practically to Pennsylvania. **Ultimate Watersports** (Ultimate Sports, 110 W. Padonia Rd., Timonium, MD 21093; 410-666-WIND; fax 410-666-9469l) started its watersports empire with windsurfing and remains devoted from its location at a spot on the Gunpowder River just as it enters the Bay. Besides rentals, instruction and camps are their forte and that includes opportunities for kayakers, too. The Upper Bay location means fresher water that's free of sea nettles, and the company sets aside an area just for windsurfers.

Other popular locations include **Sandy Point State Park** in Annapolis. Other boardsailing parks include **Point Lookout State Park** in St. Marys County and **Betterton Beach** at the mouth of the Sassafras River. Check the park and marina listings in this chapter for addresses and telephone numbers to ask about regulations.

NEARBY RECREATION

Ocean City, Maryland

Ocean City is within easy driving distance of Salisbury, Berlin, and Assateague — in fact, many would consider those a natural and worthy grouping of travel destinations. The sprawling beach town's major attraction is a ten-mile-long strip of golden sand that often is packed blanket to blanket on summer weekends. Over the years, the government has engaged in a lengthy (some might say fruitless) battle to keep that sand in place by importing tons of sand from offshore to replace what the ocean's natural cycle washes away.

None of that worries visitors much, though. They come for the sun, the sand, the carnival rides, the "World Famous French Fries" sold on Ocean City's boardwalk, the shops and restaurants, and the fishing, including the big-money, white marlin tournament.

You can reach Ocean City, or "O.C.," from the Bay via three routes. Enter the oldest, southernmost part of the city on U.S. 50 from the west; or take Md. 90 across the Assawoman Bay Bridge to what has become the city's center; or from the Delaware beach towns of Rehoboth, Dewey, and Bethany Beaches to the north (highly worthwhile destinations) via Rte. 1, which becomes the Coastal Hwy., Md. Rte. 528, once you reach Maryland. Contact: Ocean City Convention and Visitor Bureau; 800-OCO-CEAN; 410-289-8181; www.ococean.com; www.ocean-city.com.

Virginia Beach, Virginia

Rivaling the attractions of the Maryland shore, Virginia Beach draws revelers from all over Virginia and the East Coast. Virginia Beach proper offers twenty-eight miles of ocean beach and another ten miles along the Bay. Twelve of those miles are open to the public, and more beckons from nearby state and federal beaches — sun, swim, and surf fish. Atlantic Avenue, the major thoroughfare fronted by a three-mile boardwalk, has been revitalized as a pedestrian mall with public parks and benches. To reach Virginia Beach, follow Va. Rtes. 58 or 44 E. from Norfolk. Contact: Virginia Beach Visitor Information Service; 800-822-3224; www.vabeach.com/.

CHAPTER SEVEN
Antiques, Boutiques & Inlet Outlets
SHOPPING

From ship's hardware to Anne Klein suits, shopping around the Chesapeake is nothing if not diverse.

Folks who think of "antique" as a verb should find plenty to keep themselves busy. Antique specialties, of course, include decoys. Decoy hunters won't want to miss Havre de Grace, the former paradise for gun sportspeople where decoys have become the folk art stock-in-trade. One local shop worker told of an old duck decoy that garnered a rock-bottom price, selling for thousands at auction in New York.

David Trozzo

Johnson's on the Avenue, the venerable men's clothing store in Annapolis, stands across from the Statehouse.

Maryland Avenue in Annapolis, though, continues to house upscale antiques shops, although good-looking design shops have made strong inroads. The pairing makes for a complementary day on the Avenue. Antique bargain hunters, however, may want to meander south on Rte. 2 into Calvert County or into any of the more rural parts of the Bay. From Chestertown, Maryland, to Urbanna, Virginia, there's plenty to sort through.

Galleries are unlikely to exhibit much that's wildly contemporary or cutting edge, but hugely livable pieces by fine watercolorists or printmakers are widely available, especially if you're shopping in Annapolis, the Upper Eastern Shore's Talbot County, or Chestertown. Better yet, this is the perfect place to spot an intriguing piece from any fine crafts gallery.

Outlets dwell here, most notably in Queenstown, just over the Bay Bridge on Rte. 50. Shoppers will want to avoid the heavy-traffic Friday and Sunday hours when beachgoers headed to the Atlantic Ocean clog the highways and the malls.

You'll also find that certain areas, such as the historic district in Annapolis or downtown St. Michaels, offer higher concentrations of stores and boutiques that cater to the tourist trade. Look for everything from T-shirts and crab refrigerator magnets to fine paintings and nature sculpture.

A final note on store hours — in smaller towns or along rural roads, hours are likely to fluctuate considerably, especially during the off-season.

ANTIQUES

Whether you're rummaging through a dusty barn or a historic storefront, Chesapeake has more than its quota of antique shops. Prices can vary widely. If you're a bargain-lover, try an auction. One local institution on the Upper Eastern Shore is **Dixon's Antique & Furniture Auction** (Rtes. 290 and 544, Crumpton; 410-928-3006) in Queen Annes County, better known as the Crumpton Auction. People who live as sparingly as Thoreau at Walden Pond come back raving about the great finds at this vast affair. Starts at 9:00 a.m. sharp every Wednesday. Also, check out the big auction at **American Corner** (six miles north of Federalsburg on Auction Rd.; 410-754-8826). Every Thursday at 5:00 p.m. buildings full of stuff go on the block. Find everything from outboard motors to furniture.

HEAD OF THE BAY

Chesapeake City

Black Swan Antiques (219 Bohemia Ave., Chespeake City, MD 21915; 410-885-5888) Particularly good stop for those inclined toward Bay-related items. Nauticals include a fun array of binnacles, prints, and oyster cans, from Maryland Beauties to the McReady Brothers of Chincoteague.

Havre de Grace

Bank of Memories (319 St. John St., Havre de Grace, MD 21078; 410-939-4343) Dolls and *Vanity Fair* prints and an unusual amber-carved cameo can be found among the gems in the jewel case. Housed in the old First National Bank in the center of town.
Franklin Street Antiques (464 Franklin St., Havre de Grace, MD 21078; 410-939-4220) Cookie jar central, for sure. But glass drinking straw dispensers line one shelf at this chockablock-full shop. Keep an eye out for decoys, the local pride and joy.

Havre de Grace Antique Center (408 N. Union Ave., Havre de Grace, MD 21078; 410-939-4882) Likely the best antique shop in town — certainly filled with shelves aplenty with cool stuff.

Susquehanna Trading Co. (324 N. Union Ave., Havre de Grace, MD 21078; 410-939-4252) Decoys are to Havre de Grace what hammocks are to Pawley's Island, and this shop sells an enormous selection of decoys across every price range, including pieces by local son and decoy-carving star R. Madison Mitchell.

Washington Street Books & Antiques (131 N. Washington St., Havre de Grace, MD 21078; 410-939-6215) Wonderful used bookshop well worth the stop. Knowledgeable proprietor.

ANNAPOLIS/WESTERN SHORE

Annapolis

Annapolis Antique Gallery (2009 West St., Annapolis, MD 21401; 410-266-0635) Glass and china, not much furniture. An emporium of about thirty-five dealers. Take the Parole exit off Rte. 50, and you're practically there.

Baldwin & Claude Antiques (47 Maryland Ave., Annapolis, MD 21401; 410-268-1665) Maps, rare prints, books, and other antiques. Been there for twenty years.

Joan's Gems (49 Maryland Ave., Annapolis, MD 21401; 410-267-7830) Small shop filled with all kinds of antiques. Linens, china, jewelry.

Maryland Avenue Antiques (82 Maryland Ave., Annapolis, MD 21401; 410-268-5158) Specialities include advertising and toys.

Recapture The Past (69 Maryland Ave., Annapolis, MD 21401; 410-216-9067) Two floors, with linens and other cloth collectibles downstairs; glass, prints, and jewelry upstairs. Twenty-five dealers.

Ron Snyder Antiques (2011 West St., Annapolis, MD 21401; 410-266-5452) Eighteenth- and nineteenth-century furniture — and a devotee of the 100-year rule. Marilyn Snyder says that they like to start at 1830 and work back. Right next to the Annapolis Antique Gallery.

Walnut Leaf Antiques (62 Maryland Ave., Annapolis, MD 21401; 410-263-4885) Another of the venerable antique shops on this traditional antiques row, which is fast turning into Interior Design Row. Find a wide variety of lovely glass, china, and porcelains. Open Mon.–Sun.

Harwood

Muddy Creek Antiques (4452 Solomons Island Rd., Harwood, MD 21220; 800-924-6150; 410-867-2219) Your intrepid author entered this fifty-five-dealer store on a 100° day and found the following: Haviland plates of the same pattern once owned by the Mississippi gentlewoman who engineered the

From bronzed baby shoes to lace canopies, Muddy Creek Antiques in Harwood carries it all.

meeting of said author's parents; copies of the "little gypsy boy and girl" prints her mother had purchased as a young bride because they matched those that hung in the home of her aunt; and a copy of the magazine for which the author's father-in-law once served as an editor (his column was printed inside). Open Mon.–Sun., 10:00 a.m.–5:00 p.m.

Huntingtown

Bowen's Garage Antique Center (Old Town Rd., Rte. 524, Huntingtown, MD 20639; 410-257-3105) Dependable collection is offered by a group of vendors, from oak furniture to an assortment of dishware. Open Thurs.–Mon.; Mon., limited hours in winter.

Southern Maryland Antique Center (3176 Solomons Island Rd., Huntingtown, MD 20639; 410-257-1677) Keep an eye peeled for the RW&B "antiques" flag flying on the highway; this multidealer center is definitely worth a stop. Good furniture finds possible. Open Thurs.–Sun.

North Beach

Nice & Fleazy Antiques (7th & Bay Ave., North Beach, MD 20714; 410-257-3044) Longtime antiques resident in this funky little town. They have furniture, too.

St. Leonard

Chesapeake Marketplace (5015 St. Leonard Rd., St. Leonard, MD 20685; 800-655-1081; 410-586-3725) A real browsing emporium for those who can't resist flea markets. You could spend hours. Open Wed.–Sun.

JAD Center (4865 St. Leonard Rd., St. Leonard, MD 20685; 410-586-2740) Very nice selection from a handful of vendors, including sections set aside exclusively for glass and used books. Worth a stop if you're headed south to Solomons. Exit Md. Rte. 2/4 at Calvert Beach Rd., then take a left at Rte. 765.

NORTHERN NECK/MIDDLE PENINSULA

Kilmarnock, Virginia

Kilmarnock Antique Gallery (144 School St., Kilmarnock, VA 22482; 800-497-0083; 804-435-1207; www.virginia-antiques.com) We've never visited this eighty-dealer space, but have heard the locals talking about it on a trip to the Northern Neck and pass the buzz along to you. Open daily.

Urbanna, Virginia

Rose Cottage Antiques (104 Grace Ave., Urbanna, VA 23175; 804-758-3492) Fine antiques and tea. Open Tues.–Sat., 11:00 a.m.–5:00 p.m.

Nimcock Gallery (31 Cross St./P.O. Box 26, Urbanna, VA 23175; 804-758-2602) In this little frame shop, Santas are painted on crab shell ornaments for the whole family and set in a tray amidst antiques, collectibles, paintings, and prints.

Urbanna Antique Gallery (124 Rappahannock Ave., Urbanna, VA 23175; 804-758-2000) Variety of vendors peddling all kinds of stuff, from Coca-Cola boxes to unique lighters.

UPPER EASTERN SHORE

Chestertown

Blue Heron Antiques & Collectibles (204 High St., Chestertown, MD 21620; 410-778-8118) Shopping for antiques is a popular pastime in lovely Chestertown. A good place to start if you're looking for collectibles, china, crystal, or Oriental treasures.

Easton

Foxwell's Antiques & Collectibles (Rte. 50, Easton, MD 21601; 410-820-9705) With eighty dealers in one location, you'll find a variety of items from glassware to china to antique advertising in this eminently browsable shop on the highway.

Lanham-Merida Antiques and Interiors (218 N. Washington St., Easton, MD 21601; 410-763-8500) The best-quality English, Continental, and American furniture, plus paintings, prints, silver, porcelain, and crystal.

Stockley Antiques (Mulberry Hill Farm, Rte. 50, Easton, MD 21601; 410-822-9346) Not a store, exactly, but a restoration shop and historic replica furniture maker. There's a barn full of interesting pieces, and they'll custom-build period furniture.

Galena

Firehouse Antique Center (102 N. Main St., Galena, MD 21635; 410-648-5639) A good place to start exploring Galena's host of antique dealers. Multidealer shop focuses on high-quality (and high-priced) period furniture and accessories.

Oxford

Americana Antiques (111 S. Morris St., Oxford, MD 21654; 410-226-5677) Seventeenth-, eighteenth-, and early nineteenth-century American art and artifacts. A fixture in this town for three decades.

Queenstown

Chesapeake Antique Center (Md. 18 & Rte. 50, Queenstown, MD 21658; 410-827-6640) More than seventy dealers in a large exhibit space, behind Prime Outlets, that almost entirely adheres to the 100-year rule. Rules, of course, are made to be broken, exceptions made for any distinctly period, twentieth-century piece, such as Art Deco.

Rock Hall

Cattail Collections (5718 S. Main St., Rock Hall, MD 21661; 410-639-7788) Antiques, collectibles, American art, pottery, furnishings, and maritime and primitive pieces in a turn-of-the-century home. A local artisan restores and refinishes furniture and replaces cane and rush chair seats.

Royal Oak

Oak Creek Sales (25939 Royal Oak Dr., Royal Oak, MD 21662; 410-745-3193) Eclectic selection of all sorts of antiques and collectibles — the figurine saltshaker sitting next to the Depression glass. Across the street, an entire barn is devoted to antique and used furniture.

St. Michaels

Pennywhistle Antiques (408 S. Talbot St., St. Michaels, MD 21663; 410-745-9771) Known for its exceptional decoys; antiques in one room after another.

LOWER EASTERN SHORE

Berlin

Town Center Antiques (1 N. Main St., Berlin, MD 21811; 410-629-1895) Antiques and collectibles from more than seventy dealers are spread out in a big building. There's also a snack bar for when you just have to take a break.

Cambridge

Mills Antiques & Used Furniture (Rte. 50, Cambridge, MD 21613; 410-228-9866) A treasure trove and a habitual stopping point for those in the know. Mills Antiques is like the ultimate attic — relics and detritus piled high, so that you never know what you'll find. Ask for help if you have something specific in mind. A separate building sells books.

Salisbury

Holly Ridge Antiques (1411 S. Salisbury Blvd./Business Rte. 13, Salisbury, MD 21801; 410-742-4392) Specializing in eighteenth- and nineteenth-century furniture and accessories under the strict 100-year rule. Appraisals and refinishing. Open Tues.–Sat.

BOOKS

ANNAPOLIS/WESTERN SHORE

Annapolis

Barnes & Noble (Annapolis Harbour Center, Annapolis, MD 21401; 410-573-1115) Huge and popular, as one might expect. But also with a knowledgeable selection of regional and local books, ranging from Bay histories and watermen to literature penned by local writers. Probably the best stock of Chesapeake books around.

The Book Shelf (1918 A Forest Dr., Gardener Shopping Center, Annapolis, MD 21401; 410-267-6727) This one's for the locals. A good used bookstore that some of us use more than the lending library.

Briarwood Bookshop (88 Maryland Ave., Annapolis, MD 21401; 410-268-1440) The floorboards groan in this great old shop, with a good selection of

Maryland books and a variety of interesting used tomes on art, military, and other subjects of interest to sophisticated, inquiring minds. A good bulletin board, too — worth checking out to see what's going on.

Solomons

Lazy Moon Bookshop (14510 Main St./P.O. Box 1141, Solomons, MD 20688; 410-326-3720; E-mail: lazymoon@olg.com) Dependably complete offering of Chesapeake books, both new titles and old classics, like a signed copy of Calvert County son Hulbert Footner's *Rivers of the Eastern Shore*. Also operates **The Lazy Moon Annex,** essentially 5,000 first editions located in the JAD Center in the heart of the St. Leonard.

NORTHERN NECK/MIDDLE PENINSULA

Kilmarnock, Virginia

Twice Told Tales, Ltd. (75 S. Main St., Kilmarnock, VA 22482; 804-435-9201) Centrally located and easy to find, with a range of books, including quality activity books for kids.

UPPER EASTERN SHORE

Centreville

Corsica Bookshop (101 S. Commerce St., Centreville, MD 21617; 410-758-1453) The Upper Eastern Shore's most intelligently stocked bookstore, well-supplied in the classics, contemporary issues, regional books, a kids' club room for children's and juvenile literature, magazines, and gift items. Also a room for out-of-print titles.

Chestertown

The Compleat Bookseller (301 High St., Chestertown, MD 21620; 410-778-1480) Formerly a branch of the Corsica Bookshop, this fine store has a range of titles that you won't find in the big discount places.

Easton

Family Tree Bookshop (9 Goldsborough St., Easton, MD 21601; 410-820-5252) References and guidance for finding your roots are available from this specialty bookseller.
The News Center (Talbottown Shopping Center, Easton, MD 21601; 410-822-7212) Reliable bookstore with a friendly staff. Large paperback selection of

everything from Dickens to bodice-and-breeches-ripping romances, from cutting-edge contemporary fiction to paramilitary escapist yarns. Virtually complete section of regional writings. In addition, The News Center stocks the Shore's largest periodical selection, with more than 1,000 titles. A smaller News Center, without the books but with lots of magazines, is located in The Centre at Salisbury.

Queenstown

Book Warehouse (429 Outlet Center Dr., Queenstown, MD 21658; 410-827-8474) Hardcovers and paperbacks at fifty to ninety percent below retail. Good history, political science, literature, children's, and contemporary fiction sections; and a decent selection of deep discount coffee-table tomes. Located at Prime Outlets.

Tilghman

Book Bank: Crawford's Nautical Books (5782 Tilghman Island Rd./P.O. Box 336, Tilghman Island, MD 21671; 410-886-2230) More than 12,000 "watery" fiction and nonfiction titles on all things nautical, from sailing to shipbuilding to seafaring. The store buys used books and sells nautical art.

Trappe

Unicorn Book Shop (Rte. 50/Box 154, Trappe, MD 21673; 410-476-3838) Excellent rare and secondhand bookshop. Bibliophiles looking for a seasoned but serviceable copy of *Wuthering Heights* or the serious antiquarian seeking the truly rare and precious will love this place. Prices are reasonable, especially when compared to prices at similar shops in an urban area. An upstairs room holds an impressive selection of antique map reproductions. Owner Jim Dawson knows his stuff and stocks plenty of regional literature.

LOWER EASTERN SHORE

Salisbury

Atlantic Book Warehouse (2734 N. Salisbury Blvd., Salisbury, MD 21801; 410-548-9177) You'll find zero ambiance in this cavernous bookstore, but a huge selection of books; all are discounted, anywhere from ten to eighty percent. Plus calendars and magazines.

Henrietta's Attic (205 Maryland Ave., Salisbury, MD 21801; 800-546-3744; 410-546-3700) Aisles of antique and used books, watched over by the bookstore's cat and bookseller Henrietta Moore. Browse as long as you like, or ask for Moore's help in locating titles that she has in the shop or might be able to find. Collectibles, glassware, china, and genealogy materials are also packed into this "anything goes" place.

CHILDREN

ANNAPOLIS/WESTERN SHORE

Annapolis

BeBeep—A Toy Shop (Festival at Riva Shopping Center, 2327-C Forest Dr.; 410-224-4066) Quality toys.

The Giant Peach (110 Annapolis St.; 410-268-8776) Probably the most venerable children's clothing shop in town. Located in West Annapolis.

UPPER EASTERN SHORE

Chestertown

Pride & Joy (321 High St.; 410-778-2233) Children's apparel and gifts, for new arrivals up to older children.

Easton

Crackerjacks (7 S. Washington St.; 410-822-7716) Toy store selling quality games, dolls, children's books, and stuffed animals. Many imported items.

CLOTHING

ANNAPOLIS/WESTERN SHORE

Annapolis

April Cornell (16 Market Space; 410-263-4532) Bright Indian colors mark the fashions found here, created for both you and your home.

Black Market (145 Main St.; 410-263-7747) A women's shop specializing in dark-colored clothing — a counterpoint to The White House, also located on Main St.

Elanne (27 Maryland Ave.; 410-263-3300) Excellent service from one of the city's long-lived, specialty women's clothing shops. Since 1980.

Elegant Rags (216 Main St.; 410-295-RAGS) One of the new group of trendy women's clothing shops to open in the historic district, complete with gauzy slip dresses and other dreamy wares.

Fashnique (181 Main St.; 410-268-6778) Gauze, imports, 100-percent cotton and rayon clothing for women. Good selection and the sales aren't bad, either. Lots of fun jewelry.

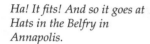

Ha! It fits! And so it goes at Hats in the Belfry in Annapolis.

David Trozzo

Hats in the Belfry (103 Main St.; 410-268-6333) Something of an impromptu performance space, because everybody has fun trying on hats. Felt hats, straw hats, including genuine Panamas, funky hats, sporty hats, Easter bonnets, and hats to garden in. Open more than twenty years.

Hazel T., Ltd. (206 Main St; 410-263-5958) Upscale, good-looking women's clothing that's breezily fashionable. Unique jewelry, too.

Hyde Park Annapolis Haberdashery (110 Dock St., Harbour Square; 410-263-0074) Classic men's clothing. Fairly conservative.

Johnson's on the Avenue (Maryland Ave. & State Circle; 410-263-6390; 410-269-6390) In the window hang traditional houndstooth wools and other fine classic menswear for civilians; inside, the Italian sweaters are folded on the counter. This Annapolis institution also has made uniforms for Navy officers for seven decades and shipped them all over the world. Noted for fine service.

Laurance Clothing (232 Main St.; 410-263-1175) Fine menswear shop, nice leisurewear for Tidewater gentlemen, and French cuffs on 100-percent cotton shirts. Very helpful staff.

Leather and Fur Shoppe (65 Maryland Ave.; 410-263-5884) This shop has been here forever and repairs leather goods too. Fine leather items.

The White House (129 Main St.; 410-267-7747) Women's shop, featuring gorgeous clothes in shades of white, ecru, cream, and other shades of tawny fawn. Companion shops located in Washington, D.C.'s Union Station and Rehoboth, DE.

Why Knot (162 Main St.; 410-263-3003) Good-looking women's clothing from one of the district's longtime shops.

NORTHERN NECK/MIDDLE PENINSULA

Irvington, Virginia

The Dandelion (4372 Irvington Rd./P.O. Box 355; 804-438-5194) Four proprietors shop the designers in New York and Atlanta — and it shows. Even a famously restless shopper wished that she'd had more time. Great women's clothing, from designer upscale to closer to home.

Urbanna, Virginia

Cyndy's Bynn (311 Virginia St.; 804-758-3756) Look for the black awning along Virginia St. Inside find a very nice shop, featuring seasonal gifts and jewelry, fine women's clothing, and a nice little selection of children's and baby's gift items.

UPPER EASTERN SHORE

Chestertown

Houston's Dockside Emporium (315 High St.; 410-778-9079) Women's sportswear, nautical gifts, scale model trains and boats, and a nice selection of unique jewelry.

Easton

Anastasia Ltd. (11 N. Harrison St.; 410-822-4814) Classic women's clothing.

Oxford

Vera C. Boutique-Creations (Morris St./P.O. Box 452; 410-226-5989) Women's and children's clothing, gifts, and jewelry; some of it made locally.

St. Michaels

Bleachers (107 S. Talbot St.; 410-745-5676) Beachy boutique offers colorful, fun clothes for adults and children. Check out the shades.

Chesapeake Bay Outfitters (100 Talbot St.; 410-745-3107) Sports clothes, quality imprinted shirts, and boat shoes. Clothing for men, women, and children.

Collections on the Bay (201 Talbot St.; 410-745-9735) Très sophisticated clothing boutique for women, with gift items, too.

Sailor of St. Michaels (214 Talbot St.; 410-745-2580) Souvenir shirts and sweat-shirts from the Shore, women's and men's sportswear, and gifts.

Shopping in St. Michaels.

David Trozzo

Shaw Bay Classics (208 S. Talbot St.; 800-426-4317; 410-745-3377) Women's classic clothing and accessories and the largest collection of Geiger of Austria boiled wool attire that you'll find anywhere in the U.S.

GALLERIES

HEAD OF THE BAY

Havre de Grace

Vincenti Decoys (353 Pennington Ave.; 410-734-7709) Not only will you find gorgeous decoys, from Patrick Vincenti's to historic collectibles, but decoy-carving materials, too. Where else are you going to find little plastic packets of glass eyes and pewter duck's feet? Decoys range from intricately hand-carved masterpieces to simple folk art.

ANNAPOLIS/WESTERN SHORE

Annapolis

The Annapolis Pottery (40 State Circle; 410-268-6153) A well-loved local institution offering a huge array of stoneware and porcelain pieces, from handy pitchers to art platters and then some.
Aurora Gallery (67 Maryland Ave.; 410-263-9150) Contemporary design pieces and fine crafts in many media. Good jewelry, too.

Old-fashioned wood planks creak beneath visitors' feet at the Dawson Gallery in Annapolis, where Tom Dawson displays fine works of art.

David Trozzo

Dawson Gallery (44 Maryland Ave.; 410-269-1299) Old-fashioned gallery with worn wooden floors showcases nineteenth-century American and European paintings. Chesapeake artists include works by Louis Feuchter, an early twentieth-century Baltimore painter who did delicate small scenes of Eastern Shore life and Otto Muhlenfeld, a Baltimore Port painter from 1871–1907.

La Petite Galerie (39 Maryland Ave.; 410-268-2425) Paintings from the nineteenth and twentieth centuries; generally traditional, representational works.

Main Street Gallery (109 Main St.; 410-280-2787) Nice space; a real mix of work. Represents about forty-five artists, primarily regional. Openings monthly from Apr.–Oct.

McBride Gallery (215 Main St.; 410-267-7077) Longtime local gallery hosts a variety of sixty artists, many from Virginia and Maryland. Generally, somewhat traditional works, many with a maritime or shoreside appeal.

Nancy Hammond Editions (64 State Circle; 410-267-7711) This longtime local silk screen artist is doing some interesting work these days with her cut-paper painted collages. Limited edition silk screen prints of Bay-related icons like herons, an annual Annapolis Christmas poster, and silk-screened utilitarian items, such as dog bowls and ties. Very Annapolis.

Obelyn Galleries (194 Green St.; 410-295-6853) Interesting mix of contemporary artists, including those from the Brandywine school.

Whitehall Gallery (57 West St.; 410-269-6161) Contemporary prints and a frame shop.

Galesville

River Gallery, Ltd. (1000 Main St.; 410-867-0954) Owned by three artists, who show the work of up to twenty consignors. Original artwork and some crafts are located in the former granary of the general store next door. Open Sat.–Sun., 11:00 a.m.–5:00 p.m., or by appt.

Leonardtown

The North End Gallery (41625 Fenwick St.; 301-475-3130) This artists' co-op offers revolving exhibitions and a range of talent, which means you may find a good deal on a nice piece of original art. Open Wed.–Sun.

Prince Frederick

Chesapeake's back roads often yield the unexpected, like these artistic treasures at the Main Street Gallery in Prince Frederick.

David Trozzo

Main Street Gallery (486 Main St.; 410-535-3334) A real fun find. Artists Nancy Collery and Jeff Klapper have turned the first floor of their home into a gallery — down to the art jewelry and photography constructions. Shows regional artists. Open long weekends, Wed.–Sat., 11:00 a.m.–5:00 p.m. most of the year; Sun., Nov.–Dec.

Solomons

Carmen's Gallery (14550 Solomons Island Rd.; 410-326-2549) Watercolors, serigraphs, and Chesapeake scenes. Primarily regional artists; exhibitions every two months.

UPPER EASTERN SHORE

Chestertown

The Finishing Touch (311 High St.; 800-292-0457; 410-778-5292) Fine framing, gifts, cards, candles, photo frames, and some truly nice handiwork from local painters and potters.

Easton

Lu-Ev Framing Shop & Gallery (25-27 E. Dover St.; 410-822-5770) Local originals and a healthy selection of prints, from Paul McGehee maritime period pieces to waterfowl art. Popular custom-frame shop.

The Wood Duck Shoppe & Gallery (8374 Ocean Gateway Dr.; 410-820-5534) Waterfowl art and carvings.

Rock Hall

Shoppes at Oyster Court (Oyster Court) A cluster of relocated watermen's buildings, behind Main St., house artists and crafters and some small boutiques. It's open year-round, Thurs.-Sun., more days open from spring to fall. Telephone numbers of the artist-shopkeepers are on the doors, so if you come when a store is closed you can call to ask that it be opened just for you.

St. Michaels

Calico Gallery (212 Talbot St.; 410-745-5370) Custom framing, artwork, cards, and a second floor filled with interesting and unusual things for kids.

LOWER EASTERN SHORE

Salisbury

The Finer Side (205 Downtown Plaza; 410-749-4081) Frequent exhibits in all kinds of media. A spacious shop inside a converted department store.

The Gallery (625 S. Division St.; 410-742-2880) Regional works in all media. Regular one-person shows and an annual Christmas exhibit, featuring four or five local artists. Custom framing and a range of gift items and crafts, such as decoys and shorebirds.

Salisbury Art & Framing (213 North Blvd., Waverly Plaza; 410-742-9522) Works by local and nationally known artists, depicting everything from seascapes of the Eastern Shore to the abstract. Prints, pottery, handmade jewelry, and custom framing.

Chincoteague, Virginia

Island Arts (6196 Maddox Blvd.; 757-336-5856) Owned by local artist Nancy West, the shop specializes in woven clothing and unique jewelry offerings. Also featured are Nancy's oil paintings, which have been exhibited nationwide.

Lott's Arts & Things (4281 Main St.; 757-336-5773) Features the silk screen artistry of Welsh native Hal Lott, known to poster collectors for his works commemorating Pony Penning and the Easter Decoy Festival.

Onley, Virginia

David Trozzo

At Turner Sculpture in Onley, Virginia, sculptor David Turner works a chunk of clay into an otter that will later be cast in bronze.

Turner Sculpture (Rte. 13/Box 128; 757-787-2818) The drive down Rte. 13 gets a little long through Virginia's Eastern Shore until you stumble upon this wonderful foundry, where William Turner, a dentist, and his son David create great blue herons, beluga whales, and even a draft horse. Their wildlife sculpture is displayed throughout the country, and if you're lucky, they'll even show you the foundry.

GIFT SHOPS & CRAFT GALLERIES

HEAD OF THE BAY

Chesapeake City

The Good Earth (208 George St., Chesapeake City, MD 21915; 410-885-2025) The pleasant splash from tabletop fountains of all sizes fills the air and would have synchronized nicely with the strum of an Irish "gourdolin." Fun, whimsical pottery at a forty-percent sale in Oct.

Maren's (200 Bohemia Ave./P.O. Box 55, Chesapeake City, MD 21915; 410-885-2475) There, in the back — that martini glass Christmas ornament, complete with olive. One Christmas present down. A nice selection of Christmas items.

ANNAPOLIS/WESTERN SHORE

Annapolis

Easy Street (8 Francis St., Annapolis, MD 21401; 410-263-5556) Among the best and most enduring of the city's upscale craft and gift galleries. Interesting blown glass pieces in particular.

The Manor House (Maryland Ave. at State Circle, Annapolis, MD 21401; 410-268-0050) Upscale and eclectic. Everything from stationery to high-end whimsical pottery. A fun place to visit.

Moon Shell Gallery (6 Fleet St., Annapolis, MD 21401; 410-263-5970) Great jewelry and other upscale items.

The Pewter Chalice (168 Main St., Annapolis, MD 21401; 800-284-3265; 410-268-6246) Tired of scouring the earth for classic "silver" baby gifts? A nice pewter selection of these and a wide range of other fine pewter pieces. One of the historic district's old-timers.

Plat du Jour (220 Main St., Annapolis, MD 21401; 410-269-1499) Filled with tempting French and Italian ceramics and fine linens. Among the most unique shops in the historic district.

Pueblo Azul (110 Dock St., Annapolis, MD 21401; 410-295-7663) A departure from the nautical-themed shops cluttered along City Dock. It's filled with Latin American pieces, including some furniture.

Sign o' the Whale (99 Main St., Annapolis, MD 21401; 410-268-2161) Local landmark in former historic customs house. High-quality gift shop. Some nice garden items.

Solomons

Harmon House (14538 Solomons Island Rd., Solomons, MD 20688; 410-326-6848) This four-shop co-op reflects very different tastes. Everything from crab tchotchkes to pottery art bowls by regional artists. A real mix.

Trendies (14636 Solomons Island Rd., Solomons, MD 20688; 410-394-0165) Located in a nineteenth-century general store, where wooden grain bins still snap shut, this is really a design store, with brushed copper thermometers and whimsically crosshatched espresso mugs. Shares the space with **The Lighthouse Angel & Gift Shop,** headquarters for gifts bearing cherubim and seraphim (410-394-0607). Open year-round; shorter hours during fall and winter.

NORTHERN NECK/MIDDLE PENINSULA

Irvington, Virginia

The Tides Inn Gift Shop (480 King Carter Dr./Box 480, Irvington, VA 22480; 804-438-4440; 804-438-5000) Fine gifts, classic styles.

Wood-A-Drift Art Shop (4474 Irvington Rd., Irvington, VA 22480; 804-438-6913) Homey, cluttered, and long in residence, this little shop offers nautical gifts, ranging from small knickknacks to drawings.

Urbanna, Virginia

Make Thyme (260 Prince George, Urbanna, VA 23175; 804-758-2101) Dried and fresh herbs of many varieties, fragrant gift items in the two-room house/shop. A Bay writer noted for his work on the lives and lore of local watermen, Larry Chowning owns this shop with his wife.

UPPER EASTERN SHORE

Easton

American Pennyroyal (5 N. Harrison St., Easton, MD 21601; 410-822-5030) A favorite among lovers of American folk art. Everything from baskets to pottery to rugs, quilts, and jewelry.

L'Atelier (9 Goldsborough St., Easton, MD 21601; 410-763-8810) High-end gift gallery, featuring ceramics, porcelain, and glass.

Rugged Roses (137 N. Harrison St., Easton, MD 21601; 410-820-9209) Clothing and gifts.

Oxford

Oxford Mews (105 S. Morris St./P.O. Box 219, Oxford, MD 21654; 410-820-8222) Like an old-fashioned general store where you can buy anything. A good selection of Bay books and gifts, specialty food products, and biking and camping gear. Bikes rent by the hour or by the day.

Queenstown

The Christmas Goose (Rte. 50, Queenstown, MD 21658; 410-827-5252) Handcrafted Christmas items like nutcrackers, ornaments, and more. Located across from the Chesapeake Outlet Center.

St. Michaels

Keepers at St. Michaels (300 S. Talbot St., St. Michaels, MD 21663; 800-549-1872; 410-745-6388) A full-line Orvis dealer with outdoor gear, clothing, plus antique and contemporary decoys. Keepers has a second store at the Ward Museum of Wildfowl Art in Salisbury (410-742-4988).

Wye Mills

Tidewater Specialties (7133 Ocean Gateway Dr., Wye Mills, MD 21679; 410-820-2076) Home accessories with hunting and dog themes.

LOWER EASTERN SHORE

Cambridge

Bay Country Shop (2709 Ocean Gateway Dr., Cambridge, MD 21613; 410-221-0700) Rustic and goose-oriented Shore items; lots of gifts.

Salisbury

The Country House (805 E. Main St., Salisbury, MD 21801; 410-749-1959) At 16,000 square feet, it's the largest country store in the East and an overwhelming experience for nonshoppers who accidentally wander inside. It has everything country that you could hope to find, plus collectibles, Christmas, and candles, and much more for the kitchen, bath, and household.

Chincoteague, Virginia

Marsha Carter Gifts (6351 Cropper St., Chincoteague, VA 23336; 757-336-3404) A boutique filled with handcrafted products like handblown glass, quilts, embroidered cotton lingerie, paintings, jewelry, pottery, and local bird carvings.

JEWELRY

ANNAPOLIS/WESTERN SHORE

Annapolis

La Belle Cezanne (117 Main St.; 410-263-1996) One of the best windows to shop in Annapolis. Great estate and other unique items.

Ron George Jewelers (205 Main St.; 410-268-3651) Stalwart business, featuring classic jewelry.

Tilghman Co. (44 State Circle; 410-268-7855) The fine old Maryland name of this business tells you that this is a traditional jewelry store, featuring classic gold and silver pieces and pearls, plus Lenox, Waterford, and fine sterling. In business since 1928; on State Circle since 1948.

W.R. Chance Jewelers (110 Main St.; 410-263-2404) Lovely work, from traditional to more contemporary. Another nice City Dock window to shop. In business for fifty years.

UPPER EASTERN SHORE

Chester

Bay Country Jewelry (1607 Postal Rd.; 410-643-8040) New and antique jewelry, appraisals.

Chestertown

Forney's Jewelers (106 S. Cross St.; 410-778-1966) Diamonds, gold, silver, pearls, colored gems, and watches, as well as silverware, pewterware, china, and brass.

Easton

Oscar Caplan & Sons Inc. (30 N. Harrison St., upstairs; 410-822-1553) Original designs are a specialty. Diamond importers, gems, estate jewelry, and watches. In business over ninety years.

Shearer the Jeweler (22 N. Washington St.; 410-822-2279) Diamonds, colored gems, watches, and original designs.

Westphal Jewelers (19 N. Harrison St.; 410-822-7774) Diamonds, colored gems, watches, and custom designs.

St. Michaels

Rings & Things (105 S. Talbot St.; 410-745-3881) Lots of rings, pins, and earrings, many with animal, nautical, or holiday themes.

LOWER EASTERN SHORE

Princess Anne

Bailey White Jewelers (30400 Mt. Vernon Rd.; 410-651-3073) Retired policeman Jonathan Bailey and his wife, Melissa, became master goldsmiths several years ago, garnered national and international awards for jewelry design, then settled down on the Lower Eastern Shore to create trademark Chesapeake jewelry originals. Their handcrafted, Bay-inspired designs include a crab, a skipjack, and an oyster, each rendered in 14K or 18K gold.

Salisbury

G.B. Heron & Co. (1307 Mt. Hermon Rd.; 410-860-0221) Custom-designed jewelry and a store full of high-quality pieces. Watch and jewelry repair by goldsmiths on the premises.

Kuhn's Jewelers (107 Downtown Plaza; 410-742-3256) Diamonds and watches are part of a full line of quality jewelry from a company established in 1853.

KITCHENWARE

ANNAPOLIS/WESTERN SHORE

Annapolis

The Gourmet's Cup (104 Annapolis St.; 410-267-6544) Always a pot of gourmet coffee brewing and a wide selection of coffees, mugs, pots, and other accoutrements beloved by the java junkie. Variety of cooking gear, from fancy knives to Vidalia relish.

UPPER EASTERN SHORE

Easton

Rowens Stationery Inc. (8-10 N. Washington St.; 410-822-2095) Along with all of its supplies for the office and the art studio, the venerable Rowens houses a nice selection of glassware, from tumblers to martini glasses. Everything from gourmet cooking supplies to serving trays with waterfowl scenes.

Talbot Kitchens (31 N. Harrison St.; 410-822-8877) Exhaustive range of kitchen accessories. Just the spot to buy that kiwi peeler for the chef who has everything.

MALLS & OUTLETS

HEAD OF THE BAY

Perryville

Prime Outlets at Perryville (68 Heather Lane; 410-378-9399) Forty-two stores include Osh Kosh, London Fog, Bon Worth, Nike, and Bugle Boy.

ANNAPOLIS/WESTERN SHORE

Annapolis

Annapolis Harbour Center (Rte. 2 & Aris T. Allen Blvd.; 410-266-5857) This place has been packed since the day it opened. Tower Records, Office Depot, Fresh Fields, Starbucks, Barnes & Noble, Old Navy, and many specialty clothing and food shops.

Annapolis Mall (Rte. 50, Jennifer & Bestgate Rds.; 410-266-5432) Over 170 stores, with Nordstrom and Lord & Taylor, The Hecht Co., Montgomery Ward, clothing, book, record, shoe, and specialty stores.

UPPER EASTERN SHORE

Queenstown

Prime Outlets-Queenstown (441 Outlet Center Dr.; 410-827-8699) New name and new management for a long-standing outlet center with more than fifty stores.

LOWER EASTERN SHORE

Crisfield

Carvel Hall Factory Outlet (Md. 413; 410-968-0500) Along with the famous Carvel Hall cutlery (serious crab pickers use their knives), there's crystal, silver, pewter, and housewares, with a lot available at good discount prices.

Salisbury

The Centre at Salisbury (2300 N. Salisbury Blvd.; 410-548-1600) A major mall with five anchor department stores (Boscov's, The Hecht Co., Montgomery Ward, Sears, and J.C. Penney), dozens of small stores, a food court, and a ten-screen cinema.

MARINE SUPPLY

HEAD OF THE BAY

Havre de Grace

Tidewater Marina Store (Bourbon St., Havre de Grace, MD 21078; 410-939-0950) Marine books and hardware, inside the marina. Keep going past the big boatyard, you'll find it.

ANNAPOLIS/WESTERN SHORE

Annapolis

Bacon & Assoc., Inc. (116 Legion Ave., Annapolis, MD 21401; 410-263-4880)

Nifty place for used equipment; noted for a broad array of secondhand sails. In business for forty years.

Boater's World (Annapolis Harbour Center, 2476 Solomons Island Rd., Annapolis, MD 21401; 410-266-7766; 301-970-2073) Discount marine supplies.

BOAT-US Marine Center (163 A Jennifer Rd., Annapolis, MD 21401; 410-573-5744) Discount supplies. Recommended by sailors.

Find whatever it takes to keep your floating prized possession going at Fawcett Boat Supplies, Inc. in Annapolis.

David Trozzo

Fawcett Boat Supplies, Inc. (110 Compromise St., Annapolis, MD 21401; 410-267-8681; E-mail: fawcboat@bellatlantic.net) Right at City Dock, Fawcett's stocks pretty much every boating thing that you'll need, like all sizes of oarlocks — not always easy to find. A local institution for fifty years and a good source of local boating information. Good selection of nautical books.

West Marine (113 Hillsmere Dr., Annapolis, MD 21401; 410-268-0129) Storefront of the big catalog chain service. Another location: 3257 Solomons Island Rd., Edgewater, MD 21037; 410-956-8920.

UPPER EASTERN SHORE

Chestertown

Chester River Marine Services Ltd. (7501 Church Hill Rd., Chestertown, MD 21620; 410-778-2240) Full-service marine store.

Oxford

Crockett Brothers Boatyard (202 Banks St., Oxford, MD 21654; 410-226-5113) Nautical supplies; boat repair and pool.

Stevensville

L&B Marine Supply (124 Kent Landing, Stevensville, MD 21666; 410-643-3600) Discount marine supply.

SPECIALTY SHOPS & GENERAL STORES

HEAD OF THE BAY

Chesapeake City

Back Creek General Store (100 Bohemia Ave., Chesapeake City, MD 21915; 410-885-5377) Circa 1861 general store, although our friendly saleslady recalled that this was a dry goods store in her youth. Now filled with everything from PJs for the kids to cobalt glass coffee cups.

ANNAPOLIS/WESTERN SHORE

Annapolis

A.L. Goodies General Store (112 Main St., Annapolis, MD 21401; 410-269-0071) The resident five-and-dime in the trendy City Dock area. Two full floors. Racks and racks of greeting cards, brass weather vanes, etc. Don't forget to buy a peanut butter cookie.

Annapolis Country Store (53 Maryland Ave., Annapolis, MD 21401; 410-269-6773) The floorboards still creak in this upscale general store, which calls itself Maryland's oldest and largest wicker shop. Also, Crabtree & Evelyn and other luxury toiletries, cookie tins, cards, and other gifts.

Art Things (2 Annapolis St., Annapolis, MD 21401; 410-268-3520) Great art supply shop, where the employees are perennially helpful and cheerful. Paints, brushes, papers, and hard-to-find items like oversized mailing tubes.

Avoca Handweavers (141-143 Main St., Annapolis, MD 21401; 410-263-1485) Avoca has been doing business in Ireland for decades and continues to make a splash in the Annapolis historic district. Exquisite handiwork. Wools, cottons, linens, clothing, and other textiles, as well as Irish glass and pottery.

Chadwick's, The British Shoppe, Ltd. (10 Annapolis St., Annapolis, MD 21401; 410-280-BRIT) Filled with all kinds of imported things British, including many foods and Woods of Windsor toiletries.

Chesapeake Trading Company (149 Main St., Annapolis, MD 21401; 410-216-9797) Books, jewelry, and outdoor clothing.

Historic Annapolis Foundation Welcome Center and Museum Store (77 Main St., Annapolis, MD 21401; 410-268-5576) Classic children's toys and museum-quality gifts in a restored eighteenth-century warehouse.

The Nature Co. (134 Main St., Annapolis, MD 21401; 410-268-3909) Shop for nature lovers: everything from whale posters and whiny, buzzing fly key chains to opal earrings and binoculars. Always fun displays.

Pepper's (133 Main St., Annapolis, MD 21401; 410-267-8722) Navy T-shirt and sweatshirt central.

Francis Keller weighs out a custom blend of tobacco at the half-century-old Smoke Shop in Annapolis.

David Trozzo

The Smoke Shop (56 Maryland Ave., Annapolis, MD 21401; 410-263-2066) Old-fashioned tobacconists in business for decades.

Solomons

Sea Gull Cove Gifts (14488 Solomons Island Rd., Solomons, MD 20688; 410-326-7182) A good stop for Solomons' souvenirs.

NORTHERN NECK/MIDDLE PENINSULA

Mathews, Virginia

Sibley's General Store (1 Main St., Mathews, VA 23109; 804-725-5857) An "old-timey country store," where you can find whatever it is that you can't find anyplace else. Oil lamp parts. New decorative flags.

Urbanna, Virginia

R.S. Bristow Store (Virginia & Cross Sts., Urbanna, VA 23175; 804-758-2210) As much a stop on the local history walking tour as your vacation shopping trip, this 1898 dry goods store offers clothing and more. R.S. Bristow Sr. opened his first retail shop in 1876.

UPPER EASTERN SHORE

Chestertown

The General Store (227½ High St., Chestertown, MD 21620; 410-778-5533) High-quality, unusual gifts, including Chestertown throws, tea and specialty foods, candles, and lighthouses.

Kerns Collection Ltd. (210 High St., Chestertown, MD 21620; 410-778-4044) High-end crafts, apparel, jewelry, and art — many with animal themes.

Twigs & Teacups (111 S. Cross St., Chestertown, MD 21620; 410-778-1708) Specialty bath products, dishes, tea things, children's books and toys, clothing, and textiles make this a difficult gift store to leave.

Oxford

Silent Poetry (201 Tilghman St., Oxford, MD 21654; 410-226-5120) Unusual gifts and works of art, including stemware and china, specialty food products, stuffed animals and toys, mood candles and fragrances, and much more.

LOWER EASTERN SHORE

Salisbury

Salisbury Pewter Outlet (2611 N. Salisbury Blvd., Salisbury, MD 21801; 800-824-4708; 410-546-1188) Watch workers create the pewterware pieces sold in this "outlet," where first-quality pieces sell for less, and you can save more with seconds, factory overruns, and discontinued items. Tours of the factory by appt. Salisbury Pewter has a second outlet on U.S. 50 in Easton (410-820-5202).

CHAPTER EIGHT
The Right Connections
INFORMATION

Annapolis was laid out around two circles: St. Anne's Episcopal Church, in the foreground, and the Statehouse, with its distinctive dome.

David Trozzo

When traveling, it's always good to know a few rules that the locals live by. Here, we offer an abbreviated encyclopedia of Bay-related information that will help you move more easily through the area. This chapter provides guidance on the following subjects:

AMBULANCE & EMERGENCY INFORMATION

Maryland

For police, fire, and ambulance emergencies in Maryland, call 911. Drivers with cellular phones can report accidents and other highway emergencies by calling #77 or 911. For additional information, contact: Maryland State Police, 1201 Reisterstown Rd., Pikesville, MD 21208; 410-486-3101.

When you're on the water, the **U.S. Coast Guard** responds to VHF marine radio Channel 16.

Maryland Department of Natural Resources Police Emergency Dispatch (410-260-8888; 410-260-8940, communications center).

Maryland Poison Center (800-492-2414).

U.S. Coast Guard Activities Baltimore (410-576-2558, general questions; 410-576-2525, search and rescue).

U.S. Coast Guard Annapolis Station (410-267-8108).

Virginia

Emergency 911 service is available throughout Virginia's Chesapeake region, on the Eastern Shore, Northern Neck, or Middle Peninsula.

Emergency telephone numbers:

For threat to life and limb: **U.S. Coast Guard Hampton Roads Group**; 757-484-8192.

For threat to property: **U.S. Coast Guard's Marine Safety Group** out of Hampton Roads; 757-483-8567. If you're farther north, from Smith Point (near Reedville) to the York River: **U.S. Coast Guard** at Milford Haven; 804-725-2125.

For boating information or to report environmental hazards (on weekday business hours): **Department of Game and Inland Fisheries,** 4010 W. Broad St., Richmond, VA 23230; 804-367-1000.

For poisonings: **Virginia Poison Center** (800-552-6337 in Virginia; 804-828-9123).

AREA CODES

Maryland has adopted a unique method for dealing with our societal need for more telephone numbers to serve all of the fax machines, modems, and telephones out there. Callers must dial area codes before telephone numbers, local or long distance. Prior to this development, Chesapeake telephone numbers almost always began with a 410 area code (except for sparse St. Marys County, where it's 301). In general, you will continue to find that's true, although new telephone numbers may come with a different area code.

Virginia area codes are the following: Hampton Roads/Tidewater region, 757; Northern Neck, 804; Washington, D.C., 202; Richmond, 804. The 703 area codes you'll run across in this book serve northern Virginia telephone numbers in the Washington, D.C. metro area.

BIBLIOGRAPHY

BOOKS YOU CAN BUY

CHILDREN'S BOOKS

Blackistone, Mick. *The Day They Left the Bay*. Acropolis, 1988.
Cummings, Priscilla. *Chadwick the Crab*. Tidewater Publishing, 1986.
Henry, Marguerite. *Misty of Chincoteague*. Rand, 1947. Many editions and publishers; this is the original.
Holland, Jeffrey. *Chessie, The Sea Monster that Ate Annapolis*. Oak Creek Publishers, 1990.
Voigt, Cynthia. *Homecoming*. Fawcett Juniper, 1981.
Wolf, Bernard. *Amazing Grace: Smith Island and the Chesapeake Watermen*. MacMillan, 1986.

COOKBOOKS

Kitching, Frances, and Dowell, Susan Stiles. *Mrs. Kitching's Smith Island Cookbook*. Tidewater Publishers, 1981.
Maryland Seafood Cookbooks, I, II, and III. Office of Seafood Marketing Division, Maryland Department of Agriculture.

FICTION

Barth, John. *The Sot-Weed Factor*. Doubleday, 1987.
_____. *Tidewater Tales*. Fawcett, 1987.
Michener, James A. *Chesapeake*. Random House, 1978.
Styron, William. *A Tidewater Morning: Three Tales from Youth*. Random House, 1993.

HISTORY & LORE

Brown, Alexander Crosby. *Steam Packets on the Chesapeake: A History of the Old Bay Line Since 1840.* Cornell Maritime, Tidewater Publishers, 1961.

Brown, Philip L. *The Other Annapolis, 1900-1950.* The Annapolis Publishing Co., 1994.

Brugger, Robert J. *Maryland: A Middle Temperament, 1634-1980.* Johns Hopkins University Press, 1988.

Burgess, Robert H. *This Was Chesapeake Bay.* Cornell Maritime Press, 1963.

Carr, Lois Green, Morgan, Philip D., and Russo, Jean B. *Colonial Chesapeake Society.* University of North Carolina, 1988.

Chowning, Larry S. *Chesapeake Legacy: Tools & Traditions.* Tidewater Publishers, 1995.

Davison, Steven G., et al. *Chesapeake Waters: Four Centuries of Controversy, Concern, and Legislation.* Tidewater Publishers, 1983, 1997.

De Gast, Robert. *The Lighthouses of the Chesapeake.* Johns Hopkins University Press, 1973.

Dize, Frances W. *Smith Island, Chesapeake Bay.* Tidewater Publishers, 1990.

Freeman, Roland L. *The Arabbers of Baltimore.* Tidewater Publishers, 1989.

Keiper, Ronald R. *The Assateague Ponies.* Tidewater Publishers, 1985.

Middleton, Arthur Pierce. *Tobacco Coast: A Maritime History of Chesapeake Bay in the Colonial Era.* Johns Hopkins University Press, 1984.

Mills, Eric. *Chesapeake Bay in the Civil War.* Tidewater Publishers, 1996.

Roundtree, Helen C., and Davidson, Thomas E. *Eastern Shore Indians of Virginia and Maryland.* University Press of Virginia, 1997.

Shomette, Donald. *Pirates on the Chesapeake: Being a True History of Pirates, Picaroons, and Sea Raiders on Chesapeake Bay, 1610-1807.* Tidewater Publishers, 1985.

Travers, Paul J. *The Patapsco, Baltimore's River of History.* Tidewater Publishers, 1990.

Wennersten, John R. *The Oyster Wars of Chesapeake Bay.* Tidewater Publishers, 1981.

Whitehead, John Hurt III. *The Watermen of the Chesapeake Bay.* Tidewater Publishers, 1979. 180 color photographs.

NATURAL HISTORY & FIELD GUIDES

Hedeen, Robert A. *The Oyster: Life and Lore of the Celebrated Bivalve.* Tidewater Publishers, 1986.

Horton, Tom. *Bay Country.* Johns Hopkins University Press, 1987.

_____. *Turning the Tide: Saving the Chesapeake Bay.* Island Press, 1991.

Kent, Bretton W. *Fossil Sharks of the Chesapeake Bay Region.* Evergreen Rees & Boyer, 1994.

Lawrence, Susannah. *The Audubon Society Field Guide to the Natural Places of the Mid-Atlantic States: Coastal.* Pantheon Books, 1984.

Lippson, Alice J., and Robert L. *Life in the Chesapeake Bay.* Johns Hopkins University Press, 1984, 1997.

Meanley, Brooke. *Birdlife at Chincoteague and the Virginia Barrier Islands.* Tidewater Publishers, 1981.

Sherwood, Arthur W. *Understanding the Chesapeake: A Layman's Guide.* Tidewater Publishers, 1973.

Taylor, John W. *Birds of the Chesapeake Bay.* Johns Hopkins University Press, 1992. Paintings and musings by the author in a coffee-table book.

Warner, William W. *Beautiful Swimmers: Watermen, Crabs and the Chesapeake Bay.* Penguin Books, 1976.

White, Christopher P. *Chesapeake Bay: A Field Guide.* Tidewater Publishers, 1989.

Williams, John Page, Jr. *Chesapeake Almanac: Following the Bay through the Seasons.* Tidewater Publishers, 1993.

PHOTOGRAPHY & ESSAY

Jander, Anne Hughes. *Crab's Hole: A Family's Story of Tangier Island.* Literary House Press, Washington College, 1994.

McWilliams, Jane Wilson, and Patterson, Carol Cushard. *Bay Ridge on the Chesapeake: An Illustrated History.* Brighton Editions, 1986.

Meyer, Eugene L., and Niemeyer, Lucian. *Chesapeake Country.* Abbeville Press, 1990.

Schubel, J.R. *The Living Chesapeake.* Johns Hopkins University Press, 1981.

Snediker, Quentin, and Jensen, Ann. *Chesapeake Bay Schooners.* Tidewater Publishers, 1992.

Warren, Mame. *Then Again . . . Annapolis, 1900-1965.* Time Exposure, 1990.

Warren, Marion E., with Warren, Mame. *Bringing Back the Bay.* Johns Hopkins University Press, 1994.

White, Dan. *Crosscurrents in Quiet Water: Portraits of the Chesapeake.* Taylor Publishing, 1987.

RECREATION

Gillelan, G. Howard. *Gunning for Sea Ducks.* Tidewater Publishers, 1988.

Shellenberger, William H. *Cruising the Chesapeake: A Gunkholer's Guide.* International Marine Publishing Co., 1990.

TRAVEL

Anderson, Elizabeth B. *Annapolis: A Walk Through History.* Tidewater Publishers, 1984.

Morrison, Russell, and Hansen, Robert. *Charting the Chesapeake.* Maryland State Archives, 1990.

Papenfuse, Edward C., et al. *Maryland, A New Guide to the Old Line State.* An update of the WPA's writer's project travel guide, *A Guide to the Old Line State,* by the staff of the Maryland State Archives. Johns Hopkins University Press, 1976.

Wiencek, Henry. *The Smithsonian Guide to Historic America, Virginia and the Capital Region.* Stewart, Tabori & Chang, 1989.

Books You Can Borrow

Barrick, Susan O. *The Chesapeake Bay Bibliography.* Virginia Institute of Marine Science, 1971. Scientific and natural history sources; look for the current volume under various authors.

Blair, Carvel Hall, and Ansel, Willits Dyer. *Chesapeake Bay: Notes & Sketches.* Tidewater Publishers, 1970.

Bodine, A. Aubrey. *Chesapeake Bay and Tidewater.* Bodine and Assoc., 1954. 3d ed., 1980. Classic black-and-white photographs by noted Baltimore *Sunday Sun* photographer.

Burgess, Robert H. *This Was Chesapeake Bay.* Tidewater Publishers, 1963. Compendium of historic accounts of watermen and Bay vessels.

Byron, Gilbert. *Early Explorations of the Chesapeake Bay.* Maryland Historical Society, 1960.

Capper, John, et al. *Chesapeake Waters: Pollution, Public Health, and Public Opinion, 1607-1972.* Originally published by the EPA, contains historic account of Bay pollution. Republished by Tidewater Publishers, 1983.

Chapelle, Suzanne Ellery Greene, et al. *Maryland, A History of Its People.* Johns Hopkins University Press, 1986.

Earle, Swepson. *The Chesapeake Bay Country.* 1923. Reprinted by Weathervane Books, 1983.

Fiske, John. *Old Virginia and her Neighbours.* Houghton, Mifflin & Co., 1897. Old-style account of the founding of Chesapeake colonies.

Footner, Hulbert. *Rivers of the Eastern Shore.* Rinehart & Co., Inc., 1944.

Gibbons, Boyd. *Wye Island.* Johns Hopkins University Press, 1977. History and natural history of unspoiled island surrounded by Wye River on Maryland's Eastern Shore.

Hildebrand, Samuel F. *Fishes of Chesapeake Bay.* TFH Publications, 1972. Originally published in 1928 by the GPO.

Klingel, Gilbert C. *The Bay.* Tradition, 1966. Natural history essay.

Lippson, Alice Jane. *The Chesapeake Bay in Maryland: An Atlas of Natural Resources.* Johns Hopkins University Press, 1973. Sponsored by the University of Maryland.

Metcalf, Paul. *Waters of Potowmack.* North Point Press, 1982. Natural and social history of the Bay's most famous tributary, with interesting anecdotes and excerpts from letters and diaries of historical figures.

Rothrock, Joseph T. and Rothrock, Jane C. *Chesapeake Odysseys: An 1883 Cruise Revisited.* Tidewater Publishers, 1984.

Schubel, J.R. *The Life and Death of the Chesapeake Bay.* University of Maryland, 1986.

Tawes, William I. *God, Man, Salt Water and the Eastern Shore.* Tidewater Publishers, 1967.

Wilstach, Paul. *Tidewater Maryland.* The Bobbs-Merrill Co., 1931. Funky classic. Reprinted several times.

CLIMATE & WEATHER

Chesapeake climate is generally mild; winter temperatures average 40° F, and summers average 76° F. The average annual rainfall amounts to a generous forty-three inches. But average temperatures tell only part of the story. Proximity to the 3,700-square-mile Bay often brings high humidity during the months of July and August, which can bring furious afternoon and evening thunderstorms in late summer when daytime temperatures are often over 90° F. Take these storms seriously; people have been struck and killed by lightning on and around the Bay. Even on the calmest day, boaters *must always* keep an eye on the windward sky (and an ear on the marine weather forecast).

By early September, humidity often has dropped considerably, although temperatures in the 80°-range continue well into the month. The average fall temperature is 62° F. Sailors love it; a steady breeze blows in the 10- to 15-knot range.

Chesapeake winters tend to be mild, with an average of fewer than ten inches of snowfall and temperatures of 30° F or more. Windchill near the water, however, can make the air seem considerably colder and may even produce dangerous chilling or frostbite.

Regardless of the season, remember that sunlight reflects brilliantly off the water. On the open Bay, rays are magnified by the water's surface, increasing the risk of sunburn and sunstroke. A hat, lip balm, and sunscreen are always recommended. Also, keep in mind that alcoholic beverages are best consumed *after* your voyage. Enforcement of drunken-boater laws can be stringent on the Bay.

To obtain updated weather reports, check Bell Atlantic's weather phone: in **Maryland** (410-936-1212); in **Virginia** (757-877-1221) Newport News; (804-268-

1212) Richmond. Hotels often carry a 24-hour weather channel with local fore-casts. The Weather Channel web site (www.weather.com) can be a traveler's best friend; for Bay-area forecasts, click on the "state" forecasts. Other good weather pages can be found at the web sites of the region's newspapers (see the heading Newspapers & Magazines). We especially like The *Washington Post* (www.weatherpost.com) for the D.C. area and the Norfolk-based *Virginian-Pilot-Ledger-Star* (www.pilotonline.com) for what's happening in that area.

ENVIRONMENT

S ave the Bay is a rallying cry around the Chesapeake Bay, the focus of a massive cleanup effort by state and federal agencies since the late 1970s. If you really want to get into the issue, there's plenty of information. Local libraries often stock scientific studies on the Bay. Or you can contact the fol-lowing point organizations:

The Chesapeake Bay headquarters for three states and the District of Columbia is the Chesapeake Bay Foundation in Annapolis.

David Trozzo

The **Chesapeake Bay Foundation** (410-268-8816 Annapolis office; www.cbf.org) with offices in Maryland, Pennsylvania, and Virginia is a non-profit organization that actively educates the three-state region about a range of Bay-related environmental issues.

The multiagency umbrella that oversees the government cleanup, the **Chesapeake Bay Program,** has a hot line (800-YOUR-BAY). The **Chesapeake Regional Information Service,** or **CRIS** (800-662-CRIS; E-mail: acb@ari.net) is the 24-hour, 7-days-per-week, hot line to call for facts and figures on the Bay or to report an illegal dumping. Sponsored by the **Alliance for the Chesapeake Bay** (www-acb-online.org).

HANDICAPPED SERVICES

Both Maryland and Virginia, well accustomed to accommodating tourists, put forth significant effort to ensure pleasant and enjoyable visits for wheelchair-bound or other disabled visitors.

In *Maryland,* the guide called *Destination Maryland*, published by the Maryland Office of Tourism Development, notes entries with accessibility for disabled persons. For free copies, contact: Maryland Office of Tourism Development, 217 E. Redwood St., Baltimore, MD 21202; 800-543-1036; 410-767-3400; www.mdisfun.org.

In *Virginia,* the Tourism Corporation offers *The Virginia Travel Guide for the Disabled*, an excellent, free comprehensive guide for the disabled that goes beyond whether or not a wheelchair-bound visitor can get in and out of doors. Contact: Virginia Tourism Corporation, 901 E. Byrd St., Richmond, VA 23219; 800-742-3935; 804-786-4484; www.virginia.org (keyword "handicapped accessible").

HOSPITALS & HEALTH CARE

Should a serious health problem arise, you are, fortunately, near some of the nation's top medical facilities.

Baltimore, Maryland

The Johns Hopkins Hospital (600 N. Wolfe St.; 410-955-2280 main emergency; Johns Hopkins Children's Center, 410-955-5680 emergency; Johns Hopkins Bayview Medical Center, 4940 Eastern Ave.; 410-550-0350 emergency).

University of Maryland Medical Center University Hospital (22 S. Greene St.; 410-328-6722 adult emergency; 410-328-6677 pediatric emergency).

Washington, D.C. area

Georgetown University Hospital (3800 Reservoir Rd. NW, Washington D.C.; 202-687-2000; 202-784-2118 emergency services).

The George Washington University Medical Center (901 23rd St. NW, Washington D.C.; 202-994-1000; 202-994-3211 emergency room). **Washington Adventist Hospital** (7600 Carroll Ave., Takoma Park, MD; 301-891-7600; 301-891-5070 emergency).

Norfolk, Virginia

Children's Hospital of the King's Daughters (601 Children's Lane; 757-668-7000; 757-668-7188 emergency).

Richmond, Virginia

Medical College of Virginia Hospitals (401 N. 12th St.; 804-828-9000; 804-828-9151 emergency).

The following local hospitals offer comprehensive medical services. All operate emergency rooms 24 hours, 7 days per week, unless otherwise noted.

HEAD OF THE BAY

Union Hospital (106 Bow St., Elkton; 410-398-4000; 410-392-7061 emergency).

ANNAPOLIS/WESTERN SHORE

Anne Arundel Medical Center (64 Franklin St., Annapolis; 410-267-1000; 410-267-1275 emergency).

NORTHERN NECK/MIDDLE PENINSULA

Rappahannock General Hospital (101 Harris Dr./P.O. Box 1449, Kilmarnock, VA; 804-435-8000; 804-435-8544 emergency).
Riverside Walter Reed Hospital (Hwy. 17/P.O. Box 1130, Gloucester, VA; 804-693-8800; 804-693-8899 emergency).

UPPER EASTERN SHORE

Kent & Queen Annes Hospital, Inc. (100 Brown St., Chestertown; 410-778-3300) Ask for emergency room.
Memorial Hospital at Easton (219 S. Washington St., Easton; 410-822-1000).

LOWER EASTERN SHORE

Dorchester General Hospital (300 Byrn St., Cambridge; 410-228-5511; for emergency room, dial 8, then 525 or 526).

Edward W. McCready Memorial Hospital (201 Hall Hwy., Crisfield; 410-968-1200, ext. 3300).

Peninsula Regional Medical Center (100 E. Carroll St., Salisbury; 410-546-6400; 410-543-7101 emergency).

LATE-NIGHT FOOD & FUEL

ANNAPOLIS/WESTERN SHORE

Chesapeake Exxon (Rtes. 50 & 450, Annapolis; 410-266-7475) Open 24 hours; fuel.

Chick & Ruth's Delly (165 Main St., Annapolis; 410-269-6737) Open 24 hours; food.

UPPER EASTERN SHORE

Fast Stop (9543 Ocean Gateway Dr., Easton; 410-822-3333) Open 24 hours; food and fuel.

Faulkner's Exxon (8147 Ocean Gateway Dr., Easton; 410-822-8219) Open 24 hours; fuel.

Royal Farm Store (301 Maple Ave., Chestertown; 410-778-0646) Open 5:00 a.m.–12:00 midnight; food.

Royal Farm Store (5th & Market Sts., Denton; 410-479-3422) Open 5:00 a.m. to midnight; food.

LOWER EASTERN SHORE

Dunkin' Donuts (Sunburst Hwy., Cambridge; 410-228-6197) Open 24 hours; food.

Shore Stop (811 Priscilla St., Salisbury; 410-548-3385) Open 24 hours; food and fuel. Keep an eye out for the **Shore Stop** stores, which are convenience store/gas stations scattered along the Delmarva Peninsula — often a welcome sight for weary travelers heading through the sparse Lower Eastern Shore. Among those open 24 hours along the Virginia shore:

Cape Charles (22177 Lankford Hwy.; 757-331-4008).
Chincoteague (Church & N. Main Sts.; 757-336-6380).
Nassowadox (7410 Lankford Hwy.; 757-442-5170).

NEWSPAPERS & MAGAZINES

The Chesapeake's proximity to major cities means that folks deep in Chesapeake country are as likely to read the *Washington Post* as their local paper. Still, the local papers are filled with information about everything from tides to VFW oyster roasts. Don't overlook them.

Maryland

Afro-American Newspapers (2519 N. Charles St., Baltimore, MD 21201; 410-554-8200; www.afroam.org) Coverage of local events with an emphasis on issues affecting the African-American community. Biweekly, Wed. and Fri.

The Capital (Annapolis) (2000 Capital Dr., Annapolis, MD 21401; 410-268-5000; www.capitalonline.com) The state capital's daily newspaper. Also publishes a comprehensive Fri. Entertainment section focusing on Annapolis-area events.

Chesapeake Bay Magazine (1819 Bay Ridge Ave., Annapolis, MD 21401; 410-263-2662) A monthly magazine featuring stories about the Bay, fishing, boating, and other water-related issues.

The Daily Banner (Cambridge) (1000 Goodwill Rd./P.O. Box 580, Cambridge, MD 21613; 410-228-3131) Published Mon.–Fri.

The Daily Times (Salisbury) (115 E Carroll St., Salisbury, MD 21801; 410-749-7171; www.shore-source.com/times/).

Kent County News (Chestertown) (P.O. Box 30, Chestertown, MD 21620; 410-778-2011) Published Thurs.

New Bay Times (P.O. Box 358, Deale, MD 20751; 410-867-0304) An eclectic weekly freebie featuring entertainment, nature, and other topics of interest to Bay readers. Look for it around Maryland's Western Shore. Published Thurs.

Publick Enterprise (P.O. Box 4520, Annapolis, MD 21401; 410-268-3527) Hefty free news magazine published twice a month; found in Annapolis businesses. Cultural events, boating news, and local personalities and history.

The Star-Democrat (Easton) (29088 Airpark Dr., Airport Industrial Park, Easton, MD 21601; 410-822-1500; www.stardem.com) Published Sun.–Fri.

The Sun, The Sunday Sun (Baltimore) (501 N. Calvert St., Baltimore, MD 21201; 800-829-8000; 410-332-6000; www.sunspot.net) Blanket coverage of Maryland, as well as a weekly entertainment tabloid on Thurs.

Washington, D.C.

The Washington Post (1150 15th St. NW, Washington, D.C. 20005; 202-334-6000; www.washingtonpost.com) The nationally oriented morning daily includes a Fri. Weekend section focusing on events in and around Washington, D.C., and often, on the Bay.

The Washington Times (3600 New York Ave. NE, Washington, D.C. 20018; 202-636-3000; www.washtimes.com) Morning daily includes a weekly entertainment section. Published Thurs.

Virginia

The Daily Press (7505 Warwick Blvd., Newport News, VA 23601; 757-247-4600; dailypress.com).

The Gazette-Journal (Gloucester-Mathews) (Main St. & Lewis Ave., Gloucester, VA 32061; 804-693-3101; Court St., Mathews, VA 23109; 804-725-2191) A local weekly. Published Thurs.

The Northern Neck News (5 Court St., Warsaw, VA 22572; 804-333-NEWS; 804-333-3655) Published Wed.

The Richmond Times Dispatch (333 E. Grace St., Richmond, VA 23201; 800-468-3383; 804-649-6000; www.gatewayva.com) The Virginia capital's morning daily. Published seven mornings a week.

The Virginian-Pilot-Ledger-Star (150 W. Brambleton Ave., Norfolk, VA 23501; 800-446-2004; 757-446-2000; www.pilotonline.com) The major seven-day-a-week paper serving the Tidewater area.

ROAD SERVICES

For a complete listing of AAA telephone numbers for the region, see Chapter Two, *Transportation*, under the heading Getting Around the Chesapeake Bay Area, in the section Maps.

HEAD OF THE BAY

Morgan's Auto Repair & Tow Service (668 W Pulaski Hwy., Elkton; 410-398-1288) Towing 24 hours.

ANNAPOLIS/WESTERN SHORE

Darden's 24-Hour Towing (87 Southgate Ave., Annapolis; 800-870-1046; 410-269-1046; 410-263-9210).

NORTHERN NECK/MIDDLE PENINSULA

Curtis Texaco Station (7043 Northumberland Hwy., Heathsville, VA; 804-580-8888) Towing 24 hours.
Dickey's Auto Recycling (Hwy. 17, Ark, VA; 804-693-4244) Towing 24 hours.

UPPER EASTERN SHORE

Mullikin's Auto Body, Inc. (9277 Ocean Gateway Dr., Easton; 410-820-8676).

LOWER EASTERN SHORE

Adkins Towing (607 Northwood Dr., Unit 8A, Salisbury; 410-749-7712).

TIDES

If you're going for a sail or leaving your crab pot in the water for a few hours, you may want to check the tide. Typical Chesapeake tide falls are only 1.5-2 feet, but it can make a big difference in the Bay's shallow waters. Keep an eye out for extra high tides if a storm is in the forecast. For information, check local newspapers, broadcast weather reports, or the monthly *Chesapeake Bay Magazine.* The *New Bay Times,* a free weekly, also publishes tides. Information is also available at any marina or bait and tackle shop.

TOURIST INFORMATION

Both Maryland and Virginia offer extensive tourist information services; travelers to Virginia, for instance, will find a range of brochures and booklets covering everything from golf to the great outdoors. Travelers headed to less-populated areas of Bay country in either state may find that the local Chamber of Commerce doesn't maintain a web site, but you can access good information about the areas via the state web sites.

Tourist information centers are scattered throughout Maryland's Chesapeake region, but are less available in Virginia's Northern Neck/Middle Peninsula. Your best bets in Virginia are the center next to the Potomac River Bridge on Rte. 301 or in the urban Tidewater area. For more information about the Bay, contact the following:

Maryland Office of Tourism Development (217 E. Redwood St., Baltimore, MD 21202; 800-543-1036; 410-767-3400; www.mdisfun.org).

Virginia Tourism Corporation (901 E. Byrd St., Richmond, VA 23219; 804-786-4484; 800-VISITVA; www.virginia.org).

HEAD OF THE BAY

Discover Harford County Tourism Council (121 N. Union Ave., Ste. B, Havre de Grace, MD 21078; 800-597-2649; 410-939-3336; www.harfordmd.com) Mon.–Fri., 9:00 a.m.–5:00 p.m.; Sat., 11:00 a.m.–4:00 p.m.

ANNAPOLIS/WESTERN SHORE

Annapolis and Anne Arundel County Conference and Visitors Bureau (26 West St., Annapolis, MD 21401; 410-268-8687; 410-280-0445; www.visit-annapolis.org) Mon.-Sun., 9:00 a.m.–5:00 p.m.

Calvert County Dept. of Economic Development (Courthouse, 175 Main St., Prince Frederick, MD 20678; 800-331-9771; 410-535-4583; 301-855-1880; www.co.cal.md.us/cced/tourism.htm) Mon.–Fri., 8:30 a.m.–4:30 p.m.

St. Mary's County Chamber of Commerce (28290 Three Notch Rd., Mechanicsville, MD 20659; 301-884-5555) Mon.–Fri., 9:00 a.m.–5:00 p.m.; Sat., Sun., 10:00 a.m.–3:00 p.m. (spring–fall).

NORTHERN NECK/MIDDLE PENINSULA

Gloucester Chamber of Commerce (6688 Main St./P.O. Box 296, Gloucester, VA 23061; 804-693-2425; www.co.gloucester.va.us).

Mathews Chamber of Commerce (P.O. Box 1126, Mathews, VA 23109; 804-725-9029).

Northern Neck Visitor Information Service (Rte. 301, Dahlgren, VA 22448; 800-453-6167).

UPPER EASTERN SHORE

Caroline County Commissioner's Office (109 Market St., Rm. 109, Denton, MD 21629; 410-479-0660).

Kent County Chamber of Commerce (400 S. Cross St., Chestertown, MD 21620; 410-810-2968).

Queen Annes County Office of Tourism (425 Piney Narrows Rd., Chester, MD 21619; 888-400-RSVP; 410-604-2100; www.qac.org).

Talbot County Chamber of Commerce (P.O. Box 1366, Easton, MD 21601; 410-822-4606; www.talbotchamber.org) For St. Michael's, Easton, Oxford, Tilghman.

LOWER EASTERN SHORE

Chincoteague Chamber of Commerce (P.O. Box 258, Chincoteague, VA 23336; 757-336-6161; www.chincoteaguechamber.com).

Dorchester Chamber of Commerce (528 Poplar St., Cambridge, MD 21613; 410-228-3575; E-mail: chamber@fastol.com).

Eastern Shore of Virginia Chamber of Commerce (P.O. Box 460, Melfa, VA 23410; 757-787-2460; www.esva.net/~esvachamber).

Somerset County Tourism Office (11440 Ocean Hwy./P.O. Box 243, Princess Anne, MD 21853; 800-521-9189; 410-651-2968; www.skipjack.net/le_shore/visitsomerset).

Wicomico County Convention & Visitors Bureau (P.O. Box 2333, Salisbury, MD 21802; 410-548-4914; E-mail: wicotour@shore.intercom.net; www.co.wicomico.md.us/tourism).

CHAPTER NINE
Urban Bay Neighbors
BALTIMORE &
NEARBY ATTRACTIONS

David Trozzo

Baltimore's expansive Inner Harbor, with its modern shopping plazas, the historic frigate Constellation, *and much more.*

The Baltimore skyline is rapidly changing, a reflection of all of the attention that the fair city by the Bay is receiving. New, vast hotels are on the horizon as city officials anticipate more and more people making their way to Charm City for business and pleasure.

BALTIMORE

It all started back in the 1970s at the **Inner Harbor,** when the waterfront was transformed into a dazzling mecca of shops, restaurants, and attractions. The energy of the Inner Harbor also has invaded other parts of the city, most notably **Federal Hill** and **Fells Point.** Where it will end? No one knows. But for now, city denizens, as well as visitors, are relishing what Baltimore has to offer. A weekend is hardly enough to catch all of the city's charms. But a good place to start is the Inner Harbor, located near some of the city's most interesting neighborhoods, where some new faces have cropped up.

The world's first **ESPN Zone** is one of three mega attractions at the famed **Power Plant** building. In addition to the interactive Zone, a grand **Barnes &**

Noble demands attention with its inventory, trendy café, and a 30,000-gallon, saltwater fish tank, and the ever-popular **Hard Rock Café** has a location here. The high-voltage Power Plant is also a fine complement to one of Baltimore's longtime attractions, the **National Aquarium in Baltimore,** and to the **Maryland Science Center,** an interactive science museum, replete with **IMAX Theater** and **Davis Planetarium** (601 Light St.; 410-685-5225, 24-hour information line; open daily; admission).

But Baltimore is not only the Inner Harbor, located near some of the city's most interesting neighborhoods. The city's cultural heart beats at **Mount Vernon,** while **Little Italy** continues to romance with its cozy eateries. **Fells Point,** an eighteenth-century fishing village, charms by day with its unique shops and galleries, but at night it transforms into a Soho of sorts; if you're ever in Baltimore during Halloween, be sure to visit Fells Point to check out the outrageous costumes. And **Federal Hill** has grown into a hot, restaurant-filled neighborhood, with the distinctive **American Visionary Art Museum** (800 Key Hwy.) right next to **Federal Hill Park.**

Food is another big thing in Charm City, so check the calorie counter at the city line. Baltimore's public markets are legendary. The most famous is **Lexington Market** (400 W. Lexington St.), established in 1782, with 140 merchants offering abundant and fresh foods of all kinds at unbelievable prices; a sandwich here can go for $2, and fresh produce sells at well below supermarket prices. Such markets are located throughout the city, the most gentrified being **Cross Street Market** (bet. Charles & Light Sts.) in Federal Hill; be sure to check out the crab cakes and sushi at **Nick's** on the Charles Street end of the market. The Fells Point's version is called the **Broadway Market** (last two blocks at south end of Broadway), offering fresh gourmet bread, as well as no-frills breakfasts.

For more refined tastes, **Charles Street** is Baltimore's "Main Street," which leads to picturesque **Mount Vernon Square,** home to many funky and trendy shops and restaurants, such as **Nouveau** (519 N. Charles St.), from funky furnishings to a great card selection, and the new hot spot **Sotto Sopra** (409 N. Charles St.), a great building with a great bar but expensive drinks. And be sure to check out the Mount Vernon institution, **Louie's Bookstore Café** (518 N. Charles St.).

Among the city's cultural jewels on Mount Vernon Square are the nation's first monument to **George Washington,** replete with 228 steps and a 360-degree view of the city, **The Walters Art Gallery,** with its expansive collections, and the famed **Peabody Conservatory of Music,** the oldest American music school. Farther up the street, in Charles Village, look for the **Baltimore Museum of Art,** adjacent to the sprawling Homewood campus, the main campus of **Johns Hopkins University.**

American history lovers will also enjoy Baltimore, once home to Babe Ruth and Edgar Allan Poe. The **Babe Ruth Museum** (216 Emory St.; 410-727-1539) is just a home run away from **Oriole Park at Camden Yards,** the city's new, old-fashioned baseball park, well worth a visit even for those who aren't baseball fans; for Baltimore Orioles game information, contact: 410-685-9800.

With the Baltimore skyline in the background, Oriole Park at Camden Yards supplies one of the country's best places to take in a ball game.

David Trozzo

Easily accessible by Interstate 95 (I-97, if you're headed north from Annapolis), Baltimore has been touted as the nation's most livable city — and for good reason. It's simple to navigate by a car, by foot, or by scenic water taxi for as little as $3 for a daylong ticket. Contact: Baltimore Area Convention and Visitors Association's Visitors Center, 301 E. Pratt St., Baltimore, MD 21202; 800-282-6632; 410-837-4636; www.baltimore.org.

BALTIMORE ATTRACTIONS

BALTIMORE MUSEUM OF ART
410-396-7101.
www.artbma.org.
10 Art Museum Dr.,
  Baltimore, MD 21201.
Open: Wed.–Fri., 11:00
  a.m.–5:00 p.m.; Sat., Sun.,
  11:00 a.m.–6:00 p.m.;
  closed Mon., Tues.
Admission: $6 adults; $4
  seniors and full-time
  students; children 18 and
  under free; all visitors
  free on Thurs.

Maryland's oldest and largest art museum has been expanded to include a new wing of modern art. The museum's best-known collection, however, is the Cone Collection, artworks collected by two Baltimore sisters who amassed one of the world's great selections of Matisse paintings. The BMA was a major contributor to the Matisse exhibit that caused a New York sensation in the early 1990s. Be sure to dine at the museum's new restaurant, Gertrude's, overlooking a sculpture garden.

BALTIMORE ZOO
410-366-5466.
Druid Hill Park, Baltimore, MD 21201.
Open: Daily, 10:00 a.m.–4:00 p.m.; Mem. Day—Labor Day weekends, 10:00 a.m.–5:30 p.m.; Jun., Jul., Aug., Sat., 10:00 a.m.–8:00 p.m.
Admission: $8.50 adults; $5 children 2–15 and adults 62 and older.

A testament to revived, inner-city zoos, the Baltimore Zoo is a favorite for locals and visitors alike. Open year-round, the zoo boasts a six-acre African Watering Hole, where the rhinos roam, and the Leopard Lair, where a new African leopard lives. Don't forget to swing by the indoor Chimpanzee Forest.

FORT McHENRY NATIONAL MONUMENT
410-962-4290.
www.bcpl.net/~etowner/patriot.htlm.
E. Fort Ave., Baltimore, MD 21201.
Open: Daily, 8:00 a.m.–4:45 p.m.
Admission: $5 adults; children 16 and under free.

Marylander Francis Scott Key wrote the words to "The Star-Spangled Banner" after witnessing the nation's flag fly high above Fort McHenry through a British naval bombardment during the War of 1812. Although historians dispute that Key actually saw the flag, there's no doubt that Fort McHenry remains one of the most popular tourist meccas in Baltimore. Situated in the industrial neighborhood of South Baltimore, Fort McHenry's expansive grounds, brick fort, and ramparts lie adjacent to the Baltimore harbor. A peaceful setting, the vast, green grounds provide a perfect picnic spot and a haven to joggers and cyclists. The fort allows visitors opportunities to explore a variety of exhibits; don't miss the free sixteen-minute movie, shown every thirty minutes, in the visitor center.

NATIONAL AQUARIUM IN BALTIMORE
410-576-3800; 410-625-0720 TTY/TDD.
www.aqua.org.
501 E. Pratt St., Baltimore, MD 21201.
Open: Jul.–Aug., daily, 9:00 a.m.–8:00 p.m.; Mar.–Jun., Sept.–Oct., Sat.–Thurs., 9:00 a.m.–5:00 p.m.; Fri., 9:00 a.m.–8:00 p.m.; Nov.–Feb., Sat.–Thurs., 10:00 a.m.–5:00 p.m.; Fri., 10:00 a.m.–8:00 p.m.
Admission: $14 adults; $10.50 seniors; $7.50 children 3–11.

Get caught in the mist at the Tropical Rain Forest at the National Aquarium, which continues to draw a continual stream of guests through the seasons. Located right in the city's fabled Inner Harbor, the National Aquarium boasts more than sharks and dolphins. Check out the Coral Reef, where a winding, downward path takes you up close to a huge tank containing the reef, with its sharks, tortoises, and other colorful inhabitants. The Marine Mammal Pavilion features performing dolphins, with shows usually on the hour. The aquarium's biggest drawback is its crowds. Lines start forming early on the weekends, and the crush of people can make viewing the exhibits a bit uncomfortable. Try visiting on Fri. evenings during the summer.

THE WALTERS ART GALLERY
410-547-9000.
www.thewalters.org.
600 N. Charles St.,
Baltimore, MD 21201.
Open: Tues.–Fri., 10:00 a.m.–4:00 p.m; Sat., Sun., 11:00 a.m.–5:00 p.m.; first Thurs. of each month, 10:00 a.m.–8:00 p.m.
Admission: $5 adults; $3 college students, senior citizens, young adults 18–25 with ID; $2 children 6–17.

With a collection of 30,000 pieces spanning three wings, the Walters presents buildings as impressive as the masterpieces that they contain. The landmark, Italian Renaissance Revival 1904 Gallery building, the four-story 1974 building, and the Hackerman House, a Greek Revival mansion, all sit at the foot of the Washington Monument in historic Mount Vernon Square. The collections include Fabergé eggs, Oriental porcelains, Egyptian, Greek, and Roman pieces, and nineteenth-century artworks, including paintings by Monet, Delacroix, and Pissarro.

BALTIMORE LODGINGS

For visitors who prefer quaint lodgings to mega hotels, consider a sampling of the city's tucked-away inns. More accommodations can be found by contacting the reservation service, Amanda's (800-899-7533; 410-225-0001).

ABACROMBIE BADGER B&B
Owners: Paul Bragaw & Collin Clarke.
410-244-7227.
www.badger-inn.com.
58 W. Biddle St., Baltimore, MD 21201.
Price: Moderate to Very Expensive.
Credit Cards: AE, D, DC, MC, V.
Handicap Access: No.

The lure of B&Bs is that they instantly make a weary traveler feel welcomed and at home, and this inn does just that and more. Located in the middle of Baltimore's modest theater and arts district, the Abacrombie Badger boasts twelve creative, theme-designed rooms, making it larger than most B&Bs, yet more intimate than a chain hotel. Clarke's flair for set design, particularly his ingenious use of fabric and paint, brings intricate detail to every room. The Abacrombie is ideal for families, with two single rooms adjoining larger rooms. Not surprising, the amenities in the rooms are first class, with Caswell-Massey toiletries, cable TV, and individual climate control. Parking is available in a lot adjoining the inn.

THE ADMIRAL FELL INN
Owner: Dominik Eckenstein.
800-292-4667; 410-522-7377.
www.admiralfell.com.
888 S. Broadway, Baltimore, MD 21201.

Long before the cult television cop drama "Homicide: Life on the Street" put Fells Point on the map, there was The Admiral Fell Inn, aptly named after the man responsible for this quaint, yet sometimes rowdy, part of Baltimore. The city's original port retains much of its eighteenth-century

Market Square at Thames St.
Price: Very Expensive.
Credit Cards: AE, DC, MC, V.
Handicap Access: Yes.
Restrictions: Smaller dogs or pets allowed on first floor with prior arrangement.

charm with Belgian brick streets, tugboats, salty taverns, and red brick row houses. This elegant inn, once a boardinghouse for sailors, embodies that charm with finely appointed rooms. Its popularity even propelled the owners to expand from thirty-seven rooms to eighty rooms in 1996. Thankfully, the flavor of the old inn has remained intact, and visitors find a quiet alternative to the Fells Point action. What's more, the inn's formal restaurant, Hamilton's, is considered one of the state's best.

The Admiral Fell Inn also offers an English pub, a casual restaurant called The Point, and opening soon on Thames St., a bakery café.

MR. MOLE BED & BREAKFAST

Owners: Paul Bragaw & Collin Clarke.
410-728-1179.
1601 Bolton St., Baltimore, MD 21201.
Price: Expensive to Very Expensive.
Credit Cards: AE, D, DC, MC, V.
Handicap Access: No.

Elegantly appointed in English-country fashion, the 1870s town house in historic Bolton Hill boasts marble fireplaces, fourteen-foot ceilings, and scores of eighteenth- and nineteenth-century antiques. The owners, also proprietors of the Abacrombie Badger B&B, take obvious pride and personal interest in their guests. Each of five suites comes with its own style and name, and all of the rooms include spacious and crystal-clean, white bathrooms, replete with hair dryers, Caswell-Massey toiletries, and thick, terry cloth robes. A breakfast of sliced meats, cheeses, fresh fruit, and homemade baked goods is served each morning.

SCARBOROUGH FAIR BED & BREAKFAST

Owners: Ellen & Ashley Scarborough.
410-837-0010.
1 E. Montgomery St., Baltimore, MD 21201.
Price: Expensive to Very Expensive.
Credit Cards: MC, V.
Handicap Access: Yes (steps into the house).

A gem, indeed. Scarborough Fair in rejuvenated Federal Hill boasts not only stellar accommodations, but also a location that other inns would envy. Guests can walk to the Inner Harbor or Fells Point (if they're up for a longer hike, during daylight hours only). Oriole Park and Ravens Stadium are a stone's throw away. What's more, Federal Hill's exceptional restaurants are in the neighborhood, and let's not forget these wonderful neighborhood streets for after-dinner strolls. Deceptively large, the inn has six fully renovated rooms. Four rooms host gas fireplaces and two have whirlpools.

Your hosts opened the inn in 1997 and have gone above and beyond in refurbishing the stately brick house on the corner of Charles & Montgomery Sts. They manage to offer today's comforts amid yesteryear's charm, and they promise that each guest will not start the day hungry; they serve a full and hearty breakfast daily. Off-street parking is included.

The following is a selection of hotels in Baltimore:

Harbor Court Hotel (550 Light St.; 410-234-0550).
Hyatt Regency Baltimore (300 Light St.; 410-528-1234).
The Tremont Plaza (222 St. Paul St.; 410-727-2222).

BALTIMORE RESTAURANTS

LA TAVOLA
410-685-1859.
248 Albemarle St.,
   Baltimore, MD 21201.
Open: Daily.
Price: Moderate to Very
   Expensive.
Cuisine: Italian.
Serving: L, D.
Credit Cards: AE, D, DC,
   MC, V.
Reservations: Yes.
Handicap Access: Limited.

The aroma of garlic permeating Baltimore's Little Italy is enough to make you walk into the first restaurant that you see. But don't. Do as Columbus did and explore. We did just that and came across a little treasure called La Tavola. While it's neither physically small nor unassuming with its bright yellow-and-black neon sign, La Tavola embodies the strengths of Little Italy and, at two years old, is still considered an upstart in this long-established neighborhood. But its offerings draw a following. Get an exceptional meal at moderate prices ($12–$16), or really live it up by ordering from the nightly specials menu ($24 median). The decor is subtle and tasteful, but cozy and casual. It's also varied, with fresh exotic seafood, such as Hawaiian escolar (similar to Arctic char) grilled to perfection with crisp green beans and red peppers. But if you're in a home-cooked-meal mood, La Tavola offers a hearty stewed veal shank in thick tomato sauce over pasta or a sautéed marscapone-stuffed veal chop. Leave room for the homemade desserts, such as the Italian staple tiramisu, the crème caramel, or fresh berries with homemade whipped cream. And, of course, La Tavola makes a cappuccino to die for.

MANGIA! MANGIA!
410-534-8999.
834 S. Luzerne Ave.,
   Baltimore, MD 21201.
Open: Daily.
Price: Inexpensive to
   Moderate.
Cuisine: Italian.
Serving: L, D.
Credit Cards: AE, D, DC,
   MC, V.
Reservations: No.
Handicap Access: Limited.

On the outside, Mangia! Mangia! looks like a spaghetti Western gone bad, with a huge 3-D fork replete with pasta adorning the façade. Upon closer inspection, however, the restaurant is a funky, happening joint, offering incredible pasta at incredible prices — and truly gigantic portions. Everything about Mangia! Mangia! is superb, from its friendly waitstaff to the creative decor. Even though the restaurant is primarily known for its variety of pasta dishes (it offers at least sixteen dishes at all times), consider the fish specials, brick-oven pizzas, and huge, fresh salads. Don't be surprised if the chef throws you an extra tuna steak, if you're there on the late side. It's evident that customers are taken care of, and they repay with repeated patronage. With that in mind, the restaurant tends to get insanely busy on weekend peak dinner hours, so consider eating there during the week or on the weekend before the dinner crowd converges between 7 and 9:30 p.m.

SOBO CAFÉ
410-752-1518.
6 W. Cross St., Baltimore,
   MD 21201.
Open: Daily.
Price: Inexpensive.
Cuisine: Eclectic/
   American.
Serving: L, D.
Credit Cards: AE, D, DC,
   MC, V.
Reservations: Yes.
Handicap Access: Yes.

A grilled tuna steak with raspberry glaze and sun-dried tomato and mushroom marmalade for $10? Baked macaroni and cheese for $3? A huge pork chop or Baltimore strip steak with garlic mashed potatoes with zucchini and red peppers, both for $10? A large Caesar salad, enough to feed a small country, for $4? Need we say more? Everything on the menu is $10 or less. And that is only one of three things that you can expect from this Federal Hill hot spot. The other two: the food is great, and the place gets packed on the weekends. But go anyway to hang out at the bar and to enjoy a beer or a glass of wine. The Sobo is warm and inviting, and there's always interesting artwork on the walls to spark the imagination and to work up an appetite.

WAYNE'S BAR-B-QUE
410-539-3810.
201 E. Pratt St., Baltimore,
   MD 21201.
Open: Daily.
Price: Inexpensive to
   Moderate.
Cuisine: Ribs/Cajun.
Serving: L, D.
Credit Cards: AE, D, DC,
   MC, V.
Reservations: No.
Handicap Access: Yes.

Located in Baltimore's urban-renewal jewel, the Inner Harbor, Wayne's Bar-B-Que touts itself as the best rib joint in Charm City. We wouldn't go that far, but for the price and location, Wayne's is a good place to sit and watch the harbor's activity, particularly on the outside deck. Despite its down and dirty Texas theme, Wayne's offers more than ribs. Shrimp Creole (downright tasty and abundant), Maryland crab soup, killer corn bread, catfish or crab cake platters, as well as a variety of so-so salads, highlight Wayne's busy menu. Wayne's does tend to get packed during the peak season, so keep in mind that service can be a bit slow.

HISTORIC TRIANGLE:
WILLIAMSBURG, JAMESTOWN & YORKTOWN

Perhaps all of America should visit **Colonial Williamsburg.** For the price of admission, the experience truly sends visitors back in time. Restored in 1926 with the aid of John D. Rockefeller, Jr., Williamsburg originally was established as Virginia's capital in 1699. In 1780, Virginians moved their capital to Richmond. But visitors to their colonial capitol can see everything from the Governor's Palace to four nearby museums, including one of the lovely James River plantations. Along Duke of Gloucester Street stand the restored homes and workshops of the eighteenth century. In all, eighty-eight original buildings stand among the 500 structures.

Williamsburg is a great town in any season, with fireplace wood smoke and bayberry candle aromas filling winter's air and dogwood, daffodils, and lilacs come spring. Formal English gardens are restored to period symmetry and perform double duty for families with children, who will love the maze. People in period costumes are everywhere. If they're not demonstrating the fine craft of smithing, they're marching in a fife-and-drum corps.

Three ticket packages (800-HISTORY, tickets) are available for Colonial Williamsburg and range from $16–$20 for children 6–12 and $27–$35 for adults. With a variety of restaurants, lodgings, and tourist attractions, Williamsburg is located midway between Richmond and Norfolk, Virginia, off I-64. Nearby are the **Busch Gardens** theme park, the daunting bargainland known as the **Williamsburg Pottery Factory,** and more. Contact: Williamsburg Area Convention & Visitors Bureau, P.O. Box 3585, Williamsburg, VA 23187; 800-368-6511; 757-253-0192; www.visitwilliamsburg.com.

Not far away stands the **Jamestown Settlement,** combining indoor gallery exhibits and outdoor living history to tell the tale of the early English colonists who came here in 1607. Docked along the riverbank are full-sized replicas of the ships that carried the settlers, *Susan Constant, Godspeed,* and *Discovery,* and onboard sailor-interpreters will tell you of their four-month voyage. A fort and Indian village complete the interpretive tale. The settlement is located just off Rte. 31, six miles west of Williamsburg, and also can be reached via the Colonial Parkway. Seasonal restaurant, gift shop, and museum are open daily, 9:00 a.m.–5:00 p.m.

The same group that operates the settlement opened the much-expanded **Yorktown Victory Center** in the mid-1990s. Nearly 1,000 different Revolutionary War artifacts are on view, and the museum offers a recreated history of the era, with costumed interpreters and hands-on exhibits. Nearby **Yorktown Battlefield** is the site of the last, climactic battle that ended the War of Independence. Contact: Jamestown-Yorktown Foundation; 888-593-4682; 757-253-4838.

URBAN VIRGINIA TIDEWATER: HAMPTON, NORFOLK & NEWPORT NEWS

Virginia's Tidewater officially includes the entire tidal shoreline of the Bay, but many refer to the cities near the mouth of the bay simply as

"Tidewater." Here, the Chesapeake meets its final tributary, the James River, and joins waters with the Atlantic Ocean. The naturally secure harbors have drawn not only commercial vessels, but the U.S. Navy. Military residents include the Naval Station Norfolk, the world's largest naval station.

Of 100 exhibits at the **Virginia Air & Space Center** (600 Settlers Landing Rd., Hampton, VA 23669; 800-296-0800; 757-727-0900; www.vasc.org), the official visitors' center of the NASA Langley Research Center, moon rocks and the Apollo 12 command module may be the standouts; there's also an IMAX theater.

Norfolk's **NAUTICUS** (Waterside Dr., Norfolk, VA 23501; 800-664-1080; 757-664-1000; www.nauticus.org) stands on the city's waterfront, with aquariums and interactive simulators that let visitors check out life beneath the sea or aboard a naval battleship. Art lovers visiting the city will also want to see the **Chrysler Museum** (245 W. Olney Rd., Norfolk, VA 23501; 757-664-6200; www.chrysler.org), with its collection of Tiffany and French and Italian paintings. Also popular with visitors is the **Mariners' Museum** (100 Museum Dr., Newport News, VA 23606; 800-581-SAIL; 757-596-2222; www.mariner.org), with its fine display of model ships. Spot-lit cases and magnifiers showcase the collection created by artist August F. Crabtree. Other galleries to visit include the **Chesapeake Bay Gallery.**

Interested in more? Contact: Newport News Tourism Development Office (888-4WE-RFUN; 757-926-3561) or Norfolk Convention and Visitors Bureau (800-368-3097).

WASHINGTON, D.C.

The nation's capital stands at the edge of Bay Country, about thirty miles west of Annapolis along the tidal portion of the Potomac River. There's a ton to see: the **Washington Monument, the Lincoln** and **Jefferson Memorials,** the **National Gallery of Art,** the **Kennedy Center for the Performing Arts,** the museums of the **Smithsonian Institution,** and, of course, the **White House,** the **Capitol,** and the **Mall** are just the beginning. The city hosts an impressive number of free museums or performances, good restaurants, and is particularly elegant in the early spring when the delicate cherry blossoms burst forth. Contact: Washington Convention and Visitors Association, 1212 New York Ave. NW, Ste. 600, Washington, D.C. 20005; 202-789-7000; www.washington.org. The *Washington Post* web site (www.washingtonpost.com) also should prove useful; click on the "Style" section.

IF TIME IS SHORT

Chesapeake Bay is huge, and your leisure time is short. What to do on a quick visit to the Bay? Consider the summer-country/winter-city yin and yang of the region and think like a native: folks down on the Eastern Shore spend the summer messing around in boats, while Annapolitans (or Chestertownians, for that matter) quickly reclaim their city the minute summer ends, and the tourists depart. We offer a seasonal taste of the region's best, set forth in somewhat idealized itineraries. You might not cram everything into a day, but you're sure to have a good time trying.

In the summer, there's no choice about the mainstay of your day. You'll spend it on the water. We suggest a day of fishing aboard a vessle chartered out of **Harrison's Sport Fishing Center** on *Tilghman Island.* They've been chartering fishing parties for sixty years, they know the local captains, and they know where the fish school. For your part, you should return with your full complement of rockfish. When you leave Harrison's, swing by **Dogwood Harbor** to see the famed sailing skipjacks, moored there until oyster season starts in the fall.

Then take a scenic, twenty-one-mile drive en route to dinner. Go back up through *St. Michaels.* If the **Chesapeake Bay Maritime Museum** is still open, stop in to see the exhibit that tells of a waterman's life — whether catching crabs or drudging oysters. Continue your drive, branching off to the right through *Royal Oak* to *Bellevue.* Catch the famed **Oxford-Bellevue Ferry** across the Tred Avon River to *Oxford,* where you can join the "cruising sailor set" at the historic **Robert Morris Inn.** Order crab cakes and strawberry pie.

As the days shorten, we think of the warm October days that can make for such lovely Indian summer sailing or the waterfowl migration that speeds along as fall fades. If it's the former you're seeking and you're an experienced sailor, you might want to contact one of the charter operations located throughout the Bay region. If you don't know how to sail, or if you have too little experience to go out alone, then you should opt instead to get out on the water aboard one of the several excursion boats that should still be operating as long as the weather holds. Also, sailing schools offer the perfect chance to get comfortable at the helm (see Chapter Six, *Recreation* for suggested charter agencies, tours, and schools). And be sure to mix with avid sailors who always reserve Columbus Day weekend for the annual **U.S. Sailboat Show,** a bustling marketplace at the **City Dock** in *Annapolis.*

Those of you inclined toward the quieter pursuit of bird-watching will want to head across the Bay Bridge to *Dorchester County,* home to the **Blackwater National Wildlife Refuge** and its great fall migration. The distinctive honks of Canada geese can be heard overhead, and snow geese pass through, too. If you're on a birding marathon, head next to the **Assateague Island National Seashore,** located on the Atlantic Ocean and likely to be very thick with birds of the Atlantic Flyway. Shorebirds are heading to tropical points south; be sure to bring a powerful spotting scope.

Now it's winter, a fine time to poke around the three-centuries-old streets of *Annapolis.* Stop by the historic **Maryland Statehouse,** where the signing of the Treaty of Paris took place, then mosey across **State Circle** to Maryland Avenue, home to a fun row of antique and high-end designer shops. Two blocks over, you'll find the **U.S. Naval Academy,** where the chapel is always worth a visit. Be sure to go downstairs to view the magificent tomb of John Paul Jones, father of the modern navy. Then stroll down the hill toward City Dock via **Prince George Street,** examining three centuries' worth of architiecture along the way. The ambitious might want to learn more; the **Historic Annapolis Foundation** offers a recorded tour narrated by Walter Cronkite that can be rented for a small fee at the **Historic Annapolis Foundation's Welcome Center and Museum Store,** located next to City Dock. And for dinner? Try **O'Leary's** for seafood or the **Wild Orchid Café** for creative cuisine, both located in *Eastport.*

When the spring sun begins to chase winter away, it's time to get outside and see the Bay again! Any of the local, state, or national parks listed in Chapter Six, *Recreation* offers a wealth of opportunities, from trails for hikers to tributaries for canoers. **Sandy Point State Park,** near Annapolis, is easy to reach since it's right off Rte. 50. Or you might want to get a dose of the ocean on *Assateague Island.* Pack your binoculars and keep an eye out for the wild ponies found along the island's thirteen miles; they shouldn't bother you if you don't bother them. The island is officially divided into three management entities: **Assateague State Park, Assateague Island National Seashore,** and **Chincoteague National Wildlife Refuge.** Birders tend to favor "the Virginia side" at *Chincoteague.*

Be sure to check with the above venues to verify hours and costs, as either (or both) may change, especially with the season. Whatever you choose to do, make sure that it includes a view of the Bay sometime during your day. There's just nothing quite like the water, under summer's rippling rays or winter's gray clouds, to stir the spirit.

Index

LODGING BY PRICE CODE

Kent Manor Inn, 65
Victoriana Inn, 64

**LOWER EASTERN
SHORE**

Inexpensive
The Washington Hotel &
Inn, 70

Inexpensive–Moderate
Econo Lodge, Princess
Anne, 77
Snow Hill Inn, 70
Somers Cove Motel, 77

Inexpensive–Expensive
Best Western, Salisbury
Plaza, 77

Sarke Plantation, 69

Moderate
Colonial Manor Inn, 74
Comfort Inn, Onley, 78
Driftwood Motor Lodge, 78
Nottingham Ridge B&B, 72
Quality Inn, 77
Sea Gate B&B, 72
Sunset Beach Inn, 77
The Tavern House, 71

Moderate–Expensive
Assateague Inn, 78
Birchwood Motel, 78
Econo Lodge, Statesman,
77
Island Manor House, 73
The Refuge Motor Inn, 78

Moderate–Very Expensive
The Atlantic Hotel, 68
The Garden & the Sea Inn,
74
Glasgow Inn B&B, 69
Island Motor Inn Resort,
78
Miss Molly's Inn, 73

Expensive
Cambridge House, 68

Expensive–Very Expensive
Channel Bass Inn, 72
Merry Sherwood Plantation,
68
Waterloo Country Inn, 70

DINING BY PRICE CODE

Price Codes
Inexpensive: up to $15
Moderate: $16 to $22
Expensive: $23 to $32
Very Expensive: $33 or more

HEAD OF THE BAY

Moderate
Schaefer's Canal House, 82
Tidewater Grille, 82

Expensive–Very Expensive
Bayard House Restaurant, 81

**ANNAPOLIS/WESTERN
SHORE**

Inexpensive
Chick & Ruth's Delly, 85
49 West Wine Bar & Gallery,
86
Pier 44, 93

Inexpensive–Moderate
Cantler's Riverside Inn, 84

Happy Harbor, 93
Ram's Head Tavern, 90

Inexpensive–Expensive
Middleton Tavern, 89

**Inexpensive–Very
Expensive**
Joss Café & Sushi Bar, 88

Moderate
CD Café, 97
McGarvey's Saloon &
Oyster Bar, 89
Pusser's Landing, 90
Saigon Place, 91
Stoney's Seafood House, 96

Moderate-Expensive
Café Normandie, 83
Carrol's Creek, 84
Ciao, 86
The Inn at Pirate's Cove, 95
La Piccola Roma, 88
Mike's Restaurant & Crab
House, 97
Riordan's Saloon, 91

Expensive
Harry Browne's, 87
O'Leary's, 94
The Wild Orchid Café, 95

Expensive–Very Expensive
Lewnes Steak House, 93
Treaty of Paris, 92

Very Expensive
Dry Dock, 98

**NORTHERN
NECK/MIDDLE
PENINSULA**

Inexpensive
Lancaster Tavern, 100
Peppermints, 101
Rocket Billy's, 103

Inexpensive–Moderate
Conrad's Upper Deck
Restaurant, 101

DINING BY CUISINE

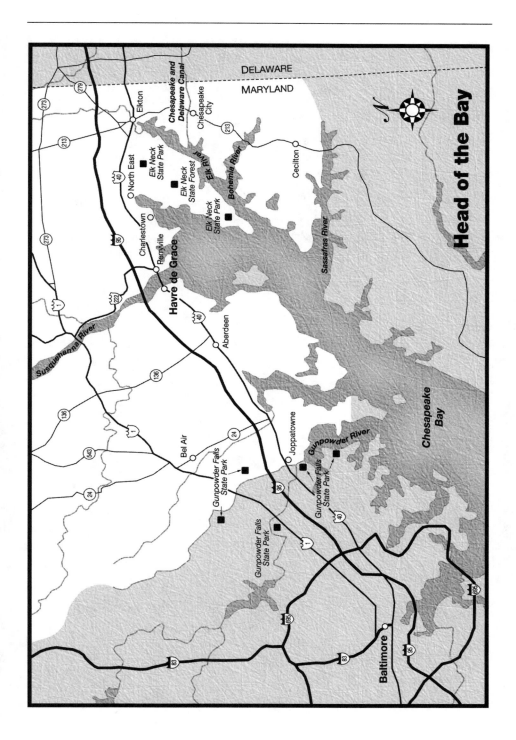

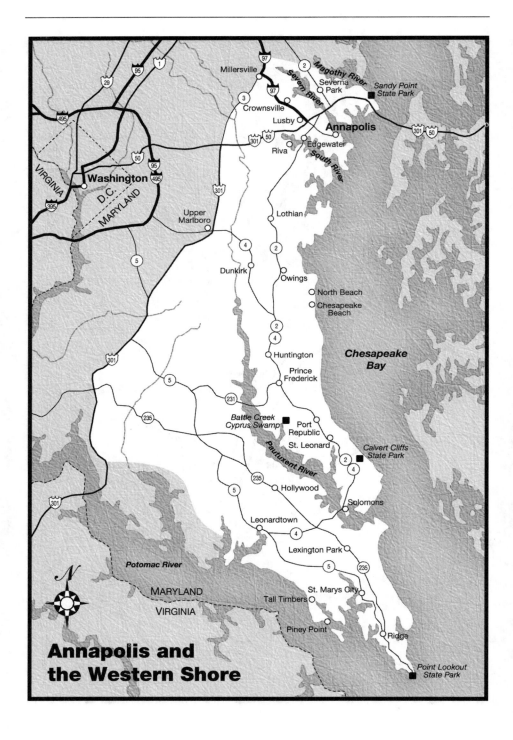

Annapolis and
the Western Shore

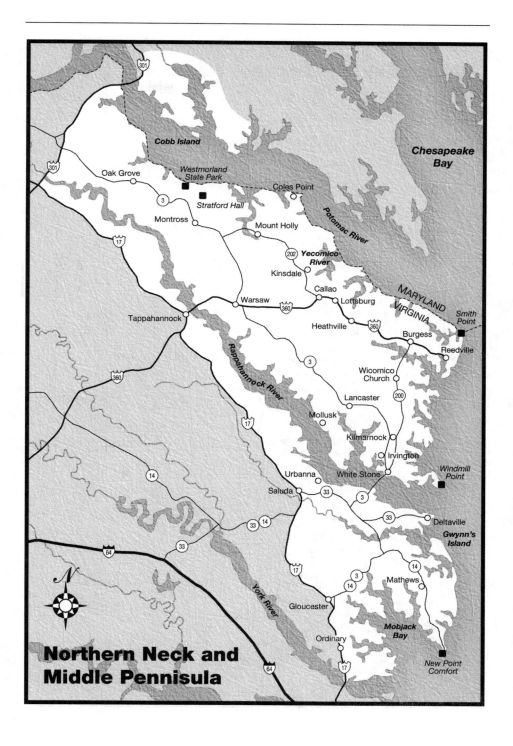

Northern Neck and Middle Pennisula

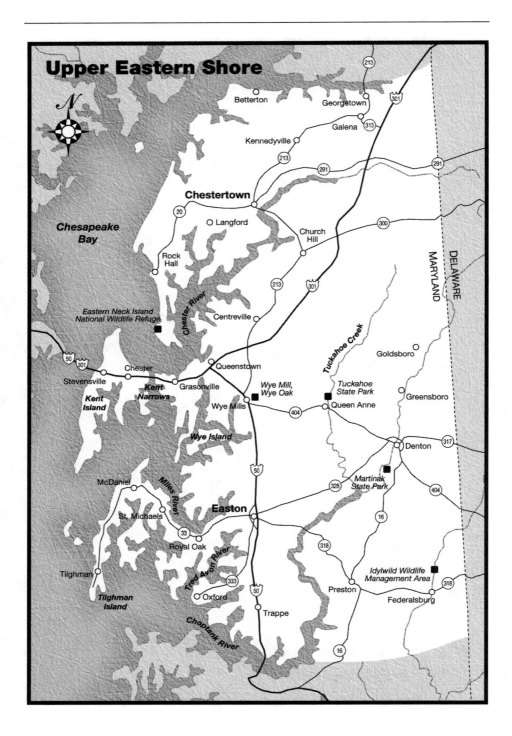

Upper Eastern Shore

Betterton
Georgetown
Galena
Kennedyville
Chestertown
Langford
Church Hill
Chesapeake Bay
Rock Hall
Chester River
Eastern Neck Island National Wildlife Refuge
Centreville
Goldsboro
Tuckahoe Creek
Chester
Queenstown
Stevensville
Grasonville
Tuckahoe State Park
Kent Narrows
Greensboro
Kent Island
Wye Mill, Wye Oak
Queen Anne
Wye Mills
Denton
Wye Island
McDaniel
Miles River
Martinak State Park
Easton
St. Michaels
Royal Oak
Preston
Tilghman
Tred Avon River
Idylwild Wildlife Management Area
Tilghman Island
Oxford
Federalsburg
Trappe
Choptank River

MARYLAND
DELAWARE

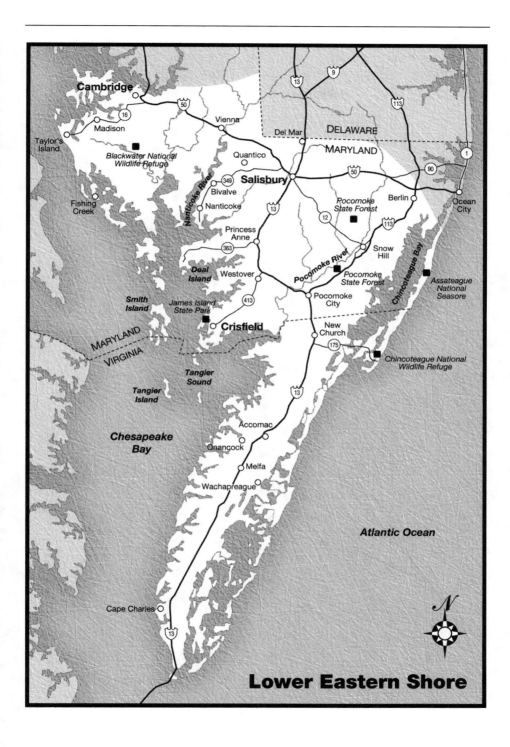

Lower Eastern Shore

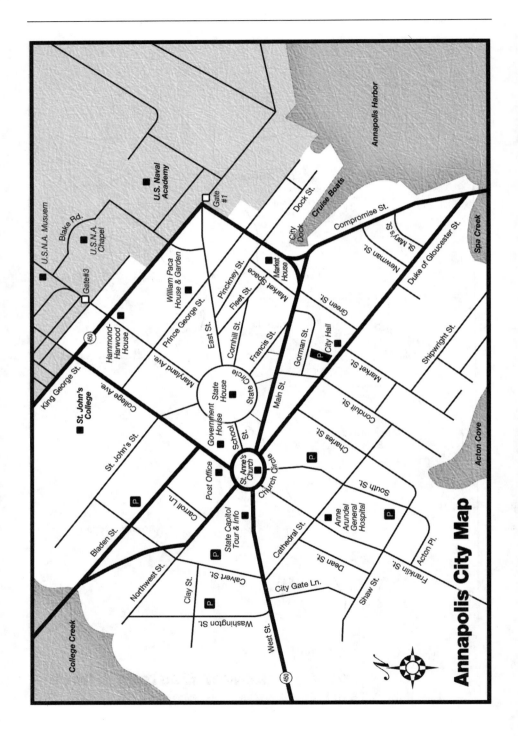

Annapolis City Map